REMEMBERING THE CIVIL WAR

REMEMBERING THE CIVIL WAR

THE CONFLICT AS TOLD BY THOSE WHO LIVED IT

EDITED BY MICHAEL BARTON
AND CHARLES KUPFER

LYONS
PRESS

Guilford, Connecticut

An imprint of The Rowman & Littlefield Publishing Group, Inc.
4501 Forbes Blvd., Ste. 200
Lanham, MD 20706
www.rowman.com

Distributed by NATIONAL BOOK NETWORK

British Library Cataloguing in Publication Information available

Library of Congress Cataloging-in-Publication Data available

ISBN 978-1-4930-5933-1 (paper)
ISBN 978-1-4930-4176-3 (electronic)

al
I/

CONTENTS

CONTENTS

1862   89

INTRODUCTION

WELCOME BACK TO THE FIGHT

Most Civil War soldiers wrote letters home, many kept diaries, and some wrote memoirs after the war was over. Civil War memoirs thence became an American literary genre. They are an account of the most momentous events in a man's life, and a record of his part in his country's history. They cover duty, boredom, fatigue, distance from home, and yearning for family. They detail the soldier's ground-level view of tactics and strategy, his admiration for his superiors or else disdain, his fellowship with comrades or else rebuke. Memoirs tell about his encounter with the enemy and the enemy's country. They reveal the shock of gore, the gasp of death, and the turns between bravery and fear. They let us imagine how, and wonder why, the author could charge against entrenched troops time and again. We read the veteran recalling the din and smoke of cannon and then the screams and smells. He might still feel the pain of a wound and its mending, but there was little talk of tears. Memoirs inform us that a singular difference between the Civil War and modern war was the fate of horses. And there was the marching, always the marching. In the end, Civil War memoirs were the veteran's last chance to answer the question, What did it all amount to? Was it worth the struggle to leave the country, or to defend it? There was much to remember and write.

Most Civil War memoirs were not published immediately after a soldier's service. Rather, they were usually the remembrances of older veterans, especially former high-ranking officers, their creation occasioned by an upcoming wartime anniversary, or a regimental reunion, or perhaps the soldier's thoughts of his own mortality. The "sentimentalized reminiscence industry," as historian David Blight calls it, was most productive after 1880. The government's stimulus to the industry was publishing *The*

War of the Rebellion: A Compilation of the Official Records of the Union and Confederate Armies, consisting of 128 volumes produced between 1880 and 1901; indeed, the most detailed memoirs could hardly have been written without the use of the *Official Records*, although one could say that memoirs were not necessarily enlivened by the author quoting dispatch after dispatch from the *OR*.

Some memoirs were written with the soldier imagining that his local community would be the audience. One of our authors, Sgt. Christian Lenker, was asked by his local newspaper, the *Pottsville Evening Chronicle*, to provide his reminiscences on a weekly basis, which he did for over three years. Some authors strived to attract a national readership, and some of those did quite well. Other memoirs were simply intended for their descendants, the authors announced at the outset. Whatever the audience, the "War of the Rebellion" is, so far, our most remembered war.

———

For this anthology we first located memoirs and comparable documents from the major battles of the war in the order that they occurred. By major battles we mean those that had the greatest number of casualties, such as Gettysburg, Chickamauga, Spotsylvania Court House, Chancellorsville, the Wilderness, Stones River, Shiloh, and Antietam. The memoirs we have chosen include many that modern historians have praised. A sampling of our choices follows.

Ambrose Bierce, for example, is an extraordinarily compelling memoirist of the Shiloh battle and the "edgiest" writer in this collection. Unlike some memoirists, he is easily readable by moderns. He has been recognized as "alone among important American writers" to have served four years in the war, where he was both wounded and embittered. We located his work in the public domain, but readers wanting more should refer to *Phantoms of a Blood-Stained Period: The Complete Civil War Writings of Ambrose Bierce* (2002), edited by Russell Duncan and David J. Klooster.

Sam Watkins's *"Co. Aytch," Maury Grays, First Tennessee Regiment; or, A Side Show of the Big Show* (1900) is a Confederate soldier's captivating reminiscence, some say the best, and a rarity coming from an enlisted man. His memories were a remarkably effective platform for Ken Burns's much-admired public television series on the Civil War. Watkins's text is a treasure chest of quotable observations.

William Tecumseh Sherman's *Memoirs of General W. T. Sherman* (1875) was one of the early Union commentaries on the war and is still greatly valued for its voice and candor. In *Patriotic Gore: Studies in the Literature of the American Civil War* (1962), literary critic Edmund Wilson called Sherman's two volumes of writing "amazing." The esteemed Library of America has republished Sherman's memoirs, an indication of their literary and historical importance. We have excerpted the original edition.

Alongside excerpts from Sherman's *Memoirs* we include those of Gen. Philip H. Sheridan, the Union commander who triumphed in the Shenandoah Valley campaign and pursued Gen. Robert E. Lee to Appomattox. After the war Sheridan led troops against the Indian tribes in the West.

The controversial Confederate general James Longstreet wrote his version of the war, *From Manassas to Appomattox: Memoirs of the Civil War in America* (1895), late in the century and as a contribution to the "resumption of fraternity." Indeed, he asserted that "*because of the war*," there was "a broader and deeper patriotism in all Americans." It may be too much to say that Longstreet was despised throughout the South after his debatable actions at Gettysburg; however, joining the Republican Party after the war and befriending Grant cannot have helped his reputation among his former comrades. We use Longstreet's memoirs a number of times in the anthology.

The recollections of Confederate general Edward Porter Alexander, first published in 1907, are highly praised today for his rich and intelligent observations. He commanded the extraordinary bombardment in advance of Pickett's charge at Gettysburg. Again, we have excerpted the public domain edition, but we recommend historian Gary Gallagher's scholarly edition for readers wanting the entire work.

Ulysses S. Grant's recollections, *Personal Memoirs of U. S. Grant*, published in 1885, are honored for their detail, restraint, and revelation of the author's personality. Plainspoken, matter-of-fact, "spare, telling and quick," as modern commentators describe them, his memoirs were published in 1885, a few months after his death from throat cancer. With Mark Twain's collaboration, Grant had submitted his final drafts a few months earlier. They sold more than 300,000 copies, sparing his family from poverty. His wife, Julia, received a first royalty payment of $200,000, a record at that time. We have excerpted the original edition; however, the Library of America offers a handsome, expertly edited, one-volume version today, including Grant's letters to his wife and a thorough chronology of his life, including even his final notes to his doctor.

Those are a few examples of highly regarded battle memoirs included in this volume. For readers interested in examining more Civil War writings, there are many online sources. The *Southern Historical Society Papers*, which began publication in 1868, featured a great variety of articles in fifty-two volumes. Speeches, documents, diaries, and brief recollections can be found in the *SHSP*. *Confederate Veteran* magazine, likewise now online, was a popular Southern outlet for brief recollections and related articles, operating between 1893 and 1932. *Annals of the War*, also now online, contains memoirs originally published in the *Philadelphia Weekly Times* beginning in 1879. An outstanding collection of 167 historic, book-length, digitized memoirs in their original format has been put online by Project Gutenberg, and they can be found at its website under the heading "US Civil War (Bookshelf)."

The second type of memoirs we have included is not tied to the chronology of battles or their outcome; rather, these memoirs touch on soldiers' lives outside of battle, such as their ordinary activities in camp or their travails as patients, prisoners, or victims. For example, two unique and popular accounts published a generation after the war are Confederate private Carlton McCarthy's *Detailed Minutiae of Soldier Life in the Army of Northern Virginia, 1861–1865* (1882) and Union soldier John Billings's *Hardtack and Coffee: The Unwritten Story of Army Life* (1887). These two volumes are among the best histories of everyday life from any period. Civil War reenactors use them as reference works today. Other non-battle writings we have chosen are Alexis de Tocqueville's observations on antebellum society in the "Prologue to War" section, Walt Whitman's and Louisa May Alcott's descriptions of hospitals, and Charles Francis Adams's and Frederick Douglass's reflections on the war. The most profound reflection is Abraham Lincoln's second inaugural address; in a sense, his own memoir of the war and its meaning.

—◦—

Some final comments are in order on a subtheme in these memoirs. Increasingly, historians are finding—or placing—slavery, race, and the mythology of the Lost Cause at the center of Southern memory. The reminiscences of Confederate soldiers often conveyed their Cause: the South's theory of states' rights and secession, its manners and way of life, and its legal and social system of racial segregation. The style of their memoirs was also linked to their Cause: they tended to be romantic and sentimental, especially on the subjects of chivalry toward women and gallantry among soldiers. Confederates believed their Cause was honorable and noble, but they claimed it was Lost because the North was simply overpowering. They thought their own warriors were superior but the North was materially greater, and that made all the difference. Their Cause deserved to prevail, but it never had a chance, they wrote to themselves.

Every modern analysis of this Lost Cause mythology is scornful of it, which is to be expected, and justified. Critics say that Southerners who found comfort in their sectional folklore were averse to accepting any responsibility for slavery, secession, and segregation. But, we may ask, what would one expect white Southerners to say after losing a war, an economy, and a social order? It has been claimed that virtually every white Southern family was touched by the war. For them, the conflict was not merely the "late unpleasantness." For us to think that they would bring confessions and apologies into their reminiscences would be unrealistic. They would be more likely to salute their comrades, decorate graves, and erect statues, which is what they did. They were more prone to say, as Sam Watkins did, that they were "only trying to protect their homes and families, their property, their constitution and their laws, that had been guaranteed to them as a heritage forever by their forefathers. They died for the faith that each state was a separate sovereign government, as laid down by the Declaration of Independence and the Constitution of our fathers." For Confederates, believing such principles was more sustaining than denying them.

The irony of the Lost Cause mythology is that it seems to have helped the sections reconcile with one another. Northerners could be entertained by the myth as well as Southerners could be solaced by it. Moreover, it could be argued that Northerners had their own Won Cause mythology of the war. In any case, what was forgotten in this arrangement was the construction of an African-American memory of the war. Frederick Douglass reminded his audiences of that omission and their need for a usable past.

If we want something of a closing statement on this issue for now, it could be found in the work of David Blight. His prize-winning book *Race and Reunion: The Civil War in American Memory* begins with a quotation from Thucydides: "The People made their recollection fit in with their sufferings." That is an apt and understanding description of Southern memory.

We have designed this book for general readers, not Civil War specialists, so we have not included scholarly apparatuses such as extensive footnotes and a bibliography. Our intention has been to present Civil War memoirs on their own terms and let the reader comment. Our hope is that readers will follow the urging of Clara Barton (editor Michael Barton's ancestor), who said that when you read a Civil War memoirist, "I charge you listen and believe him."

PROLOGUE TO WAR

THE PRESENT AND PROBABLE FUTURE CONDITION OF THE THREE RACES THAT INHABIT THE TERRITORY OF THE UNITED STATES

1835
ALEXIS DE TOCQUEVILLE

Alexis de Tocqueville's Democracy in America *has been called both the best book about democracy and the best book about America. The French aristocrat wrote it after visiting the United States in 1831. His official task was to study the American prison system, a model for reform at that time; he did so, but then he went on to study the nation at large, being that territory east of the Mississippi River, during an extensive trip with his colleague Gustave de Beaumont. An analysis of Tocqueville's provocative observations and conclusions could fill books, but here our concern is focused on his comparison of the North and South. Tocqueville was a student of the American character, or what we would refer to now as American culture and its subcultures. His conclusion was that race, and slavery, counted for everything in explaining the difference between the two sections. He died in 1859, too soon to see the Civil War commence, but we can say he saw it coming.*

The dangers which threaten the American Union do not originate in the diversity of interests or of opinions, but in the various characters and passions of the Americans. The men who inhabit the vast territory of the United States are almost all the issue of a common stock; but the effects of the climate, and more especially of slavery, have gradually introduced very striking differences between the British settler of the Southern States and the British settler of the North. In Europe it is generally believed that slavery has rendered the interests of one part of the Union contrary to those of another part; but I by no means remarked this to be the case: slavery has not created interests in the South contrary to those of the North, but it has modified the character and changed the habits of the natives of the South.

I have already explained the influence which slavery has exercised upon the commercial ability of the Americans in the South; and this same influence equally extends to their manners. The slave is a servant who never remonstrates, and who submits to everything without complaint. He may sometimes assassinate, but he never withstands, his master. In the South there are no families so poor as not to have slaves. The citizen of the Southern States of the Union is invested with a sort of domestic dictatorship, from his earliest years; the first notion he acquires in life is that he is born to command, and the first habit which he contracts is that of being obeyed without resistance. His education tends, then, to give him the character of a supercilious and a hasty man; irascible, violent, and ardent in his desires, impatient of obstacles, but easily discouraged if he cannot succeed upon his first attempt.

The American of the Northern States is surrounded by no slaves in his childhood; he is even unattended by free servants, and is usually obliged to provide for his own wants. No sooner does he enter the world than the idea of necessity assails him on every side: he soon learns to know exactly the natural limit of his authority; he never expects to subdue those who withstand him, by force; and he knows that the surest means of obtaining the support of his fellow-creatures, is to win their favor. He therefore becomes patient, reflecting, tolerant, slow to act, and persevering in his designs.

In the Southern States the more immediate wants of life are always supplied; the inhabitants of those parts are not busied in the material cares of life, which are always provided for by others; and their imagination is diverted to more captivating and less definite objects. The American of the South is fond of grandeur, luxury, and renown, of gayety, of pleasure, and above all of idleness; nothing obliges him to exert himself in order to subsist; and as he has no necessary occupations, he gives way to indolence, and does not even attempt what would be useful.

But the equality of fortunes, and the absence of slavery in the North, plunge the inhabitants in those same cares of daily life which are disdained by the white population of the South. They are taught from infancy to combat want, and to place comfort above all the pleasures of the intellect or the heart. The imagination is extinguished by the trivial details of life, and the ideas become less numerous and less general, but far more practical and more precise. As prosperity is the sole aim of exertion, it is excellently well attained; nature and mankind are turned to the best pecuniary advantage, and society is dexterously made to contribute to the welfare of each of its members, whilst individual egotism is the source of general happiness.

The citizen of the North has not only experience, but knowledge: nevertheless he sets but little value upon the pleasures of knowledge; he esteems it as the means of attaining a certain end, and he is only anxious to seize its more lucrative applications. The citizen of the South is more given to act upon impulse; he is more clever, more frank, more generous, more intellectual, and more brilliant. The former, with a greater degree of activity, of common-sense, of information, and of general aptitude, has the characteristic good and evil qualities of the middle classes. The latter has the tastes, the prejudices, the weaknesses, and the magnanimity of all aristocracies. If two men are united in society, who have the same interests, and to a certain extent the same opinions, but different characters, different acquirements, and a different style of civilization, it is probable that these men will not agree. The same remark is applicable to a society of nations. Slavery, then, does not attack the American Union directly in its interests, but indirectly in its manners.

Source: Alexis de Tocqueville, *Democracy in America*, trans. Henry Reeve (New York, 1838; Project Gutenberg, 2006), vol. 1, chap. 18, pt. 7, http://www.gutenberg.org/ebooks/815.

THE RAID OF JOHN BROWN AT HARPER'S FERRY AS I SAW IT

OCTOBER 16-18, 1859
REV. SAMUEL VANDERLIP LEECH, USA

Rev. Leech's account of John Brown's raid at Harper's Ferry, Virginia, and his trial and execution afterward, has sermonic qualities. It tells a story with facts in great detail but also moral significance. The event might be called the starting battle of the Civil War, although "Bleeding Kansas" might also qualify. Rev. Leech was proudly anti-slavery but he was also anti-idiotic, anti-senseless, anti-unreasonable, and anti-ridiculous, words he used to describe the raid and its intentions. The trial was not a charade of justice; proper form was followed. Some of Brown's testimony and his final words may be surprising to us, given the image we might have of a ruthless fanatic. Brown knew what he was doing, and so did his captors.

The town of Harper's Ferry is located in Jefferson County, West Virginia. Lucerne, in Switzerland, does not excel it in romantic grandeur of situation. On its northern front the Potomac sweeps along to pass the national capital, and the tomb of Washington, in its silent flow towards the sea. On its eastern side the Shenandoah hurries to empty its waters into the Potomac, that in perpetual wedlock they may greet the stormy Atlantic. Across the Potomac the Maryland Heights stand out as the tall sentinels of Nature. Beyond the Shenandoah are the Blue Ridge mountains, fringing the westward boundary of Loudon County, Virginia. Between these rivers, and nestling inside of their very confluence, reposes Harper's Ferry. Back of its hills lies the famous Shenandoah Valley, celebrated for its natural scenery, its historic battles and "Sheridan's Ride." At Harper's Ferry the United States authorities early located an Arsenal and an Armory.

Before the Civil War, the Baltimore Conference of the Methodist Episcopal Church was constituted of five extensive districts in Virginia, stretching from Alexandria to Lewisburg and two great districts north of the Potomac, including the cities of Washington and Baltimore. The first three years of my ministerial life I spent on Shepherdstown, West Loudon and Hillsboro Circuits, being then all in Virginia. The State of West Virginia, now embracing Harper's Ferry, had not been organized by Congress as a war measure out of the territory of the mother State. Our Methodist Episcopal Church was theoretically an anti-slavery organization; but our Virginia and Maryland members held thousands of inherited and many purchased slaves. These were generally well-cared for and contented. Being close to the free soil of Pennsylvania they could have gotten there in a night had they wished to escape bondage, and then they could have easily reached Canada by that Northern aid, called the "Underground Railroad."

On the Sunday night when John Brown and his men invaded Virginia, I slept within a half mile of Harper's Ferry. That day I inaugurated revival services at my westward appointment called "Ebenezer," in Loudon County two miles from Harper's Ferry. I was twenty-two years of age.

Three months before this raid Captain John Brown with two of his sons, Owen and Oliver, and Jeremiah G. Anderson, calling themselves "Isaac Smith and Sons" rented a small farm on the Maryland side of the Potomac four miles from Harper's Ferry. It was known as the "Booth-Kennedy Place." They also carried on across the mountains at Chambersburg, Pennsylvania, a small hardware store managed by John H. Kagi. It was a depot for the munitions of war to be hauled to their Maryland farm. Another of Brown's men, John E. Cook, sold maps in the vicinity. He was a relative of Governor Willard of Indiana who secured the services of Hon. Daniel W. Voorhees, Attorney General of Indiana, to defend Cook at his after trial in Virginia. It was a time of profound national peace. Brown and his men represented themselves as geologists, miners and speculators. They had a mule and wagon with which to haul their boxes from Chambersburg. A wealthy merchant of Boston, Mr. George Luther Stearns, Chairman of the Massachusetts Aid Society had financed Brown's Kansas border warfare work, as well as his approaching Harper's Ferry raid. Other Northern friends assisted. Brown had completed his preparations and collected his twenty-one helpers early in October, 1859. He had hidden in an old log cabin on the place 200 Sharpe's rifles, 13,000 rifle cartridges, 950 long iron pikes, 200 revolving pistols, 100,000 pistol caps, 40,000 percussion caps, 250 pounds of powder, 12 reams of cartridge paper and other warlike materials. He organized his twenty-two men, himself included, into a "Military Provisional Government" to superintend the possible uprising of the slaves of Virginia. Thirteen of these men had engaged in border warfare in Kansas, in a successful effort to prevent Kansas from becoming a slave state. He, sixteen other white men and five negroes, constituted his entire Virginia army. The white men were Captain John Brown, Adjutant General John H. Kagi, Captains Owen Brown, Oliver Brown, Watson Brown, Aaron D. Stephens, John E. Cook, Dauphin Adolphus Thompson, George P. Tidd, William Thompson and Edwin Coppoc. The Lieutenants were Jeremiah G. Anderson, Albert Hazlitt and William Henry Leeman. The privates numbered eight. Three of them were white men and five were negroes. The whites were Francis J. Merriam, Barclay Coppoc and Steward Taylor. The negroes were Dangerfield Newby, Osborne P. Anderson, John A. Copeland, Sherrard Lewis Leary and Shields Green.

On Sunday morning, October 16th, 1859, Brown assembled his men and informed them that on that night their invasion into Virginia would take place. They took the oath of allegiance to the "Provisional Government." Adjutant General Kagi presented to each officer his commission.

The contents of the Armory, Arsenal and Hall's Rifle Works were daily open to public inspection. Captain John Brown well knew that Daniel Whelan was the only watchman, during the nighttime, at the Armory grounds. He believed that if he could secure the arms and ammunition in these buildings, carry them into the vastnesses of the adjacent mountains, and then unfurl the flag of freedom for all slaves who would flock to his standard, the result would be a general uprising of the negro population throughout the border states. A more idiotic and senseless theory never entered an American mind. In the superlative degree it was unreasonable and ridiculous. I personally know of the general loyalty of the slaves to their masters in that locality, at that period in our national history. Federal generals were astonished at the devotion of the negroes to their masters everywhere in the South after the war had begun. This was especially true along the border states. But John Brown—honest, enthusiastic and intensely fanatical on the slavery question—issued his commands. On this Sunday he assigned to each his earliest work. Captain Owen Brown, Barclay Coppoc and Francis J. Merriam were to remain at the farm to guard the arms and ammunition. Hence only nineteen left the Kennedy farm. They were to walk down the river road on the Maryland side to the Maryland end of the Baltimore and Ohio railroad bridge. The Virginia end was close to the depot, hotel, Armory and the Arsenal. Captain John Brown was to ride in the wagon with the necessary guns, pistols and tools. Captains Cook and Tidd were to go in advance and cut the telegraph wires on the Maryland side. Captain Stephens and Adjutant General Kagi were to capture Mr. Williams, the guard of the bridge. Captain Watson Brown and Taylor were to hold up the passenger train due from the west at 1:40 A. M. It would be bound for Washington and Baltimore. Captain Oliver Brown and Thompson were to hold the bridges spanning the two rivers. Captain Dauphin Adolphus Thompson and Lieutenant Anderson were to hold the first building in the Armory grounds popularly known afterwards as "John Brown's Fort." It was the engine house where Brown held his most distinguished prisoners. From the portholes of it that they made after his entrance, his men did their final fighting. Captain Coppoc and Lieutenant Hazlitt were to hold the Arsenal outside and opposite the Armory gates. Adjutant General Kagi and Copeland were to seize and retain Hall's Rifle Works. They were half of a mile up the western shore of the Shenandoah. Captain Stephens, and such men as he might select, were to go out to the home of Colonel Lewis W. Washington, the grand nephew of General George Washington, and bring him and some of his adult male slaves, to the engine house. They were also to secure the swords presented to General George Washington by Frederick the Great and by General Lafayette. For this object Stephens selected as his helpers Captains Tidd and Cook and privates Leary, Green and Anderson.

Brown made the raid at 11:30 that night. Mr. Williams the bridge guard was captured by Stephens and Kagi. The watchman at the Armory, Daniel Whelan, refused Brown and his men admission to the grounds. They broke the locks with tools, captured Whelan, and took possession of the Armory and also of the Arsenal outside. The following prisoners were brought in early on Monday and placed in the engine house: Jesse W. Graham who was master workman, Colonel Lewis W. Washington, Terance Byrne, John M. Allstadt, John Donohue, who was clerk of the railroad company; Benjamin F. Mills, the master armorer; Armstead M. Ball, the master machinist; Archibald M. Kitzmiller, assistant superintendent; Isaac Russell, a Justice of the Peace; George D. Shope, of Frederick and J. Bird, Arsenal armorer. The white prisoners were to be held as hostages and the blacks were to be armed and placed in Brown's army. Cook and Tidd evidently mistrusted their surroundings. During the night they made their way back to the farm and hastily escaped into Pennsylvania. Captain Watson Brown and Taylor held up the train bound for Baltimore, detaining it for three hours. The colored porter of the depot, Shepherd Hayward, went out on the bridge to hunt for Williams. He was brutally shot by one of Brown's bridge guards. Hayward managed to crawl to the baggage room where he died at noon on Monday. Dr. John Starry dressed his wounds and ministered to his every want. The physician was under the impression that a band of train robbers had captured the depot. He told this to Mr. Kitzmiller before Kitzmiller's imprisonment. Captain E. P. Dangerfield, clerk to the paymaster, entered the grounds and was hustled into the engine house quite early in the morning. Numerous arriving workmen were imprisoned in an adjoining building. Colonel Washington said that fully sixty men were imprisoned by eight o'clock on Monday morning.

The citizens were hearing of the situation. Newby and Green, negroes, were stationed at the junction of High and Shenandoah streets. Newby shot at and killed Captain George W. Turner, a graduate of West Point. Green shot and killed Mr. Thomas Boerley, a grocer. Dr. Claggett attended Boerley, who also soon died. After the mulatto had shot Turner, a man named Bogert entered the residence of Mrs. Stephenson by a rear door. Having no bullet he put a large nail into his gun, went up stairs and shot Newby, the nail cutting his throat from ear to ear. He was also shot in the stomach by some one else. I saw him die, in great agony, with an infuriated crowd around him.

About ten o'clock in the morning, armed citizens crossed the Potomac and Shenandoah rivers to prevent the escape by the bridges, or by water, of any of the raiders. Some walked down the Maryland river road and wounded Captain Oliver Brown on the bridge. He reached the engine house but soon died beside his father. Citizens seized the uninjured prisoner, Captain Thompson, and put him under guard at the Galt hotel. Captain Stephens tried to reach the hotel to propose, as he stated, terms of surrender. George Chambers wounded him, and then assisted him into the Galt hotel, where his wounds were dressed. About eleven o'clock in the morning the Jefferson Guards from Charlestown commanded by Captain J. W. Rowen arrived. A half hour passed and the Hamtramck guards under Captain V. M. Butler came to the Ferry. They were followed by the Shepherdstown Mounted Troop commanded by Captain Jacob Reinhart. Then a military company from Martinsburg twenty miles distant reached the place, under the command of Captain Alburtis. Colonels W. R. Baylor and John T. Gibson took the general direction of the military affairs. Some soldiers crossed the Shenandoah along with armed citizens to intercept the four raiders Kagi, Leary, Leeman and Copeland, when they should be driven out of Hall's Rifle Works. These raiders also had in these works one of Colonel Washington's slaves pressed into their service. All of them ran out into the river to swim across to the Loudon County shore. All were shot to death in the river with the exception of Copeland. He threw up his hands and surrendered. During the excitement Hazlitt and the negro Anderson left the Arsenal and, undetected, escaped into Pennsylvania. Early in the morning Captain Owen Brown, Barclay Coppoc and Merriam had deserted the Kennedy farm and gone north. Thus seven of the twenty-two men fled to the North. Cook and Hazlitt were captured. They were returned to Virginia, tried and executed.

By 2 o'clock p.m., the town and hills swarmed with militia and citizens. Brown had barricaded the engine house doors with the engine and reel. Inside were Captains John Brown and his son Watson; also Captain Oliver Brown, who was soon dead; Shields Green, Captain Edwin Coppoc, Lieutenant Jeremiah G. Anderson, Captain Dauphin Adolphus Thompson and ten white prisoners. The numerous prisoners, mostly workmen, in the adjoining structure had all escaped from the grounds, Brown having no port-holes on that side of his fort. The militia were afraid to fire into the port-holes for fear of killing some of the prominent prisoners. About 4 o'clock the Mayor, Mr. Fontaine Beckham, aged sixty years, who was also station agent of the railroad company, went out on the platform unarmed. He was shot dead by the negro Shields Green. Captain Watson Brown in the engine house received his death wound soon afterwards. Mayor Beckham was very much beloved by the people. A number of citizens hurried into the hotel and brutally seized Captain Thompson, threw him over the wall into the Potomac and riddled him with bullets. Mrs. Foulke of the hotel, and her colored porter, went to the platform and brought in the dead body of the Mayor.

As night was settling on the excited city a military company from Winchester, Virginia, commanded by Captain B. B. Washington, arrived by a Shenandoah Valley train. Shortly thereafter a Baltimore and Ohio railroad train brought several companies of soldiers from Frederick, Maryland. They were commanded by Colonel Shriver. Soon several independent companies from Baltimore, accompanied by the Second Light Brigade, arrived under the general command of General Charles C. Edgerton. Colonel Robert E. Lee of the United States army overtook these troops at Sandy Hook, a mile and a half below the Ferry on the Maryland side. He had come from Washington with several companies of marines. He was accompanied by Lieutenant J. E. B. Stuart, afterwards a famous Confederate Cavalry General; also by Major Russell and by Lieutenant Israel Green, who died several months ago in the West. All were regular army officers.

Colonel Lee regarded it as unwise to attack the engine house that night, fearing that Colonel Lewis W. Washington or other prisoners might be killed. Early in the morning he sent Lieutenant J. E. B. Stuart, who had once held Brown as a prisoner in Kansas, to demand an immediate and unconditional surrender. Brown refused to trust himself and men to the United States officers. About this time Colonel Robert E. Lee got within range of Captain Coppoc's rifle. Prisoners said that Mr. Graham knocked the muzzle aside. Lee's life was saved.

Had he been then killed who knows that the battles of Antietam, Gettysburg, and the final conflicts north of the Appomattox would have ever been fought? On the Confederate side no abler general or more magnificent man, ever sat on a saddle than Robert E. Lee. He was the son of "Light Horse Harry Lee," a brave Major General of the Revolutionary War. He was the father of William Henry Fitzhugh Lee, who became a Major General of the Confederate forces of Virginia, at a later date. General Robert E. Lee made a brilliant record in the Mexican war as Chief Engineer of the United States army. After surrendering his decimated army to General Ulysses S. Grant, at Appomattox, he accepted the political situation with dignity. He became President of the Washington University at Lexington, Virginia. The South lavished on him every possible honor. During the late summer the Virginia legislature placed in the National Hall of Fame, at the United States Capitol, two fine statues of two representative men of their state. One was the statue of General George Washington; the other that of General Robert E. Lee.

By the advice of Colonel Lewis W. Washington all of Brown's prisoners mounted the fire engine and the reel carriage and lifted up their hands when the attack began. Three marines undertook to batter down the doors with heavy sledgehammers. They were not successful. Then twelve marines struck the doors with the end of a strong ladder. They opened. Lieutenant Green entered first of all amidst a shower of bullets. Discovering Brown reloading his rifle he sprang on him with his sword and cut his head and stomach. The raider Captain Anderson rose to shoot Green. A marine named Luke Quinn ran his bayonet through him. Another raider shot Luke Quinn who soon died. Two other marines were wounded. I saw Captains Anderson and Watson Brown as they lay dying on the grass after their capture. The dead body of Captain Oliver Brown lay beside them. Captain Watson Brown had been dying for sixteen hours. Captain John Brown, bleeding profusely, and Captain Stephens from the hotel, were carried into the paymaster's office. Brown's long grey beard was stained with wet blood. He was bare headed. His shirt and trousers were grey in color. His trousers were tucked into the top of his boots. Captain Coppoc and the negro Green were also taken prisoners. They were not wounded.

As Brown lay on the floor of the paymaster's office he was very cool and courageous. Governor Henry A. Wise, United States Senator J. M. Mason of Virginia and Honorable Clement L. Vallandingham of Ohio plied him with many questions. To all he gave intelligent and fearless replies. He refused to involve his Northern financiers and advisers. He took the entire responsibility on himself. He told Governor Wise that he, Brown, was simply "An instrument in the hands of Providence." He said to some newspaper correspondents and others: "I wish to say that you had better—all you people of the South—prepare for a settlement of this question. You may dispose of me very easily. I am nearly disposed of now. But this question is yet to be settled—this negro question I mean. The end is not yet." Before thirteen months had passed one of the greatest Americans of any century, Abraham Lincoln, had been elected President of the United States; the Republican party was for the first time dominating national affairs and, soon thereafter, the Civil War was begun which culminated in the physical freedom of every slave in this Republic.

On Wednesday Captains John Brown, Stephens and Coppoc, along with Copeland and Green, were removed to the county jail at Charlestown, ten miles south of Harper's Ferry. Being acquainted with the jailor, Captain John Avis, I was permitted to visit Brown on one occasion. Captain Aaron D. Stephens was lying on a cot in the same room. I was told that Brown had ordered out of his room a Presbyterian minister named Lowrey when he had proposed to offer prayer. He had also said to my first colleague, Rev. James H. March, "You do not know the meaning of the word Christianity. Of course I regard you as a gentleman, but only as a heathen gentleman." I was advised to say nothing to him about prayer. He had told other visitors that he wanted no minister to pray with him who would not be willing to die to free a slave. I was not conscious that I was ready for martyrdom from Brown's standpoint. I have never been anxious to die to save the life of any body. My life is as valuable to me and my family as any other man's is to him and his family. But young as I was, I hated American slavery. I was a "boy minister" of a great anti-slavery denomination of Christians. For more than a century the Methodist Episcopal Church has carried in its Disciplines its printed testimony against slavery. It is to-day the largest fully organized anti-slavery society on earth. I would have gladly offered prayer in Brown's room at Charlestown if an honorable opportunity had been afforded.

At his preliminary examination before five justices, Colonel Davenport presiding, Brown said: "Virginians! I did not ask for quarter at the time I was taken. I did not ask to have my life spared. Your governor assured me of a fair trial. If you seek my blood you can have it at any time without this mockery of a trial. I have no counsel. I have not been able to advise with any one. I know nothing of the feelings of my fellow prisoners and am utterly unable to attend to my own defense. If a fair trial is to be allowed there are mitigating circumstances to be urged. But, if we are forced with a mere form, a trial for execution, you might spare yourselves that trouble. I am ready for my fate."

Two very able Virginia attorneys were assigned as a matter of State form as counsel for Brown. They were Honorable Charles J. Faulkner of Martinsburg, afterwards United States Envoy Extraordinary to France, and Judge Green, Ex-Mayor of Charlestown. The county grand jury indicted Brown on three separate charges: first, conspiracy with slaves for purposes of insurrection; second, treason against the commonwealth of Virginia; third, murder in the first degree. Mr. Faulkner withdrew from the case and Mr. Lawson Botts took his place. Mr. Samuel Chilton a learned lawyer of Washington, D. C., and Judge Henry Griswold of Ohio, another distinguished attorney, volunteered their services as counsel for John Brown and were accepted. Some of Brown's friends sent an excellent young lawyer named George H. Hoyt from Boston, as additional counsel. These attorneys made an able defense, whatever may have been their private opinion as to Brown's guilt or innocence. The prosecuting attorney for the State of Virginia was Andrew Hunter, an exceptionally brilliant orator and able lawyer. He was a courtly and commanding speaker. He was gifted with a rich and powerful voice. After the indictment of Brown by the court of justices, the prosecuting attorney of Jefferson county, Mr. Charles B. Harding left the prosecution almost exclusively to Mr. Andrew Hunter, who represented the State. So too, after the arrival of Brown's chosen outside counsel, Judge Green and Mr. Lawson Botts withdrew, in good taste, from his defense.

At the regular trial Brown's counsel requested a postponement on account of the prisoner's health. But Dr. Mason, his physician, attested the physical ability of his patient to undergo the strain. The State was spending almost a thousand dollars a day for military guards and other items. When Brown's counsel presented telegrams from his relatives asking for delay until they could forward proofs of his insanity, Brown said, "I will say, if the court will allow me, that I look on this as a miserable artifice and trick of those who ought to take a different course in regard to me if they take any at all. I view it with contempt more than otherwise. I am perfectly unconscious of insanity and I reject, so far as I am capable, any attempts to interfere in my behalf on that score."

On the last day of the trial, October 31st, after six hours of argument by Hunter, Chilton and Griswold, the jury delivered the following verdict: "Guilty of treason, and of conspiring and advising with slaves and others to rebel; and of murder in the first degree." On Wednesday, November the 2nd, he was brought into court to receive his sentence. The County Clerk, Robert H. Brown, asked: "Have you anything to say why sentence should not be passed on you?" Brown, leaning on a cane, slowly arose from his chair and with plaintive emphasis addressed Judge Parker as follows:

"I have, may it please the court, a few words to say. In the first place I deny everything but what I have all along admitted, the design on my part to free the slaves. I certainly intended to have made a clean thing of that matter as I did last winter when I went into Missouri and took slaves without the snapping of a gun on either side, moved them through the country and finally left them in Canada. I designed to have done the same thing again on a larger scale. That was all I intended. I never did intend murder or treason, or the destruction of property, or to excite or incite slaves to rebellion or to make insurrection. I have another objection and that is that it is unjust that I should suffer such a penalty. Had I interfered in the manner which I admit, and which I admit has been fairly proved, for I admire the truthfulness and candor of the greater portion of the witnesses who have testified in this case, had I so interfered in behalf of the rich, the powerful, the intelligent, the so-called great; or in behalf of any of their friends, either father, mother, sister, brother, wife or children, or any of that class, and suffered and sacrificed what I have in this interference, it would have been all right and every man in this court would have deemed it an act worthy of reward rather than punishment. This court acknowledges as I suppose the validity of the law of God. I see a book kissed here which I suppose is the Bible, or at least the New Testament. That teaches me that all things whatsoever I would that men should do to me I should do even unto them. It teaches me further to 'Remember them that are in bonds as bound with them.' I endeavored to act up to that instruction. I say that I am yet too young to understand that God is any respecter of persons. I believe that to have interfered as I have done, as I have always admitted freely I have done, in behalf of His despised poor was not wrong but right. Now if it is deemed necessary that I should forfeit my life for the furtherance of the ends of justice, and mingle my blood further with the blood of my children and with the blood of millions in this slave country whose rights are disregarded by wicked, cruel and unjust enactments, I submit. So let it be done.

"Let me say one word further. I feel entirely satisfied with the treatment I have received on my trial. Considering all the circumstances it has been more generous than I expected. But I feel no consciousness of guilt. I never had any design against the life of any person, nor any disposition to commit treason or excite slaves to rebellion or make any general insurrection. I never encouraged any man to do so but always discouraged any idea of the kind.

"Let me say a word in regard to the statements made by some of those connected with me. I hear it has been stated by some of them that I induced them to join me. But the contrary is true. I do not say this to injure them, but as regards their weakness. There is not one of them but joined me of his own accord and the greater part of them at their own expense. A number of them I never saw, and never had a word of conversation with, till the day they came to me, and that was for the purpose I have stated. Now I am done."

Brown's statement was not exactly sustained by the facts. Why had he collected the Sharpe's rifles, the pikes, the kegs of powder, many thousands of caps and much warlike material at the Kennedy farm? Why did he and other armed men, break into the United States Armory and Arsenal, make portholes in the engine house, shoot and kill citizens and surround their own imprisoned persons with prominent men as hostages? But everybody in the courthouse believed the old man when he said that he did everything with a solitary motive, the liberation of the slaves.

Judge Parker could, under his oath, do nothing else than to sentence him to be hung. He fixed the date for Friday, the second of December. Brown's counsel appealed to the Supreme Court of Virginia. Its five judges unanimously sustained the action of the Jefferson county court.

Brown was hung on the bright and beautiful morning of December 2nd at 11:15 o'clock. At his request Andrew Hunter wrote his will. He then visited his fellow prisoners who were all executed at a later date. He rode to his death between Sheriff Campbell and Captain Avis in a furniture wagon drawn by two white horses. He did not ride seated on his coffin as some of his chief eulogists have affirmed. The wagon was escorted to the scaffold by State military companies. No citizens were allowed near to the jail. Hence he did not kiss any negro baby as he emerged from his prison, as Mr. Whittier has described in a poem on the event and as artists have memorialized in paintings. The utter absurdity of such an incident occurring under such surroundings any Virginian will see. Avis, Campbell and Hunter publicly denied it. But the story will doubtless have immortality. In one of the companies of soldiers walked the actor John Wilkes Booth, the infamous assassin of Abraham Lincoln. At the head of the Lexington cadets walked Professor Thomas Jefferson Jackson, who became an able Confederate General and is best known to the world as "Stonewall Jackson." As the party neared the gallows Brown gazed on the glorious panorama of mountain and landscape scenery. Then he said: "This is a beautiful country." He wore a black slouch hat with the front tipped up. Reaching the scaffold the numerous State troops formed into a hollow square. Brown mounted the platform without trepidation. Standing on the drop he said to the sheriff and his assistants: "Gentlemen! I thank you for your kindness to me. I am ready at any time. Do not keep me waiting." The drop fell and in ten minutes Dr. Mason pronounced him dead.

That evening Mrs. Brown and her friends received the casket at Harper's Ferry and accompanied it to the old home at North Elba, N. Y.

His funeral, as reported by the metropolitan papers, took place there six days after his execution. An immense concourse was in attendance. The conspicuous and brilliant orator, Wendell Phillips, delivered the address. He closed it with these words: "In this cottage he girded himself and went forth to battle. Fuller success than his heart ever dreamed of God had granted him. He sleeps in the blessings of the crushed and the poor. Men believe more firmly in virtue now that such a man has lived."

Source: Rev. Samuel Vanderlip Leech, *The Raid of John Brown at Harper's Ferry as I Saw It* (Washington, DC: DeSoto, 1909; Project Gutenberg, 2001), http://www.gutenberg .org/ebooks/35427.

A DECLARATION OF THE IMMEDIATE CAUSES WHICH INDUCE AND JUSTIFY THE SECESSION OF THE STATE OF MISSISSIPPI FROM THE FEDERAL UNION

JANUARY 9, 1861

The valuable purpose of documents such as Mississippi's Ordinance of Secession is to show what was set forth as the official and candid reason for their leaving the Union. Reading their plain language one wonders how any contemporary of theirs could say the determinative reason for Southern secession was a studied commitment to states' rights or differences with Northern states over tariffs. As Lincoln said, all knew that slavery was somehow the cause of the war. The way Mississippi politicians saw it, secession was necessary not merely because cotton was king, but because the slaves who picked it constituted "the greatest material interest of the world." There was money in slavery, in short. There's some racialist reasoning for secession thrown in too—slavery must be protected because Africans could take the sun better.

In the momentous step which our State has taken of dissolving its connection with the government of which we so long formed a part, it is but just that we should declare the prominent reasons which have induced our course.

Our position is thoroughly identified with the institution of slavery—the greatest material interest of the world. Its labor supplies the product, which constitutes by far the largest and most important portions of commerce of the earth. These products are peculiar to the climate verging on the tropical regions, and by an imperious law of nature, none but the black race can bear exposure to the tropical sun. These products have become necessities of the world, and a blow at slavery is a blow at commerce and civilization. That blow has been long aimed at the institution, and was at the point of reaching its consummation. There was no choice left us but submission to the mandates of abolition, or dissolution of the Union, whose principles had been subverted to work out our ruin.

That we do not overstate the dangers to our institution, a reference to a few facts will sufficiently prove.

The hostility to this institution commenced before the adoption of the Constitution and was manifested in the well-known Ordinance of 1787, in regard to the Northwestern Territory.

The feeling increased, until, in 1819-20, it deprived the South of more than half the vast territory acquired from France.

The same hostility dismembered Texas and seized upon all the territory acquired from Mexico.

It has grown until it denies the right of property in slaves, and refuses protection to that right on the high seas, in the Territories, and wherever the government of the United States had jurisdiction.

It refuses the admission of new slave States into the Union, and seeks to extinguish it by confining it within its present limits, denying the power of expansion.

It tramples the original equality of the South under foot.

It has nullified the Fugitive Slave Law in almost every free State in the Union, and has utterly broken the compact which our fathers pledged their faith to maintain.

It advocates negro equality, socially and politically, and promotes insurrection and incendiarism in our midst.

It has enlisted its press, its pulpit and its schools against us, until the whole popular mind of the North is excited and inflamed with prejudice.

It has made combinations and formed associations to carry out its schemes of emancipation in the States and wherever else slavery exists.

It seeks not to elevate or to support the slave, but to destroy his present condition without providing a better.

It has invaded a State, and invested with the honors of martyrdom the wretch whose purpose was to apply flames to our dwellings, and the weapons of destruction to our lives.

It has broken every compact into which it has entered for our security.

It has given indubitable evidence of its design to ruin our agriculture, to prostrate our industrial pursuits and to destroy our social system.

It knows no relenting or hesitation in its purposes; it stops not in its march of aggression, and leaves us no room to hope for cessation or for pause.

It has recently obtained control of the Government, by the prosecution of its unhallowed schemes, and destroyed the last expectation of living together in friendship and brotherhood.

Utter subjugation awaits us in the Union, if we should consent longer to remain in it. It is not a matter of choice, but of necessity. We must either submit to degradation, and to the loss of property worth four billions of money, or we must secede from the Union framed by our fathers, to secure this as well as every other species of property. For far less cause than this, our fathers separated from the Crown of England.

Our decision is made. We follow their footsteps. We embrace the alternative of separation; and for the reasons here stated, we resolve to maintain our rights with the full consciousness of the justice of our course, and the undoubting belief of our ability to maintain it.

Source: Secession of Mississippi from the Federal Union and the Ordinance of Secession (Jackson, MS: Mississippian Book and Job Printing Office, 1861), https://en.wikisource .org/wiki/Secession_of_Mississippi_from_the_Federal_Union_and_the_ordinance_of _secession.

THE CORNER-STONE SPEECH

ALEXANDER H. STEPHENS, CSA
MARCH 21, 1861

In tandem with Mississippi's justification for secession is Alexander Stephens's speech made just prior to the war's inauguration. Here he first underscores the advantages of the new Confederate constitution (the same argument as his is made today for limiting a president to one six-year term). But more important than the new political science in the South would be the confirmation of ancient racial science. It would be difficult to concoct a more fundamentalist argument than his for the protection and perpetuation of negro slavery, given his presumptions, which we moderns do not accept. Frederick Douglass, in a sense, would take the same path and insist years later that the Civil War was a war of ideas—right ideas and wrong ideas. Blacks, Stephens argued, were not merely second-rate humans. They were profoundly inferior, and their continuance in that position would be the "corner-stone" on which the South would be constructed. Again, states' rights are not the issue the South would actually fight for. The issue would be, in Stephens's way of thinking, white rights. These were the true natural rights, and he considered his logic the equivalent of Galileo's.

I was remarking that we are passing through one of the greatest revolutions in the annals of the world. Seven States have within the last three months thrown off an old government and formed a new. This revolution has been signally marked, up to this time, by the fact of its having been accomplished without the loss of a single drop of blood.

This new constitution, or form of government, constitutes the subject to which your attention will be partly invited. In reference to it, I make this first general remark: it amply secures all our ancient rights, franchises, and liberties. All the great principles of Magna Charta are retained in it. No citizen is deprived of life, liberty, or property, but by the judgment of his peers under the laws of the land. The great principle of religious liberty, which was the honor and pride of the old constitution, is still maintained and secured. All the essentials of the old constitution, which have endeared it to the hearts of the American people, have been preserved and perpetuated. Some changes have been made. Some of these I should have preferred not to have been made; but other important changes do meet my cordial approbation. They form great improvements upon the old constitution. So, taking the whole new constitution, I have no hesitancy in giving it as my judgment that it is decidedly better than the old.

Allow me briefly to allude to some of these improvements. The question of building up class interests, or fostering one branch of industry to the prejudice of another under the exercise of the revenue power, which gave us so much trouble under the old constitution, is put at rest forever under the new. We allow the imposition of no duty with a view of giving advantage to one class of persons, in any trade or business, over those of another. All, under our system, stand upon the same broad principles of perfect equality. Honest labor and enterprise are left free and unrestricted in whatever pursuit they may be engaged. This old thorn of the tariff, which was the cause of so much irritation in the old body politic, is removed forever from the new.

Again, the subject of internal improvements, under the power of Congress to regulate commerce, is put at rest under our system. The power, claimed by construction under the old constitution, was at least a doubtful one; it rested solely upon construction. We of the South, generally apart from considerations of constitutional principles, opposed its exercise upon grounds of its inexpediency and injustice. Notwithstanding this opposition, millions of money, from the common treasury had been drawn for such purposes. Our opposition sprang from no hostility to commerce, or to all necessary aids for facilitating it. With us it was simply a question upon whom the burden should fall. In Georgia, for instance, we have done as much for the cause of internal improvements as any other portion of the country, according to population and means. We have stretched out lines of railroads from the seaboard to the mountains; dug down the hills, and filled up the valleys at a cost of not less than $25,000,000. All this was done to open an outlet for our products of the interior, and those to the west of us, to reach the marts of the world. No State was in greater need of such facilities than Georgia, but we did not ask that these works should be made by appropriations out of the common treasury. The cost of the grading, the superstructure, and the equipment of our roads was borne by those who had entered into the enterprise. Nay, more not only the cost of the iron no small item in the aggregate cost was borne in the same way, but we were compelled to pay into the common treasury several millions of dollars for the privilege of importing the iron, after the price was paid for it abroad. What justice was there in taking this money, which our people paid into the common treasury on the importation of our iron, and applying it to the improvement of rivers and harbors elsewhere? The true principle is to subject the commerce of every locality, to whatever burdens may be necessary to facilitate it. If Charleston harbor needs improvement, let the commerce of Charleston bear the burden. If the mouth of the Savannah river has to be cleared out, let the sea-going navigation which is benefited by it, bear the burden. So with the mouths of the Alabama and Mississippi river. Just as the products of the interior, our cotton, wheat, corn, and other articles, have to bear the necessary rates of freight over our railroads to reach the seas. This is again the broad principle of perfect equality and justice, and it is especially set forth and established in our new constitution.

Another feature to which I will allude is that the new constitution provides that cabinet ministers and heads of departments may have the privilege of seats upon the floor of the Senate and House of Representatives and may have the right to participate in the debates and discussions upon the various subjects of administration. I should have preferred that this provision should have gone further, and required the President to select his constitutional advisers from the Senate and House of Representatives. That would have conformed entirely to the practice in the British Parliament, which, in my judgment, is one of the wisest provisions in the

British constitution. It is the only feature that saves that government. It is that which gives it stability in its facility to change its administration. Ours, as it is, is a great approximation to the right principle....

Another change in the constitution relates to the length of the tenure of the presidential office. In the new constitution it is six years instead of four, and the President rendered ineligible for a re-election. This is certainly a decidedly conservative change. It will remove from the incumbent all temptation to use his office or exert the powers confided to him for any objects of personal ambition. The only incentive to that higher ambition which should move and actuate one holding such high trusts in his hands, will be the good of the people, the advancement, prosperity, happiness, safety, honor, and true glory of the confederacy.

But not to be tedious in enumerating the numerous changes for the better, allow me to allude to one other though last, not least. The new constitution has put at rest, forever, all the agitating questions relating to our peculiar institution, African slavery, as it exists amongst us the proper status of the negro in our form of civilization. This was the immediate cause of the late rupture and present revolution. Jefferson in his forecast, had anticipated this, as the "rock upon which the old Union would split." He was right. What was conjecture with him, is now a realized fact. But whether he fully comprehended the great truth upon which that rock stood and stands, may be doubted. The prevailing ideas entertained by him and most of the leading statesmen at the time of the formation of the old constitution, were that the enslavement of the African was in violation of the laws of nature; that it was wrong in principle, socially, morally, and politically. It was an evil they knew not well how to deal with, but the general opinion of the men of that day was that, somehow or other in the order of Providence, the institution would be evanescent and pass away. This idea, though not incorporated in the constitution, was the prevailing idea at that time. The constitution, it is true, secured every essential guarantee to the institution while it should last, and hence no argument can be justly urged against the constitutional guarantees thus secured, because of the common sentiment of the day. Those ideas, however, were fundamentally wrong. They rested upon the assumption of the equality of races. This was an error. It was a sandy foundation, and the government built upon it fell when the "storm came and the wind blew."

Our new government is founded upon exactly the opposite idea; its foundations are laid, its corner-stone rests, upon the great truth that the negro is not equal to the white man; that slavery subordination to the superior race is his natural and normal condition. This, our new government, is the first, in the history of the world, based upon this great physical, philosophical, and moral truth. This truth has been slow in the process of its development, like all other truths in the various departments of science. It has been so even amongst us. Many who hear me, perhaps, can recollect well, that this truth was not generally admitted, even within their day. The errors of the past generation still clung to many as late as twenty years ago. Those at the North, who still cling to these errors, with a zeal above knowledge, we justly denominate fanatics. All fanaticism springs from an aberration of the mind from a defect in reasoning. It is a species of insanity. One of the most striking characteristics of insanity, in many instances, is forming correct conclusions from fancied or erroneous premises; so with the anti-slavery fanatics. Their conclusions are right if their premises were. They assume that the negro is equal, and hence conclude that he is entitled to equal privileges and rights with the white man. If their premises were correct, their conclusions would be logical and just but their premise being wrong, their whole argument fails. I recollect once of having heard a gentleman from one of the northern States, of great power and ability, announce in the House of Representatives, with imposing effect, that we of the South would be compelled, ultimately, to yield upon this subject of slavery, that it was as impossible to war successfully against a principle in politics, as it was in physics or mechanics. That the principle would ultimately prevail. That we, in maintaining slavery as it exists with us, were warring against a principle, a principle founded in nature, the principle of the equality of men. The reply I made to him was, that upon his own grounds, we should, ultimately, succeed, and that he and his associates, in this crusade against our institutions, would ultimately fail. The truth announced, that it was as impossible to war successfully against a principle in politics as it was in physics and mechanics, I admitted; but told him that it was he, and those acting with him, who were warring against a principle. They were attempting to make things equal which the Creator had made unequal.

In the conflict thus far, success has been on our side, complete throughout the length and breadth of the Confederate States. It is upon this, as I have stated, our social fabric is firmly planted; and I cannot permit myself to doubt the ultimate success of a full recognition of this principle throughout the civilized and enlightened world.

As I have stated, the truth of this principle may be slow in development, as all truths are and ever have been, in the various branches of science. It was so with the principles announced by Galileo, it was so with Adam Smith and his principles of political economy. It was so with Harvey, and his theory of the circulation of the blood. It is stated that not a single one of the medical profession, living at the time of the announcement of the truths made by him, admitted them. Now, they are universally acknowledged. May we not, therefore, look with confidence to the ultimate universal acknowledgment of the truths upon which our system rests? It is the first government ever instituted upon the principles in strict conformity to nature, and the ordination of Providence, in furnishing the materials of human society. Many governments have been founded upon the principle of the subordination and serfdom of certain classes of the same race; such were and are in violation of the laws of nature. Our system commits no such violation of nature's laws. With us, all of the white race, however high or low, rich or poor, are equal in the eye of the law. Not so with the negro. Subordination is his place. He, by nature, or by the curse against Canaan, is fitted for that condition which he occupies in our system. The architect, in the construction of buildings, lays the foundation with the proper material—the granite; then comes the brick or the marble. The substratum of our society is made of the material fitted by nature for it, and by experience we know that it is best, not only for the superior, but for the inferior race, that it should be so. It is, indeed, in conformity with the ordinance of the Creator. It is not for us to inquire into the wisdom of His ordinances, or to question them. For His own purposes, He has made one race to differ from another, as He has made "one star to differ from another star in glory." The great objects of humanity are best attained when there is conformity to His laws and decrees, in the formation of governments as well as in all things else. Our confederacy is founded upon principles in strict conformity with these laws. This stone which was rejected by the first builders "is become the chief of the corner" the real "corner-stone" in our new edifice.

Source: Henry Cleveland, *Alexander H. Stephens, in Public and Private: With Letters and Speeches, Before, During, and Since the War* (Philadelphia: National Publishing Company, 1866), pp. 717–29.

1861

Fort Sumter following the Confederate attack, April 14, 1861

THE BOMBARDMENT

APRIL 12, 1861
BRIG. GEN. ABNER DOUBLEDAY, USA

It is ironic that Abner Doubleday is primarily remembered for the claim—never made by him, and popularized years after his death in 1893—that he invented baseball in a cow pasture near Cooperstown, New York. The irony is that while that tale is purely mythic, Doubleday's life and military career were full of actual feats worthy of remembrance. Grandson of a minuteman and son of a War of 1812 veteran who served in Congress, Doubleday was born and raised in New York State. He graduated from the United States Military Academy in 1842, serving in the Mexican and Seminole wars. As the Civil War drew near, Doubleday was a captain at Fort Sumter, second in command to Col. John L. Gardner. With the fort under siege from secessionist Charleston, where artillery stood ready to stop the naval resupply ordered by President Lincoln, it was Doubleday's cannon that fired the first response to Confederate shells. Later he fought with distinction at Second Bull Run, Antietam, and Gettysburg. Here, he recalls that fateful time when the irrepressible conflict finally erupted into fighting.

As soon as the outline of our fort [Sumter] could be distinguished, the enemy carried out their programme. It had been arranged, as a special compliment to the venerable Edmund Ruffin, who might almost be called the father of secession, that he should fire the first shot against us, from the Stevens battery on Cummings Point, and I think in all the histories it is stated that he did so; but it is attested by Dr. Crawford and others who were on the parapet at the time, that the first shot really came from the mortar battery at Fort Johnson. Almost immediately afterward a ball from Cummings Point lodged in the magazine wall, and by the sound seemed to bury itself in the masonry about a foot from my head, in very unpleasant proximity to my right ear. This is the one that probably came with Mr. Ruffin's compliments. In a moment the firing burst forth in one continuous roar, and large patches of both the exterior and interior masonry began to crumble and fall in all directions. The place where I was had been used for the manufacture of cartridges, and there was still a good deal of powder there, some packed and some loose. A shell soon struck near the ventilator, and a puff of dense smoke entered the room, giving me a strong impression that there would be an immediate explosion. Fortunately, no sparks had penetrated inside.

Nineteen batteries were now hammering at us, and the balls and shells from the ten-inch columbiads, accompanied by shells from the thirteen-inch mortars which constantly bombarded us, made us feel as if the war had commenced in earnest.

When it was broad daylight, I went down to breakfast. I found the officers already assembled at one of the long tables in the mess-hall. Our party were calm, and even somewhat merry. We had retained one colored man to wait on us. He was a spruce-looking mulatto from Charleston, very active and efficient on ordinary occasions, but now completely demoralized by the thunder of the guns and crashing of the shot around us. He leaned back against the wall, almost white with fear, his eyes closed, and his whole expression one of perfect despair. Our meal was not very sumptuous. It consisted of pork and water, but Dr. Crawford triumphantly brought forth a little farina, which he had found in a corner of the hospital.

When this frugal repast was over, my company was told off in three details for firing purposes, to be relieved afterward by Seymour's company. As I was the ranking officer, I took the first detachment, and marched them to the casemates, which looked out upon the powerful iron-clad battery of Cummings Point.

In aiming the first gun fired against the rebellion I had no feeling of self-reproach, for I fully believed that the contest was inevitable, and was not of our seeking. The United States was called upon not only to defend its sovereignty, but its right to exist as a nation. The only alternative was to submit to a powerful oligarchy who were determined to make freedom forever subordinate to slavery. To me it was simply a contest, politically speaking, as to whether virtue or vice should rule.

My first shot bounded off from the sloping roof of the battery opposite without producing any apparent effect. It seemed useless to attempt to silence the guns there; for our metal was not heavy enough to batter the work down, and every ball glanced harmlessly off, except one, which appeared to enter an embrasure and twist the iron shutter, so as to stop the firing of that particular gun.

I observed that a group of the enemy had ventured out from their intrenchments to watch the effect of their fire, but I sent them flying back to their shelter by the aid of a forty-two-pounder ball, which appeared to strike right in among them. . . .

Our firing now became regular, and was answered from the rebel guns which encircled us on the four sides of the pentagon upon which the fort was built. The other side faced the open sea. Showers of balls from ten-inch columbiads and forty-two-pounders, and shells from thirteen-inch mortars poured into the fort in one incessant stream, causing great flakes of masonry to fall in all directions. When the immense mortar shells, after sailing high in the air, came down in a vertical direction, and buried themselves in the parade-ground, their explosion shook the fort like an earthquake.

Our own guns were very defective, as they had no breech-sights. In place of these, Seymour and myself were obliged to devise notched sticks, which answered the purpose, but were necessarily very imperfect.

Our fort had been built with reference to the penetration of shot when the old system of smooth-bore guns prevailed. The balls from a new Blakely gun on Cummings Point, however, had force enough to go entirely through the wall which sheltered us, and some of the fragments of brick which were knocked out wounded several of my detachment. None were seriously hurt except Sergeant Thomas Kirnan, of my company. His contusions were severe, but did not keep him out of the fight.

After three hours' firing, my men became exhausted, and Captain Seymour came, with a fresh detachment, to relieve us. He has a great deal of humor in his composition, and said, jocosely, "Doubleday, what in the world is the matter here, and what is all this uproar about?"

I replied, "There is a trifling difference of opinion between us and our neighbors opposite, and we are trying to settle it."

"Very well," he said; "do you wish me to take a hand?"

I said, "Yes, I would like to have you go in."

"All right," he said. "What is your elevation, and range?"

I replied, "Five degrees, and twelve hundred yards."

"Well," he said, "here goes!" And he went to work with a will.

Part of the fleet was visible outside the bar about half-past ten A.M. It exchanged salutes with us, but did not attempt to enter the harbor, or take part in the battle. In fact, it would have had considerable difficulty in finding the channel, as the marks and buoys had all been taken up.... After the event much obloquy was thrown upon the navy because it did not come in and engage the numerous batteries and forts, and open for itself a way to Charleston; but this course would probably have resulted in the sinking of every vessel....

When Seymour's three hours were up, I relieved him, and continued the firing. As our balls bounded off the sloping iron rails like peas upon a trencher, utterly failing to make any impression, and as the shot from the Blakely gun came clear through our walls, Anderson directed that the men should cease firing at that particular place. I regretted very much that the upper tier of guns had been abandoned, as they were all loaded and pointed, and were of very heavy calibre. A wild Irish soldier, however, named John Carmody, slipped up on the parapet, and, without orders, fired the pieces there, one after another, on his own account. One of the ten-inch balls so aimed made quite an impression on the Cummings Point battery; and if the fire could have been kept up, it might possibly have knocked the iron-work to pieces.

After my detachment had abandoned the casemate opposite the Blakely gun, to my great astonishment the battery I had left recommenced firing. I could not imagine who could have taken our places. It seems that a group of the Baltimore workmen had been watching our motions, and had thus learned the duties of a cannoneer. In spite of their previous determination not to take part in the fight, they could not resist the fun of trying their hand at one of the guns. It was already accurately pointed, and the ball struck the mark in the centre. The men attributed it to their own skill, and when I entered they were fairly in convulsions of laughter. One of them, in answer to my question, gasped out, "I hit it square in the middle." After this first attempt, each of them was desirous of trying his skill at aiming. The result was, that we soon had them organized into a firing-party....

The night was an anxious one for us, for we thought it probable that the launches, filled with armed men from the fleet, might take advantage of the darkness to come in with provisions and supplies. Then, too, it was possible that the enemy might attempt a night attack. We were on the alert, therefore, with men stationed at all the embrasures; but nothing unusual occurred. The batteries fired upon us at stated intervals all night long. We did not return the fire, having no ammunition to waste.

On the morning of the 13th, we took our breakfast—or, rather, our pork and water—at the usual hour, and marched the men to the guns when the meal was over.

From 4 to 6.30 A.M. the enemy's fire was very spirited. From 7 to 8 A.M. a rain-storm came on, and there was a lull in the cannonading. About 8 A.M. the officers' quarters were ignited by one of Ripley's incendiary shells, or by shot heated in the furnaces at Fort Moultrie. The fire was put out; but at 10 A.M. a mortar shell passed through the roof, and lodged in the flooring of the second story, where it burst, and started the flames afresh. This, too, was extinguished; but the hot shot soon followed each other so rapidly that it was impossible for us to contend with them any longer. It became evident that the entire block, being built with wooden partitions, floors, and roofing, must be consumed, and that the magazine, containing three hundred barrels of powder, would be endangered; for, even after closing the metallic door, sparks might penetrate through the ventilator. The floor was covered with loose powder, where a detail of men had been at work manufacturing cartridge-bags out of old shirts, woolen blankets, etc.

While the officers exerted themselves with axes to tear down and cut away all the wood-work in the vicinity, the soldiers were rolling barrels of powder out to more sheltered spots, and were covering them with wet blankets. The labor was accelerated by the shells which were bursting around us; for Ripley had redoubled his activity at the first signs of a conflagration. We only succeeded in getting out some ninety-six barrels of powder, and then we were obliged to close the massive copper door, and await the result. A shot soon after passed through the intervening shield, struck the door, and bent the lock in such a way that it could not be opened again. We were thus cut off from our supply of ammunition, but still had some piled up in the vicinity of the guns. Anderson officially reported only four barrels and three cartridges as on hand when we left.

By 11 A.M. the conflagration was terrible and disastrous. One-fifth of the fort was on fire, and the wind drove the smoke in dense masses into the angle where we had all taken refuge. It seemed impossible to escape suffocation. Some lay down close to the ground, with handkerchiefs over their mouths, and others posted themselves near the embrasures, where the smoke was somewhat lessened by the draught of air. Every one suffered severely. I crawled out of one of these openings, and sat on the outer edge; but Ripley made it lively for me there with his case-shot, which spattered all around. Had not a slight change of wind taken place, the result might have been fatal to most of us.

Our firing having ceased, and the enemy being very jubilant, I thought it would be as well to show them that we were not all dead yet, and ordered the gunners to fire a few rounds more. I heard afterward that the enemy loudly cheered Anderson for his persistency under such adverse circumstances.

The scene at this time was really terrific. The roaring and crackling of the flames, the dense masses of whirling smoke, the bursting of the enemy's shells, and our own which were exploding in the burning rooms, the crashing of the shot, and the sound of masonry falling in every direction, made the fort a pandemonium. When at last nothing was left of the building but the blackened walls and smoldering embers, it became painfully evident that an immense amount of damage had been done. There was a tower at each angle of the fort. One of these, containing great quantities of shells, upon which we had relied, was almost completely shattered by successive explosions. The massive wooden gates, studded with iron nails, were burned, and the wall built behind them was now a mere heap of débris, so that the main entrance was wide open for an assaulting party. The sally-ports were in a similar condition, and the numerous windows on the gorge side, which had been planked up, had now become all open entrances.

About 12.48 P.M. the end of the flag-staff was shot down, and the flag fell. It had been previously hanging by one halyard, the other having been cut by a piece of shell. The exultation of the enemy, however, was short-lived. Peter Hart found a spar in the fort, which answered very well as a temporary flag-staff. He nailed the flag to this, and raised it triumphantly by nailing and tying the pole firmly to a pile of gun-carriages on the parapet. This was gallantly done, without undue haste, under Seymour's supervision, although the enemy concentrated all their fire upon the spot to prevent Hart from carrying out his intention. From the beginning, the rebel gunners had been very ambitious to shoot the flag down, and had wasted an immense number of shots in the attempt.

Source: Abner Doubleday, *Reminiscences of Forts Sumter and Moultrie in 1860–'61* (New York: Harper and Brothers, 1876; Project Gutenberg, 2008), chap. 10, http://www .gutenberg.org/ebooks/24972.

Confederate fortifications at Manassas, Virginia

THE BATTLE OF BULL RUN

JULY 21, 1861
CHARLES CARLETON COFFIN, USA

"On to Richmond!" went the cry from impatient Northerners, fully expecting Union troops to overwhelm nascent Confederate forces in a frontal assault on Virginia's capital. But the forces of USA Brig. Gen. Irvin McDowell were no more seasoned than the Southern troops under CSA Brig. Gen. P. G. T. Beauregard. The Union attack was halted, the Confederate counterattack aided by the fierce presence of a Virginia Military Institute professor, Thomas J. Jackson, whose battlefield indefatigability earned him his famous sobriquet, Stonewall. As they retreated after fierce fighting, Union soldiers and supporters realized the war was unlikely to be short and glorious. There to document the sobering action was Charles Carleton Coffin, a patriotic Republican reporter from New Hampshire who closely covered Abraham Lincoln's victorious 1860 campaign. Unable to enlist due to a crippling leg injury suffered while working on the railroad, Coffin would make his mark as a war correspondent. He covered battles from Bull Run to Appomattox, earning army goodwill for his accurate reporting and gaining the trust of the soldiers whose hardships he recounted and even shared. Here, he lays out the action at First Bull Run.*

The first great battle of the war was fought near Bull Run, in Virginia. There had been skirmishing along the Potomac, in Western Virginia, and Missouri; but upon the banks of this winding stream was fought a battle which will be forever memorable. The Rebels call it the battle of

Manassas. It has been called also the battle of Stone Bridge and the battle of Warrenton Road.

Bull Run is a lazy, sluggish stream, a branch of the Occoquan River, which empties into the Potomac. It rises among the Bull Run Mountains, and flows southeast through Fairfax County. Just beyond the stream, as you go west from Washington, are the plains of Manassas—level lands, which years ago waved with corn and tobacco, but the fields long since were worn out by the thriftless farming of the slaveholders, and now they are overgrown with thickets of pine and oak.

Two railroads meet upon the plains, one running northwest through the mountain gaps into the valley of the Shenandoah, and the other running from Alexandria to Richmond, Culpepper, and the Southwest. The junction, therefore, became an important place for Rebel military operations. There, in June, 1861, General Beauregard mustered his army, which was to defeat the Union army and capture Washington. The Richmond newspapers said that this army would not only capture Washington, but would also dictate terms of peace on the banks of the Hudson. Hot-headed men, who seemed to have lost their reason through the influence of slavery and secession, thought that the Southern troops were invincible. They were confident that one Southerner could whip five Yankees. Ladies cheered them, called them chivalrous sons of the South, and urged them on to the field.

But General Beauregard, instead of advancing upon Washington, awaited an attack from the Union army, making Bull Run his line of defense, throwing up breastworks, cutting down trees, and sheltering his men beneath the thick growth of the evergreen pines.

The army of the Union, called the Army of the Potomac, assembled at Arlington Heights and Alexandria. General McDowell was placed in command. Half of his soldiers were men who had enlisted for three months, who had suddenly left their homes at the call of the President. Their term of service had nearly expired. The three years' men had been but a few days in camp. Military duties were new. They knew nothing of discipline, but they confidently expected to defeat the enemy and move on to Richmond. Few people thought of the possibility of defeat.

Let us walk up the valley of Bull Run and notice its fords, its wooded banks, the scattered farm-houses, and fields of waving grain. Ten miles from the Occoquan we come to the railroad bridge. A mile farther up is McLean's Ford; another mile carries us to Blackburn's, and another mile brings us to Mitchell's. Above these are Island Ford, Lewis Ford, and Ball's Ford. Three miles above Mitchell's there is a stone bridge, where the turnpike leading from Centreville to Warrenton crosses the stream. Two miles farther up is a place called Sudley Springs—a cluster of houses, a little stone church, a blacksmith's shop. The stream there has dwindled to a brook, and gurgles over a rocky bed.

Going back to the stone bridge, and standing upon its parapet, you may look east to Centreville, about four miles distant, beautifully situated on a high ridge of land, but a very old, dilapidated place when you get to it. Going west from the bridge, you see upon your right hand a swell of land, and another at your left hand, south of the turnpike. A brook trickles by the roadside. Leaving the turnpike, and ascending the ridge on the north side, you see that towards Sudley Springs there are other swells of land, with wheat-fields, fences, scattered trees, and groves of pines and oaks. Looking across to the hill south of the turnpike, a half-mile distant, you see the house of Mr. Lewis, and west of it Mrs. Henry's, on the highest knoll. Mrs. Henry is an old lady, so far advanced in life that she is helpless. Going up the turnpike a mile from the bridge, you come to the toll-gate, kept by Mr. Mathey. A cross-road comes down from Sudley Springs, and leads south towards Manassas Junction, six miles distant. Leave the turnpike once more, and go northwest a half-mile, and you come to the farm of Mr. Dogan. There are farm-sheds and haystacks near his house.

This ground, from Dogan's to the ridge east of the toll-gate, across the turnpike and the trickling brook to Mr. Lewis's and Mrs. Henry's, is the battle-field. You see it—the ridges of land, the houses, haystacks, fences, knolls, ravines, wheat-fields, turnpike, and groves of oak and pine—a territory about two miles square.

On Saturday, June 20th, General Johnston, with nearly all the Rebel army of the Shenandoah, arrived at Manassas. Being General Beauregard's superior officer, he took command of all the troops. He had about thirty thousand men.

On Thursday, General Richardson's brigade of General McDowell's army had a skirmish with General Longstreet's brigade at Blackburn's

Ford, which the Rebels call the battle of Bull Run, while that which was fought on the 21st they call the battle of Manassas. General Beauregard expected that the attack would be renewed along the fords, and posted his men accordingly.

Going down to the railroad bridge, we see General Ewell's brigade of the Rebel army on the western bank guarding the crossing. General Jones's brigade is at McLean's Ford. At Blackburn's Ford is General Longstreet's, and at Mitchell's Ford is General Bonham's. Near by Bonham's is General Earley's, General Bartow's, and General Holmes's. General Jackson's is in rear of General Bonham's. At Island Ford is General Bee and Colonel Hampton's legion, also Stuart's cavalry. At Ball's Ford is General Cocke's brigade. Above, at the Stone Bridge, is the extreme left of the Rebel army, General Evans's brigade. General Elzey's brigade of the Shenandoah army is on its way in the cars, and is expected to reach the battle-field before the contest closes. General Johnston has between fifty and sixty pieces of artillery and about one thousand cavalry. General McDowell had also about thirty thousand men and forty-nine pieces of artillery. His army was in four divisions,—General Tyler's, General Hunter's, General Heintzelman's, and General Miles's. One brigade of General Tyler's and General Miles's division was left at Centreville to make a feint of attacking the enemy at Blackburn's and Mitchell's Fords, and to protect the rear of the army from an attack by Generals Ewell and Jones. The other divisions of the army—five brigades, numbering eighteen thousand men, with thirty-six cannon—marched soon after midnight, to be ready to make the attack by sunrise on Sunday morning.

General Tyler, with General Keyes's brigade, General Sherman's, and General Schenck's, marched down the turnpike towards the Stone Bridge, where General Evans was on the watch. General Tyler had twelve pieces of artillery,—two batteries, commanded by Ayer and Carlisle.

It is sunrise as they approach the bridge—a calm, peaceful Sabbath morning. The troops leave the turnpike, march into a cornfield, and ascend a hill overlooking the bridge. As you stand there amid the tasseled stalks, you see the stream rippling beneath the stone arches, and upon the other bank breastworks of earth and fallen trees. Half hid beneath the oaks and pines are the Rebel regiments, their gun-barrels and bayonets flashing in the morning light. Beyond the breastworks upon the knolls are the farmhouses of Mr. Lewis and Mrs. Henry.

Captain Ayer, who has seen fighting in Mexico, brings his guns upon the hill, wheels them into position, and sights them towards the breastworks. There is a flash, a puff of smoke, a screaming in the air, and then across the stream a handful of cloud bursts into view above the Rebel lines. The shell has exploded. There is a sudden movement of the Rebel troops. It is the first gun of the morning. And now, two miles down the Run, by Mitchell's Ford, rolling, echoing, and reverberating through the forests, are other thunderings. General Richardson has been waiting impatiently to hear the signal gun. He is to make a feint of attacking. His cannonade is to begin furiously. He has six guns, and all of them are in position, throwing solid shot and shells into the wood where Longstreet's men are lying.

All of Ayer's guns are in play, hurling rifled shot and shells, which scream like an unseen demon as they fly over the cornfield, over the meadow lands, to the woods and fields beyond the stream.

General Hunter and General Heintzelman, with their divisions, have left the turnpike two miles from Centreville, at Cub Run bridge, a rickety, wooden structure, which creaks and trembles as the heavy cannon rumble over. They march into the northwest, along a narrow road—a round-about way to Sudley Springs. It is a long march. They started at two o'clock, and have had no breakfast. They waited three hours at Cub Run, while General Tyler's division was crossing, and they are therefore three hours behind the appointed time. General McDowell calculated and intended to have them at Sudley Springs by six o'clock, but now it is nine. They stop a half-hour at the river-crossing to fill their canteens from the gurgling stream.

Looking south from the little stone church, you see clouds of dust floating over the forest-trees. The Rebels have discovered the movement, and are marching in hot haste to resist the impending attack. General Evans has left a portion of his command at Stone Bridge, and is hastening with the remainder to the second ridge of land north of the turnpike. He plants his artillery on the hill, and secretes his infantry in a thicket of pines. General Bee is on the march, so is General Bartow and General

Jackson, all upon the double-quick. Rebel officers ride furiously, and shout their orders. The artillerymen lash their horses to a run. The infantry are also upon the run, sweating and panting in the hot sunshine. The noise and confusion increase. The booming deepens along the valley, for still farther down, by Blackburn's Ford, Hunt's battery is pouring its fire upon Longstreet's, Jones's, and Ewell's men.

The Union troops at Sudley Springs move across the stream. General Burnside's brigade is in advance. The Second Rhode Island infantry is thrown out, deployed as skirmishers. The men are five paces apart. They move slowly, cautiously, and nervously through the fields and thickets.

Suddenly, from bushes, trees, and fences there is a rattle of musketry. General Evans's skirmishers are firing. There are jets of flame and smoke, and a strange humming in the air. There is another rattle, a roll, a volley. The cannon join. The first great battle has begun. General Hunter hastens to the spot, and is wounded almost at the first volley, and compelled to leave the field. The contest suddenly grows fierce. The Rhode Island boys push on to closer quarters, and the Rebels under General Evans give way from a thicket to a fence, from a fence to a knoll.

General Bee arrives with his brigade to help General Evans. You see him swing up into line west of Evans, towards the haystacks by Dogan's house. He is in such a position that he can pour a fire upon the flank of the Rhode Island boys, who are pushing Evans. It is a galling fire, and the brave fellows are cut down by the raking shots from the haystacks. They are almost overwhelmed. But help is at hand. The Seventy-first New York, the Second New Hampshire, and the First Rhode Island, all belonging to Burnside's brigade, move toward the haystacks. They bring their guns to a level, and the rattle and roll begin. There are jets of flame, long lines of light, white clouds, unfolding and expanding, rolling over and over, and rising above the tree-tops. Wilder the uproar. Men fall, tossing their arms; some leap into the air, some plunge headlong, falling like logs of wood or lumps of lead. Some reel, stagger, and tumble; others lie down gently as to a night's repose, unheeding the din, commotion, and uproar. They are bleeding, torn, and mangled. Legs, arms, bodies, are crushed. They see nothing. They cannot tell what has happened. The air is full of fearful noises. An unseen storm sweeps by. The trees are splintered, crushed, and broken as if smitten by thunderbolts. Twigs and leaves fall to the ground. There is smoke, dust, wild talking, shouting, hissings, howlings, explosions. It is a new, strange, unanticipated experience to the soldiers of both armies, far different from what they thought it would be.

Far away, church-bells are tolling the hour of Sabbath worship, and children are singing sweet songs in many a Sunday school. Strange and terrible the contrast! You cannot bear to look upon the dreadful scene. How horrible those wounds! The ground is crimson with blood. You are ready to turn away, and shut the scene forever from your sight. But the battle must go on, and the war must go on till the wicked men who began it are crushed, till the honor of the dear old flag is vindicated, till the Union is restored, till the country is saved, till the slaveholder is deprived of his power, and till freedom comes to the slave. It is terrible to see, but you remember that the greatest blessing the world ever received was purchased by blood—the blood of the Son of God. It is terrible to see, but there are worse things than war. It is worse to have the rights of men trampled in the dust; worse to have your country destroyed, to have justice, truth, and honor violated. You had better be killed, torn to pieces by cannon-shot, than lose your manhood, or yield that which makes you a man. It is better to die than give up that rich inheritance bequeathed us by our fathers, and purchased by their blood.

The battle goes on. General Porter's brigade comes to the aid of Burnside, moving towards Dogan's house. Jackson's Rebel brigade is there to meet him. Arnold's battery is in play—guns pouring a constant stream of shot and shells upon the Rebel line. The Washington Artillery, from New Orleans, is replying from the hill south of Dogan's. Other Rebel batteries are cutting Burnside's brigade to pieces. The men are all but ready to fall back before the terrible storm. Burnside sends to Porter for help—he asks for the brave old soldiers, the regulars, who have been true to the flag of their country, while many of their former officers have been false. They have been long in the service, and have had many fierce contests with the Indians on the Western plains. They are as true as steel. Captain Sykes commands them. He leads the way. You see them, with steady ranks, in the edge of the woods east of Dogan's house. They have been facing southwest, and now they turn to the southeast. They pass through the grove of pines, and enter the open field. They are cut through and through with solid shot, shells burst around them, men drop from the ranks, but the battalion does not falter. It sweeps on close up to the cloud of flame and smoke rolling from the hill north of the turnpike. Their muskets come to a level. There is a click, click, click, along the line. A broad sheet of flame, a white, sulphurous cloud, a deep roll like the angry growl of thunder. There is sudden staggering in the Rebel ranks. Men whirl round, and drop upon the ground. The line wavers, and breaks. They run down the hill, across the hollows, to another knoll. There they rally, and hold their ground a while. Hampton's legion and Cocke's brigade come to their support. Fugitives are brought back by the officers, who ride furiously over the field. There is a lull, and then the strife goes on, a rattling fire of musketry, and a continual booming of the cannonade.

General Heintzelman's division was in rear of General Hunter's on the march. When the battle begun the troops were several miles from Sudley Church. They were parched with thirst, and when they reached the stream they, too, stopped and filled their canteens. Burnside's and Porter's brigades were engaged two hours before Heintzelman's division reached the field. Eight regiments had driven the Rebels from their first position.

General Heintzelman marched upon the Rebels west of Dogan's house. The Rebel batteries were on a knoll, a short distance from the toll-gate. Griffin and Ricketts opened upon them with their rifled guns. Then came a great puff of smoke. It was a Rebel caisson blown up by one of Griffin's shells. It was a continuous, steady artillery fire. The gunners of the Rebel batteries were swept away by the unerring aim of Griffin's gunners. They changed position again and again, to avoid the shot. Mingled with the constant crashing of the cannonade was an irregular firing of muskets, like the pattering of rain-drops upon a roof. At times there was a quicker rattle, and heavy rolls, like the fall of a great building.

General Wilcox swung his brigade round upon Jackson's flank. The Rebel general must retreat or be cut off, and he fell back to the toll-gate, to the turnpike, across it, in confusion, to the ridge by Mrs. Henry's. Evans's, Bee's, Bartow's, and Cocke's brigades, which have been trying to hold their ground against Burnside and Porter's brigades, by this movement, are also forced back to Mr. Lewis's house. The Rebels do not all go back. There are hundreds who rushed up in hot haste in the morning lying bleeding, torn, mangled, upon the wooded slopes. Some are prisoners.

I talked with a soldier of one of the Virginia regiments. We were near the Stone Bridge. He was a tall, athletic young man, dressed in a gray uniform trimmed with yellow braid.

"How many soldiers have you on the field?" I asked.

"Ninety thousand."

"Hardly that number, I guess."

"Yes, sir. We have got Beauregard's and Johnston's armies. Johnston came yesterday and a whole lot more from Richmond. If you whip us to-day, you will whip nigh to a hundred thousand."

"Who is in command?"

"Jeff Davis."

"I thought Beauregard was in command."

"Well, he was; but Jeff Davis is on the field now. I know it; for I saw him just before I was captured. He was on a white horse."

While talking, a shell screamed over our heads and fell in the woods. The Rebel batteries had opened again upon our position. Another came, and we were compelled to leave the spot.

The prisoner may have been honest in his statements. It requires much judgment to correctly estimate large armies. He was correct in saying that Jeff Davis was there. He was on the ground, watching the progress of the battle, but taking no part. He arrived in season to see the close of the contest.

After Burnside and Porter had driven Evans, Bee, and Bartow across the turnpike, General Sherman and General Keyes crossed Bull Run above the Stone Bridge and moved straight down the stream. Schenck's brigade and Ayer's and Carlisle's batteries were left to guard the rear.

Perhaps you had a brother or a father in the Second New Hampshire, or in the Seventy-first New York, or in some other regiment; or perhaps when the war is over you may wish to visit the spot and behold the ground where the first great battle was fought. You will wish to see just where they stood. Looking, then, along the line at one o'clock, you see nearest the stream General Keyes's brigade, composed of the First,

Second, and Third Connecticut regiments and the Fourth Maine. Next is Sherman's brigade, composed of the Sixty-ninth and Seventy-ninth New York Militia, the Thirteenth New York Volunteers, and the Second Wisconsin. Between these and the toll-gate you see first, as you go west, Burnside's brigade, composed of the First and Second Rhode Island, the Seventy-first New York Militia, and the Second New Hampshire, and the Second Rhode Island battery; extending to the toll-house is Porter's brigade. He has Sykes's battalion of regulars, and the Eighth and Four-teenth regiments of New York Militia and Arnold's battery. Crossing the road which comes down from Sudley Springs, you see General Franklin's brigade, containing the Fifth Massachusetts Militia, the First Minnesota Volunteers, and the Fourth Pennsylvania Militia. Next you come to the men from Maine and Vermont, the Second, Fourth, and Fifth Maine, and the Second Vermont, General Howard's brigade. Beyond, upon the extreme right, is General Wilcox with the First Michigan and the Eleventh New York. Griffin's and Rickett's batteries are near at hand. There are twenty-four regiments and twenty-four pieces of artillery. There are two companies of cavalry. If we step over to the house of Mr. Lewis, we shall find General Johnston and General Beauregard in anxious consulta-tion. General Johnston has sent officers in hot haste for reinforcements. Brigades are arriving out of breath—General Cocke's, Holmes's, Long-street's, Earley's. Broken regiments, fragments of companies, and strag-glers are collected and brought into line. General Bonham's brigade is sent for. All but General Ewell's and General Jones's; they are left to pre-vent General Miles from crossing at Blackburn's Ford and attacking the Rebel army in the rear. General Johnston feels that it is a critical moment. He has been driven nearly two miles. His flank has been turned. His loss has been very great, and his troops are beginning to be disheartened. They have changed their opinions of the Yankees.

General Johnston has Barley's brigade, composed of the Seventh and Twenty-fourth Virginia, and the Seventh Louisiana; Jackson's brigade, composed of the Second, Fourth, Fifth, Twenty-seventh, and Thirty-third Virginia, and the Thirteenth Mississippi; Bee's and Bartow's brigades united, composed of two companies of the Eleventh Mississippi, Sec-ond Mississippi, First Alabama, Seventh and Eighth Georgia; Cocke's brigade, the Eighteenth, Nineteenth, and Twenty-eighth Virginia, seven companies of the Eighth, and three of the Forty-ninth Virginia; Evans's brigade, composed of Hampton's legion, Fourth South Carolina, and Wheat's Louisiana battalion; Holmes's brigade, composed of two regiments of Virginia infantry, the First Arkansas, and the Second Tennessee. Two regiments of Bonham's brigade, and Elzey's brigade were brought in before the conflict was over. Putting the detached companies into regiments, Johnston's whole force engaged in this last struggle is thirty-five regiments of infantry, and about forty pieces of artillery, all gathered upon the ridge by Mr. Lewis's and Mrs. Henry's.

There is marching to and fro of regiments. There is not much order. Regiments are scattered. The lines are not even. This is the first battle, and officers and men are inexperienced. There are a great many stragglers on both sides; more, probably, from the Rebel ranks than from McDowell's army, for thus far the battle has gone against them. You can see them scattered over the fields, beyond Mr. Lewis's.

The fight goes on. The artillery crashes louder than before. There is a continuous rattle of musketry. It is like the roaring of a hail-storm. Sherman and Keyes move down to the foot of the hill, near Mr. Lewis's. Burnside and Porter march across the turnpike. Franklin and Howard and Wilcox, who have been pushing south, turn towards the southeast. There are desperate hand-to-hand encounters. Cannon are taken and retaken. Gunners on both sides are shot while loading their pieces. Hundreds fall, and other hundreds leave the ranks. The woods toward Sudley Springs are filled with wounded men and fugitives, weak, thirsty, hungry, exhausted, worn down by the long morning march, want of sleep, lack of food, and the excitement of the hour.

Across the plains, towards Manassas, are other crowds,—disappointed, faint-hearted, defeated soldiers, fleeing for safety.

"We are defeated!"

"Our regiments are cut to pieces!"

"General Bartow is wounded and General Bee is killed!"

Thus they cry, as they hasten towards Manassas. Officers and men in the Rebel ranks feel that the battle is all but lost. Union officers and men feel that it is almost won.

The Rebel right wing, far out upon the turnpike, has been folded back upon the center; the center has been driven in upon the left wing, and the left wing has been pushed back beyond Mr. Lewis's house. Griffin's and Rickett's batteries, which had been firing from the ridge west of the toll-gate, were ordered forward to the knoll from which the Rebel batteries had been driven.

"It is too far in advance," said General Griffin.

"The Fire Zouaves will support you," said General Barry.

"It is better to have them go in advance till we come into position; then they can fall back," Griffin replied.

"No; you are to move first, those are the orders. The Zouaves are already to follow on the double-quick."

"I will go; but, mark my words, they will not support me."

The battery galloped over the fields, descended the hill, crossed the ravine, advancing to the brow of the hill near Mrs. Henry's, followed by Rickett's battery, the Fire Zouaves, and the Fourteenth New York. In front of them, about forty or fifty rods position, and opened a fire so terrible and destructive that the Rebel batteries and infantry were driven beyond the crest of the hill.

The field was almost won. Read what General Johnston says: "The long contest against fivefold odds, and heavy losses, especially of field officers, had greatly discouraged the troops of General Bee and Colonel Evans. The aspect of affairs was critical."

The correspondent of the *Charleston Mercury* writes: "When I entered on the field at two o'clock, the fortunes of the day were dark. The remnants of the regiments, so badly injured or wounded and worn, as they staggered out gave gloomy pictures of the scene. We could not be routed, perhaps, but it is doubtful whether we were destined to a victory."

The correspondent of the *Richmond Dispatch* writes: "Fighting for hours under a hot sun, without a drop of water near, the conduct of our men could not be excelled; but human endurance has its bounds, and all seemed about to be lost."

The battle surges around the house of Mrs. Henry. She is lying there amidst its thunders. Rebel sharpshooters take possession of it, and pick off Rickett's gunners. He turns his guns upon the house. Crash!

crash! crash! It is riddled with grape and canister. Sides, roof, doors, and windows are pierced, broken, and splintered. The bed-clothes are cut into rags, and the aged woman instantly killed. The Rebel regiments melt away. The stream of fugitives toward Manassas grows more dense. Johnston has had more men and more guns engaged than McDowell; but he has been steadily driven. But Rebel reinforcements arrive from an unexpected quarter—General Smith's brigade, from the Shenandoah. It comes into action in front of Wilcox. There are from two to three thousand men. General Smith is wounded almost at the first fire, and Colonel Elzey takes command. General Bonham sends two regiments, the Second and Eighth South Carolina. They keep south of Mrs. Henry's, and march on till they are in position to fire almost upon the backs of Griffin's and Rickett's gunners. They march through a piece of woods, reach the top of the hill, and come into line. Captain Imboden, of the Rebel battery, who is replying to Griffin, sees them. Who are they? He thinks they are Yankees flanking him. He wheels his guns, and is ready to cut them down with grape and canister. Captain Griffin sees them, and wheels his guns. Another instant, and he will sweep them away. He believes them to be Rebels. His gunners load with grape and canister.

"Do not fire upon them; they are your supports!" shouts Major Barry, riding up.

"No, sir; they are Rebels."

"They are your supports, just ordered up."

"As sure as the world, they are Rebels."

"You are mistaken, Captain; they are your supports."

The cannoneers stand ready to pull the lanyards, which will send a tornado through those ranks.

"Don't fire!" shouts the Captain.

The guns are wheeled again towards Mrs. Henry's, and the supposed supports are saved from destruction at the hand of Captain Griffin.

Captain Imboden, before ordering his men to fire upon the supposed Yankees, gallops nearer to them, to see who they are. He sees them raise their guns. There is a flash, a rattle and roll. Griffin's and Rickett's men and their horses go down in an instant! They rush on with a yell. There is sharp, hot, decisive work. Close musket-shots and sabre-strokes. Men are trampled beneath the struggling horses.

There are shouts and hurrahs. The few soldiers remaining to support Griffin and Rickett fire at the advancing Rebel brigade, but the contest is unequal; they are not able to hold in check the three thousand fresh troops. They fall back. The guns are in the hands of the Rebels. The day is lost. At the very moment of victory the line is broken. In an instant all is changed. A moment ago we were pressing on, but now we are falling back. Quick almost as the lightning's flash is the turning of the tide. All through a mistake! So great events sometimes hang on little things.

The unexpected volley, the sudden onset, the vigorous charge, the falling back, produces confusion in the Union ranks. Officers and men, generals and soldiers alike, are confounded. By a common impulse they begin to fall back across the turnpike. Unaccountably to themselves, and to the Rebel fugitives streaming towards Manassas, they lose strength and heart. The falling back becomes a retreat, a sudden panic and a rout. Regiments break and mix with others. Soldiers drop their guns and cartridge-boxes, and rush towards the rear.

I had watched the tide of battle through the day. Everything was favorable. The heat was intense, and I was thirsty. A soldier came past with a back-load of canteens freshly filled.

"Where did you find the water?"

"Over there in the woods, in the rear of Schenck's brigade."

I passed the brigade. Ayers's and Carlisle's batteries were there. I found the spring beyond a little hillock. While drinking, there was sudden confusion in Schenck's brigade. There was loud talking, cannon and musketry firing, and a sudden trampling of horses. A squadron of Rebel cavalry swept past within a few rods of the spring, charging upon Schenck's brigade. The panic tide had come rolling to the rear. Ayers lashed his horses to a gallop, to reach Cub Run bridge. He succeeded in crossing it. He came into position to open upon the Rebels and to check their pursuit. The road was blocked with wagons. Frightened teamsters cut their horses loose and rode away. Soldiers, officers, and civilians fled towards Centreville, frightened at they knew not what. Blenker's brigade was thrown forward from Centreville to the bridge, and the rout was stopped. The Rebels were too much exhausted, too much amazed at the sudden and unaccountable breaking and fleeing of McDowell's army, to improve the advantage. They followed to Cub Run bridge, but a few cannon and musket shots sent them back to the Stone Bridge.

But at Blackburn's Ford General Jones crossed the stream to attack the retreating troops. General Davies, with four regiments and Hunt's battery, occupied the crest of a hill looking down towards the ford. The Rebels marched through the woods upon the bank of the stream, wound along the hillside, filed through a farm-yard and halted in a hollow within a quarter of a mile of General Davies's guns.

"Lie down," said the General, and the four regiments dropped upon the ground. The six cannon and the gunners alone were in sight.

"Wait till they come over the crest of the hill; wait till I give the word," said the General to Captain Hunt.

The men stand motionless by their pieces. The long column of Rebels moves on. There is an officer on his horse giving directions. The long dark line throws its lengthening shadows upward in the declining sunlight, toward the silent cannon.

"Now let them have it!" The guns are silent no longer. Six flashes of light, and six sulphurous clouds are belched towards the moving mass. Grape and canister sweep them down. The officer tumbles from his horse, and the horse staggers to the earth. There are sudden gaps in the ranks. They stop advancing. Officers run here and there. Another merciless storm—another—another. Eighteen flashes a minute from those six pieces! Like grass before the mower the Rebel line is cut down. The men flee to the woods, utterly routed.

The attempt to cut off the retreat signally failed. It was the last attempt of the Rebels to follow up their mysterious victory. The rearguard remained in Centreville till morning recovering five cannon which had been abandoned at Cub Run, which the Rebels had not secured, and then retired to Arlington.

So the battle was won and lost. So the hopes of the Union soldiers changed to sudden, unaccountable fear, and so the fear of the Rebels became unbounded exultation.

The sun had gone down behind the Blue Mountains, and the battle-clouds hung thick and heavy along the winding stream where the conflict had raged. It was a sad night to us who had gone out with such high hopes, who had seen the victory so nearly won and so suddenly lost. Many of our wounded were lying where they had fallen. It was a terrible night to them. Their enemies, some of them, were hard-hearted and cruel. They fired into the hospitals upon helpless men. They refused them water to quench their burning thirst. They taunted them in their hour of triumph, and heaped upon them bitterest curses. They were wild with the delirium of success, and treated their prisoners with savage barbarity. Any one who showed kindness to the prisoners or wounded was looked upon with suspicion. Says an English officer in the Rebel service:

> *I made it my duty to seek out and attend upon the wounded, and the more so when I found that the work of alleviating their sufferings was performed with evident reluctance and want of zeal by many of those whose duty it was to do it. I looked upon the poor fellows only as suffering fellow-mortals, brothers in need of help, and made no distinction between friend and foe; nay, I must own that I was prompted to give the preference to the latter, for the reason that some of our men met with attention from their relations and friends, who had flocked to the field in numbers to see them. But in doing so I had to encounter opposition, and was even pointed at by some with muttered curses as a traitor to the cause of the Confederacy for bestowing any attention on the "d—— Yankees."*

Notwithstanding the inhuman treatment they received at the hands of their captors, there were men on that field who never quailed—men with patriotism so fervent, deep, and unquenchable, that they lay down cheerfully to their death-sleep. This officer in the Rebel service went out upon the field where the fight had been thickest. It was night. Around him were the dying and the dead. There was a young Union officer, with both feet crushed by a cannon-shot. There were tears upon his cheeks.

"Courage, comrade!" said the officer, bending over him; "the day will come when you will remember this battle as one of the things of the past."

"Do not give me false hopes, sir. It is all up with me. I do not grieve that I must die, for with these stumps I shall not live long."

He pointed to his mangled feet, and added: "I weep for my poor, distracted country. Had I a second life to live, I would willingly sacrifice it for the cause of the Union!"

His eyes closed. A smile lighted his countenance, as if, while on the border of another world, he saw once more those who were dearest on earth or in heaven. He raised himself convulsively, and cried, "Mother! Father!"

He was dead.

He sleeps upon the spot where he fell. His name is unknown, but his devotion to his country shall shine forevermore like a star in heaven!

When the Union line gave way, some of the soldiers were so stupefied by the sudden change that they were unable to move, and were taken prisoners. Among them was a Zouave, in red trousers. He was a tall, noble fellow. Although a prisoner, he walked erect, unabashed by his captivity. A Virginian taunted him, and called him by hard names.

"Sir," said the Zouave, "I have heard that yours was a nation of gentlemen, but your insult comes from a coward and a knave. I am your prisoner, but you have no right to fling your curses at me because I am unfortunate. Of the two, I consider myself the gentleman."

The Virginian hung his head in silence, while other Rebel soldiers assured the brave fellow that he should not again be insulted. So bravery, true courage, and manliness will win respect even from enemies.

No accurate reports have been made of the number of men killed and wounded in this battle; but each side lost probably from fifteen hundred to two thousand men.

It was a battle which will always have a memorable place in the history of this Rebellion, because having won a victory, the slaveholders believed that they could conquer the North. They became more proud and insolent. They manifested their terrible hate by their inhuman treatment of the prisoners captured. They gave the dead indecent burial. The Rebel soldiers dug up the bones of the dead Union men, and carved them into ornaments, which they sent home to their wives and sweethearts. One girl wrote to her lover to "be sure and bring her Old Lincoln's skelp" (scalp), so that the women as well as the men became fierce in their hatred. I have seen the letter, which was found upon a prisoner.

The North, although defeated, was not discouraged. There was no thought of giving up the contest, but, as you remember, there was a great uprising of the people, who determined that the war should go on till the Rebellion was crushed.

Source: Charles Carleton Coffin, *My Days and Nights on the Battle-Field* (Boston: Dana Estes and Company, 1887; Project Gutenberg, 2009), chap. 3, http://www.gutenberg.org/ebooks/28571.

EVERYDAY LIFE IN
CAMP AND FIELD

It was Napoleon who observed that an army travels on its stomach, but logistics were hardly smooth in a Confederate army hurriedly built from scratch. It was a struggle to feed thousands of men in the field at the best of times, and Confederate authorities struggled to invent and maintain a supply system. Frequently, victuals were late, inadequate, or in short supply, and the Confederate troops learned to supplement their scanty rations by foraging around the countryside, sometimes to the dismay of locals. All in all, supplies were a challenge to the Confederacy throughout the war. **Pvt. Carlton McCarthy**, *a Virginian born in 1847, here recounts the situation. McCarthy's Civil War memoirs appeared in 1882, and he was elected mayor of Richmond in 1904.*

Pvt. Sam Watkins, CSA, also recounts the haphazard, feast-or-famine nature of a soldier's diet. His memoir, Co. Aytch, *appeared in 1882, recounting his experiences as a soldier in Company H, 1st Tennessee Infantry Regiment. Watkins joined at the beginning of the war and was one of a very few who survived till the war's end. His book is widely considered one of the war's finest literary productions, noted for its honesty as well as its good humor and fetching prose style.*

***John D. Billings**'s 1887* Hardtack and Coffee: The Unwritten Story of Army Life *is a Union equivalent to Watkins's book. Billings served with the 10th Massachusetts Volunteer Light Artillery. His unit fought many battles, including The Wilderness, Spotsylvania,*

Cold Harbor, Petersburg, and Appomattox. Civil War armies were either in camp, on the march, or in combat. Enhanced by the pen-and-ink illustrations of Charles Reed, Billings's volume narrates camp life and movement rather than battles. With no small amount of humor, Billings provides an accurate and detailed look at the living conditions of typical Union soldiers.

Alf Burnett was a Cincinnati writer with considerable national appeal as the war began. He enlisted in the 5th Ohio and was soon hired by his hometown newspapers to provide colorful nuggets about soldiers and their stories. Incidents of the War: Humorous, Pathetic, and Descriptive is his impressionistic collection of anecdotes and letters covering what he saw. He covered topics ranging from slavery to combat, from field hospitals to army protocol. Here, he describes how Union soldiers whiled away their time in camp with sports and games.

COOKING AND EATING

PVT. CARLTON McCARTHY, CSA

Rations in the Army of Northern Virginia were alternately superabundant and altogether wanting. The quality, quantity, and frequency of them depended upon the amount of stores in the hands of the commissaries, the relative position of the troops and the wagon trains, and the many accidents and mishaps of the campaign. During the latter years and months of the war, so uncertain was the issue as to time, quantity, and composition, that the men became in large measure independent of this seeming absolute necessity, and by some mysterious means, known only to purely patriotic soldiers, learned to fight without pay and to find subsistence in the field, the stream, or the forest, and a shelter on the bleak mountain side.

Sometimes there was an abundant issue of bread, and no meat; then meat in any quantity, and no flour or meal; sugar in abundance, and no coffee to be had for "love or money;" and then coffee in plenty, without a grain of sugar; for months nothing but flour for bread, and then nothing but meal (till all hands longed for a biscuit); or fresh meat until it was nauseating, and then salt-pork without intermission.

To be one day without anything to eat was common. Two days' fasting, marching and fighting was not uncommon, and there were times when no rations were issued for three or four days. On one march, from Petersburg to Appomattox, no rations were issued to Cutshaw's battalion of artillery for one entire week, and the men subsisted on the corn intended for the battery horses, raw bacon captured from the enemy, and the water of springs, creeks, and rivers.

Union soldiers cooking

A soldier in the Army of Northern Virginia was fortunate when he had his flour, meat, sugar, and coffee all at the same time and in proper quantity. Having these, the most skillful axeman of the mess hewed down a fine hickory or oak, and cut it into "lengths." All hands helped to "tote" it to the fire. When wood was convenient, the fire was large, the red coals abundant, and the meal soon prepared.

The man most gifted in the use of the skillet was the one most highly appreciated about the fire, and as tyrannical as a Turk; but when he raised the lid of the oven and exposed the brown-crusted tops of the biscuit, animosity subsided. The frying-pan, full of "grease," then became the centre of attraction. As the hollow-cheeked boy "sopped" his biscuit, his poor, pinched countenance wrinkled into a smile, and his sunken eyes glistened with delight. And the coffee, too—how delicious the aroma of it, and how readily each man disposed of a quart! The strong men gathered round, chuckling at their good luck, and "cooing" like a child with a big piece of cake. Ah, this was a sight which but few of those who live and die are permitted to see!

And now the last biscuit is gone, the last drop of coffee, and the frying-pan is "wiped" clean. The tobacco-bag is pulled wide open, pipes are scraped, knocked out, and filled, the red coal is applied, and the blue smoke rises in wreaths and curls from the mouths of the no longer hungry, but happy and contented soldiers. Songs rise on the still night air, the merry laugh resounds, the woods are bright with the rising flame of the fire, story after story is told, song after song is sung, and at midnight the soldiers steal away one by one to their blankets on the ground, and sleep till reveille. Such was a meal when the mess was fortunate.

How different when the wagons have not been heard from for forty-eight hours. Now the question is, how to do the largest amount of good to the largest number with the smallest amount of material? The most experienced men discuss the situation and decide that "somebody" must go foraging. Though the stock on hand is small, no one seems anxious to leave the small certainty and go in search of the large uncertainty of supper from some farmer's well-filled table; but at last several comrades start out, and as they disappear the preparations for immediate consumption commence. The meat is too little to cook alone, and the flour will scarcely make six biscuits. The result is that "slosh" or "coosh" must do. So the bacon is fried out till the pan is half full of boiling grease. The flour is mixed with water until it flows like milk, poured into the grease and rapidly stirred till the whole is a dirty brown mixture. It is now ready to be served. Perhaps some dainty fellow prefers the more imposing "slapjack." If so, the flour is mixed with less water, the grease reduced, and the paste poured in till it covers the bottom of the pan, and, when brown on the underside, is, by a nimble twist of the pan, turned and browned again. If there is any sugar in camp it makes a delicious addition.

About the time the last scrap of "slapjack" and the last spoonful of "slosh" are disposed of, the unhappy foragers return. They take in the situation at a glance, realize with painful distinctness that they have sacrificed the homely slosh for the vain expectancy of apple butter, shortcake, and milk, and, with woeful countenance and mournful voice, narrate their adventure and disappointment thus: "Well, boys, we have done the best we could. We have walked about nine miles over the mountain, and haven't found a mouthful to eat. Sorry, but it's a fact. Give us our biscuits." Of course there are none, and, as it is not contrary to army etiquette to do so, the whole mess professes to be very sorry. Sometimes, however, the foragers returned well laden with good things, and as good comrades should, shared the fruits of their toilsome hunt with their comrades.

Foragers thought it not indelicate to linger about the house of the unsuspecting farmer till the lamp revealed the family at supper, and then modestly approach and knock at the door. As the good-hearted man knew that his guests were "posted" about the meal in progress in the next room, the invitation to supper was given, and, shall I say it, accepted with an unbecoming lack of reluctance.

The following illustrates the ingenuity of the average forager. There was great scarcity of meat, and no prospect of a supply from the wagons. Two experienced foragers were sent out, and as a farmer about ten miles from the camp was killing hogs, guided by soldier instinct, they went directly to his house, and found the meat nicely cut up, the various pieces of each hog making a separate pile on the floor of an outhouse. The proposition to buy met with a surprisingly ready response on the part of the farmer. He offered one entire pile of meat, being one whole hog, for such a small sum that the foragers instantly closed the bargain, and as promptly opened their eyes to the danger which menaced them. They gave the old gentleman a ten-dollar bill and requested change. Pleased with their honest method he hastened away to his house to obtain it. The two honest foragers hastily examined the particular pile of pork which the simple-hearted farmer designated as theirs, found it very rank and totally unfit for food, transferred half of it to another pile, from which they took half and added to theirs, and awaited the return of the farmer. On giving them their change, he assured them that they had a bargain. They agreed that they had, tossed good and bad together in a bag, said good-by, and departed as rapidly as artillerymen on foot can. The result of the trip was a "pot-pie" of large dimensions; and some six or eight men gorged with fat pork declared that they had never cared for and would not again wish to eat pork—especially pork-pies.

A large proportion of the eating of the army was done in the houses and at the tables of the people, not by the use of force, but by the wish and invitation of the people. It was at times necessary that whole towns should help to sustain the army of defense, and when this was the case, it was done voluntarily and cheerfully. The soldiers—all who conducted themselves properly—were received as honored guests and given the best in the house. There was a wonderful absence of stealing or plundering, and even when the people suffered from depredation they attributed the cause to terrible necessity rather than to wanton disregard of the rights of property. And when armed guards were placed over the smoke-houses and barns, it was not so much because the commanding general doubted the honesty as that he knew the necessities of his troops. But even pinching hunger was not held to be an excuse for marauding expeditions.

The inability of the government to furnish supplies forced the men to depend largely upon their own energy and ingenuity to obtain them. The officers, knowing this, relaxed discipline to an extent which would seem, to a European officer, for instance, ruinous. It was no uncommon sight to see a brigade or division, which was but a moment before marching in solid column along the road, scattered over an immense field searching for the luscious blackberries. And it was wonderful to see how promptly and cheerfully all returned to the ranks when the field was gleaned. In the fall of the year a persimmon tree on the roadside would halt a column and detain it till the last persimmon disappeared.

The sutler's wagon, loaded with luxuries, which was so common in the Federal army, was unknown in the Army of Northern Virginia, for two reasons: the men had no money to buy sutlers' stores, and the country no men to spare for sutlers. The nearest approach to the sutler's wagon was the "cider cart" of some old darkey, or a basket of pies and cakes displayed on the roadside for sale.

The Confederate soldier relied greatly upon the abundant supplies of eatables which the enemy was kind enough to bring him, and he cheerfully risked his life for the accomplishment of the twofold purpose of whipping the enemy and getting what he called "a square meal." After a battle there was general feasting on the Confederate side. Good things, scarcely ever seen at other times, filled the haversacks and the stomachs of the "Boys in Gray." Imagine the feelings of men half famished when they rush into a camp at one side, while the enemy flees from the other, and find the coffee on the fire, sugar at hand ready to be dropped into the coffee, bread in the oven, crackers by the box, fine beef ready cooked, desiccated vegetables by the bushel, canned peaches, lobsters, tomatoes, milk, barrels of ground and roasted coffee, soda, salt, and in short everything a hungry soldier craves. Then add the liquors, wines, cigars, and tobacco found in the tents of the officers and the wagons of the sutlers, and, remembering the condition of the victorious party, hungry, thirsty, and weary, say if it did not require wonderful devotion to duty, and great self-denial to push on, trampling under foot the plunder of the camp, and pursue the enemy till the sun went down.

When it was allowable to halt, what a glorious time it was! Men, who a moment before would have been delighted with a pone of cornbread and a piece of fat meat, discuss the comparative merits of peaches and milk and fresh tomatoes, lobster and roast beef, and, forgetting the briar-root pipe, faithful companion of the vicissitudes of the soldier's life, snuff the aroma of imported Havanas.

In sharp contrast with the mess-cooking at the big fire was the serious and diligent work of the man separated from his comrades, out of reach of the woods, but bent on cooking and eating. He has found a coal of fire, and having placed over it, in an ingenious manner, the few leaves and twigs near his post, he fans the little pile with his hat. It soon blazes. Fearing the utter consumption of his fuel, he hastens to balance on the little fire his tin cup of water. When it boils, from some secure place in his clothes he takes a little coffee and drops it in the cup, and almost instantly the cup is removed and set aside; then a slice of fat meat is laid on the coals, and when brown and crisp, completes the meal—for the "crackers," or biscuit, are ready. No one but a soldier would have undertaken to cook with such a fire, as frequently it was no bigger than a quart cup.

Crackers, or "hard tack" as they were called, are notoriously poor eating, but in the hands of the Confederate soldier were made to do good duty. When on the march and pressed for time, a piece of solid fat pork and a dry cracker was passable or luscious, as the time was long or short since the last meal. When there was leisure to do it, hardtack was soaked well and then fried in bacon grease. Prepared thus, it was a dish which no Confederate had the weakness or the strength to refuse.

Sorghum, in the absence of the better molasses of peace times, was greatly prized and eagerly sought after. A "Union" man living near the Confederate lines was one day busy boiling his crop. Naturally enough, some of "our boys" smelt out the place and determined to have some of the sweet fluid. They had found a yearling dead in the field hard by, and in thinking over the matter determined to sell the Union man if possible. So they cut from the dead animal a choice piece of beef, carried it to the old fellow and offered to trade. He accepted the offer, and the whole party walked off with canteens full.

Artillerymen, having tender consciences and no muskets, seldom, if ever, shot stray pigs; but they did sometimes, as an act of friendship, wholly disinterested, point out to the infantry a pig which seemed to need shooting, and by way of dividing the danger and responsibility of the act, accept privately a choice part of the deceased.

On one occasion, when a civilian was dining with the mess, there was a fine pig for dinner. This circumstance caused the civilian to remark on the good fare. The "forager" replied that pig was an uncommon dish, this one having been kicked by one of the battery horses while stealing corn, and instantly killed. The civilian seemed to doubt the statement after his teeth had come down hard on a pistol bullet, and continued to doubt, though assured that it was the head of a horse-shoe nail.

The most melancholy eating a soldier was ever forced to do, was, when pinched with hunger, cold, wet, and dejected, he wandered over the deserted field of battle and satisfied his cravings with the contents of the haversacks of the dead. If there is anything which will overcome the natural abhorrence which a man feels for the enemy, the loathing of the bloated dead, and the awe engendered by the presence of death, solitude, and silence, it is hunger. Impelled by its clamoring, men of high principle and tenderest humanity become for the time void of sensibility, and condescend to acts which, though justified by their extremity, seem afterwards, even to the doers, too shameless to mention.

When rations became so very small that it was absolutely necessary to supplement them, and the camp was permanently established, those men who had the physical ability worked for the neighborhood farmers at cutting cord-wood, harvesting the crops, killing hogs, or any other farm-work. A stout man would cut a cord of wood a day and receive fifty cents in money, or its equivalent in something eatable. Hogs were slaughtered for the "fifth quarter." When the corn became large enough to eat, the roasting ears, thrown in the ashes with the shucks on, and nicely roasted, made a grateful meal. Turnip and onion patches also furnished delightful and much-needed food, good raw or cooked.

Occasionally, when a mess was hard pushed for eatables, it became necessary to resort to some ingenious method of disgusting a part of the mess, that the others might eat their fill. The "pepper treatment" was a common method practiced with the soup, which once failed. A shrewd fellow, who loved things "hot," decided to have plenty of soup, and to accomplish his purpose, as he passed and repassed the boiling pot, dropped in a pod of red pepper. But, alas! for him, there was another man like minded who adopted the same plan, and the result was that all the mess waited in vain for that pot of soup to cool.

The individual coffee-boiler of one man in the Army of Northern Virginia was always kept at the boiling point. The owner of it was an enigma to his comrades. They could not understand his strange fond-ness for "red-hot" coffee. Since the war he has explained that he found the heat of the coffee prevented its use by others, and adopted the plan of placing his cup on the fire after every sip. This same character never troubled himself to carry a canteen, though a great water drinker. When he found a good canteen he would kindly give it to a comrade, reserving the privilege of an occasional drink when in need. He soon had an inter-est in thirty or forty canteens and their contents, and could always get a drink of water if it was to be found in any of them. He pursued the same plan with blankets, and always had plenty in that line. His entire outfit was the clothes on his back and a haversack accurately shaped to hold one half pone of corn bread.

Roasting-ear time was a trying time for the hungry private. Having been fed during the whole of the winter on salt meat and coarse bread, his system craved the fresh, luscious juice of the corn, and at times his hon-esty gave way under the pressure. How could he resist? He didn't—he took some roasting ears! Sometimes the farmer grumbled, sometimes he quarreled, and sometimes he complained to the officers of the depredations of "the men." The officers apologized, ate what corn they had on hand, and sent their "boy" for some more. One old farmer conceived the happy plan of inviting some privates to his house, stating his grievances, and securing their coöperation in the effort to protect his corn. He told them that of course *they* were not the *gentlemen* who took his corn! Oh no! of course *they* would not do such a thing; but wouldn't they please speak to the others and ask them please not to take his corn? Of course! certainly! oh, yes! they would remonstrate with their comrades. How they burned, though, as they thought of the past and contemplated the near future. As they returned to camp through the field they filled their haversacks with the silky ears, and were met on the other side of the field by the kind farmer and a file of men, who were only too eager to secure the plucked corn "in the line of duty."

A faithful officer, worn out with the long, weary march, sick, hungry, and dejected, leaned his back against a tree and groaned to think of his inability to join in the chase of an old hare, which, he knew, from the wild yells in the wood, his men were pursuing. But the uproar approached him—nearer, nearer, and nearer, until he saw the hare bounding towards him with a regiment at her heels. She spied an opening made by the folds of the officer's cloak and jumped in, and he embraced his first meal for forty-eight hours.

An artilleryman, camped for a day where no water was to be found easily, awakened during the night by thirst, went stumbling about in search of water; and to his great delight found a large bucketful. He drank his fill, and in the morning found that what he drank had washed a bullock's head, and was crimson with its blood.

Some stragglers came up one night and found the camp silent. All hands asleep. Being hungry they sought and to their great delight found a large pot of soup. It had a peculiar taste, but they "worried" it down, and in the morning bragged of their good fortune. The soup had defied the stomachs of the whole battery, being strongly impregnated with the peculiar flavor of defunct cockroaches.

Shortly before the evacuation of Petersburg, a country boy went hunting. He killed and brought to camp a muskrat. It was skinned, cleaned, buried a day or two, disinterred, cooked, and eaten with great relish. It was splendid.

During the seven days' battles around Richmond, a studious private observed the rats as they entered and emerged from a corn-crib. He killed one, cooked it privately, and invited a friend to join him in eating a fine squirrel. The comrade consented, ate heartily, and when told what he had eaten, forthwith disgorged. But he confesses that up to the time when he was enlightened he had greatly enjoyed the meal.

It was at this time, when rats were a delicacy, that the troops around Richmond agreed to divide their rations with the poor of the city, and they were actually hauled in and distributed. Comment here would be like complimenting the sun on its brilliancy.

Orators dwell on the genius and skill of the general officers; historians tell of the movements of divisions and army corps, and the student of the art of war studies the geography and topography of the country and the returns of the various corps: they all seek to find and to tell the secret of success or failure. The Confederate soldier knows the elements of his success—courage, endurance, and devotion. He knows also by whom he was defeated—sickness, starvation, death. He fought not men only, but food, raiment, pay, glory, fame, and fanaticism. He endured privation, toil, and contempt. He won, and despite the cold indifference of all and the hearty hatred of some, he will have for all time, in all places where generosity is, a fame untarnished.

Source: Carlton McCarthy, *Detailed Minutiae of Soldier Life in the Army of Northern Virginia, 1861–1865* (Richmond, VA: Carlton McCarthy and Company, 1882; Project Gutenberg, 2008), chap. 5, http://www.gutenberg.org/ebooks/25603.

PLEASE PASS THE BUTTER

CPL. SAM R. WATKINS, CSA

For several days the wagon train continued on until we had arrived at the part of country to which we had been directed. Whether they bought or pressed the corn, I know not, but the old gentleman invited us all to take supper with him. If I have ever eaten a better supper than that I have forgotten it. They had biscuit for supper. What! Flour bread? Did my eyes deceive me? Well, there were biscuit—sure enough flourbread—and sugar and coffee—genuine Rio—none of your rye or potato coffee, and butter—regular butter—and ham and eggs, and turnip greens, and potatoes, and fried chicken, and nice clean plates—none of your tin affairs—and a snow-white table-cloth and napkins, and white-handled knives and silver forks. At the head of the table was the madam, having on a pair of golden spectacles, and at the foot the old gentleman. He said grace. And, to cap the climax, two handsome daughters. I know that I had never seen two more beautiful ladies. They had on little white aprons, trimmed with jaconet edging, and collars as clean and white as snow. They looked good enough to eat, and I think at that time I would have given ten years of my life to have kissed one of them. We were invited to help ourselves. Our plates were soon filled with the tempting food and our tumblers with California beer. We would have liked it better had it been twice as strong, but what it lacked in strength we made up in quantity. The old lady said, "Daughter, hand the gentleman the butter." It was the first thing that I had refused, and the reason that I did so was because my plate was full already. Now, there is nothing that will offend a lady so quick as to refuse to take butter when handed to you. If you should say, "No, madam, I never eat butter," it is a direct insult to the lady of the house. Better, far better, for you to have remained at home that day. If you don't eat butter, it is an insult; if you eat too much, she will make your ears burn after you have left. It is a regulator of society; it is a civilizer; it is a luxury and a delicacy that must be touched and handled with care and courtesy on all occasions. Should you desire to get on the good side of a lady, just give a broad, sweeping, slathering compliment to her butter. It beats kissing the dirty-faced baby; it beats anything. Too much praise cannot be bestowed upon the butter, be it good, bad, or indifferent to your notions of things, but to her, her butter is always good, superior, excellent. I did not know this characteristic of the human female at the time, or I would have taken a delicate slice of the butter. Here is a sample of the colloquy that followed:

"Mister, have some butter?"

"Not any at present, thank you, madam."

"Well, I insist upon it; our butter is nice."

"O, I know it's nice, but my plate is full, thank you."

"Well, take some anyhow."

One of the girls spoke up and said: "Mother, the gentleman don't wish butter."

"Well, I want him to know that our butter is clean, anyhow."

"Well, madam, if you insist upon it, there is nothing that I love so well as warm biscuit and butter. I'll thank you for the butter."

I dive in. I go in a little too heavy. The old lady hints in a delicate way that they sold butter. I dive in heavier. That cake of butter was melting like snow in a red hot furnace. The old lady says, "We sell butter to the soldiers at a mighty good price."

I dive in afresh. She says, "I get a dollar a pound for that butter," and I remark with a good deal of nonchalance, "Well, madam, it is worth it," and dive in again. I did not marry one of the girls.

Source: Sam R. Watkins, *"Co. Aytch," Maury Grays, First Tennessee Regiment; or, A Side Show of the Big Show*, 2nd. ed. (self-pub., 1882; Chattanooga, TN: Chattanooga Times, 1900), chap. 8, http://www.fullbooks.com/Co-Aytch-1.html.

LIFE IN TENTS

JOHN BILLINGS, USA

The last chapter I described quite fully the principal varieties of shelter that our troops used in the war. To this I wish to detail their daily life in those tents when they settled down in camp.

Enter with me into a Sibley tent which is not stockaded. If it is cold weather, we shall find the cone-shaped stove, which I have already mentioned, setting in the centre. These stoves were useless for cooking purposes, and the men were likely to burn their blankets on them in the night, so that many of the troops utilized them by building a small brick or stone oven below, in which they did their cooking, setting the stove on top as a part of the flue. The length of pipe furnished by the government was not sufficient to reach the opening at the top, and the result was that unless the inmates bought more to piece it out, the upper part of such tents was as black and sooty as a chimney tine.

The dozen men occupying a Sibley tent slept with their feet towards the centre. The choice place to occupy was that portion opposite the door, as one was not then in the way of passers in and out, although he was himself more or less of a nuisance to others when he came in. The tent was most crowded at meal times, for, owing to its shape, there can be no standing or sitting erect except about the centre. But while there was more or less growling at accidents by some, there was much forbearance by others, and, aside from the vexations arising from the constitutional blundering of the Jonahs and the Beats, whom I shall describe later, these little knots were quite family-like and sociable.

The manner in which the time was spent in these tents—and, for that matter, in all tents—varied with the disposition of the inmates. It was not always practicable for men of kindred tastes to band themselves under the same canvas, and so just as they differed in their avocations as citizens, they differed in their social life, and many kinds of pastimes went on simultaneously. Of course, all wrote letters more or less, but there were a few men who seemed to spend the most of their spare time in this occupation. Especially was this so in the earlier part of a man's war experience. The side or end of a hardtack box, held on the knees, constituted the writing-desk on which this operation was performed.

It is well remembered that in the early months of the war silver money disappeared, as it commanded a premium, so that, change being scarce, postage stamps were used instead. This was before scrip was issued by the government to take the place of silver; and although the use of stamps as change was not authorized by the national government, yet everybody took them, and the soldiers in particular just about to leave for the war carried large quantities away with them. They were not all in the best of condition. This could hardly be expected when they had been through so many hands. They were passed about in little envelopes, containing twenty-five and fifty cents in value. Many an old soldier can recall his disgust on finding what a mess his stamps were in either from rain, perspiration, or compression, as he attempted, after a hot march, to get one for a letter. If he could split off one from a welded mass of perhaps a hundred or more, he counted himself fortunate. Of course they could be soaked out after a while, but he would need to dry them on a griddle afterwards, they were so sticky. It was later than this that the postmaster-general issued an order allowing soldiers to send letters without pre-payment; but, if I recollect right, it was necessary to write on the outside "Soldier's Letter." I recall in this connection a verse that was said to have appeared on a letter of this kind. It ran as follows:

> *Soldier's letter, nary red,*
> *Hardtack and no soft bread,*
> *Postmaster, please put it through,*
> *I've nary cent, but six months due.*

There were a large number of fanciful envelopes got up during the war. I heard of a young man who had a collection of more than seven thousand such, all of different designs. I have several in my possession which I found among the numerous letters written home during wartime. One is bordered by thirty-four red stars—the number of States then in the Union—each star bearing the abbreviated name of a State. At the left end of the envelope hovers an eagle holding a shield and streamer, with this motto, "Love one another." Another one bears a representation of the earth in space, with "United States" marked on it in large letters, and the American eagle above it. Enclosing all is the inscription, "What God has joined, let no man put asunder." A third has a medallion portrait of Washington, under which is, "A Southern Man with Union Principles." A fourth displays a man sitting among money-bags, on horseback, and driving at headlong speed. Underneath is the inscription, "Rode off for the South. All that the Seceding States ask is to be let alone." Another has a negro standing grinning, a hoe in his hand. He is represented as saying, "Massa can't have dis chile, dat's what's de matter"; and beneath is the title, "The latest contraband of war." Then there are many bearing the portraits of early Union generals. On others Jeff Davis is represented as hanged; while the national colors appear in a hundred or more ways on a number—all of which, in a degree at least, expressed, some phase of the sentiments popular at the North. The Christian Commission also furnished envelopes gratuitously to the armies, bearing their stamp and "Soldier's letter" in one corner.

Besides letter-writing the various games of cards were freely engaged in. Many men played for money. Cribbage and euchre were favorite games. Reading was a pastime quite generally indulged in, and there was no novel so dull, trashy, or sensational as not to find some one so bored with nothing to do that he would wade through it. I, certainly, never read so many such before or since. The mind was hungry for something, and took husks when it could get nothing better. A great deal of good might have been done if the Christian Commission or some other organization planned to furnish the soldiers with good literature, for in that way many might have acquired a taste for the works of the best authors who would not have been likely acquired except under just such a condition as they were then in, viz., a want of some entertaining pastime. There would then have been much less gambling and sleeping away of daylight than there was.

Religious tracts were scattered among the soldiers by thousands, it is true, and probably did some good. I heard a Massachusetts soldier say, not long ago, that when his regiment arrived in New York en route for the seat of war, the men were presented with "a plate of thin soup and a Testament." This remark to me was very suggestive. It reminded me of the vast amount of mistaken or misguided philanthropy that was expended upon the army by good Christian men and women, who, with the best of motives urging them forward no doubt, often labored under the delusion that the army was composed entirely of men thoroughly bad, and governed their actions accordingly. That there were bad men in the army is too well known to be denied if one cared to deny it; and, while I may forgive, I cannot forget a war governor who granted pardon to several criminals that were serving out sentences in prison, if they would enlist. But the morally bad soldiers were in the minority. The good men should have received some consideration, and the tolerably good even more. Men are only children of an older growth; they like to be appreciated at their worth at least, and the nature of many of the tracts was such that they defeated the object aimed at in their distribution.

Chequers was a popular game among the soldiers, backgammon less so, and it was only rarely that the statelier and less familiar game of chess was to be observed on the board. There were some soldiers who rarely joined in any games. In this class were to be found the illiterate members of a company. Of course they did not read or write, and they rarely played cards. They were usually satisfied to lie on their blankets, and talk with one another, or watch the playing. Yes, they did have one pastime—the proverbial soldier's pastime of smoking. A pipe was their omnipresent companion, and seemed to make up to them in sociability for whatsoever they lacked of entertainment in other directions. Then there were a few men in every organization who engaged in no pastimes and joined in no social intercourse. These men were irreproachable as soldiers, it may have been, doing without grumbling everything that was expected of them in the line of military or fatigue duty, but they seemed shut up within an impenetrable shell, and would lie on their blankets silent while all others joined in the social round; or, perhaps, would get up and go out of the tent as if its lively social atmosphere was uncongenial, and walk up and down the parade or company street alone. Should you address them, they would answer pleasantly but in monosyllables; and if the conversation was continued, it must be done in the same way. They could not be drawn out. They would cook by themselves, eat by themselves, camp by themselves on the march—in fact, keep by themselves at all times as much as possible. Guard duty was the one occupation which seemed most suited to their natures, for it provided them with the exclusiveness and comparative solitude that their peculiar mental condition craved. But these men were the exceptions. They were few in number, and the more noticeable on that account. They only served to emphasize the fact that the average soldier was a sociable being.

One branch of business which was carried on quite extensively was the making of pipes and rings as mementos of a camp or battlefield. The pipes were made from the root of the mountain laurel when it could be had, and often ornamented with the badges of the various corps, either in relief or inlaid. The rings were made sometimes of dried horn or hoof, very often of bone, and some were fashioned out of large gutta-percha buttons which were sent from home.

The evenings in camp were less occupied in game-playing, I should say, than the hours off duty in the daytime; partly, perhaps, because the tents were rather dimly lighted, and partly because of a surfeit of such recreations by daylight. But, whatever the cause, I think old soldiers will generally agree in the statement that the evenings were the time of sociability and reminiscence. It was then quite a visiting time among soldiers of the same organization. It was then that men from the same town or neighborhood got together and exchanged some gossip. Each one would produce recent letters giving interesting information about mutual friends or acquaintances, telling that such a girl or old schoolmate was married; that such a man had enlisted in such a regiment; that another was wounded and at home on furlough; that such another had been exempted from the forthcoming draft because he had lost teeth; that yet another had suddenly gone to Canada on important business—which was a favorite refuge for all those who were afraid of being forced into the service. And when the draft finally was ordered, such chucklings as these old schoolmates or fellow-townsmen would exchange as they again compared notes; first, to think that they themselves had voluntarily responded to their country's appeal, and, second, to hope that some of the croakers they left at home might be drafted and sent to the front at the point of the bayonet, interchanging sentiments of the following character:

"There's A, he was always urging others to go, and declaring he would himself make one of the next quota. I want to see him out here with a government suit on."

"Yes, and there's B, who has lots of money. If he's drafted, he'll send a substitute. The government ought not to allow any able-bodied man, even if he has got money, to send a substitute."

"Then there's C, who declared he'd die on his doorstep rather than be forced into the service. I only hope that his courage will be put to the test."

Such are fair samples of the remarks these fellow-soldiers would exchange with one another during an evening visitation. Then, there were many men not so fortunate as to have enlisted with acquaintances, or to be near them in the army. These were wont to lie on their blankets, and join in the general conversation, or exchange ante-war experiences, and find much of interest in common; but, whatever the number or variety of the evening diversions, there is not the slightest doubt that home, its inmates, and surroundings were more thought of and talked of then than in all the rest of the twenty-four hours.

In some tents vocal or instrumental music was a feature of the evening. There was probably not a regiment in the service that did not boast at least one violinist, one banjoist, and a bone player in its ranks—not to mention other instruments generally found associated with these—and one or all of them could be heard in operation, either inside or in a company street, most any pleasant evening. However unskillful the artists, they were sure to be the center of an interested audience. The usual medley of comic songs and negro melodies comprised the greater part of the entertainment, and, if the space admitted, a jig or clog dance was stepped out on a hard-tack box or other crude platform. Sometimes a real negro was brought in to enliven the occasion by patting and dancing "Juba," or singing his quaint music. There were always plenty of them in or near camp ready to fill any gap, for they "Massa Linkum's Sojers." But the men played tricks of all descriptions on them, descending at times to most shameful abuse until some one interfered. There were a few of the soldiers who were not satisfied to play a reasonable practical joke, but must bear down with all that the good-natured Ethiopians could stand, and, having the fullest confidence in the friendship of the soldiers, these poor fellows stood much more than human nature should be called to endure without a murmur. Of course they were on the lookout a second time. There was one song which the boys of the old Third Corps used to sing in the fall of 1863, to the tune of "When Johnny comes marching home," which is an amusing jingle of historical facts. I have not heard it sung since that time, but it ran substantially as follows:

> *We are the boys of Potomac's ranks,*
> *Hurrah! Hurrah!*
> *We are the boys of Potomac's ranks,*
> *We ran with McDowell,*
> *retreated with Banks,*
> *And we'll all drink stone blind —*
> *Johnny, fill up the bowl.*
> *We fought with McClellan, the Rebs, shakes and fever.*
> *Hurrah! Hurrah!*
> *Then we fought with McClellan, the Rebs, shakes and fever.*
> *But Mac joined the navy on reaching James River,*
> *And we'll all drink, etc.*
> *Then they gave us John Pope,*
> *our patience to tax.*
> *Hurrah ! Hurrah!*
> *Then they gave us John Pope,*
> *our patience to tax.*
> *Who said that out West he'd seen naught but Gray backs*
> *He said his headquarters were in the saddle,*
> *Hurrah! Hurrah!*
> *He said his headquarters were in the saddle,*
> *But Stonewall Jackson made him skedaddle.*
> *Then Mac was recalled, but after Antietam,*

Hurrah! Hurrah!
Abe gave him a rest,
he was too slow to beat 'em.
Oh, Burnside then he tried his luck.
Hurrah! Hurrah!
Oh, Burnside then he tried his luck,
But in the mud so fast got stuck.
Then Hooker was taken to fill the bill,
Hurrah! Hurrah!
Then Hooker was taken to fill the bill.
But he got a black eye at Chancellorsville.
Next came General Meade, a slow old plug,
Hurrah! Hurrah!
A slow old plug,
For he let them away at Gettysburg.

I think that there were other verses, and some of the above may have got distorted with the lapse of time. But they are essentially correct.

Here is the revised prayer of the soldier while on the celebrated "Mud March" of Burnside:

Now I lay me down to sleep
in mud that's many fathoms deep;
If I'm not here when you awake,
Just hunt me up with an oyster rake.

It was rather interesting to walk through a company street of an evening, and listen to a few words of the conversation in progress in the tents—all lighted up, unless some one was saving or had consumed his allowance of candle. It would read much like a chapter from the telephone—noted down by a listener from one end of the line only. Then to peer into the tents, as one went along, just time enough to see what was going on, and excite the curiosity of the inmates as to the identity of the intruder, was a feature of such a walk. While the description I have been giving applies in some particulars to life in Sibley tents, yet, so far as much of it is concerned, it describes equally well the life of the private soldier in any tent. But the tent of the army was the shelter or dog tent, and the life of the private soldier in log huts under these tents requires treatment by itself in many respects. I shall therefore leave it for consideration in another chapter.

Source: John Billings, *Hard Tack and Coffee* (Boston: G. M. Smith and Co., 1887), chap. 4, https://archive.org/details/hardtackcoffee00bill.

ON THE MARCH

PVT. CARLTON McCARTHY, CSA

Who does not know all about the marching of soldiers? Those who have never marched with them and some who have. The varied experience of thousands would not tell the whole story of the march. Every man must be heard before the story is told, and even then the part of those who fell by the way is wanting.

Orders to move! Where? when? what for?—are the eager questions of the men as they begin their preparations to march. Generally nobody can answer, and the journey is commenced in utter ignorance of where it is to end. But shrewd guesses are made, and scraps of information will be picked up on the way. The main thought must be to "get ready to move." The orderly sergeant is shouting "Fall in!" and there is no time to lose. The probability is that before you get your blanket rolled up, find your frying pan, haversack, axe, etc., and "fall in," the roll-call will be over, and some "extra duty" provided.

No wonder there is bustle in the camp. Rapid decisions are to be made between the various conveniences which have accumulated, for some must be left. One fellow picks up the skillet, holds it awhile, mentally determining how much it weighs, and what will be the weight of it after carrying it five miles, and reluctantly, with a half-ashamed, sly look, drops it and takes his place in ranks. Another having added to his store of blankets too freely, now has to decide which of the two or three he will leave. The old water-bucket looks large and heavy, but one stout-hearted, strong-armed man has taken it affectionately to his care.

This is the time to say farewell to the breadtray, farewell to the little piles of clean straw laid between two logs, where it was so easy to sleep;

farewell to those piles of wood, cut with so much labor; farewell to the girls in the neighborhood; farewell to the spring, farewell to "our tree" and "our fire," good-by to the fellows who are not going, and a general good-by to the very hills and valleys.

Soldiers commonly threw away the most valuable articles they possessed. Blankets, overcoats, shoes, bread and meat—all gave way to the necessities of the march; and what one man threw away would frequently be the very article that another wanted and would immediately pick up; so there was not much lost after all.

The first hour or so of the march was generally quite orderly, the men preserving their places in ranks and marching in solid column; but soon some lively fellow whistles an air, somebody else starts a song, the whole column breaks out with roars of laughter; "route step" takes the place of order, and the jolly singing, laughing, talking, and joking that follows no one could describe.

Now let any young officer who sports a new hat, coat, saddle, or anything odd, or fine, dare to pass along, and how nicely he is attended to. The expressions of good-natured fun, or contempt, which one regiment of infantry was capable of uttering in a day for the benefit of such passers-by, would fill a volume. As one thing or another in the dress of the "subject" of their remarks attracted attention, they would shout, "Come out of that hat!—you can't hide in thar!" "Come out of that coat, come out—there's a man in it!" "Come out of them boots!" The infantry seemed to know exactly what to say to torment cavalry and artillery, and generally said it. If any one on the roadside was simple enough to recognize and address by name a man in the ranks, the whole column would kindly respond, and add all sorts of pleasant remarks, such as, "Halloa, John, here's your brother!" "Bill! oh, Bill! here's your ma!" "Glad to see you! How's your grandma?" "How d 'ye do!" "Come out of that 'biled shirt'!"

Troops on the march were generally so cheerful and gay that an outsider, looking on them as they marched, would hardly imagine how they suffered. In summer time, the dust, combined with the heat, caused great suffering. The nostrils of the men, filled with dust, became dry and feverish, and even the throat did not escape. The "grit" was felt between the teeth, and the eyes were rendered almost useless. There was dust in eyes, mouth, ears, and hair. The shoes were full of sand, and the dust, penetrating the clothes, and getting in at the neck, wrists, and ankles, mixed with perspiration, produced an irritant almost as active as cantharides. The heat was at times terrific, but the men became greatly accustomed to it, and endured it with wonderful ease. Their heavy woolen clothes were a great annoyance; tough linen or cotton clothes would have been a great relief; indeed, there are many objections to woolen clothing for soldiers, even in winter. The sun produced great changes in the appearance of the men: their skins, tanned to a dark brown or red, their hands black almost, and long uncut beard and hair, burned to a strange color, made them barely recognizable to the home folks.

If the dust and the heat were not on hand to annoy, their very able substitutes were: mud, cold, rain, snow, hail and wind took their places. Rain was the greatest discomfort a soldier could have; it was more uncomfortable than the severest cold with clear weather. Wet clothes, shoes, and blankets; wet meat and bread; wet feet and wet ground; wet wood to burn, or rather not to burn; wet arms and ammunition; wet ground to sleep on, mud to wade through, swollen creeks to ford, muddy springs, and a thousand other discomforts attended the rain. There was no comfort on a rainy day or night except in "bed,"—that is, under your blanket and oil-cloth. Cold winds, blowing the rain in the faces of the men, increased the discomfort. Mud was often so deep as to submerge the horses and mules, and at times it was necessary for one man or more to extricate another from the mud holes in the road. Night marching was attended with additional discomforts and dangers, such as falling off bridges, stumbling into ditches, tearing the face and injuring the eyes against the bushes and projecting limbs of trees, and getting separated from your own company and hopelessly lost in the multitude. Of course, a man lost had no sympathy. If he dared to ask a question, every man in hearing would answer, each differently, and then the whole multitude would roar with laughter at the lost man, and ask him "if his mother knew he was out?"

Very few men had comfortable or fitting shoes, and fewer had socks, and, as a consequence, the suffering from bruised and inflamed feet was terrible. It was a common practice, on long marches, for the men to take off their shoes and carry them in their hands or swung over the shoulder.

Bloody footprints in the snow were not unknown to the soldiers of the Army of Northern Virginia!

When large bodies of troops were moving on the same road, the alternate "halt" and "forward" was very harassing. Every obstacle produced a halt, and caused the men at once to sit and lie down on the roadside where shade or grass tempted them; about the time they got fixed they would hear the word "forward!" and then have to move at increased speed to close up the gap in the column. Sitting down for a few minutes on a long march is pleasant, but it does not always pay; when the march is resumed the limbs are stiff and sore, and the man rather worsted by the halt.

About noon on a hot day, some fellow with the water instinct would determine in his own mind that a well was not far ahead, and start off in a trot to reach it before the column. Of course another and another followed, till a stream of men were hurrying to the well, which was soon completely surrounded by a thirsty mob, yelling and pushing and pulling to get to the bucket as the windlass brought it again and again to the surface. But their impatience and haste would soon overturn the windlass, and spatter the water all around the well till the whole crowd were wading in mud, the rope would break, and the bucket fall to the bottom. But there was a substitute for rope and bucket. The men would hasten away and get long, slim poles, and on them tie, by the straps a number of canteens, which they lowered into the well and filled; and unless, as was frequently the case, the whole lot slipped off and fell to the bottom, drew them to the top and distributed them to their owners, who at once threw their heads back, inserted the nozzles in their mouths and drank the last drop, hastening at once to rejoin the marching column, leaving behind them a dismantled and dry well. It was in vain that the officers tried to stop the stream of men making for the water, and equally vain to attempt to move the crowd while a drop remained accessible. Many, who were thoughtful, carried full canteens to comrades in the column, who had not been able to get to the well; and no one who has not had experience of it knows the thrill of gratification and delight which those fellows felt when the cool stream gurgled from the battered canteen down their parched throats.

In very hot weather, when the necessities of the service permitted, there was a halt about noon, of an hour or so, to rest the men and give them a chance to cool off and get the sand and gravel out of their shoes. This time was spent by some in absolute repose; but the lively boys told many a yarn, cracked many a joke, and sung many a song between "Halt" and "Column forward!" Some took the opportunity, if water was near, to bathe their feet, hands, and face, and nothing could be more enjoyable.

The passage of a cider cart (a barrel on wheels) was a rare and exciting occurrence. The rapidity with which a barrel of sweet cider was consumed would astonish any one who saw it for the first time, and generally the owner had cause to wonder at the small return in cash. Sometimes a desperately enterprising darkey would approach the column with a cartload of pies, "so-called." It would be impossible to describe accurately the taste or appearance of those pies. They were generally similar in appearance, size, and thickness to a pale specimen of "Old Virginia" buckwheat cakes, and had a taste which resembled a combination of rancid lard and crab apples. It was generally supposed that they contained dried apples, and the sellers were careful to state that they had "sugar in 'em" and were "mighty nice." It was rarely the case that any "trace" of sugar was found, but they filled up a hungry man wonderfully.

Men of sense, and there were many such in the ranks, were necessarily desirous of knowing where or how far they were to march, and suffered greatly from a feeling of helpless ignorance of where they were and whither bound—whether to battle or camp. Frequently, when anticipating the quiet and rest of an ideal camp, they were thrown, weary and exhausted, into the face of a waiting enemy, and at times, after anticipating a sharp fight, having formed line of battle and braced themselves for the coming danger, suffered all the apprehension and got themselves in good fighting trim, they were marched off in the driest and prosiest sort of style and ordered into camp, where, in all probability, they had to "wait for the wagon," and for the bread and meat therein, until the proverb, "Patient waiting is no loss," lost all its force and beauty.

Occasionally, when the column extended for a mile or more, and the road was one dense moving mass of men, a cheer would be heard away ahead—increasing in volume as it approached, until there was one universal shout. Then some favorite general officer, dashing by, followed by his staff, would explain the cause. At other times, the same cheering and enthusiasm would result from the passage down the column of some obscure and despised officer, who knew it was all a joke, and looked mean and sheepish accordingly. But no *man* could produce more prolonged or hearty cheers than the "old hare" which jumped the fence and invited the column to a chase; and often it was said, when the rolling shout arose: "There goes old General Lee or a Molly Cotton Tail!"

The men would help each other when in real distress, but their delight was to torment any one who was unfortunate in a ridiculous way. If, for instance, a piece of artillery was fast in the mud, the infantry and cavalry passing around the obstruction would rack their brains for words and phrases applicable to the situation, and most calculated to worry the cannoners, who, waist deep in the mud, were tugging at the wheels.

Brass bands, at first quite numerous and good, became very rare and their music very poor in the latter years of the war. It was a fine thing to see the fellows trying to keep the music going as they waded through the mud. But poor as the music was, it helped the footsore and weary to make another mile, and encouraged a cheer and a brisker step from the lagging and tired column.

As the men tired, there was less and less talking, until the whole mass became quiet and serious. Each man was occupied with his own thoughts. For miles nothing could be heard but the steady tramp of the men, the rattling and jingling of canteens and accoutrements, and the occasional "Close up, men—close up!" of the officers.

The most refreshing incidents of the march occurred when the column entered some clean and cozy village where the people loved the troops. Matron and maid vied with each other in their efforts to express their devotion to the defenders of their cause. Remembering with tearful eyes the absent soldier brother or husband, they yet smiled through their tears, and with hearts and voices welcomed the coming of the road-stained troops. Their scanty larders poured out the last morsel, and their bravest words were spoken, as the column moved by. But who will tell the bitterness of the lot of the man who thus passed by his own sweet home, or the anguish of the mother as she renewed her farewell to her darling boy? Then it was that men and women learned to long for the country where partings are no more.

As evening came on, questioning of the officers was in order, and for an hour it would be, "Captain, when are we going into camp?" "I say, lieutenant, are we going to — or to — ?" "Seen anything of our wagon?" "How long are we to stay here?" "Where's the spring?" Sometimes these questions were meant simply to tease, but generally they betrayed anxiety of some sort, and a close observer would easily detect the seriousness of the man who asked after "our wagon," because he spoke feelingly, as one who wanted his supper and was in doubt as to whether or not he would get it. People who live on country roads rarely know how far it is from anywhere to any where else. This is a distinguishing peculiarity of that class of people. If they do know, then they are a malicious crew. "Just over the hill there," "Just beyond those woods," "'Bout a mile," "Round the bend," and other such encouraging replies, mean anything from a mile to a day's march!

An accomplished straggler could assume more misery, look more horribly emaciated, tell more dismal stories of distress, eat more and march further (to the rear), than any ten ordinary men. Most stragglers were real sufferers, but many of them were ingenious liars, energetic foragers, plunder hunters and gormandizers. Thousands who kept their place in ranks to the very end were equally as tired, as sick, as hungry, and as hopeless, as these scamps, but too proud to tell it or use it as a means of escape from hardship. But many a poor fellow dropped in the road and breathed his last in the corner of a fence, with no one to hear his last fond mention of his loved ones. And many whose ambition it was to share every danger and discomfort with their comrades, overcome by the heat, or worn out with disease, were compelled to leave the ranks, and while friend and brother marched to battle, drag their weak and staggering frames to the rear, perhaps to die pitiably alone, in some hospital.

After all, the march had more pleasure than pain. Chosen friends walked and talked and smoked together; the hills and valleys made themselves a panorama for the feasting of the soldiers' eyes; a turnip patch here and an onion patch there invited him to occasional refreshment; and it was sweet to think that "camp" was near at hand, and rest, and the journey almost ended.

Source: Carlton McCarthy, *Detailed Minutiae of Soldier Life in the Army of Northern Virginia, 1861–1865* (Richmond, VA: Carlton McCarthy and Company, 1882; Project Gutenberg, 2008), chap. 4, http://www.gutenberg.org/ebooks/25603.

SPORTS IN CAMP

ALF BURNETT, USA

There are, at all times, sunny sides as well as the dark and melancholy picture, in camp life. Men whose business is that of slaughter—men trained to slay and kill, will, amid the greatest destruction of life, become oblivious to all surrounding scenes of death and carnage.

I have seen men seated amid hundreds of slain, quietly enjoying a game of "seven-up," or having *a little draw*. Yet let them once return to their homes, and enjoy the society and influence of the gentler sex, and they will soon forget the excitement and vices of camp, and return to the more useful and ennobling enjoyments of life.

Yesterday a lively time, generally, was had in camp. After the drilling of the division, a grand cock-fight occurred on the hill. Some of the boys, who are regular game-fanciers, brought some splendid chickens, and, as a consequence, a good deal of money changed hands. The birds fought nobly: three were killed, one of them killing his opponent the first round, and instantly crowing, much to the amusement of the Sports. This fighting with gaffs is not a cruel sport, as one or the other is soon killed.

Snakes are not so prevalent in these parts as they were when we first came: then it was not uncommon to find a nice little "garter" quietly ensconced in one's pocket, or in your pantaloon leg, or taking a nap in one corner of your tent.

A prize-fight occurred in the division a few days ago. A couple of sons of *Ethiopia*, regular young bucks, feeling their dignity insulted by various epithets hurled at each other, from loud-mouthing adjourned to fight it out in the woods—a big crowd following to enjoy the fun. A ring was soon formed, and at it they went, *a la* Sayers and Heenan. Umpires were improvised for the occasion, and time-keepers, etc., chosen.

The first clash was a *butter* and a *rebutter*, their heads coming together, fairly making the *wool* fly. This was round first.

Round 2d.—35th Ohio darkey came boldly to the scratch; as he only weighed sixty-five pounds more than his opponent, and with the *slight* difference of one foot six inches higher, he pitched in most valiantly, and received a splendid hit on the sconce, which made him feel as if a *flea* bit him. After full ten minutes skirmishing, during which time neither struck the other, both retired to the further *corner* of the *ring*, until time was called.

Round 3d.—Minnesota Ethiopian, who had been weakening in the pulse for some time, came up shaky, and was received with laughter by his opponent; but the little fellow hit out splendidly, and launched an eye-shutter at the stalwart form of the 35th darkey. First blood claimed for the 2d Minnesota.

Round 4th was, per agreement, a rough and tumble affair, as the spectators were growing impatient; and such "wool-carding" was never before exhibited. Both fought plucky; but the 2d Minnesota having but just recovered from a *sick of fitness*, as he said, was about being overpowered, when the officer of the day interfered; and thus ended the dispute for the time. Betters *drew* their money, as the fight was a *draw*.

Source: Alf Burnett, *Incidents of the War: Humorous, Pathetic and Descriptive* (Cincinnati, OH: Rickey and Carroll, 1863; Project Gutenberg, 2007), chap. 10, http://www.gutenberg.org/ebooks/23733.

1862

REPORT ON THE BATTLE OF PEA RIDGE

MARCH 7-8, 1862
COL. EUGENE A. CARR, USA

United States Army Col. Eugene A. Carr, West Pointer, fought for the North at the Battle of Pea Ridge, March 7–8, 1862. This crucial Trans-Mississippi clash, also known as the Battle of Elkhorn Tavern, saw Union forces under Brig. Gen. Samuel R. Curtis move into northwestern Arkansas and defeat a Confederate counterattack led by Maj. Gen. Earl Van Dorn, thus securing Missouri for the Union and putting Confederate forces in Arkansas on the defensive. Here is the text of Carr's official report.

Hdqrs. Fourth Div., Camp near Elkhorn Tavern
Benton County, Arkansas, March 10, 1862
Sir: Pursuant to Paragraph I of General Orders, No. 5, dated Headquarters Army of the Southwest, Pea Ridge, Ark., March 9, 1862, directing commanders of divisions to report as soon as practicable the movements and casualties in their respective divisions during the campaign, I have the honor to report as follows:

On the 9th of February, at Lebanon, Mo., the General organized the Fourth Division and placed it under my command. I had previously conducted the operations of the cavalry expedition and the force under Colonel Osterhaus up to the time when the general commanding the district arrived in person at Lebanon. The troops ordered to constitute the Fourth Division were:

First Brigade, Colonel Dodge commanding: Fourth Iowa Volunteers, Colonel Dodge; Thirty-fifth Illinois Volunteers, Colonel Smith; First Iowa Battery, Lieutenant David.

Second Brigade: Colonel Vandever commanding: Ninth Iowa Volunteers, Colonel Vandever; Twenty-fourth Missouri Volunteers, Colonel Boyd; Dubuque battery, Captain Hayden; third battalion of the Third Illinois Cavalry, under Majors Ruggles, McConnell, and Captain Maus.

With this command I started from Lebanon, Mo., on the 10th of February, and arrived at Marshfield on the 12th, where the whole army had assembled. On the 13th we marched within 8 miles of Springfield, I leading the advance on the direct road, and my advance of cavalry, under Major McConnell, together with Major Bowen and Colonel Wright's cavalry, and the mountain howitzers, under Captain Stephens, skirmished the enemy during the latter part of the day's march. I placed a picket of four companies, Third Illinois Cavalry, a mile and a half in advance, at the fork of the road, immediately after arriving in camp. This picket was attacked by the enemy, but gallantly held its ground and drove the enemy away. The next morning at 4 o'clock my division took the advance in the direction of Springfield. Upon arriving 5 miles from Springfield, before daylight in the morning, I halted to wait for the other divisions to come up and deploy, but a company of the Fourth Iowa, which had been thrown forward as skirmishers, did not receive the orders to halt, but marched into Springfield and took it, with some prisoners and stores, the enemy having evacuated in the night.

The next day the Third and Fourth Divisions moved on to McCulla's Store, 29 miles. The next day my division led. The cavalry advance, composed of the Third Illinois Cavalry, the cavalry of the Third Division, and the mountain howitzers, overtook the rear guard of the enemy's artillery and infantry on Flat Creek, and brought them to bay. The Dubuque battery was brought up, and under the personal supervision of the General fired upon the enemy, doing him considerable damage, but the infantry could not come up until it was too late to pursue any farther.

The next day the Third Division led, proceeded by all the cavalry, including the Third Illinois. They had a skirmish after passing Keetsville, and in Cross Timber Hollow a party with Colonel Davis, commanding Third Division, who went forward to reconnoiter, consisting of three companies of the Third Illinois Cavalry and about a company of the First Missouri, charged the enemy's pickets and ran them to their camp, my men having several men and horses wounded and 1 horse killed.

The next day, my division leading, with Ellis', Wright's, and McConnell's cavalry, came upon the enemy at Sugar Creek. The general ordered a charge of cavalry, which was gallantly executed, supported by the mountain howitzers under Major Bowen, who was wounded in the wrist. My cavalry, though in rear of the column, advanced well up by flanking to the left, and did considerable execution. I came on as rapidly as possible with the Second Brigade, under Colonel Vandever, and opened with the Dubuque battery, Captain Hayden, the enemy having made a stand about a mile and a half from the creek. He was quite obstinate, and showed some good artillery practice at our battery, disabling two horses, but Captain Hayden finally drove him away, and we camped where we were. I have since learned that the enemy had come to that point from Cross Hollow to assist Price and intended to fight us there, but that his heart failed him and he retreated in considerable confusion before my Second Brigade, and that if we had pursued at that time we might have routed him and done him considerable damage; but the positive order of the general, based upon the reason that it was too late in the day to go as far as Cross Hollow and fight a battle—and that point had long been spoken of as one where the enemy intended to make a determined stand—forbade my going farther.

The next day we waited for General Sigel's division to come up. The next we marched to Osage Springs, when we found that the enemy had decamped from Cross Hollow. My division was then moved to that place, Colonel Phelps' regiment of Missouri Volunteers having been assigned to the Second Brigade and Colonel Boyd's regiment relieved. While at Cross Hollow Lieutenant Jones, of the First Iowa Battery, received his commission as captain and took command, relieving Lieutenant David. The ammunition of that battery and also the Dubuque battery was defective, the powder being poor, the charges too light, and the fuses uncertain. I was told that the ammunition was put up by contractors, and on the day of battle the blood of our soldiers paid over again the unjust debt which had once been paid from the public Treasury.

On the 24th of February an expedition of cavalry and artillery, under General Asboth, was sent to Fayetteville. My cavalry led the charge into the town, capturing several prisoners. During my occupation of Cross Hollow, up to the 5th of March, several parties went out in different

directions, Colonel Dodge making two expeditions and Colonel Vandever one, taking a good many prisoners and killing some of the enemy.

On the 5th of March his cavalry appeared in strong force on the Fayetteville road and captured some of our wagons and men which were out
foraging. We at the same time received intelligence that he was advancing
in force. The general directed me to move back to Sugar Creek, to which
place he had ordered the other divisions and where he intended to fight. I
moved that night, but on account of the loss of my wagons was obliged to
destroy a few stores and some camp equipage and valuable private baggage.

Battle of the 7th. Having heard that the enemy had made his appearance on the west of us, General Curtis had called us in consultation on
the morning of the 7th about changing front in that direction, when news
came from the rear (north) that parties of the enemy were in close vicinity to the Elkhorn Tavern, where our depot of supplies had been placed,
together with the provost-marshal's guard and prisoners. The general
immediately directed me to send a brigade to that point, and I gave the
order to Colonel Dodge, who was present. Elkhorn Tavern was about a
mile and a half north of our camp, the ground being smooth and gradually ascending, with open fields on each side of the road from about
three-quarters of a mile from camp to within about a hundred yards of
the house. The house is situated on the west side of the Springfield and
Fayetteville road, at the head of a gorge known as Cross Timber Hollow
(the head of Sugar Creek), through which the road runs about 7 miles
north towards Keetsville. Behind the house to the west is a rocky hill
about 150 feet high, running off in a ridge towards the northwest. In
front of the house is a level ridge, on which a road runs towards the east,
having on the south side the smooth slope, mostly timbered, and on its
north side the heads of rugged gorges running down into Cross Timber
Hollow. About a half a mile from the tavern on the north side of this road
is Clemens' house, with a field mostly on the south side of the road of
about 20 acres. About the Elk-horn Tavern is an open space of about 10
acres. With these two exceptions the ground is mostly covered with trees
and underbrush, which comes up close to the tavern on the north side. As
I left the general to go with my leading brigade he remarked to me that I
would clean out that hollow in a very short time.

On arriving at the tavern I found that the enemy were trying to flank around to the east beyond Clemens' house. I sent out the cavalry, under Major McConnell, to skirmish them, followed by Colonel Dodge, with his regiment and two pieces; ordered Captain Jones to remain with two pieces as a reserve at the tavern, and took two other pieces myself down the road, which led down the hollow 300 or 400 yards to where the bushes were open enough to see a little to the front and to the right, bringing Colonel Smith, with the Thirty-fifth Illinois, to support the battery, and opened fire on a battery on a bluff on our right front. They immediately replied, and as long as my guns staid there there was a perfect storm of shot, shell, and grape.

In the mean time Dodge had driven back the enemy on the right flank and frustrated his first attempt to outflank us. I then sent back to the general a request to send forward Vandever's brigade; brought Jones' two pieces down the road, which took some time, owing to the fact that they had gone with Dodge instead of remaining as reserve. About that time one of the pieces which I had became disabled by a cartridge sticking half way down and was sent off.

The enemy seemed to have the range exactly. Colonel Smith, Thirty-fifth Illinois, was wounded in the head by a shell, which took off a part of his scalp. He received a bullet in his shoulder and his horse was killed all about the same time. Colonel Smith and his regiment showed the utmost gallantry, and deserve great credit for their steadiness in supporting the battery as well as for their conduct. Subsequently, when fighting the enemy's infantry near the same point, just before Colonel Smith was wounded, five or six ammunition chests burst, one after the other. Captain Jones and Lieutenant Gainbell were wounded by my side, and all but one of the pieces were disabled. This one piece was commanded by Corporal Leebert, First Iowa Battery, and was the only gun which was in the action from beginning to end, and both Corporal Leebert and his cannoneers deserve great credit for coolness, gallantry, and activity through the entire action.

About this time General Curtis came up to see how we were getting along. At this juncture two pieces of the Dubuque battery arrived, under Lieutenant Wright, and General Earl Van Dorn, and were served with admirable zeal and activity. Lieutenant Wright showed great coolness and skill during the entire action and was slightly wounded. The remainder of

the Dubuque battery then came, and continued firing until I became satisfied that it was disadvantageous to remain there any longer, and retired
to the top of the hill. I had then been struck three times. I then sent word
to the general that I had need of re-enforcements, having become satisfied that it was no small party merely to annoy the road with whom I was
contending, but a very considerable force—perhaps his main body. From
subsequent information I learn that it consisted of between 10,000 and
15,000 men, comprising all the Missourians, some of whom were called
Confederate troops, and were under Colonel Little; all the Missouri State
Guards, under General Price. There were other rebel forces, including
Indians, the whole commanded by General Van Dorn in person, with
about twenty guns, some of which were rifled, while I had not quite 2,500
men now on the field, with twelve guns, which came up successively, were
disabled, and ran out of ammunition in such a manner that I could never
have more than five playing at the same time.

I know of the following divisions being engaged there, viz: Frost's,
Slack's, Parsons', Rains', and Little's; also the following batteries: Guibor's,
Clark's, MacDonald's, and Wade's. Against this force my division, with
the slight assistance mentioned further on, held its ground for upwards
of seven hours. After retiring from my first advanced position down the
road there was a lull in the action, and I went over to see Colonel Dodge,
who was about three-quarters of a mile distant, near the road running to
the east, along the ridge and beyond Clemens' house. During this time
the enemy advanced up the hollow in the brush along the main road, and
Colonel Vandever ordered forward the infantry, when there ensued a desperate conflict with small-arms, our men driving them back to the foot of
the hill, where the enemy opened his batteries. As our wounded men were
being brought back by their comrades from this desperate encounter many
of them would hurrah for the Union and utter expressions of joy that they
had had an opportunity to suffer for the cause. Colonel Vandever, Ninth
Iowa, commanding the brigade, exhibited the utmost coolness and bravery.
He was everywhere where his presence was most needed, cheering and
encouraging his men, who, however, needed but little encouragement, and
directing their efforts to the best advantage. His horse was hit twice. Colonel Phelps, commanding Phelps' regiment of six-months' Missourians, had

three horses shot under him and received a contusion from a shell. Both he and his regiment behaved nobly. Major Geiger, of the same regiment, had his horse shot under him. Major Weston, Twenty-fourth Missouri Volunteers, had three or four companies on provost guard duty, a part of which were stationed on the hill, and did good service in protecting the flanks. Captain Hayden, commanding the Dubuque battery, acted with his usual coolness in superintending the operation of his guns. He had two horses killed under him. Maj. William H. Coyl, Ninth Iowa, was here wounded in the shoulder. His gallantry had been very conspicuous.

I sent word to Colonel Dodge to draw his forces near. After our men retired from the range of the battery there was another short lull, when the enemy advanced, and there was another desperate encounter, in which the enemy failed to drive us out of the edge of the timber, but was driven back himself, we being materially assisted by two mountain howitzers, under Major Bowen, and his lieutenant, Madison, which had been sent up by the general. It was at this time that one of the guns of Hayden's battery was lost in the attempt to place it on the top of the hill, by going into a large body of the enemy who were concealed in the brush. There was now a lull for a considerable time, the enemy being engaged in arranging his forces for a final attack. From the tavern I could not see him on account of the thick brushes, but on the right, the timber being more open, Colonel Dodge saw him plainly advancing and placing his batteries and outflanking.

At this time I was satisfied that the enemy was too strong for me, although my troops had fought with the most heroic gallantry, and I would have retired but for the following reasons: The position which I now held would, if occupied by the enemy, have commanded our camp. We had some stores in a barn near the tavern, and I was constantly expecting re-enforcements, which I knew the general was using every effort to get up to me, and if they arrived in time we could hold the ridge, which would be as valuable to us as to the enemy, and the general sent me word repeatedly to "persevere." I therefore determined to hang on to the last extremity. Knowing that every moment saved brought my re-enforcements nearer, I sent what was left of the Thirty-fifth Illinois to Dodge, as it belonged to his brigade. I received about this time a battalion of the Eighth Indiana and three field pieces, all of which I placed in position at the tavern, but soon after the enemy opened on Dodge with artillery and infantry, and I sent the last-arrived troops to him.

While Colonel Vandever was closing in the gap thus occasioned the enemy commenced swarming up the road and hollow and through the brush in front of us. My troops fought with most heroic courage and devotion, officers exposing themselves freely, cheering and encouraging their men, but it was impossible to withstand such overpowering numbers, and the men retreated across the field, but rallied very handsomely along the fence not far back.

Lieut. Col. F. J. Herron, Ninth Iowa, had his horse shot under him, was wounded, and taken prisoner. He had commanded his regiment during the entire engagement, and his courage and conduct won the admiration of all, and will add to the laurels he gained at the battle of Wilson's Creek. Here my horse was hit three times. The artillery fired until the last moment, and in consequence thereof lost two pieces, several of the men being shot down while trying to attach them to the limber. The three pieces of artillery lost that day by Captain Hay-den's battery were recovered by our troops on the next day.

Upon retiring to the fence above mentioned we fortunately met General Curtis, with re-enforcements under General Asboth, advancing. The commanding general conducted the remainder of the operation in person.

During all this time Colonel Dodge had sustained a constant engagement with the enemy. He had placed himself on the hither side of the field near Clemens' house, and though immediately outnumbered and in point-blank range of grape, held his position until his ammunition gave out, when he retired a short distance, waited for the enemy's approach, gave him a last volley, which checked and turned him, and then marched off the field with colors flying, and bringing his wounded men along. Colonel Dodge had three horses shot under him, one of them being struck with 20 balls, and received a slight wound in the hand. Lieut. Col. J. Galligan, Fourth Iowa, was wounded in the hand. Lieut. Col. William P. Chandler, Thirty-fifth Illinois, was taken prisoner while rallying a squad of men to check the enemy, who were very near the left flank. Maj. John McConnell, with two battalions of the Third Illinois Cavalry, supported the right during the entire engagement, and

Colonel Dodge speaks in the highest terms of their conduct. They were much under fire of artillery. They skirmished constantly, and frequently dismounted to fight on foot. Some of the men whose horses were disabled joined the infantry and fought out the battles with them. Captain Sparks was wounded. Captain Davis had a horse shot under him.

The Second Battalion of the Third Illinois Cavalry supported the left, and was a part of the time placed on top of the hill to the west of the tavern, skirmishing with the troops there, some of whom were Indians. Lieut. S. F. Dolloff received a dangerous wound in the thigh. Lieut. W. S. Lee had a horse shot under him.

The total loss of the division was 97 killed, 488 wounded, and 78 missing; total, 663.

We brought onto the ground 1,790 infantry and 469 cavalry; twelve smooth-bore guns, with 204 men.

In giving the above narrative I have spoken of those officers and troops whom I personally noticed or whose conduct has been specially reported to me. There are many others deserving of whom I have not yet heard. All the troops behaved with such gallantry and devotion that it is the proudest boast of my life to have commanded them.

My staff were of the greatest service to me. First Lieut. T. W. Sullivan, adjutant Third Illinois Cavalry, acting assistant adjutant-general of the Fourth Division, rode the same horse on which he made the gallant charge at Dug Springs, where both he and his horse were desperately wounded. He carried a great many orders and went forward many times to reconnoiter, exposing himself freely. His horse was wounded. Lieut. L. Shields, Fourth Iowa, acting aide, was of great assistance. He had a horse shot under him while conducting a battalion of the Eighth Indiana to Colonel Dodge. Lieut. O. A. Bowen, Ninth Iowa, acting aide, was of great service, transmitting, &c. Mr. John E. Phelps, who has been acting aide since February 17, was with me in all the hottest parts of the engagement, and was wounded in the leg. Sergt. Maj. James William Wooster, of my regiment, was killed while trying to disengage an artillery team in front of the troops.

After the engagement we lay en bivouac in front of the enemy until morning, when the action was again renewed. My division, being on the right, did not come in contact with the enemy. Captain Hayden's battery, however, did excellent service, having been posted by the general in person so as to cross-fire on the enemy. The First Iowa Battery also, under Lieutenant David, did good execution with what little ammunition he had been able to obtain during the night, and the Third Illinois Cavalry, as on the previous day, was of great benefit to us by skirmishing on the flanks.

Before closing I wish to remark on the facts that Colonel Dodge, with a large part of his brigade, by special direction of the general, had been out the night before the battle until 12 o'clock, blockading the road by which the enemy traveled an hour or two afterwards to get in our rear. This blockading delayed the enemy and was of great advantage to us. Also Colonel Vandever, with a large part of his regiment, Phelps', and the Third Illinois Cavalry, composing more than half his brigade, being on detached service, made a march of 40 miles the day before the battle to join us. The horses had absolutely nothing to eat from the morning of the 6th till the evening of the 8th. These facts show that my division was tired when it went into action, account for the absence of some of the men, who were absolutely worn-out, and demonstrate what our soldiers cheerfully endure for the cause.

I inclose herewith reports of Col. G. M. Dodge, Fourth Iowa, and of Col. William Vandever, Ninth Iowa, with the accompanying papers; likewise the report of Col. David Shunk, commanding battalion of Eighth Indiana.

Very respectfully, your obedient servant,
E. A. Carr
Colonel, Commanding Division.
Capt. T. I. McKenny,
Actg. Asst. Adjt. Gen., Army of the Southwest

Source: The War of the Rebellion: A Compilation of the Official Records of the Union and Confederate Armies, ser. 1, vol. 8, and "The Pea Ridge Campaign" by Franz Sigel, in *Battles and Leaders of the Civil War*, vol. 1, ed. Clarence C. Buel and Robert U. Johnson; available at http://www.ironbrigader.com/2016/02/27/colonel-eugene-carrs-report-battle-pea-ridge.

THE *MONITOR* VS. THE *MERRIMACK*

MARCH 9, 1862
LT. SAMUEL DANA GREEN, USN

On March 14, 1862, United States Navy Lt. Samuel Dana Green wrote a description of the famous ironclad duel between the USS Monitor *and CSS* Virginia *(Merrimack) on March 9, 1862, in the Battle of Hampton Roads. Serving aboard the* Monitor, *Green had particular praise for his ship's commander, Lt. John Worden, as can be seen in Green's firsthand account. Originally set down in a letter to Green's parents, the original is displayed at the United States Naval Academy, in Annapolis, and became a well-known pamphlet for the Naval Historical Foundation.*

At 11 a.m. on Thursday we started down the harbor in company with the gun-boats *Sachem* and *Currituck*. We went along very nicely and when we arrived at Governor's Island, the steamer *Seth Low* came along side and took us in tow. We went out passed the Narrows with a light wind from the West and very smooth water. The weather continued the same all Thursday night. I turned out at six o'clock on Friday morning, and from that time until Monday at 7 p.m. I think I lived ten good years. About noon the wind freshened and the sea was quite rough. In the afternoon the sea was breaking over our decks at a great rate, and coming in our hawse pipe, forward, in perfect floods. Our berth deck hatch leaked in spite of all we could do, and the water came down under the Tower like a waterfall. It would strike the pilothouse and go over the Tower in most beautiful curves. The water came through the narrow eyeholes in the pilothouse with such force as to knock the helmsman completely round from the wheel. At 4 p.m.

An artist's depiction of the "terrific battle" between the *Monitor* and *Merrimack*
LIBRARY OF CONGRESS

the water had gone down our smoke stacks and blowers to such an extent that the blowers gave out, and the Engine Room was filled with gas. Then Mother occurred a scene I shall never forget. Our Engineers behaved like heroes every one of them. They fought with the gas, endeavoring to get the blowers to work, until they dropped down—apparently as dead as men ever were. I jumped in the Engine Room with my men as soon as I could and carried them on top of the Tower to get fresh air. I was nearly suffocated with the gas myself, but got on deck after everyone was out of the Engine Room just in time to save myself. Three firemen were in the same condition as the Engineers. Then times looked rather blue I can assure you. We had no fear as long as the Engine could be kept going, to pump out the water, but when that stopped the water increased rapidly. I immediately rigged the hand pump on the berth deck, but we were obliged to lead the hose out over the Tower; there was not force enough in the pump to throw the water out. Our only resource now was to bail, and that was useless as we had to pass the buckets up through the Tower, which made it a very long operation. What to do now we did not know. We had done all in our power and must let things take their own course. Fortunately the wind was off shore, so we hailed the tugboat, and told them to steer directly for the shore in order to get in smooth water. After five hours of hard steaming, we got near the land and in smooth water. At 8 p.m. we managed to get the engines to go in everything comparatively quiet again. The Captain had been up nearly all the previous night, and as we did not like to leave the deck without one of us being there, so I told him I would keep the watch from 8 to 12, he take it from 12 to 4, and I would relieve him from 4 to 8. Well the first watch passed off very nicely, smooth sea, clear sky, the moon out and the old tank going along five and six knots very nicely. All I had to do was to keep awake and think over the narrow escape we had in the afternoon. At 12 o'clock things looked so favorable, that I told the Captain he need not turn out, I would lay down with my clothes on, and if any thing happened, I would turn out and attend to it. He said very well and I went to my room and hoped to get a little nap. I had scarcely got to my bunk, when I was startled by the most infernal noise that I ever heard in my life. The *Merrimac*'s firing on Sunday last was music to it.

We were just passing a shoal and the sea suddenly became very rough and right ahead. It came up with tremendous force through our anchor-well and forced the air through our hawse pipe where the chain comes and then the water would come through in a perfect stream clear to our berth deck over the Ward Room table. The noise resembled the death groans of twenty men, and certainly was the most dismal, awful sound I ever heard. Of course the Captain and myself were on our feet in a moment and endeavoring to stop the hawse pipe. We succeeded partially but now the water commenced to come down our blowers again and we feared the same accident that happened in the afternoon. We tried to hail the Tug Boat, but the wind being directly ahead, they could not hear us, and we had no way of signaling to them as the steam whistle which father recommend had not been put on. We commenced to think then the *Monitor* would never see daylight. We watched carefully every drop of water that went down the blowers and sent continually to ask the Firemen how the blowers were going. His only answer was slowly, but could not be kept going much longer unless we could stop the water from coming down. The sea was washing completely over our decks and it was dangerous for a man to go on them so we could do nothing to the blowers. In the midst of all this our wheel ropes jumped off the steering wheel (owing to the pitching of the ship) and became jammed. She now commenced to sheer about at awful rate and we thought our hawser must certainly part. Fortunately it was a new one and held on well. In the course of half an hour we fixed the wheel ropes and now our blowers were the only difficulty. About 3 o'clock on Saturday morning, the sea became a little smoother, though still rough, and going down our blowers to some extent. The never failing answer from the Engine Room, "Blowers going slowly, but cant go much longer." From 4 a.m. until daylight, was certainly the longest hour and a half, I ever spent. I certainly thought old *Sol* had stopped in China and never intended to pay us another visit. At last however we could see and made the Tug Boat understand to go nearer in shore and get in smooth water, which we did at about 8 a.m. Things were again a little quiet, but every thing wet and uncomfortable below. The decks and air Ports leaked and the water still came down the hatches and under the Tower. I was busy all day, making out my Station Bills and attending to different things that constantly required my attention. At 3 p.m. we parted our hawser, but fortunately it was quite smooth, and we secured it without difficulty. At 4 p.m. we passed Cape Henry and heard heavy firing in the direction of Fortress Monroe. As we approached it increased, and we immediately cleated ship for action. When about half way between Fortress Monroe and Cape Henry, we spoke [with] a pilot boat. He told us the *Cumberland* was sunk and the *Congress* was on fire and had surrendered to the *Merrimac*. We did not credit it, at first, but as we approached Hampton Roads, we could see the fine old *Congress* burning brightly, and we knew then it must be so. Badly indeed did we feel, to think those two fine old vessels had gone to their last homes, with so many of their brave crews. Our hearts were very full and we vowed vengeance on the "Merrimac," if it should ever be our lot to fall in with her. At 9 p.m. we anchored near the frigate *Roanoke*, the flagship, Captain Marston (the Major's brother.) Captain Worden immediately went on board, and received orders to proceed to New Port News, and protect the *Minnesota* (which was aground) from the *Merrimac*. We immediately got underweigh [*sic*] and arrived at the *Minnesota* at 11 p.m. I went all board in our cutter and asked the Captain what his prospects were of getting off. He said he should try to get afloat at 2 a.m. when it was high water. I asked him if we could render him any assistance, to which he replied No. I then told him we should do all in our power to protect him from the attacks of the *Merrimac*. He thanked me kindly and wished us success. Just as I arrived back to the *Monitor*, the *Congress* blew up, and certainly a grander sight was never seen, but it went straight to the marrow of our bones. Not a word was said, but deep did each man think, and wish he was by the side of the *Merrimac*. At 1 a.m. we anchored near the *Minnesota*. The Captain and myself remained on deck, waiting for the *Merrimac*. At 3 a.m. we thought the *Minnesota* was afloat and coming down on us, so we got underweigh as soon as possible and stood out of the Channel. After backing and filling about for an hour we found we were mistaken and anchored again. At daylight we discovered the *Merrimac* at anchor with several vessels under Sewall's Point. We immediately made every preparation for battle. At 8 a.m. on Sunday the *Merrimac* got underweigh, accompanied by several Steamers, and started direct for the *Minnesota*. When a mile distant she fired two guns at the *Minnesota*. By this time our anchor was up, the men at quarters, the guns loaded, and everything ready for action. As the *Merrimac* came closer, the Captain passed the word to commence firing. I triced up the port, run the gun out, and fired the first gun, and thus commenced the great battle between the" Monitor" and the "Merrimac."

Now mark the condition our men and officers were in. Since Friday morning, 48 hours, they had had no rest, and very little food, as we could not conveniently cook. They had been hard at work all night, and nothing to eat for breakfast except hard bread, and were thoroughly worn out. As for myself, I had not slept a wink for 51 hours, and had been on my feet almost constantly. But after the first gun was fired, we forgot all fatigues, hard work and every thing else, and went to work fighting as hard as men ever fought. We loaded and fired as fast as we could. I pointed and fired the guns myself. Every shot I would ask the Captain the effect, and the majority of them were encouraging. The Captain was in the Pilot House directing the movements of the vessel. Acting Master Stodder was stationed at the wheel which turns the Tower, but as he could not manage it, he was relieved by Stimers. The speaking trumpet from the Tower to the pilot House was broken, so we passed the word from the Captain to myself on the berth deck, by Pay Master Keeler and Captain's Clerk Toffey.

Five times during the engagement we touched each other, and each time I fired a gun at her, and I will vouch the 168 lbs. penetrated her sides. Once she tried to run us down with her iron prow, but did no damage whatever. After fighting for two hours, we hauled off for half an hour to hoist shot in the Tower. At it we went again as hard as we could. The Shot, Shell, grape, canister, musket and rifle balls flew about us in every direction but did us no damage. Our Tower was struck several times, and though the noise was pretty loud, it did not effect us any. Stodder and one of the men were carelessly leaning against the Tower, when a shot struck the Tower exactly opposite to them, and disabled them for an hour or two. At about 11:30 the Captain sent for me. I went forward, and there stood as noble a man as lives, at the foot of the ladder of the Pilot House. His face was perfectly black with powder and iron, and he was apparently perfectly blind. I asked him what was the matter. He said a shot had struck the pilothouse exactly opposite his eyes and blinded him, and he thought the Pilot House was damaged. He told me to take charge of the ship and use my own discretion. I lead him to his room and laid him on the sofa, and then took his position. On examining the Pilot House I found the iron hatch on top had been knocked about half way off, and the second iron log from the Top, on the forward side was completely cracked through. We still continued firing, the Tower being under the direction of Stimers. We were between two fires. The *Minnesota* on one side and the *Merrimac* on the other. The latter was retreating to Sewell's Point and the *Minnesota* had struck us twice on the Tower. I knew if another shot should strike our Pilot House in the same place, our steering apparatus would be disabled and we should be at the mercy of the Batteries on Sewall's Point. The *Merrimac* was retreating towards the latter place. We had strict orders to act on the defensive and protect the *Minnesota*. We had evidently finished the *Merrimac* as far as the *Minnesota* was concerned, our pilot house was damaged and we had strict orders, not to follow the *Merrimac* up; therefore, after the *Merrimac* had retreated, I went to the *Minnesota* and remained by her until she was afloat. Genl. Wool and Secretary Fox both have complimented me very highly for acting as I did, and said it was the strict military plan to follow. This is the reason we did not sink the *Merrimac*, and everyone here capable of judging says we acted exactly right.

The fight was over now and we were victorious. My men and myself were perfectly black with smoke and powder. All my under clothes were perfectly black and my person was in the same condition. As we ran along side the *Minnesota*, Secretary Fox hailed us, and told us we had fought the greatest Naval battle on record and behaved as gallantly as men could. He saw the whole fight. I felt proud and happy then mother, and felt fully repaid for all I had suffered. When our noble Captain heard the *Merrimac* had retreated he said he was perfectly happy and willing to die, since he had saved the *Minnesota*. Oh how I love and venerate that man.

Source: Samuel Dana Green, *An Eye-witness Account of the Battle between the U.S.S. Monitor and the C.S.S. Virginia (formerly U.S.S. Merrimack) on March 9th, 1862* (Washington, DC: Naval Historical Foundation, n.d.), http://www.navyhistory.org/ eye-witness-account-battle-between-uss-monitor-css-virginia.

WHAT I SAW OF SHILOH

APRIL 6-7, 1862
LT. AMBROSE BIERCE, USA

Union forces pressed their advantage in the West. Led by Maj. Gen. Ulysses S. Grant, the Army of the Tennessee followed the Tennessee River deep into the breakaway state before being challenged at Pittsburg Landing by Confederate troops headed by Gen. Albert Sidney Johnston and Gen. P. G. T. Beauregard. Moving speedily from their base at Corinth, Mississippi, the Southerners hit the Northern army hard, fighting to drive them away from the security of the river and into nearby swamps. Union forces gave ground and another Confederate victory looked to be unfolding. But Grant, reinforced by Maj. Gen. Don Carlos Buell's Army of Ohio, halted the retreat and ordered a counterattack. After intense fighting, Confederate forces withdrew toward Corinth, sacrificing their earlier gains. Present at the Union victory was Lt. Ambrose Bierce, of the 9th Indiana. A valiant soldier, Bierce compiled a heroic service record stretching from Philippi to Kennesaw Mountain, where he sustained a head wound. After the war he emerged as one of the most renowned American authors of the nineteenth century, specializing in sharp journalism and realistic fiction. Here, the famous writer focuses on his experiences at Shiloh.

This is a simple story of a battle; such a tale as may be told by a soldier who is no writer to a reader who is no soldier.

The morning of Sunday, the sixth day of April, 1862, was bright and warm. Reveille had been sounded rather late, for the troops, wearied with

An artist's depiction of the Battle of Shiloh, 1862

long marching, were to have a day of rest. The men were idling about the embers of their bivouac fires; some preparing breakfast, others looking carelessly to the condition of their arms and accoutrements, against the inevitable inspection; still others were chatting with indolent dogmatism on that never-failing theme, the end and object of the campaign. Sentinels paced up and down the confused front with a lounging freedom of mien and stride that would not have been tolerated at another time. A few of them limped unsoldierly in deference to blistered feet. At a little distance in rear of the stacked arms were a few tents out of which frowsy-headed officers occasionally peered, languidly calling to their servants to fetch a basin of water, dust a coat or polish a scabbard. Trim young mounted orderlies, bearing dispatches obviously unimportant, urged their lazy nags by devious ways amongst the men, enduring with unconcern their good-humored raillery, the penalty of superior station. Little negroes of not very clearly defined status and function lolled on their stomachs, kicking their long, bare heels in the sunshine, or slumbered peacefully, unaware of the practical waggery prepared by white hands for their undoing.

Presently the flag hanging limp and lifeless at headquarters was seen to lift itself spiritedly from the staff. At the same instant was heard a dull, distant sound like the heavy breathing of some great animal below the horizon. The flag had lifted its head to listen. There was a momentary lull in the hum of the human swarm; then, as the flag drooped the hush passed away. But there were some hundreds more men on their feet than before; some thousands of hearts beating with a quicker pulse.

Again the flag made a warning sign, and again the breeze bore to our ears the long, deep sighing of iron lungs. The division, as if it had received the sharp word of command, sprang to its feet, and stood in groups at "attention." Even the little blacks got up. I have since seen similar effects produced by earthquakes; I am not sure but the ground was trembling then. The mess-cooks, wise in their generation, lifted the steaming camp-kettles off the fire and stood by to cast out. The mounted orderlies had somehow disappeared. Officers came ducking from beneath their tents and gathered in groups. Headquarters had become a swarming hive.

The sound of the great guns now came in regular throbbings—the strong, full pulse of the fever of battle. The flag flapped excitedly, shaking out its blazonry of stars and stripes with a sort of fierce delight. Toward the knot of officers in its shadow dashed from somewhere—he seemed to have burst out of the ground in a cloud of dust—a mounted aide-de-camp, and on the instant rose the sharp, clear notes of a bugle, caught up and repeated, and passed on by other bugles, until the level reaches of brown fields, the line of woods trending away to far hills, and the unseen valleys beyond were "telling of the sound," the farther, fainter strains half drowned in ringing cheers as the men ran to range themselves behind the stacks of arms. For this call was not the wearisome "general" before which the tents go down; it was the exhilarating "assembly," which goes to the heart as wine and stirs the blood like the kisses of a beautiful woman. Who that has heard it calling to him above the grumble of great guns can forget the wild intoxication of its music?

The Confederate forces in Kentucky and Tennessee had suf-fered a series of reverses, culminating in the loss of Nashville. The blow was severe: immense quantities of war material had fallen to the vic-tor, together with all the important strategic points. General Johnston withdrew Beauregard's army to Corinth, in northern Mississippi, where he hoped so to recruit and equip it as to enable it to assume the offensive and retake the lost territory.

The town of Corinth was a wretched place—the capital of a swamp. It is a two days' march west of the Tennessee River, which here and for a hundred and fifty miles farther, to where it falls into the Ohio at Paducah, runs nearly north. It is navigable to this point—that is to say, to Pittsburg Landing, where Corinth got to it by a road worn through a thickly wooded country seamed with ravines and bayous, rising nobody knows where and running into the river under sylvan arches heavily draped with Spanish moss. In some places they were obstructed by fallen trees. The Corinth road was at certain seasons a branch of the Tennessee River. Its mouth was Pittsburg Landing. Here in 1862 were some fields and a house or two; now there are a national cemetery and other improvements.

It was at Pittsburg Landing that Grant established his army, with a river in his rear and two toy steamboats as a means of communication with the east side, whither General Buell with thirty thousand men was moving from Nashville to join him. The question has been asked, Why did General Grant occupy the enemy's side of the river in the face of a superior force before the arrival of Buell? Buell had a long way to come; perhaps Grant was weary of waiting. Certainly Johnston was, for in the gray of the morning of April 6th, when Buell's leading division was *en bivouac* near the little town of Savannah, eight or ten miles below, the Confederate forces, having moved out of Corinth two days before, fell upon Grant's advance brigades and destroyed them. Grant was at Savannah, but hastened to the Landing in time to find his camps in the hands of the enemy and the remnants of his beaten army cooped up with an impassable river at their backs for moral support. I have related how the news of this affair came to us at Savannah. It came on the wind—a messenger that does not bear copious details.

On the side of the Tennessee River, over against Pittsburg Landing, are some low bare hills, partly inclosed by a forest. In the dusk of the evening of April 6 this open space, as seen from the other side of the stream—whence, indeed, it was anxiously watched by thousands of eyes, to many of which it grew dark long before the sun went down—would have appeared to have been ruled in long, dark lines, with new lines being constantly drawn across. These lines were the regiments of Buell's leading division, which having moved up from Savannah through a country presenting nothing but interminable swamps and pathless "bottom lands," with rank overgrowths of jungle, was arriving at the scene of action breathless, footsore and faint with hunger. It had been a terrible race; some regiments had lost a third of their number from fatigue, the men dropping from the ranks as if shot, and left to recover or die at their leisure. Nor was the scene to which they had been invited likely to inspire the moral confidence that medicines physical fatigue. True, the air was full of thunder and the earth was trembling beneath their feet; and if there is truth in the theory of the conversion of force, these men were storing up energy from every shock that burst its waves upon their bodies. Perhaps this theory may better than another explain the tremendous endurance of men in battle. But the eyes reported only matter for despair.

Before us ran the turbulent river, vexed with plunging shells and obscured in spots by blue sheets of low-lying smoke. The two little steamers were doing their duty well. They came over to us empty and went back crowded, sitting very low in the water, apparently on the point of capsizing. The farther edge of the water could not be seen; the boats came out of the obscurity, took on their passengers and vanished in the darkness. But on the heights above, the battle was burning brightly enough; a thousand lights kindled and expired in every second of time. There were broad flushings in the sky, against which the branches of the trees showed black. Sudden flames burst out here and there, singly and in dozens. Fleeting streaks of fire crossed over to us by way of welcome. These expired in blinding flashes and fierce little rolls of smoke, attended with the peculiar metallic ring of bursting shells, and followed by the musical humming of the fragments as they struck into the ground on every side, making us wince, but doing little harm. The air was full of noises. To the right and the left the musketry rattled smartly and petulantly; directly in front it sighed and growled. To the experienced ear this meant that the death-line was an arc of which the river was the chord. There were deep, shaking explosions and smart shocks; the whisper of stray bullets and the hurtle of conical shells; the rush of round shot. There were faint, desultory cheers, such as announce a momentary or partial triumph. Occasionally, against the glare behind the trees, could be seen moving black figures, singularly distinct but apparently no longer than a thumb. They seemed to me ludicrously like the figures of demons in old allegorical prints of hell. To destroy these and all their belongings the enemy needed but another hour of daylight; the steamers in that case would have been doing him fine service by bringing more fish to his net. Those of us who had the good fortune to arrive late could then have eaten our teeth in impotent rage. Nay, to make his victory sure it did not need that the sun should pause in the heavens; one of the many random shots falling into the river would have done the business had chance directed it into the engine-room of a steamer. You can perhaps fancy the anxiety with which we watched them leaping down.

But we had two other allies besides the night. Just where the enemy had pushed his right flank to the river was the mouth of a wide bayou, and here two gunboats had taken station. They too were of the toy sort, plated perhaps with railway metals, perhaps with boiler-iron. They staggered under a heavy gun or two each. The bayou made an opening in the high bank of the river. The bank was a parapet, behind which the gunboats crouched, firing up the bayou as through an embrasure. The enemy was at this disadvantage: he could not get at the gunboats, and he could advance only by exposing his flank to their ponderous missiles, one of which would have broken a half-mile of his bones and made nothing of it. Very annoying this must have been—these twenty gunners beating back an army because a sluggish creek had been pleased to fall into a river at one point rather than another. Such is the part that accident may play in the game of war.

As a spectacle this was rather fine. We could just discern the black bodies of these boats, looking very much like turtles. But when they let off their big guns there was a conflagration. The river shuddered in its banks, and hurried on, bloody, wounded, terrified! Objects a mile away sprang toward our eyes as a snake strikes at the face of its victim. The report stung us to the brain, but we blessed it audibly. Then we could hear the great shell tearing away through the air until the sound died out in the distance; then, a surprisingly long time afterward, a dull, distant explosion and a sudden silence of small-arms told their own tale.

There was, I remember, no elephant on the boat that passed us across that evening, nor, I think, any hippopotamus. These would have been out of place. We had, however, a woman. Whether the baby was somewhere on board I did not learn. She was a fine creature, this woman; somebody's wife. Her mission, as she understood it, was to inspire the failing heart with courage; and when she selected mine I felt less flattered by her pref-erence than astonished by her penetration. How did she learn? She stood on the upper deck with the red blaze of battle bathing her beautiful face, the twinkle of a thousand rifles mirrored in her eyes; and displaying a small ivory-handled pistol, she told me in a sentence punctuated by the thunder of great guns that if it came to the worst she would do her duty like a man! I am proud to remember that I took off my hat to this little fool.

Along the sheltered strip of beach between the river bank and the water was a confused mass of humanity—several thousands of men. They were mostly unarmed; many were wounded; some dead. All the camp-following tribes were there; all the cowards; a few officers. Not one of them knew where his regiment was, nor if he had a regiment. Many had not. These men were defeated, beaten, cowed. They were deaf to duty and dead to shame. A more demented crew never drifted to the rear of broken battalions. They would have stood in their tracks and been shot down to a man by a provost-marshal's guard, but they could not have been urged up that bank. An army's bravest men are its cowards. The death which they would not meet at the hands of the enemy they will meet at the hands of their officers, with never a flinching.

Whenever a steamboat would land, this abominable mob had to be kept off her with bayonets; when she pulled away, they sprang on her and were pushed by scores into the water, where they were suffered to drown one another in their own way. The men disembarking insulted them, shoved them, struck them. In return they expressed their unholy delight in the certainty of our destruction by the enemy.

By the time my regiment had reached the plateau night had put an end to the struggle. A sputter of rifles would break out now and then, followed perhaps by a spiritless hurrah. Occasionally a shell from a far-away battery would come pitching down somewhere near, with a whir crescendo, or flit above our heads with a whisper like that made by the wings of a night bird, to smother itself in the river. But there was no more fighting. The gunboats, however, blazed away at set intervals all night long, just to make the enemy uncomfortable and break him of his rest.

For us there was no rest. Foot by foot we moved through the dusky fields, we knew not whither. There were men all about us, but no camp-fires; to have made a blaze would have been madness. The men were of strange regiments; they mentioned the names of unknown generals. They gathered in groups by the wayside, asking eagerly our numbers. They recounted the depressing incidents of the day. A thoughtful officer shut their mouths with a sharp word as he passed; a wise one coming after encouraged them to repeat their doleful tale all along the line.

Hidden in hollows and behind clumps of rank brambles were large tents, dimly lighted with candles, but looking comfortable. The kind of comfort they supplied was indicated by pairs of men entering and reap-pearing, bearing litters; by low moans from within and by long rows of dead with covered faces outside. These tents were constantly receiving the wounded, yet were never full; they were continually ejecting the dead, yet were never empty. It was as if the helpless had been carried in and murdered, that they might not hamper those whose business it was to fall to-morrow.

The night was now black-dark; as is usual after a battle, it had begun to rain. Still we moved; we were being put into position by somebody. Inch by inch we crept along, treading on one another's heels by way of keeping together. Commands were passed along the line in whispers; more commonly none were given. When the men had pressed so closely together that they could advance no farther they stood stock-still, shel-tering the locks of their rifles with their ponchos. In this position many fell asleep. When those in front suddenly stepped away those in the rear, roused by the tramping, hastened after with such zeal that the line was soon choked again. Evidently the head of the division was being piloted at a snail's pace by some one who did not feel sure of his ground. Very often we struck our feet against the dead; more frequently against those who still had spirit enough to resent it with a moan. These were lifted carefully to one side and abandoned. Some had sense enough to ask in their weak way for water. Absurd! Their clothes were soaken, their hair dank; their white faces, dimly discernible, were clammy and cold. Besides, none of us had any water. There was plenty coming, though, for before midnight a thunderstorm broke upon us with great violence. The rain, which had for hours been a dull drizzle, fell with a copiousness that stifled us; we moved in running water up to our ankles. Happily, we were in a forest of great trees heavily "decorated" with Spanish moss, or with an enemy standing to his guns the disclosures of the lightning might have been inconvenient. As it was, the incessant blaze enabled us to consult our watches and encouraged us by displaying our numbers; our black, sinuous line, creeping like a giant serpent beneath the trees, was apparently interminable. I am almost ashamed to say how sweet I found the companionship of those coarse men.

So the long night wore away, and as the glimmer of morning crept in through the forest we found ourselves in a more open country. But where? Not a sign of battle was here. The trees were neither splintered nor scarred, the underbrush was unmown, the ground had no footprints but our own. It was as if we had broken into glades sacred to eternal silence. I should not have been surprised to see sleek leopards come fawning about our feet, and milk-white deer confront us with human eyes.

A few inaudible commands from an invisible leader had placed us in order of battle. But where was the enemy? Where, too, were the riddled regiments that we had come to save? Had our other divisions arrived during the night and passed the river to assist us? or were we to oppose our paltry five thousand breasts to an army flushed with victory? What protected our right? Who lay upon our left? Was there really anything in our front?

There came, borne to us on the raw morning air, the long, weird note of a bugle. It was directly before us. It rose with a low, clear, deliberate warble, and seemed to float in the gray sky like the note of a lark. The bugle calls of the Federal and the Confederate armies were the same: it was the "assembly"! As it died away I observed that the atmosphere had suffered a change; despite the equilibrium established by the storm, it was electric. Wings were growing on blistered feet. Bruised muscles and jolted bones, shoulders pounded by the cruel knapsack, eyelids leaden from lack of sleep—all were pervaded by the subtle fluid, all were unconscious of their clay. The men thrust forward their heads, expanded their eyes and clenched their teeth. They breathed hard, as if throttled by tugging at the leash. If you had laid your hand in the beard or hair of one of these men it would have crackled and shot sparks.

I suppose the country lying between Corinth and Pittsburg Landing could boast a few inhabitants other than alligators. What manner of people they were it is impossible to say, inasmuch as the fighting dispersed, or possibly exterminated them; perhaps in merely classing them as non-saurian I shall describe them with sufficient particularity and at the same time avert from myself the natural suspicion attaching to a writer who points out to persons who do not know him the peculiarities of persons whom he does not know. One thing, however, I hope I may without offense affirm of these swamp-dwellers—they were pious. To what deity their veneration was given—whether, like the Egyptians, they worshiped the crocodile, or, like other Americans, adored themselves, I do not presume to guess. But whoever, or whatever, may have been the divinity whose ends they shaped, unto Him, or It, they had builded a temple. This humble edifice, centrally situated in the heart of a solitude, and conveniently accessible to the supersylvan crow, had been christened Shiloh Chapel, whence the name of the battle. The fact of a Christian church—assuming it to have been a Christian church—giving name to a wholesale cutting of Christian throats by Christian hands need not be dwelt on here; the frequency of its recurrence in the history of our species has somewhat abated the moral interest that would otherwise attach to it.

Owing to the darkness, the storm and the absence of a road, it had been impossible to move the artillery from the open ground about the Landing. The privation was much greater in a moral than in a material sense. The infantry soldier feels a confidence in this cumbrous arm quite unwarranted by its actual achievements in thinning out the opposition. There is something that inspires confidence in the way a gun dashes up to the front, shoving fifty or a hundred men to one side as if it said, "*Permit me!*" Then it squares its shoulders, calmly dislocates a joint in its back, sends away its twenty-four legs and settles down with a quiet rattle which says as plainly as possible, "I've come to stay." There is a superb scorn in its grimly defiant attitude, with its nose in the air; it appears not so much to threaten the enemy as deride him.

Our batteries were probably toiling after us somewhere; we could only hope the enemy might delay his attack until they should arrive. "He may delay his defense if he like," said a sententious young officer to whom I had imparted this natural wish. He had read the signs aright; the words were hardly spoken when a group of staff officers about the brigade commander shot away in divergent lines as if scattered by a whirlwind, and galloping each to the commander of a regiment gave the word. There was a momentary confusion of tongues, a thin line of skirmishers detached itself from the compact front and pushed forward, followed by its diminutive reserves of half a company each—one of which platoons it was my fortune to command. When the straggling line of skirmishers had swept four or five hundred yards ahead, "See," said one of my comrades, "she moves!" She did indeed, and in fine style, her front as straight as a string, her reserve regiments in columns doubled on the center, following in true subordination; no braying of brass to apprise the enemy, no fifing and drumming to amuse him; no ostentation of gaudy flags; no nonsense. This was a matter of business.

In a few moments we had passed out of the singular oasis that had so marvelously escaped the desolation of battle, and now the evidences of the previous day's struggle were present in profusion. The ground was tolerably level here, the forest less dense, mostly clear of undergrowth, and occasionally opening out into small natural meadows. Here and there were small pools—mere discs of rainwater with a tinge of blood. Riven and torn with cannon-shot, the trunks of the trees protruded bunches of splinters like hands, the fingers above the wound interlacing with those below. Large branches had been lopped, and hung their green heads to the ground, or swung critically in their netting of vines, as in a hammock. Many had been cut clean off and their masses of foliage seriously impeded the progress of the troops. The bark of these trees, from the root upward to a height of ten or twenty feet, was so thickly pierced with bullets and grape that one could not have laid a hand on it without covering several punctures. None had escaped. How the human body survives a storm like this must be explained by the fact that it is exposed to it but a few moments at a time, whereas these grand old trees had had no one to take their places, from the rising to the going down of the sun. Angular bits of iron, concavo-convex, sticking in the sides of muddy depressions, showed where shells had exploded in their furrows. Knapsacks, canteens, haversacks distended with soaken and swollen biscuits, gaping to disgorge, blankets beaten into the soil by the rain, rifles with bent barrels or splintered stocks, waist-belts, hats and the omnipresent sardine-box—all the wretched debris of the battle still littered the spongy earth as far as one could see, in every direction. Dead horses were everywhere; a few disabled caissons, or limbers, reclining on one elbow, as it were; ammunition wagons standing disconsolate behind four or six sprawling mules. Men? There were men enough; all dead, apparently, except one, who lay near where I had halted my platoon to await the slower movement of the line—a Federal sergeant, variously hurt, who had been a fine giant in his time. He lay face upward, taking in his breath in convulsive, rattling snorts, and blowing it out in sputters of froth which crawled creamily down his cheeks, piling itself alongside his neck and ears. A bullet had clipped a groove in his skull, above the temple; from this the brain protruded in bosses, dropping off in flakes and strings. I had not previously known one could get on, even in this unsatisfactory fashion, with so little brain. One of my men, whom I knew for a womanish fellow, asked if he should put his bayonet through him. Inexpressibly shocked by the cold-blooded proposal, I told him I thought not; it was unusual, and too many were looking.

It was plain that the enemy had retreated to Corinth. The arrival of our fresh troops and their successful passage of the river had disheartened him. Three or four of his gray cavalry videttes moving amongst the trees on the crest of a hill in our front, and galloping out of sight at the crack of our skirmishers' rifles, confirmed us in the belief; an army face to face with its enemy does not employ cavalry to watch its front. True, they might be a general and his staff. Crowning this rise we found a level field, a quarter of a mile in width; beyond it a gentle acclivity, covered with an undergrowth of young oaks, impervious to sight. We pushed on into the open, but the division halted at the edge. Having orders to conform to its movements, we halted too; but that did not suit; we received an intimation to proceed. I had performed this sort of service before, and in the exercise of my discretion deployed my platoon, pushing it forward at a run, with trailed arms, to strengthen the skirmish line, which I overtook some thirty or forty yards from the wood. Then—I can't describe it—the forest seemed all at once to flame up and disappear with a crash like that of a great wave upon the beach—a crash that expired in hot hissings, and the sickening "spat" of lead against flesh. A dozen of my brave fellows tumbled over like ten-pins. Some struggled to their feet, only to go down again, and yet again. Those who stood fired into the smoking brush and doggedly retired. We had expected to find, at most, a line of skirmishers similar to our own; it was with a view to overcoming them by a sudden *coup* at the moment of collision that I had thrown forward my little reserve. What we had found was a line of battle, coolly holding its fire till it could count our teeth. There was no more to be done but get back across the open ground, every superficial yard of which was throwing up its little jet of mud provoked by an impinging bullet. We got back, most of us, and I shall never forget the ludicrous incident of a young officer who had taken part in the affair walking up to his colonel, who had been a calm and apparently impartial spectator, and gravely reporting: "The enemy is in force just beyond this field, sir."

In subordination to the design of this narrative, as defined by its title, the incidents related necessarily group themselves about my own personality as a center; and, as this center, during the few terrible hours of the engagement, maintained a variably constant relation to the open field already mentioned, it is important that the reader should bear in mind the topographical and tactical features of the local situation. The hither side of the field was occupied by the front of my brigade—a length of two regiments in line, with proper intervals for field batteries. During the entire fight the enemy held the slight wooded acclivity beyond. The debatable ground to the right and left of the open was broken and thickly wooded for miles, in some places quite inaccessible to artillery and at very few points offering opportunities for its successful employment. As a consequence of this the two sides of the field were soon studded thickly with confronting guns, which flamed away at one another with amazing zeal and rather startling effect. Of course, an infantry attack delivered from either side was not to be thought of when the covered flanks offered inducements so unquestionably superior; and I believe the riddled bodies of my poor skirmishers were the only ones left on this "neutral ground" that day. But there was a very pretty line of dead continually growing in our rear, and doubtless the enemy had at his back a similar encouragement.

The configuration of the ground offered us no protection. By lying flat on our faces between the guns we were screened from view by a straggling row of brambles, which marked the course of an obsolete fence; but the enemy's grape was sharper than his eyes, and it was poor consolation to know that his gunners could not see what they were doing, so long as they did it. The shock of our own pieces nearly deafened us, but in the brief intervals we could hear the battle roaring and stammering in the dark reaches of the forest to the right and left, where our other divisions were dashing themselves again and again into the smoking jungle. What would we not have given to join them in their brave, hopeless task! But to lie inglorious beneath showers of shrapnel darting divergent from the unassailable sky—meekly to be blown out of life by level gusts of grape—to clench our teeth and shrink helpless before big shot pushing noisily through the consenting air—this was horrible! "Lie down, there!" a captain would shout, and then get up himself to see that his order was obeyed. "Captain, take cover, sir!" the lieutenant-colonel would shriek, pacing up and down in the most exposed position that he could find.

O those cursed guns!—not the enemy's, but our own. Had it not been for them, we might have died like men. They must be supported, forsooth, the feeble, boasting bullies! It was impossible to conceive that these pieces were doing the enemy as excellent a mischief as his were doing us; they seemed to raise their "cloud by day" solely to direct aright the streaming procession of Confederate missiles. They no longer inspired confidence, but begot apprehension; and it was with grim satisfaction that I saw the carriage of one and another smashed into matchwood by a whooping shot and bundled out of the line.

The dense forests wholly or partly in which were fought so many battles of the Civil War, lay upon the earth in each autumn a thick deposit of dead leaves and stems, the decay of which forms a soil of surprising depth and richness. In dry weather the upper stratum is as inflammable as tinder. A fire once kindled in it will spread with a slow, persistent advance as far as local conditions permit, leaving a bed of light ashes beneath which the less combustible accretions of previous years will smolder until extinguished by rains. In many of the engagements of the war the fallen leaves took fire and roasted the fallen men. At Shiloh, during the first day's fighting, wide tracts of woodland were burned over in this way and scores of wounded who might have recovered perished in slow torture. I remember a deep ravine a little to the left and rear of the field I have described, in which, by some mad freak of heroic incompetence, a part of an Illinois regiment had been surrounded, and refusing to surrender was destroyed, as it very well deserved. My regiment having at last been relieved at the guns and moved over to the heights above this ravine for no obvious purpose, I obtained leave to go down into the valley of death and gratify a reprehensible curiosity.

Forbidding enough it was in every way. The fire had swept every superficial foot of it, and at every step I sank into ashes to the ankle. It had contained a thick undergrowth of young saplings, every one of which had been severed by a bullet, the foliage of the prostrate tops being afterward burnt and the stumps charred. Death had put his sickle into this thicket and fire had gleaned the field. Along a line which was not that of extreme depression, but was at every point significantly equidistant from the heights on either hand, lay the bodies, half buried in ashes; some in the unlovely looseness of attitude denoting sudden death by the bullet, but by far the greater number in postures of agony that told of the tormenting flame. Their clothing was half burnt away—their hair and beard entirely; the rain had come too late to save their nails. Some were swollen to double girth; others shriveled to manikins. According to degree of exposure, their faces were bloated and black or yellow and shrunken. The contraction of muscles which had given them claws for hands had cursed each countenance with a hideous grin. Faugh! I cannot catalogue the charms of these gallant gentlemen who had got what they enlisted for.

It was now three o'clock in the afternoon, and raining. For fifteen hours we had been wet to the skin. Chilled, sleepy, hungry and disappointed—profoundly disgusted with the inglorious part to which they had been condemned—the men of my regiment did everything doggedly.

The spirit had gone quite out of them. Blue sheets of powder smoke, drifting amongst the trees, settling against the hillsides and beaten into nothingness by the falling rain, filled the air with their peculiar pungent odor, but it no longer stimulated. For miles on either hand could be heard the hoarse murmur of the battle, breaking out near by with frightful distinctness, or sinking to a murmur in the distance; and the one sound aroused no more attention than the other.

We had been placed again in rear of those guns, but even they and their iron antagonists seemed to have tired of their feud, pounding away at one another with amiable infrequency. The right of the regiment extended a little beyond the field. On the prolongation of the line in that direction were some regiments of another division, with one in reserve. A third of a mile back lay the remnant of somebody's brigade looking to its wounds. The line of forest bounding this end of the field stretched as straight as a wall from the right of my regiment to Heaven knows what regiment of the enemy. There suddenly appeared, marching down along this wall, not more than two hundred yards in our front, a dozen files of gray-clad men with rifles on the right shoulder. At an interval of fifty yards they were followed by perhaps half as many more; and in fair supporting distance of these stalked with confident mien a single man! There seemed to me something indescribably ludicrous in the advance of this handful of men upon an army, albeit with their left flank protected by a forest. It does not so impress me now. They were the exposed flanks of three lines of infantry, each half a mile in length. In a moment our gunners had grappled with the nearest pieces, swung them half round, and were pouring streams of canister into the invaded wood. The infantry rose in masses, springing into line. Our threatened regiments stood like a wall, their loaded rifles at "ready," their bayonets hanging quietly in the scabbards. The right wing of my own regiment was thrown slightly backward to threaten the flank of the assault. The battered brigade away to the rear pulled itself together.

Then the storm burst. A great gray cloud seemed to spring out of the forest into the faces of the waiting battalions. It was received with a crash that made the very trees turn up their leaves. For one instant the assailants paused above their dead, then struggled forward, their bayonets glittering in the eyes that shone behind the smoke. One moment, and those unmoved men in blue would be impaled. What were they about? Why did they not fix bayonets? Were they stunned by their own volley? Their inaction was maddening! Another tremendous crash!—the rear rank had fired! Humanity, thank Heaven! is not made for this, and the shattered gray mass drew back a score of paces, opening a feeble fire. Lead had scored its old-time victory over steel; the heroic had broken its great heart against the commonplace. There are those who say that it is sometimes otherwise.

All this had taken but a minute of time, and now the second Confederate line swept down and poured in its fire. The line of blue staggered and gave way; in those two terrific volleys it seemed to have quite poured out its spirit. To this deadly work our reserve regiment now came up with a run. It was surprising to see it spitting fire with never a sound, for such was the infernal din that the ear could take in no more. This fearful scene was enacted within fifty paces of our toes, but we were rooted to the ground as if we had grown there. But now our commanding officer rode from behind us to the front, waved his hand with the courteous gesture that says *apres vous*, and with a barely audible cheer we sprang into the fight. Again the smoking front of gray receded, and again, as the enemy's third line emerged from its leafy covert, it pushed forward across the piles of dead and wounded to threaten with protruded steel. Never was seen so striking a proof of the paramount importance of numbers. Within an area of three hundred yards by fifty there struggled for front places no fewer than six regiments; and the accession of each, after the first collision, had it not been immediately counterpoised, would have turned the scale.

As matters stood, we were now very evenly matched, and how long we might have held out God only knows. But all at once something appeared to have gone wrong with the enemy's left; our men had somewhere pierced his line. A moment later his whole front gave way, and springing forward with fixed bayonets we pushed him in utter confusion back to his original line. Here, among the tents from which Grant's people had been expelled the day before, our broken and disordered regiments inextricably intermingled, and drunken with the wine of triumph, dashed confidently against a pair of trim battalions, provoking a tempest of hissing lead that made us stagger under its very weight. The sharp onset of another against our flank sent us whirling back with fire at our heels and fresh foes in merciless pursuit—who in their turn were broken upon the front of the invalided brigade previously mentioned, which had moved up from the rear to assist in this lively work.

As we rallied to reform behind our beloved guns and noted the ridiculous brevity of our line—as we sank from sheer fatigue, and tried to moderate the terrific thumping of our hearts—as we caught our breath to ask who had seen such-and-such a comrade, and laughed hysterically at the reply—there swept past us and over us into the open field a long regiment with fixed bayonets and rifles on the right shoulder. Another followed, and another; two—three—four! Heavens! where do all these men come from, and why did they not come before? How grandly and confidently they go sweeping on like long blue waves of ocean chasing one another to the cruel rocks! Involuntarily we draw in our weary feet beneath us as we sit, ready to spring up and interpose our breasts when these gallant lines shall come back to us across the terrible field, and sift brokenly through among the trees with spouting fires at their backs. We still our breathing to catch the full grandeur of the volleys that are to tear them to shreds. Minute after minute passes and the sound does not come. Then for the first time we note that the silence of the whole region is not comparative, but absolute. Have we become stone deaf? See; here comes a stretcher-bearer, and there a surgeon! Good heavens! a chaplain!

The battle was indeed at an end.

And this was, O so long ago! How they come back to me—dimly and brokenly, but with what a magic spell—those years of youth when I was soldiering! Again I hear the far warble of blown bugles. Again I see the tall, blue smoke of camp-fires ascending from the dim valleys of Wonderland. There steals upon my sense the ghost of an odor from pines that canopy the ambuscade. I feel upon my cheek the morning mist that shrouds the hostile camp unaware of its doom, and my blood stirs at the ringing rifle-shot of the solitary sentinel. Unfamiliar landscapes, glittering with sunshine or sullen with rain, come to me demanding recognition, pass, vanish and give place to others. Here in the night stretches a wide and blasted field studded with half-extinct fires burning redly with I know not what presage of evil. Again I shudder as I note its desolation and its awful silence. Where was it? To what monstrous inharmony of death was it the visible prelude?

O days when all the world was beautiful and strange; when unfamiliar constellations burned in the Southern midnights, and the mockingbird poured out his heart in the moon-gilded magnolia; when there was something new under a new sun; will your fine, far memories ever cease to lay contrasting pictures athwart the harsher features of this later world, accentuating the ugliness of the longer and tamer life? Is it not strange that the phantoms of a blood-stained period have so airy a grace and look with so tender eyes?—that I recall with difficulty the danger and death and horrors of the time, and without effort all that was gracious and picturesque? Ah, Youth, there is no such wizard as thou! Give me but one touch of thine artist hand upon the dull canvas of the Present; gild for but one moment the drear and somber scenes of to-day, and I will willingly surrender an other life than the one that I should have thrown away at Shiloh.

Source: Ambrose Bierce, *The Collected Works of Ambrose Bierce*, vol. 1 (New York: Neale Publishing Company, 1909), http://books.google.com/books?id=9Zepl6EEquwC&amp ;oe=UTF-8.

The Seven Pines battlefield, with a howitzer cannon in the foreground

THE BATTLE OF SEVEN PINES

MAY 31-JUNE 1,1862
BRIG. GEN. HENRY NAGLEE, USA

Philadelphia-born Henry Morris Naglee graduated from West Point in 1835. He put his education to work in the civilian world as a civil engineer before rejoining the army and serving as a captain during the Mexican-American War. Pleased by what he saw in California, Naglee moved there and became a winery owner, credited with starting the state's brandy industry. Rejoining the army at the start of the Civil War, Naglee gained command of a brigade in the Army of the Potomac's IV Corps. At Fair Oaks, or Seven Pines, his unit won plaudits for its performance, and Naglee fought with distinction even as his horse was killed and he received multiple wounds. Mustering out in 1864, he returned to his brandy business and supported George McClellan's unsuccessful presidential bid that year. Like many who served with "The Little Napoleon," Naglee remained fiercely loyal to McClellan.

The Battle of Seven Pines was a part of McClellan's Peninsular Campaign, during which the Union took advantage of its command of the Chesapeake Bay to land troops along the James River, moving up the Virginia Peninsula, in what was ultimately a fruitless attempt to get at Richmond. The battle, near the Chickahominy River, was intense but inconclusive, notable for the wounds that incapacitated Confederate commander Gen. Joseph E. Johnston. Persistent Southern attacks managed to stem IV Corps' advance, but bitter fighting ended without a clear victor. Here, Naglee describes the combat.

Lieutenant: Before alluding to the occurrences of the 31st of May, it would probably add to a better understanding of the subject to refer to the advance of my Brigade on the 24th, 25th and 26th, a week previous.

Having crossed the railroad bridge, and examined the Chickahominy from the railroad to Bottom's Bridge, on the 20th, and made a reconnaissance from the "Chimney," near Bottom's Bridge to within two miles of the James River, on the Quaker road, on the 23d, Gen. McClelland ordered me to make a reconnaissance of the road and country by the Williamsburg road, as far as the Seven Pines, on Saturday, the 24th, with instructions, "If possible, to advance to the Seven Pines, or the forks of the direct road to Richmond, and the road turning to the right into the road leading from New-Bridge to Richmond, and to hold that point as practicable." Under these instructions, with the a addition of two batteries of Col. Bailey's New-York First Artillery, and Col. Gregg's Cavalry, we pushed the reconnaissance, not without considerable opposition, to the Seven Pines on the day referred to; one mile and a half beyond the Pines on the following day, and to a line perpendicular to the railroad from Richmond to West Point, intersecting at midway between the fifth and sixth mile post, on the day following the last, and on the day after, the 27th, extended it across to the Nine-Mile road, where it was intersected by the road to Garnett's house, and thence by this road bearing to the right. Our picket lines extended to the Chickahominy. This line, from the river across the railroad to the Williamsburg road, about three miles long, was picketed at first by the First Brigade, and afterwards by Casey's Division, but placed more directly under the charge and protection of the regiments of the First Brigade, which were encamped along its entire length for that purposes.

The picket line proposed to be kept up, and the supports to the same, from the left of the above picket line on the Williamsburg road to the White Oak Swamp, were especially intrusted to Gen. Couch. This was the line of our advance on Saturday, the 31st of May, at 12 M., when two shells thrown into our camp inst announced the hostile intentions of the enemy. No alarm was felt by any one, for it was seldom that twenty-four hours passed that we did not exchange similar salutations.

Soon after it was reported that an attack was impending, the usual orders were issued, and within half an hour the troops moved to positions that were assigned to them by Gen. Casey. Being at this time on the "Nine-Mile road." near a breastwork fronting the "Old Tavern," then under construction, and surging, from the discharges of musketry becoming frequent, that something serious was intended, I hastened in the direction indicated by the fire, and soon arrived upon the ground, on the Williamsburg road, about three-quarters of a mile in front of the "Seven Pines," where I found Gen. Casey, who had placed the One Hundredth New-York, Col. Brown, on the left of that road, behind a field of large timber that had been cut down. On the right of the same road was placed Capt. Spratt's New-York Battery of four pieces. On the right of this were three companies of the Eleven Maine, Col. Plaisted; and on the right of the Eleventh Maine were eight companies of the One Hundred and Fourth Pennsylvania, Col. Davis. Four companies of the Eleventh Maine were on picket duty, out, being driven in, formed with the Fifty-sixth New-York, Lieut.-Col. Jaudan, at his encampment, in line of battle, parallel with and about 800 yards in rear of the picket line—200 yards to the left of the railroad. Col. Dodge's Fifty-second Pennsylvania, supporting the picket line on the extreme right, formed at his encampment, on the Nine-Mile road, three-quarters of a mile in rear of the large Garnett field. The remaining companies of the One Hundred and Fourth Pennsylvania and Eleventh Maine were on picket duty along the large field in the direction of the Chickahominy.

Soon after my arrival upon the ground—about 1 o'clock p.m.—the fire then being frequent, and from the direction of the main Richmond Stage Road, Gen. Casey gave an order to the One Hundredth New-York, and One Hundred and Fourth Pennsylvania and Eleventh Maine to charge, when, as reported by Col. Davis, the regiments sprang forward "toward the enemy with a tremendous yell, in our way was a high worm fence, which cut our former line of battle, but the boys sprang over it, into the same enclosure with the enemy, where we formed and renewed the fight. The battle now raged with great fury, and the wing was much hotter than before. Spratt's Battery during this time had kept up a lively fire in the same direction. At about 3 p.m., the enemy being largely reinforced, pressed us in front and flank, and seeing that we could not hold our position much longer, unless reinforced, I dispatched an officer to Gen. Casey for that purpose. The Colonel of the One Hundredth New-York being killed, the Colonel of the One Hundred and Fourth Pennsylvania severely wounded, the Major mortally wounded, the Lieutenant-Colonel absent, half of our men having been killed or wounded, the enemy, ten times our number, within a few feet of us—one of them striking Sergeant Porter, the left guide of the One Hundred and Fourth, over the neck with his musket—several of the Eleventh Maine being bayoneted, and receiving no reinforcements, we were ordered, with Spratt's Battery, to retire; but, unfortunately, the horses of one of the pieces being killed, we were compelled to abandon that piece."

The enemy endeavored to follow up this success, and was advancing in closed columns, when our troops having been sufficiently withdrawn, Col. Bailey, of the First New-York Artillery, at my request, directed the fire of the batteries of Fitch and Bates, situated in and near the redoubt, to be concentrated upon the advancing mass. At every discharge of grape and canister wide gaps were opened in his tanks, which were filled as soon as opened; still, he pressed on, until, after many trials, with immense loss, finding that he was "advancing into the very jaws of death," with sullen hesitation he concluded to desist at this point.

I congratulated Col. Bailey upon his gallant conduct and good services, as heretofore described, and suggested that in the event of being compelled to abandon another piece, he should instruct his gunners to spike before leaving it. He went into the redoubt to give these orders, when he was shot by a rifle ball through the forehead, and died a few minutes after, the State losing a gallant soldier, and his artillerymen a friend to whom they were entirely devoted. Soon after this, Major Van Valkenburgh, of the same artillery, was killed by a rifle ball whilst actively engaged in working these batteries, and but a little while after, Lieut. Rumsey, the Adjutant in the same manner. All of the field and Staff officers being killed. I assumed the direction of the batteries composing the First New-York Artillery.

No reinforcements having been sent to us, and desirous of following up the success above referred to, about 3 1/2 p.m., I rode to the rear, and led up the Fifty-fifth New-York, Lieut.-Col. Thourete, and placed it in line perpendicular to the Williamsburg road, about fifty yards in advance of the redoubt, the left resting a short distance from the road. Before setting into position they were compelled to march over the bodies of their killed and wounded comrades, and soon after found themselves fully engaged. Leaving the Fifty-fifth, my attention was directed towards the right, where I found the Fifty-sixth New-York, with the Eleventh Maine, who, after four hour's contest, had fallen back about four hundred yards, and were again placed by me, at four hours and ten minutes, in a depression in the ground, about midway between the Williamsburg road and the railroad, and about three hundred yards in front of the Nine Mile road. Nearby I found the Fifty-second Pennsylvania, which had been ordered from the right, and I placed them in echelon to the right, and in front of the Fifty-sixth, with the right resting upon and in rear of a large pond. At this time the fire here had considerably slackened, but was considerably increasing on the left. Returning in about an hour, to the left, I found the Fifty-fifth engaged to their utmost extent, and ascertained for the first time that the enemy had discovered what I had long feared, that there were none of our troops between the White Oak Swamp and a line parallel with and but two hundred yards from the Williamsburg road. He had more than an hour before discovered this, and with sharpshooters concealed in the woods, to the left and rear of the redoubt and rifle-pits, they had killed many of our most valuable officers, had picked off the cannoneers, and had killed from three to four horses out of every team attached to the First New-York Artillery, and, at the time of my return, had driven our men from the rifle-pits. No time was to be lost; Fitch's Battery was ordered to the rear. The battery under Lieut. Hart was next ordered to retire, but it was soon found that but one limber could be moved. I ordered the pieces to be spiked; but after spiking the pieces in the redoubt, those on the outside of it were in the possession of the enemy. By way of precaution, I had ordered the prologues to be fixed to the sections of Regan's Battery, still firing up the Williamsburg road, and ordered it to retire firing, until in the abattis that crosses the road. I then withdrew the Fifty-fifth, under the protection of its fire. This regiment had fought most gallantly, suffered severely, and contributed much, in the end, towards saving Regan's Battery from falling into the hands of the enemy. And then the entire field in front of, and including the redoubt, was in possession of the enemy, who had pressed to within a few yards of us, it being necessary to support many of the wounded horses, to keep them from falling in the traces. At 5:15 p.m. we brought the last sections of Bailey's First New-York Artillery from the field, they being at this time literally filled with iron and lead. Returning rapidly to my Fifty-sixth New-York, Eleventh Maine and Fifty-second Pennsylvania, my anticipations here were realized; being successful in running our left flank, the enemy had opened a most destructive cross fire upon them from the pieces near the redoubt that had not been spiked; and this, with the fire from their immediate front, was no longer to be ordered, and they were withdrawn and marched down the Nine Mile road and placed in position, in rear of this road, about three hundred yards from the Seven Pines, where soon their services were required. In the meanwhile, Col. Neil, of the Twenty-third Pennsylvania, had come upon the ground occupied by Col. Dodge, and induced him to advance in front, and in the right of the position that had been assigned to him, whilst he, Col. Neil, occupied that which the Fifty-second Pennsylvania evacuated. But these dispositions were scarcely made before the masses of the enemy broke through, and a few minutes sufficed to leave the half of Dodge's command upon the ground, and to force Neil, precipitately from his position.

The remaining portion of the Fifty-second—for it was now reduced to a little over one hundred men—were conducted along the Nine Mile Road to the Seven Pines, where, finding the rifle-pits occupied, they took possession of a fence and some outhouses, and did most effective service. Afterward, they crossed to the left of Couch's position, and advanced two hundred yards, into and along the woods, to the left and front of the Seven Pines, where they remained actively employed until near dark, when the enemy advancing rapidly in masses to the rear of the Nine Mile road, inclined toward the Williamsburg road, sweeping everything from the field, our forces making one general, simultaneous movement to the rear, which did not stop until all had arrived at the line of defense, one mile in that direction. The Fifty-second having their retreat cut off, escaped by passing through the woods to the left and rear, to the sawmill at the White Oak Swamp, and thence to the line above referred to, where they rejoined their comrades of the First Brigade. Following down the Nine Mile road, after Dodge retired from his first position, about 500 yards from the intersection of the Seven Pines, I found Col. J. Adams commanding the First Long Island, which was placed across the road, a portion of the right flank being in rear of it, with the left flank extending to the front and left. Advising Col. Adams of the rapid approach of the enemy—of the direction he was coming, and of the position of the Fifty-sixth and One Hundred and Fourth Pennsylvania on his left, he withdrew the left flank of the Long Island to the rear of the Nine Mile road, making a continuous line with the above, and the men were ordered to the down, that they should escape the murderous fire that was incessantly pouring in from the front. Scarcely was this done before the Eighty-seventh New-York, Col. Stephen E. Dodge, of Kearney's Division, Heintzelman's Corps, came along the Nine Mile road, with rapid step, cheering most vociferously, passed the Fifty-sixth New-York, One Hundred and Fourth Pennsylvania, and First Long Island about fifty yards, received a volley, broke, and passed the whole of them, running over the backs of those lying down, the latter remaining undisturbed until ordered to rise and meet the accumulated force that was bearing all before it. Volley after volley was given and received. An order was given to charge, but one hundred yards brought us into such close proximity with the enemy, "that a sheet of fire was blazing in our faces." The ranks on both sides were rapidly thinning; but still the great disparity in our numbers continued. So close were the contending forces, that our men in many instances, whilst at a charge, poured their fire into the breasts of the enemy, within a few feet from the points of their bayonets. This dreadful contest lasted until nearly dark. My Fifty-sixth and One Hundred and Fourth suffered dreadfully, lost the greater part of their officers and men, and were compelled to give way, carrying their wounded with them.

It was then, in the language of Lieut. Haney, of the One Hundred and Fourth, "that I (Lieut. Haney) and Lieut. Ashenfelder and others led Capt. Corcoran, Capt. Swatzlander, and Lieut. Hendric off the field. It was about half an hour before dark. We went down the Nine Mile road, and along the Williamsburg road. The fighting was nearly over. Our troops were all retiring. We saw the enemy, not over seventy-five yards in our rear, and no troops between us and them. All of our forces were moving back, little regard being paid to brigade, regimental, or even company organization. Kearney's troops came, but did not stay long. Capt. Corcoran becoming continually weaker, we were compelled to carry him."

Fully confirming the statements of my officers, I assert that I saw no running, and there was no panic, but all moved off together, with a single purpose, and that one, to make a stand upon the line of defenses, one mile in the rear, the only one of sufficient capacity to enable us to defend ourselves against vastly superior numbers, until our reinforcements could be brought together.

Company I, Capt. Morrill, and Company E, Lieut. Sabine, of the Eleventh Maine, were on picket duty along the Garnett field, in front of which several rebel regiments marched about dark. Some of the men crawled into the wheat, and shot three of the field officers as they marched by. When Sedgwick crossed the Chickahominy, they immediately communicated with him, remained all night upon the picket line, with the enemy in their front and rear, and on Sunday, at 9 a.m., came in, bringing more prisoners than the entire number of men in their ranks.

Second Lieut. Rice, of the Eleventh Maine, was very sick in the hospital, where there was a number of the same regiment. After the fight grew warm, he exclaimed; "Boys, every one of you that can hold up his head, follow me." More than twenty followed him. He shouldered a musket, and all joined their regiment, and fought most gallantly. Rice, after seventeen rounds, delivered with deadly effect, for he was an excellent shot, was severely wounded in the thigh, and was carried from the field.

Company E, One Hundred and Fourth Pennsylvania, Capt. Harvey, Lieut. Croll, and fifty-eight men, were extended on picket duty from the railroad to the corner, at the intersection of the Nine Mile road with the road to Garnett's house; when, about 3 p.m., the enemy approached, but left them unmolested after firing some scattering shots, during which time we took thirteen prisoners. After 5 p.m., the enemy again appeared in force along this entire line. With the assistance of their supports, he was held in check for nearly an hour, when, finding themselves surrounded, they were taken prisoners. Capt. Harvey was placed in charge of an officer with five men, and was marching off, when a shell struck and killed the officer. The Captain, taking advantage of the confusion, made his escape, four of the men following his example.

On Saturday, Lieut.-Col. Hoyt, of the Fifty-second Pennsylvania, was in charge of the Pioneers of the First Brigade, and two companies of the same regiment, building a bridge which I had directed to be built across the Chickahominy. Remaining upon the ground, and informing himself of the proceedings upon the extreme right, he rendered most valuable service by advising Gen. Sumner, as soon as he crossed the swamp, of the precise position of our forces, and those of the enemy. After which, the enemy having pressed down between the railroad and Gen. Sumner, Lieut.-Col. Hoyt, with the above, and some of the One Hundredth New-York, that were driven in from the picket lines, near the Chickahominy, remained with Gen. Sumner until Sunday, and behaved well. After leaving the battlefield, at dark, the brigade, numbering over 1,000, was marched to the right rifle-pits of the rear defenses, but vacated them at the request of Gen. Kearney, and occupied those on the left, with the other brigades of Casey's Division, where we remained under arms, in the rain, all night.

I have shown, in the history of the battle of the Seven Pines, the conduct of every one of the regiments of the First Brigade, from the time the first volley was fired, at noon, until the enemy, having driven our troops from the around, near dark, cut off the retreat of the Fifty-second, by the Williamsburg road, and was still annoyed by its deadly fire.

The list of casualties shows that there were taken into the action 64 officers and 1,669 men; and that 35 officers and 603 men were killed, wounded and taken prisoners, being 42 per cent of the former and 37 per cent of the latter. Of the 93 of the Eleventh Maine that were led into the fight by Col. Plaisted, 52 were killed and wounded.

The brigade was among the last enlisted. It had been reduced more than one-half by sickness. That it fought well none can deny, for it lost 638 of its number; bodies were found over every part of the field, and where these bodies lay were found double the number of the enemy.

The enemy, more generous than our friends, admit "that we fought most desperately, and against three entire divisions of his army, with two in reserve that, later in the day, were brought in." For three and a half hours we contested every inch of ground with the enemy, and did not yield in that time the half of a mile. We fought from 12 p.m. until 3 1/2 p.m., with but little assistance, and until dark, with our comrades of other regiments and of other divisions, wherever we could be of service, and when, at dark, the enemy swept all before him, we were the last to leave the ground.

I am most happy to refer to the kind treatment extended by the enemy to many of the wounded of the brigade that were taken prisoners.

Since the battle of Seven Pines, now nearly three weeks, a force ten times that of Casey and Couch has not been able to regain the line of outposts established by the First Brigade on the 26th of May; our present line being half a mile in rear thereof.

None of the brigade, regimental or company baggage was lost. Some of the shelter tents, knapsacks, and blankets, fell into the hands of the enemy, which was the natural consequence of being encamped in close proximity with the outposts.

Conduct such as this, if it be not worthy of commendation, should not call forth censure, for censure undeserved chills the ardor and daring of the soldier, and dishonors both the living and the dead.

Very respectfully, &c.,

Naglee, Brigadier-General.

To Lieut. Foster, A.A.A. General, Casey's Division, Army of the Potomac.

Source: "The Battle of Seven Pines," *New York Times*, August 11, 1862, p. 4.

THE SEVEN DAYS BATTLES

JUNE 25-JULY 1, 1862
LT. AUGUSTUS A. DEAN, CSA

When CSA Gen. Joseph E. Johnston was seriously wounded at Fair Oaks, or Seven Pines, Confederate leaders needed to select a new commander. President Jefferson Davis chose Robert E. Lee, who promptly set about dealing with the threat McClellan's men posed on the Virginia Peninsula. The Seven Days Battles, fought from June 25 to July 1, 1862, saw the aggressive and relentless Lee push Union forces back down the Peninsula toward the campaign's starting point, where they were scant threat to Richmond. The series of Confederate attacks, from Beaver Dam Creek / Mechanicsville to Malvern Hill, saw McClellan's men pushed back step-by-step. Losses on both sides were heavy. The Army of the Potomac remained intact as a fighting force, but no one could deny the fact that, during the Seven Days, Lee relieved pressure on the Confederate capital and got the best of his Northern counterpart.

Augustus "Gus" Dean joined Company G, 2nd South Carolina Rifles, in January 1862. By late June, he and his unit were in Virginia, part of Lee's counterattack, determinedly driving the bluecoats away from Richmond and back down the Peninsula. Dean was in the thick of the fighting and noticed—among other things—how superior Yankee blankets, knapsacks, and canteens were to those supplied by Southern quartermasters. Dean recalls his experiences in what amounted to Lee's introductory campaign as commander of Confederate forces.

I was mustered into the service of the Confederate States on January 11, 1862, at Anderson, S. C. Court House by Major Boggs. I was a member of Company G, Second South Carolina Rifle Regiment. The company was required to take an oath to serve the Confederate States honestly and faithfully against all enemies or opposers whatsoever; I thought so often of the oath afterwards, and how many of the men lacked so much of doing what they were supposed to do.

The company left home a few days after being mustered into service. We went on to Sullivan's Island and remained there a few days. We then went to Johns Island and to Wadmalaw Island. We then went back on the mainland and remained on the coast till the 26th of May. While on the coast we did not do any fighting but had to drill and stand guard a great deal and sometimes go on picket. I recollect one night Berry Harbin and I were on picket on the bank of a river. We had to go through a swamp to get to the place. There was another river just to the left so we were in the fork of the two rivers. The swamp was all around us, and no way to get out of there but along a path, and the Yankees were camped not far from us on the other side of the river. We were put there directly after dark and had to stay there till midnight. One of us had to be awake all the time. Berry Harbin was so uneasy that he was miserable for fear the Yankees would cross the river and come around behind us and capture us. A porpoise or large fish of some kind came along and made a noise like someone had hit the water with a plank. It scared Berry almost to death but I was asleep some of the time. Yet Berry was a good soldier; I recollect so well how he acted in the second battle of Manassas. While on the coast we moved camp often. Each company had a wagon to haul our tents and cooking utensils, besides a number of other wagons. But after going to Virginia it was very different for we had no tents a great deal of the time and we had to carry our cooking utensils with us ourselves or do without.

We left the coast May 26, 1862, and reached Richmond May 30, about sundown. We stayed that night at the edge of the city and Oh My! How it rained that night. It came down in torrents, and as the men had no tents they had to stand and take it. James Jones and I got under an ambulance and though we did not keep dry, it was better than being out in the rain. The next day, May 31, we were marched two or three miles in the direction of Seven Pines but did not have to go into the battle. We were near enough to hear the firing though, and I was about as close as I wished to be. There was some fighting done Sunday morning, the first of June. We were fresh troops and had not had any hard service so we were kept either on picket or near the picket line nearly all of the time till the Seven Days battles started June 25. It rained a great deal during June. Where the land was level, the water stood on the ground all the time in many places and made it very disagreeable for us. Our company stayed at some old houses a good deal. One of them had fallen down but the boards were still on it. Some the others and I would crawl under it when it rained to keep out the rain, though we generally got wet. There were seven or eight dead horses within seventy or a hundred yards of where we stayed that were killed in the battle of Seven Pines. We had to endure the stench while we were there. We used water out of a well that was right by the road and which had no cover over it. It was so full we could dip the water with a cup. When it rained muddy water from the road ran into the well.

A number of horses were killed in the battle of Seven Pines that smelled bad near us but there were fields between our camp and the picket line where clover was growing. The road got so bad that the men marched through the fields. Wagons, ambulances, and artillery also went through the fields. A great deal of the clover was mashed into the ground and rotted. It smelt worse to me than the dead horses; it was one of the most sickening smells that I ever smelt. Though it was less than a month from the time our regiment went to Richmond till the Seven Days fight commenced, two-thirds of our company was sick by that time and a number had died.

The Seven Days battle commenced on Wednesday, June 26, 1862. There was not much fighting done that day, more fighting done the next day. A brigade that we belonged to until a few days before the fighting began was in the fight on Thursday and was pretty bad cut up. A good many of the men were killed and wounded. The three principal battles were Gaines Mill, on Friday, June 27th, Frasier's Farm on the 30th, and Malvern Hill on July 1. On Thursday evening about dark we crossed the Chickahominy River and camped not far from where we crossed. The next morning, Friday the 27th, we started early and went down on the east side of the river. We passed through a number of camps where the Yankees had been but had left, though a few tents were about all they had left. About ten or eleven o'clock we were halted and stacked arms in a field. We were ordered to leave our guns though it was very warm. There was a piece of weeds not more than fifty yards in front of us where the trees were large and no undergrowth. The shade certainly looked tempting but we were not allowed to go near it, though there were no Yankees about. After remaining there for an hour and a half or two hours we were ordered to fall in and take arms, march out into the road, and turn down toward the Mill. After going a short distance Col. Moore gave the command "Halt, Front, Load, Load at will." What a feeling that produced in me. I knew it meant going into battle, or expecting to, and I might be a corpse before night. We marched on down to the mill and turned down the branch a short distance, then went up the hill in the direction of the enemy. We were ordered to lie down. The firing commenced in front of us. It was about the heaviest infantry firing that I ever heard in my life. There were a great many cannons firing too and the minie balls passed over our heads by the hundreds. It seemed to me that a great many of them just passed over the hill and then turned right toward my head. I was almost sticking my nose in the ground I was so afraid that one of them would hit me. We lay there for some time while the battle was raging in front of us. While there an officer rode up in front of our regiment and ordered us forward. A good many of the men jumped right up, but Col. Moore ordered us to lie down and the officer ordered us forward again. Many of us got up the second time. Col. Moore ordered us to lie down and said he was the officer to get orders from. After that we paid but little attention to that fellow. He may have been sent back to bring up reinforcements, but I think he was drinking and was trying to lead us into the battle and distinguish himself. He should have been with his own command. Soon afterwards, Col. Moore ordered us forward. I thought as soon as we got to the top of the hill, fifty or seventy-five yards distant, that we would see the whole face of the earth covered with dead men, the firing had been so tremendous. We could not see a single one till we had gone nearly half a mile; the fighting was so much further than I had thought. It was while we were moving forward that the shells from the enemy's guns were flying and bursting around us, which made it extremely unpleasant for us. One shell passed very near us, and J. L. Humphreys jumped behind a bunch of sprouts not much more than knee high and not larger than my finger. This reminded me of the old saying that a drowning man will catch at a straw and a man in battle will jump behind one when a shell comes near him.

Source: Augustus A. Dean, *Recollections of Army Life During the Civil War 1861–1865*, https://psscamp1428.blogspot.com/2013/05/part 1 recolations-of-army-life-during .html.

GAINES'S MILL

JUNE 27, 1862
THEO V. BROWN, HOSPITAL STEWARD, USA

By the time of the Peninsular Campaign, hospital steward Theo V. Brown had four years of military experience. He had served out west in the Mormon and Indian campaigns, and now found himself amidst McClellan's Army of the Potomac, aiming for Richmond. Military medicine at this time was a difficult specialty. Doctors were under great pressure to save those soldiers who could be healed and sent back into the ranks, for manpower was a crucial strategic factor on both sides. Yet combat medicine was in its infancy: surgical methods were direct and horribly painful; concepts of hygiene were hazy at best; patients suffered without benefit of later advances in antiseptic cleanliness or antibiotics. Some wounds were death sentences; infection and illness often finished those who survived the fighting. North or South, a Civil War field hospital was a frightful place of screams, struggle, and severed limbs.

Here, Brown lays out his memories of caring for the fallen at Gaines's Mill, the battle that convinced McClellan to abandon his Peninsula approach. This was a tactical loss for the Union, which saw Brig. Gen. Fitz John Porter's soldiers yield to the largest Confederate attack of the war. Fifty-seven thousand men under Lee pressured Porter's troops, who nevertheless maintained order and withdrew across the Chickahominy River. The battle is sometimes called "First Cold Harbor," since it took place near the same spot as the 1864 Cold Harbor battle.

I received my warrant as a Hospital Steward, United States Army, shortly after we took the field in March 1862, and was assigned to duty with the 3rd Inf.

Thus I had been a soldier and combatant-non-combatant four years; had helped to put down the Mormon rebellion; had been on scouts after Indians, and had participated in the siege of Yorktown and McClellan's siege of Richmond, but had not as yet heard the song of unfriendly bullet or shriek of bellicose shell, when, one fine morning—how green the woods and fields, how clear the sky, how sweet the warbling of the birds, how grateful the mingled odor of meadow and forest that memorable day!—we were ordered to pack up our tents, take our beds upon our backs and march. Some of us, blessed with a keener instinct than the rest, did sniff the breeze and smell the battle from afar.

GRAND STRATEGY

Then we marched several hundred yards in the direction of Richmond, only seven miles distant. With a caution that beat all, we marched through some cornfields (we being the First Brigade, Second Division, Fifth Corps, Army of the Potomac); but as we did not detect any Johnnies in that direction, soon concluded to look for them in the opposite direction. Several of us had a little knowledge of geography, and as Richmond lay between ourselves and the Pacific Ocean, and only a few miles away, we could not quite comprehend why we should be marched straight for the Atlantic Ocean. However, as our superiors were supposed to know more about marches and countermarches than we, we trusted them blindly to lead us Richmond, even should we have to cross the Atlantic to get there. What a funny world this would be were the bright beacon, Faith, eliminated from its mysteries.

After this wandering around in an aimless yet expectant manner for three or four hours, we ascended, about noon, a little knoll upon which stood a substantial dwelling, which somehow reminded us that it was dinner time and that our stomachs were empty, though dire presentiments of a dinnerless day possessed our souls, and in this, at least, were not disappointed.

A battery was in position on this knoll, which seemed to fire minute shots in the direction of Richmond, since there was neither sight nor sound of an enemy; yet there were mysterious hints that a great battle was in progress. Presently, like a peal of thunder from a clear sky, a piece of iron, with its peculiar and highly disagreeable falsetto notes, came sailing over us—we did not even catch the report of the gun from which it was fired.

What made me look about so frantically for a hole in the ground? Surely, if I, enjoying all the rights and privileges of a non-combatant, must run the risk of coming in personal contact with such a barbarous vehicle of savage warfare, I might as well resume my original character as an armed warrior, with its alluring vista of promotions and brevets, which to the hapless combatant-non-combatant must ever prove a mere *ignis fatuus*.

However, five minutes, ten, passed without the advent of more such meteorites, and my nervous system resumed the even tenor of its way.

"So this a great battle!" I chuckled to myself. "Well, if so, I am ready to fight one every day as a pre-prandial appetizer."

Alas! Just then a shell burst in the air over us, followed soon by another, then another. Now a party of four comes toward us, bearing on a litter a man whose thigh has been penetrated by a fragment of shell.

"What will my stomach do, that has always proven so refractory in the presence of human blood?" I ask myself in fear and despair. Thank the stars! My stomach is too engrossed with its own safety to sympathize officiously with the blood of a fellow-man, and I am able to assist at the application of a temporary dressing. Hardly is this done when I hear the command. "Fall in," given in a sharp, decisive tone that presages no good and in a moment the regiment is quickstepping it past the battery, which is now firing briskly, and heading for a narrow valley which, God help me, now shows a long line of rebel infantry advancing to the attack, while the rising ground behind glistens with objects that my fast-beating heart tells me are hostile cannon; and toward these we are still marching.

THE SONG OF THE BULLET

I look at Dr. Sternberg with a glance he well understands, and which says: "Remember that we are non-combatants, and that our duty is to the man we left behind." The Doctor is pale, but resolute, and answers my glance with one that says, "Follow me!" accompanied with an attempt at a smile. So, though still dissenting from my superior as to the propriety of going farther in that direction, I conclude to make a virtue of necessity, keep cool and trust to luck, as every good soldier does.

We are on much higher ground than the advancing line of rebel infantry, and still four or five hundred yards from that line, when I become conscious of something sounding like "z-zip" constantly passing my ear, and it is fully ten minutes before I learn that not insects peculiar to that locality, as it first I thought, but bullets, are when at last my eyes were opened to the true character of the sound, my pulse did not beat one iota more quickly. Not so when occasionally a shell came our way; then force of habit, established by the hustling railroad iron, again and again overcame me, and the momentary frantic search for a hole in the ground was not to be resisted.

When within a couple hundred yards of the enemy, the regiment formed in line of battle, and the other regiments formed in line of battle, and the other regiments of the brigade formed on its left and began firing. Dr. Sternberg and I, with our hospital force, consisting of four hospital attendants, the regimental band, and all the drummers and fifers, took position 100 yards behind the fighting line and planted our red flag, both to direct the wounded and to inform the hostile artillery of our character and mission. One of the hospital attendants carried the field case of surgical instruments, another the hospital knapsack, containing anesthetics, styptics, and bandages, and another led the Doctor's horse; the rest carried litters, pails filled with water, wash basins and canteens.

Dr. Sternberg now unlimbered his pocket-case of instruments, and I did the same, little as I knew of their use. Indeed, little did I know of medicine and less of surgery, though the men, on some of whom I had, in my ignorant and therefore daring dispensation of strong doses, worked rapid cures in slight yet painful ailments such as colic and cholera morbus, had the utmost confidence in my knowledge and skill.

Being the only hospital corps on the spot, a stream of slightly wounded men, guided by our red flag and stretchers, soon came to us from all sides. Imitating my superior closely, I would say:

"My poor fellow, where are you hurt?"

"Right here in my arm."

Finding no wound of exit, I would feel for the bullet, compass the surrounding parts with the thumb and forefinger of my left hand, cut down to the bullet, insert the little finger of my right hand under it, yank it out, put a bandage around the arm, and be ready for the next man, full of the feeling that if one of the everzipping bullets should mark me for its own, a reserved seat in the regions of everlasting bliss was at my disposal; such the satisfaction that springs from a sense of duty well performed. How some of the wounds healed that I made by cutting crosswise instead of lengthwise, I never learned.

GALLANT SYKES

During this time I noticed our Division Commander. Gen. George Sykes, cantering past, followed by one orderly, as cool and unconcerned as though out for a pleasure-ride after dinner. A soldierly man, indeed; *sans puer et sans reproche!*

I also noticed, soon after the fight began, a cloud of stragglers (to use a mild term) all along the line as far as the eye could reach, going to the rear—removing themselves out of the way of bullets without apparent excuse of any kind; and there seemed to be no one whose duty if was to stop them, and none was afterwards punished. This the more extraordinary when it is borne in mind that these men were Regulars; it must not be forgotten, however, that a majority of the officers of the Regular Army cast their lot with the rebellion, and most of the loyal minority were appointed to higher commands in the volunteer force, leaving the Regulars rather poorly officered with new men, appointed, for the most part from civil life. In fact, it may be asserted that the Regulars were volunteers at the beginning of the war, and the volunteers Regulars at its close.

We had been occupied in the manner stated not more than an hour, doing little real good, since all the wounded that came to us could have been better attended to at the field hospitals farther to the rear (I doubt that we were instrumental in saving a single life), when the regimental commander, Maj. N.B. Rossell, who had gone into action mounted on a showy horse, was shot through the left breast, and his Adjutant, Dr. Sternberg and I accompanied the litter which bore him from the field, to the orchard hospital about a half-mile away; none of us, I fear, very sorry for the excuse to leave the fighting line. The farmhouses and orchards were already crowded with severely wounded, dying and dead Zouaves, members of the 5thNY, a splendid body of brave men, and we deposited the Major in the shade of a tree. As we did so, he addressed Dr. Sternberg, in a voice still audible and natural: "Can you do nothing for me, Doctor?" "Nothing, Major," answered the Doctor, sadly. "Then all stand aside and let me speak to the Adjutant," said the dying officer, and whispering a last message to his loved ones in that officer's ear, he promptly breathed his last.

Soon after this our line of battle gave way to the victorious rebels, a panic seized the host of stragglers in the rear, and a wild rush for the bridges over the [Chickahominy] began, in which we were forced to participate, leaving our wounded and dead in the hands of the enemy. This was the battle of Gaines' Mill, fought June 27, 1862.

During the time we were on the battlefield, the artillery of both sides played but an insignificant part, presumably for the reason that the two lines of battle were too close to each other for the artillery to get in its work. The musketry-fire of the two opposing lines sounded to me like the noise made by the combustion of a big heap of firecrackers on a Fourth of July. Occasionally a shell exploded near us, much to our disgust, the hostile batteries apparently finding amusement in annoying us, though they surely knew our occupation.

When, late that night, I wrapped myself in my one blanket under an oak tree, to seek rest and oblivion of the day's sad experiences, I said to myself that we, the hospital party, could have probably done much more good had we stayed farther away from the battlefield, as it seemed to me that a man will either die from loss of blood immediately after being hit in a vital spot, or the missile will have acted as a styptic through contusion of the smaller vessels and the consequent formation of the blood-clot, acting as a plug, which will hold good for a day or two. Our presence on the battlefield was, in my opinion, calculated simply to swell the list of dead and wounded, and of pensioners. I also resolved that any future war I should participate in should not find me in the role of a combatant-non-combatant.

Source: Theo V. Brown, *Gaines's Mill: A Hospital Steward's Sketchy Picture of a Day with Bullets and Bandages*, National Museum of Civil War Medicine, http://civilwarmed.org/explore/bibs/memoirs/steward-memoirs.

BATTLE OF BOONEVILLE

JULY 1, 1862
GEN. PHILIP H. SHERIDAN, USA

The Union's victory at Shiloh put the Confederates on the defensive in the western theater. CSA Gen. Braxton Bragg was anxious to recapture the lost rail junction at Corinth, Mississippi, which had recently served as local rebel headquarters before falling to a Northern advance led by Maj. Gen. Henry W. Halleck, USA. Halleck had expected to besiege Corinth, but the Confederates slipped out toward Tupelo on May 29, 1862. It was there that they plotted their counterattack, aimed at recapturing Corinth and driving Union forces out of northern Mississippi. Fully anticipating such a move, USA Col. Philip H. Sheridan occupied and fortified Booneville, south of the rail junction and astride Bragg's expected path. Sheridan's men withstood the initial onrush, then hit rebel flanks with cavalry units 2nd Michigan and 2nd Iowa. Firing their new Colt repeater rifles to devastating effect, these Northern horsemen repulsed the attack, threatening the Confederate rear. CSA Brig. Gen. James R. Chalmers had no choice but to retreat. Sheridan's pursuit was immediate, and although the Southern men escaped into swampy terrain, his tenacity made it clear that federal forces had another gritty fighter whose aggressive leadership would mark him for prominence and glory when he was promoted and brought east to pacify Virginia's Shenandoah Valley.

Preparations for the Booneville Campaign

In the course of the afternoon I turned over all my property to my successor, and about 8 o'clock that evening made my appearance at the camp of the Second Michigan Cavalry, near Farmington, Mississippi. The regiment was in a hubbub of excitement making preparations for the raid, and I had barely time to meet the officers of my command, and no opportunity at all to see the men, when the trumpet sounded to horse. Dressed in a coat and trousers of a captain of infantry, but recast as a colonel of cavalry by a pair of well-worn eagles that General Granger had kindly given me, I hurriedly placed on my saddle a haversack, containing some coffee, sugar, bacon, and hard bread, which had been prepared, and mounting my horse, I reported my regiment to the brigade commander as ready for duty.

The expedition referred to by General Halleck in his parting conversation was composed of the Second Michigan and Second Iowa regiments of cavalry, formed into a brigade under command of Colonel Washington L. Elliott, of the Second Iowa. It was to start on the night of the 27th of May at 12 o'clock, and proceed by a circuitous route through Iuka, Miss., to Booneville, a station on the Mobile and Ohio Railroad, about twenty-two miles below Corinth, and accomplish all it could in the way of destroying the enemy's supplies and cutting his railroad communications.

The weather in that climate was already warm, guides unobtainable, and both men and horses suffered much discomfort from the heat, and fatigue from the many delays growing out of the fact that we were in almost total ignorance of the roads leading to the point that we desired to reach. In order that we might go light we carried only sugar, coffee, and salt, depending on the country for meat and bread. Both these articles were scarce, but I think we got all there was, for our advent was so unexpected by the people of the region through which we passed that, supposing us to be Confederate cavalry, they often gave us all they had, the women and servants contributing most freely from their reserve stores.

Before reaching Booneville I had the advance, but just as we arrived on the outskirts of the town the brigade was formed with the Second Iowa on my right, and the whole force moved forward, right in front, preceded by skirmishers. Here we encountered the enemy, but forced him back with little resistance. When we had gained possession of the station,

Colonel Elliott directed me to take the left wing of my regiment, pass to the south, and destroy a bridge or culvert supposed to be at a little distance below the town on the Mobile and Ohio Railroad. The right wing, or other half of the regiment, was to be held in reserve for my support if necessary. I moved rapidly in the designated direction till I reached the railroad, and then rode down it for a mile and a half, but found neither bridge nor culvert. I then learned that there was no bridge of any importance except the one at Baldwin, nine miles farther down, but as I was aware, from information recently received, that it was defended by three regiments and a battery, I concluded that I could best accomplish the purpose for which I had been detached—crippling the road—by tearing up the track, bending the rails, and burning the cross-ties. This was begun with alacrity at four different points, officers and men vying with one another in the laborious work of destruction. We had but few tools, and as the difficulties to overcome were serious, our progress was slow, until some genius conceived the idea that the track, rails and ties, might be lifted from its bed bodily, turned over, and subjected to a high heat; a convenient supply of dry fence-rails would furnish ample fuel to render the rails useless. In this way a good deal of the track was effectively broken up, and communication by rail from Corinth to the south entirely cut off. While we were still busy in wrecking the road, a dash was made at my right and rear by a squadron of Confederate cavalry. This was handsomely met by the reserve under Captain Archibald P. Campbell, of the Second Michigan, who, dismounting a portion of his command, received the enemy with such a volley from his Colt's repeating rifles that the squadron broke and fled in all directions. We were not molested further, and resumed our work, intending to extend the break toward Baldwin, but receiving orders from Elliott to return to Booneville immediately, the men were recalled, and we started to rejoin the main command.

In returning to Booneville, I found the railroad track above where I had struck it blocked by trains that we had thus cut off, and the woods and fields around the town covered with several thousand Confederate soldiers. These were mostly convalescents and disheartened stragglers belonging to General Beauregard's army, and from them we learned that Corinth was being evacuated. I spent some little time in an endeavor to get these demoralized men into an open field, with a view to some future disposition of them; but in the midst of the undertaking I received another order from Colonel Elliott to join him at once. The news of the evacuation had also reached Elliott, and had disclosed a phase of the situation so different from that under which he had viewed it when we arrived at Booneville, that he had grown anxious to withdraw, lest we should be suddenly pounced upon by an overwhelming force from some one of the columns in retreat. Under such circumstances my prisoners would prove a decided embarrassment, so I abandoned further attempts to get them together—not even paroling them, which I thought might have been done with but little risk.

In the meantime the captured cars had been fired, and as their complete destruction was assured by explosions from those containing ammunition, they needed no further attention, so I withdrew my men and hastened to join Elliott, taking along some Confederate officers whom I had retained from among four or five hundred prisoners captured when making the original dash below the town. . . .

THE BATTLE OF BOONEVILLE

On the morning of July 1, 1862, a cavalry command of between five and six thousand men, under the Confederate General James R. Chalmers, advanced on two roads converging near Booneville. The head of the enemy's column on the Blackland and Booneville road came in contact with my pickets three miles and a half west of Booneville. These pickets, under Lieutenant Leonidas S. Scranton, of the Second Michigan Cavalry, fell back slowly, taking advantage of every tree or other cover to fire from till they arrived at the point where the converging roads joined. At this junction there was a strong position in the protecting timber, and here Scranton made a firm stand, being reinforced presently by the few men he had out as pickets on the road to his left, a second company I had sent him from camp, and subsequently by three companies more, all now commanded by Captain Campbell. This force was dismounted and formed in line, and soon developed that the enemy was present in large numbers. Up to this time Chalmers had shown only the heads of his columns, and we had doubts as to his purpose, but now that our resistance forced him to deploy two regiments on the right and left of the road, it became apparent that he meant business, and that there was no time to lose in preparing to repel his attack.

Full information of the situation was immediately sent me, and I directed Campbell to hold fast, if possible, till I could support him, but if compelled to retire he was authorized to do so slowly, taking advantage of every means that fell in his way to prolong the fighting. Before this I had stationed one battalion of the Second Iowa in Booneville, but Colonel Edward Hatch, commanding that regiment, was now directed to leave one company for the protection of our camp a little to the north of the station, and take the balance of the Second Iowa, with the battalion in Booneville except two sabre companies, and form the whole in rear of Captain Campbell, to protect his flanks and support him by a charge should the enemy break his dismounted line.

While these preparations were being made, the Confederates attempted to drive Campbell from his position by a direct attack through an open field. In this they failed, however, for our men, reserving their fire until the enemy came within about thirty yards, then opened on him with such a shower of bullets from our Colt's rifles that it soon became too hot for him, and he was repulsed with considerable loss. Foiled in this move, Chalmers hesitated to attack again in front, but began overlapping both flanks of Campbell's line by force of numbers, compelling Campbell to retire toward a strong position I had selected in his rear for a line on which to make our main resistance. As soon as the enemy saw this withdrawing he again charged in front, but was again as gallantly repelled as in the first assault, although the encounter was for a short time so desperate as to have the character of a hand-to-hand conflict, several groups of friend and foe using on each other the butts of their guns. At this juncture the timely arrival of Colonel Hatch with the Second Iowa gave a breathing-spell to Campbell, and made the Confederates so chary of further direct attacks that he was enabled to retire; and at the same time I found opportunity to make disposition of the reinforcement to the best advantage possible, placing the Second Iowa on the left of the new line and strengthening Campbell on its right with all the men available.

In view of his numbers, the enemy soon regained confidence in his ability to overcome us, and in a little while again began his flanking movements, his right passing around my left flank some distance, and approaching our camp and transportation, which I had forbidden to be moved out to the rear. Fearing that he would envelop us and capture the camp and transportation, I determined to take the offensive. Remembering a circuitous wood road that I had become familiar with while making the map heretofore mentioned, I concluded that the most effective plan would be to pass a small column around the enemy's left, by way of this road, and strike his rear by a mounted charge simultaneously with an advance of our main line on his front. I knew that the attack in rear would be a most hazardous undertaking, but in the face of such odds as the enemy had the condition of affairs was most critical, and could be relieved, only by a bold and radical change in our tactics; so I at once selected four sabre companies, two from the Second Michigan and two from the Second Iowa, and placing Captain Alger, of the former regiment, in command of them, I informed him that I expected of them the quick and desperate work that is usually imposed on a forlorn hope.

To carry out the purpose now in view, I instructed Captain Alger to follow the wood road as it led around the left of the enemy's advancing forces, to a point where it joined the Blackland road, about three miles from Booneville, and directed him, upon reaching the Blackland road, to turn up it immediately, and charge the rear of the enemy's line. Under no circumstances was he to deploy the battalion, but charge in column right through whatever he came upon, and report to me in front of Booneville, if at all possible for him to get there. If he failed to break through the enemy's line, he was to go ahead as far as he could, and then if any of his men were left, and he was able to retreat, he was to do so by the same route he had taken on his way out. To conduct him on this perilous service I sent along a thin, sallow, tawny-haired Mississippian named Beene, whom I had employed as a guide and scout a few days before, on account of his intimate knowledge of the roads, from the public thoroughfares down to the insignificant by-paths of the neighboring swamps. With such guidance I felt sure that the column would get to the desired point without delay, for there was no danger of its being lost or misled by taking any of the many by-roads which traversed the dense forests through which it would be obliged to pass. I also informed Alger that I should take the reserve and join the main line in front of Booneville for the purpose of making an advance of my whole force, and that as a signal he must have his men cheer loudly when he struck the enemy's rear, in order that my attack might be simultaneous with his.

I gave him one hour to go around and come back through the enemy, and when he started I moved to the front with the balance of the reserve, to put everything I had into the fight. This meant an inestimable advantage to the enemy in case of our defeat, but our own safety demanded the hazard. All along our attenuated line the fighting was now sharp, and the enemy's firing indicated such numerical strength that fear of disaster to Alger increased my anxiety terribly as the time set for his cheering arrived and no sound of it was heard.

Relying, however, on the fact that Beene's knowledge of the roads would prevent his being led astray, and confident of Alger's determination to accomplish the purpose for which he set out, as soon as the hour was up I ordered my whole line forward. Fortunately, just at this moment a locomotive and two cars loaded with grain for my horses ran into Booneville from Corinth. I say fortunately, because it was well known throughout the command that in the morning, when I first discovered the large numbers of the enemy, I had called for assistance; and my troops, now thinking that reinforcements had arrived by rail from Rienzi, where a division of infantry was encamped, and inspired by this belief, advanced with renewed confidence and wild cheering. Meantime I had the engineer of the locomotive blow his whistle loudly, so that the enemy might also learn that a train had come; and from the fact that in a few moments he began to give way before our small force, I thought that this stratagem had some effect. Soon his men broke, and ran in the utmost disorder over the country in every direction. I found later, however, that his precipitous retreat was due to the pressure on his left from the Second Iowa, in concert with the front attack of the Second Michigan, and the demoralization wrought in his rear by Alger, who had almost entirely accomplished the purpose of his expedition, though he had failed to come through, or so near that I could hear the signal agreed upon before leaving Booneville.

After Alger had reached and turned up the Blackland road, the first thing he came across was the Confederate headquarters; the officers and orderlies about which he captured and sent back some distance to a farm-house. Continuing on a gallop, he soon struck the rear of the enemy's line, but was unable to get through; nor did he get near enough for me to hear his cheering; but as he had made the distance he was to travel in the time allotted, his attack and mine were almost coincident, and the enemy, stampeded by the charges in front and rear, fled toward Blackland, with little or no attempt to capture Alger's command, which might readily have been done. Alger's troopers soon rejoined me at Booneville, minus many hats, having returned by their original route. They had sustained little loss except a few men wounded and a few temporarily missing. Among these was Alger himself, who was dragged from his saddle by the limb of a tree that, in the excitement of the charge, he was unable to flank. The missing had been dismounted in one way or another and run over by the enemy in his flight; but they all turned up later, none the worse except for a few scratches and bruises.

My effective strength in this fight was 827 all told, and Alger's command comprised ninety officers and men. Chalmers's force was composed of six regiments and two battalions, and though I have been unable to find any returns from which to verify his actual numbers yet, from the statements of prisoners and from information obtained from citizens along his line of march, it is safe to say that he had in the action not less than five-thousand men. Our casualties were not many—forty-one in all. His loss in killed and wounded was considerable, his most severely wounded—forty men—falling into our hands, having been left at farmhouses in the vicinity of the battlefield.

The victory in the face of such odds was most gratifying, and as it justified my disinclination—in fact, refusal—to retire from Booneville without fighting (for the purpose of saving my transportation, as directed by superior authority when I applied in the morning for reinforcements), it was to me particularly grateful. It was also very valuable, in view of the fact that it increased the confidence between the officers and men of my brigade and me, and gave us for the balance of the month not only comparative rest, but entire immunity from the dangers of a renewed effort to gobble my isolated outpost. In addition to all this, commendation from my immediate superiors was promptly tendered through oral and written congratulations; and their satisfaction at the result of the battle took definite form a few days later, in the following application for my promotion, when, by an expedition to Ripley, Miss., most valuable information as to the enemy's location and plans was captured:

Headquarters Army of the Mississippi,
July 30, 1862—3:05 p.m.
Major General Halleck,
Washington, D.C.

Brigadiers scarce; good ones scarce. Asboth goes on the month's leave you gave him ten months since; Granger has temporary command. The undersigned respectfully beg that you will obtain the promotion of Sheridan. He is worth his weight in gold. His Ripley expedition has brought us captured letters of immense value, as well as prisoners, showing the rebel plans and dispositions, as you will learn from District Commander.

W. S. Rosecrans, Brigadier–General
C. C. Sullivan,
G. Granger,
W. L. Elliott,
A. Asboth

Source: Philip H. Sheridan, *Personal Memoirs of P. H. Sheridan* (New York: Charles L. Webster & Company, 1888; Project Gutenberg, 2004), vol. 1, chap. 9, http://www.gutenberg .org/ebooks/4362.

SECOND MANASSAS

AUGUST 29-30, 1862
LT. JOHN H. WORSHAM, CSA

It was called Bull Run in the North, Manassas in the South. But no matter what it was called, the place in northern Virginia had massive psychological as well as strategic significance during the Civil War. The first battle fought there disabused Northerners of their expectations for a quick and easy war. At Second Bull Run / Manassas, much larger armies clashed—Union forces led by Maj. Gen. John Pope, Confederate forces by Gen. Robert E. Lee. Pope was in pursuit of CSA Maj. Gen. Stonewall Jackson, who had recently captured Manassas Junction, a major Union supply depot. The wily Jackson retreated to strong positions, where he was reinforced by Confederates led by CSA Maj. Gen. James Longstreet. Pope, dazzled by dreams of trapping Jackson and apparently not cognizant of Longstreet's presence, pressed what he thought was his advantage. But Union attacks ran headlong into massive Confederate artillery bombardment, and 25,000 Confederates under Longstreet smashed into federal flanks. It might have been a total disaster, and only the most determined rearguard defense allowed Union forces to withdraw in relative order to safer positions.

John H. Worsham, 21st Virginia Infantry, Terry's Brigade, fought in this battle. His memoirs used the term "Foot Cavalry," a nod to the capacity of Jackson's men for rapid and long-distance marching that seemed impossible to onlookers, and especially foes. Worsham's 2nd Brigade racked up one of the most illustrious unit records on either side during the entire war. Again and again, battle after battle, Worsham and his cohort usually found themselves in the fiercest combat conceivable. In 1864, at Winchester, he sustained wounds that left him permanently disabled. Worsham's memoirs constitute one of the most valuable firsthand records of service under Stonewall Jackson, and here, he recapitulates the Confederate victory at Second Bull Run / Manassas.

Longstreet having joined Jackson and Gen. Lee having completed his plans, the army broke camp on August 20th and marched in the direction of Pope's army. Jackson crossed the Rapidan river at Summerville Ford. Pope had retreated behind the Rappahannock river, and we made that river our objective point. After trying several fords with the seeming intention of crossing, the morning of the 25th found us near the village of Jeffersonton in Culpeper county. Here we received orders to cook three days' rations, and be ready to move as soon as possible. Soon afterwards, orders were given to fall in; but many of the men had not prepared their rations for want of time, the half baked biscuit and the raw dough were left. This for many was nothing to eat for some time, probably days! The wagon train having remained behind, and everything being in light marching trim, indicated that something of importance was on hand.

As soon as the column was formed, we were hurried off on the march, passing through the village of Amissville, and crossing the Rappahannock at Hinson's mill; thence several miles right through the country, through fields, over ditches and fences, through woods until we came to a public road. This we took, passing the village of Orleans and marching steadily until we passed Salem, about 8 or 9 o'clock at night. Here we halted in the road, stacked arms, and were told we could lie down and rest, having marched about twenty-six miles. Early the next morning we were up and on the march again, passing through Bull Run Mountain at Thoroughfare Gap, thence through Hay Market and Gainesville, not stopping until ten or eleven o'clock at night; marching about the same distance as the day before, and again stopping in the road. Many of the men lay down right where they stopped in the road, being so completely used up from the march and heat as not to have energy to move to one side. We were near Bristow Station, and not far from Manassas Junction, and far in Pope's rear, "the man that had no rear." (?) Gen. Jackson now sent a force ahead to capture Manassas, which was done during the night with small loss to us. Immense quantities of stores were captured with several trains of railroad cars, eight pieces of artillery with caissons and horses, etc., complete, a number of wagons, several hundred prisoners, and several hundred negroes, who had been persuaded to run away from their owners. Early the next morning Ewell's division marched in the direction of Bristow, the remainder of the corps to Manassas Junction, which place our division reached about 7 or 8 o'clock in the morning. The Second Brigade was filed by regiments to the right of the road, in an open field and near the storehouses, where arms were stacked, and we were ordered to rest and remain near our guns.

Not long after this it was rumored that a force from Washington was approaching to drive us away. A. P. Hill's division was sent forward to meet them, and soon put them to rout. They consisted of a brigade of infantry with some artillery, sent down to brush away a small raiding force, as they supposed us to be.

A scene around the storehouses was now witnessed, but cannot be described. Were you, when a boy, on some special occasion allowed to eat as much of everything you wanted? Were you ever a soldier, who had eaten nothing but roasting ears for two days? Well, if you have ever been either, you may probably have some conception of what followed. Only those who participated can ever appreciate it. Remember, that many of those men were hurried off on the march on the morning of the 25th with nothing to eat, that it was now the 27th, add we had marched in this time about sixty miles. The men who had prepared their rations did not have enough for two days, much less for three, and, after dividing with such comrades as had none, everything had long been eaten. Now here are vast storehouses filled with everything to eat, and sutler's stores filled with all the delicacies, potted ham, lobster, tongue, candy, cakes, nuts, oranges, lemons, pickles, catsup, mustard, etc. It makes an old soldier's mouth water now, to think of the good things captured there. A guard was placed over everything in the early part of the day, rations were issued to the men, but not by weight and measure to each man. A package or two of each article was given to each company. These are some of the articles issued to F Company. The first thing brought us was a barrel of cakes, next, a bag of hams. We secured a camp kettle, made a fire, and put a ham on to boil; and we had hardly gotten it underway before a barrel of sugar and coffee, the Yanks had it mixed, and a bag of beans were sent us. After a consultation, we decided to empty the ham out of the kettle, as we could take that along raw, and in its place put the beans on the fire, as they were something we were fond of and had not had for a long time. About the time they commenced to get warm, a bag of potatoes was brought us; over the kettle goes, and the potatoes take the place of the beans. We now think our kettle is all right, as potatoes cook in a short time, but here comes a package of desiccated vegetables, and the kettle is again emptied, and the vegetables are placed on the fire, as soup is so good. We were also given a barrel of syrup. This was a liberal and varied bill of fare for our company, which was small then.

Gen. Jackson's idea was that he could care for the stores until Gen. Lee came up, and turn the remainder over to him, hence he placed the guard over them. The enemy began to make such demonstrations that he decided he could not hold the place, therefore the houses were thrown open, and every man was told to help himself. Our kettle of soup was left to take care of itself. Men who were starving a few hours before, and did not know when they would get another mouthful, were told to help themselves. Well, what do you think they did? Begin to eat. Oh, no. They discussed what they should eat, and what they should take with them, as orders were issued for us to take four days' rations with us. It was hard to decide what to take, some filled their haversacks with cakes, some with candy, others oranges, lemons, canned goods, etc. I know one who took nothing but French mustard, filled his haversack and was so greedy that he put one more bottle in his pocket. This was his four days' rations, and it turned out to be the best thing taken, because he traded it for meat and bread, and it lasted him until we reached Frederick City. All good times have an end, and, as night approached, preparations were made to burn everything that we could not carry; and not long after sunset the stores were set on fire. Our division, taking up our march as soon as the fires got well under way, marched several hours, when our brigade was ordered to a road on our left for picket duty. At daybreak we found ourselves on the Warrenton and Alexander pike near Groveton.

There was only one field officer in our brigade at this time, and Gen. Jackson had assigned Col. Bradley T. Johnson temporarily to command it. The Irish battalion was commanded by a major, the 48th Va. Regt. by a lieutenant, the 42d by a captain, and the 21st by a captain. The Second Brigade remained about Groveton until late in the evening. Col. Johnson had orders to make demonstrations and the biggest show he could, so as to delay the enemy as long as possible from any advance in this direction; and well did he do it. At one time he had one regiment on top of a hill, with its colors under the next hill, just high enough to show over its top; a regiment with its colors on the next hill, etc., thus making the appearance of a long line of battle. We had two pieces of artillery, and as one body of the enemy was seen, one or both pieces of artillery were brought into view, and when the enemy moved, the cannons were limbered up and moved also to some far hill, and the movement was repeated.

Early in the morning, while the 21st Va. Regt. was on one of these hills lying down in line, the enemy ran a cannon out on a hill, unlimbered, and fired a shot at us, hitting one of the men of Company K, tearing the heel of his shoe off, but not injuring him. This was the first cannon shot from either side at Second Manassas, and the only one fired at that time, as the piece limbered up and withdrew in a trot. When the 21st regiment soon afterwards was deployed as skirmishers, and stationed across the Warrenton pike, a Yankee artilleryman rode into our line, thinking it was his. He was the first prisoner taken.

The inmates of the Groveton house now abandoned it,—a lady, bareheaded, and her servant woman, running out of the front door, having a little girl between them, each holding her by one of her hands, the child crying loudly. They crossed the pike, climbed over the fence, and went directly south through the fields, and were soon lost to sight. In their excitement they did not even close the door to their deserted home.

The Yankee wagon train was seen on a road south of us, on its way to Washington; the two pieces of artillery were run out and commenced to fire at them, causing a big stampede. It was now about eleven or twelve o'clock, and we retired to a wood north of the pike, formed the brigade into line of battle, stacked arms, and lay down in position.

None of the men had seen or heard anything of the remainder of our corps, and we had no idea as to where they were, and it was singular that "Old Jack" had not made his accustomed appearance along the front, the artillery fire not even bringing him. The men were much puzzled and mystified by this. Col. Johnson sent to the 21st Va. Regt. for a lieutenant and six men to report with arms. etc., at once to him; one of the men from F Company, the writer, was designated by name. On reporting, they were ordered to drive a squad of Yankees away from a house in sight. This they did in quick order, although they had to cross an open field and get over three fences before reaching the house. We remained at the house a while, and seeing that we were about to be cut off, we retired to the brigade without loss. This was the first musket fire of Second Manassas, and it may be said that the battle had commenced, the enemy being seen in several directions towards our front. The officer returning to Col. Johnson made his report, when the colonel retained the "F" man, the writer, and ordered him to go out to the front as far as possible without being seen by the enemy, and keep a lookout, reporting to him any body of the enemy seen approaching, and, in order to get along the better, to leave his arms. I crept to the front until I reached a bush on top of a slight elevation, where I lay down for several hours, observing the movements of several small bodies of the enemy, mostly cavalry. While I was lying down behind the bush, an incident occurred that has always puzzled me. I heard the quick step of a horse to my right and rear, and looking around I saw a horseman in full gallop, coming from the north and going along a small country road that joined the Warrenton pike at Groveton house. Arriving at the gap in the fence along the road, he wheeled his horse and rode directly towards me as I lay down in the field; and it was done in such a deliberate way as to impress the vidette that his presence was known before the horseman came along the road. He did not draw rein until he was almost on the vidette, when he asked if the vidette knew where Gen. Jackson was. Receiving a negative reply, he wheeled his horse and rode back to the gap, turned into the road, and was off at full gallop towards Groveton house. This man was riding a black mare, and wore a long linen duster and dark pants; there was something so suspicious about his movements and dress, that the vidette would have taken him to Col. Johnson if he had

had his gun. There was a squad of Yankees at the Groveton house, and when the rider reached it, several of them ran from the front of the house and surrounded him. He dismounted and went with them to the front of the house while one of their number led the horse into the back yard and tied him. This was hardly done before a body of our cavalry charged up the Warrenton pike, and captured the party. The vidette had seen that detachment coming along the road a few minutes before, and could have warned the man riding the horse of the Yankees' presence, but a distrust came over him as soon as I saw him.

About 4 o'clock in the afternoon the vidette was startled by a long line of skirmishers stepping out of the wood in his front and advancing. Jumping to my feet, I started towards Col. Johnson and having gone only a short distance, I saw their line of battle following. Now that fellow just "dusted" made his report to Col. Johnson, who called the line to attention, and gave the command, "Right face! double quick! march!" and away we went northward through the woods. All of us were wondering what had become of Jackson, but when we were through the woods, the first man we saw was "Old Jack," and looking beyond, we could see that his command was massed in a large field, arms stacked, batteries parked, and everything resting. Col. Johnson rode up to him and made his report. Gen. Jackson turned at once to his staff, gave each an order, and, in a minute, the field was in a perfect hubbub,—men riding in all directions, infantry rushing to arms, cannoneers to their guns and the drivers mounting. We saw the master hand now. In the time I am taking to tell this, one heard the sharp command of an officer, "Right face, forward march," and saw a body of skirmishers march out of that confused mass right up to "Old Jack," where the officer gave the command, "File right," and the next instant the command to deploy. The movement was done in the twinkling of an eye. Forward they went to meet the enemy. Gen. Jackson had waited to see this; he now turned to Col. Johnson and told him to let his men stack arms and rest, as they had been on duty since the day before; he would not call on them if he could avoid it; and off he went with the advance skirmishers. Another body of them had, in the meantime, marched out and filed to the left, and gone forward. A column of infantry unwound itself out of that mass, marched up to the point where the skirmishers had been filed to the right, fronted, and went forward. Another was now filing to the left, while the third column moved straight ahead, a part of the artillery following each column of infantry. This was the most perfect movement of troops I saw during the war. The crack of muskets and the bang of artillery told us that the lines had met, and the fire in a few minutes was terrific. An officer soon came, however, ordering the Second Brigade to report on the extreme left of Jackson's line, where the whole brigade was formed as skirmishers, ordered forward and, after going a certain distance, halted, and ordered to lie down. We stayed there all night, sleeping on our arms. The enemy did not appear in our front; but our right had a hard fight, in which the enemy were defeated, retreating during the night. Brig. Gen. Taliaferro, commanding Jackson's division, and Maj. Gen. Ewell were amongst our wounded.

The next morning, August 29th, the Second Brigade marched to the right of Jackson's line, on top of a large hill, where there were several pieces of artillery. We stayed there about an hour, and were shelled severely by the enemy, who had made their appearance from another direction than that of the evening before.

Jackson now took position behind an unfinished railroad, which ran parallel to and north of the Warrenton pike, and, I suppose, about a mile from it. Jackson's division was on the right, Ewell's next, and A. P. Hill's on the left. The Second Brigade marched from the hill to the left about half a mile, where we joined our division and formed two lines of battle, in a wood and near its edge, facing south. In our front there was a narrow neck of open land, about three hundred yards wide; on the west, the wood ran along this field about three hundred yards to a point where the field joined a larger field. A short distance around the angle of the wood was the hill which we occupied early in the morning, and Jackson had now several batteries of artillery on it. On the east, the woods ran along the field for six hundred yards to a point where the field joined a large field; this large field ran east and west and at its far side the Warrenton pike ran. About two hundred yards in our front was a part of the abandoned railroad, running across the open neck from the wood on the east to near that of the west. The eastern end of the road was in a valley, where there was a fill for about one hundred yards, extending to a hill through which a cut ran out on the level ground just before it reached the west wood. The reader will notice now that in front of the railroad there was a short strip of wood on the west side and a long strip on the east. Our skirmishers were stationed at the railroad; we were ordered to lie down in line, guns in hand, and directed to rush for the railroad as soon as an order to forward should be given. Col. Johnson came along the line, stopped about ten yards in front of F Company, took out his pipe, filled it and lighted it, and quietly sat on the ground, leaning against a small sapling.

Everything was perfectly quiet, but this did not last long. The stillness in our front was broken by a shot, and almost in the same instant a shell went crashing through the trees overhead. This was the signal for a severe shelling of our woods; a man was wounded. Col. Johnson immediately arose, went to him, sent him to the rear, and stopped long enough to talk to the men around him, and quiet their uneasiness. He came back and resumed his seat. This was repeated several times. The enemy now advanced and engaged our skirmishers at the railroad, some of the balls aimed at them occasionally reached our line, and wounded some of the men. Col. Johnson invited several of the men who were becoming uneasy to come and sit by him, and he had about a dozen around him, talking and laughing. Our skirmishers were now being driven from the railroad, and soon they retired to the line of battle. The enemy were now some distance north of the railroad in our front. The brigade being called to attention, instantly was on its feet, and when the order was given to forward, it rushed to the front. Reaching the field, we emptied our guns into the enemy, and charged them with empty guns. They turned and ran, leaving many dead and wounded on our side of the railroad. Approaching these men, lying on the ground about one hundred yards from us, I noticed one of them on his back, gesticulating with his hands, raising them up, moving them violently backward and forward. I thought he was trying to attract our attention, so that we might not injure him in our advance. When I reached him, I recognized by his shoulder straps that he was a Yankee captain, and one of our captains, who was running on my left, said he was making the masonic sign of distress. Arriving at the railroad, the 21st Va. Regt. occupied the bank, and the remainder of the Second

Brigade occupied the cut on our right. We loaded and fired at the retreating enemy, and soon cleared the field.

Expecting a renewal of the attack by the enemy, we remained at the railroad, and, after a short halt, the announcement "Here they come!" was heard. A line of battle marched out of the far end of the east wood into the field, halted, dressed the line, and moved forward. They were allowed to come within about one hundred yards of us, when we opened fire. We could see them stagger, halt, stand a short time, break, and run. At this time, another line made its appearance, coming from the same point. It came a little nearer. They, too, broke and ran. Still another line came nearer, broke and ran. The whole field seemed to be full of Yankees and some of them advanced nearly to the railroad. We went over the bank at them, the remainder of the brigade following our example. The enemy now broke and ran, and we pursued, firing as fast as we could. We followed them into the woods, and drove them out on the other side, where we halted and were ordered back to the railroad. We captured two pieces of artillery in the woods, and carried them back with us. As we returned a Yankee battery of eight guns had full play on us in the field, and our line became a little confused; we halted, every man instantly turned and faced the battery. As we did so, I heard a thud on my right, as if one had been struck with a heavy fist. Looking around I saw a man at my side standing erect, with his head off, a stream of blood spurting a foot or more from his neck. As I turned farther around, I saw three others lying on the ground, all killed by this cannon shot. The man standing was a captain in the 42d Va. Regt., and his brains and blood bespattered the face and clothing of one of my company, who was standing in my rear. This was the second time I saw four men killed by one shot. The other occurred in the battle of Cedar Run, a few weeks earlier. Each time the shot struck as it was descending,—the first man had his head taken off, the next was shot through the breast, the next through the stomach, and the fourth had all his bowels torn out.

We went back to our position in the woods, formed our old line of battle in two lines, and lay down as before. Immediately our attention was called to a line of battle filing into position in our front, but nearly at right angles to us. What did this mean? Were the enemy making preparations to storm us again? General Starke, our division commander, arrived, his attention was called to the line, he used his glass, and, after a careful survey, called a courier, and directed him to go to the right around the hill in our front, and find out who they were. The Yankees were shelling our woods heavily, but the excitement was so great that the men, who had orders to lie down for protection, were all standing up watching the line form, which grew longer each moment. Our courier, after a short stay, was seen coming as fast as his horse could run, and before he reached General Starke, cried out, "It is Longstreet!" A great cry that Longstreet had come was taken up by the men all down the line. The courier now told General Starke that the man sitting on a stump, whom we had noticed before, was General Lee; and that Longstreet said he had gotten up in time to witness our charge, which, he said, was splendid!

This put new life into Jackson's men, who had heard nothing of Longstreet. They knew that if Pope with his large army would put forth energy, he could greatly damage us; but every thought was changed now. We only wished for a renewal of the attack, but were afraid he would not attack us after his repulse on the morning and the presence of Longstreet! He did attack A. P. Hill's division on the left, and met with the same kind of repulse that we had given him. A part of Longstreet's command became heavily engaged also. This ended the second day's fighting, and the Second Brigade was jubilant over its share of Second Manassas so far.

The cannonading commenced early on the morning of the 30th with skirmishing in front that at times became active. About noon, expecting an attack, the Second Brigade moved to the railroad, taking position as on the day before. About 2 or 3 o'clock we heard on our right, the sound of "Here they come!" and almost instantly we saw a column of the enemy march into the field from the point at which they appeared the day before, dressing the line and advancing on us. Every man in our line shifted his cartridge box to the front, unstrapped it and his cap box, gave his gun a second look, and took his position to meet the coming enemy, who were rapidly approaching. We allowed them to come about the same distance as on the day before, and then opened fire, with about the same result. Other lines advanced, each getting nearer us; the field was filled with Yanks as on the day before, but in much greater numbers, and their advance continued. Every man in the Second Brigade at this moment remembered Cedar Run, each one loaded his gun with care, raised it deliberately to his shoulder, took deadly aim, and pulled the trigger! We were fighting now as I never saw it done, we behind the railroad bank and in the cut, which made a splendid breastwork, the enemy crowded in the field, their men falling fast, as we could plainly see. Our ammunition was failing, our men taking it from the boxes of dead and wounded comrades. The advance of the enemy continued; by this time they were at the bank, they mounting it, our men mounting too, some with guns loaded, some with bayonets fixed, some with muskets clubbed, and some with large rocks in their hands. (Col. Johnson in his official report says he saw a man's skull crushed by a rock in the hands of one of his brigade.) A short struggle on top of the bank, and in front of the cut, and the battle was ours! The enemy were running! and then went up that yell that only Confederates could make! Some men were wild with excitement, hats were off, some up in the air! It was right here that Lieut. Rawlings, commanding F Company, was killed!—his hat in one hand, his sword in the other, cheering his men to victory! He was struck in the head by a rifle ball, and fell dead.

After the flying enemy we went, through the field in our front, to the woods on the left, through that into the next field, where we could see our line advancing in all directions, our artillery firing over our heads! Some of the artillery following in the pursuit, and nearing a hill, ran up, unlimbered, and fired rapidly through openings in our advancing line, thousands of muskets fired, the men giving the old yell! It was one of those inspiring scenes, which its actors will never forget, and made a staunch soldier of a recruit!

We kept up the pursuit until eight or nine o'clock in the night, when we halted, and were allowed to rest until morning. The man, "with headquarters in the saddle," who "had no rear," was taught the second lesson of Jackson's tactics. He wished now that he had a rear, as he was putting forth all his efforts to find Washington with its fortifications, which was forty-five or fifty miles in his rear, when we commenced our movement.

The loss in our brigade was small. Among the killed was Lieut. Edward G. Rawlings, commanding F Company. He was as good a soldier as the war produced, a magnificent specimen of manhood, tall and erect, over six feet in his stockings, weighing about two hundred pounds, with endurance in proportion to his size. I have often heard him say he could march forever, if his feet would not become sore. He was kind and gentle, always at his post doing his duty.

To Jackson belongs the chief honor of Second Manassas, as in the first battle of Manassas, and the position held by the Second Brigade was one of the points on which the enemy made many desperate and repeated assaults; in all of which they were repulsed with great loss. I saw more of their dead lying on the ground in our front than I saw in the same space during the war.

One of our company wrote home that he was shot all to pieces, having twenty-seven holes shot through his blanket. In his next letter he explained that his blanket was folded, and one shot going through it, made the twenty-seven holes!

Source: John H. Worsham, *One of Jackson's Foot Cavalry: His Experience and What He Saw During the War 1861–1865* (New York: Neale Publishing Company, 1912), https://archive.org/details/oneofjacksonsfoowors.

BATTLE OF ANTIETAM

SEPTEMBER 17, 1862
GEN. JAMES LONGSTREET, CSA

Emboldened by victories such as Second Bull Run / Manassas, General Lee and Confederate president Jefferson Davis resolved upon the invasion of Maryland. If successful, this move northward across the Potomac would prompt the border slave state, heretofore cagily neutral, to join the Confederacy. This would cut off Washington, DC, from the rest of the United States. The plan was bold, audacious even. The campaign is remembered partly thanks to the beloved poem "Barbara Fritchie," by John Greenleaf Whittier, in which an elderly loyal woman defiantly flies the Stars and Stripes as Jackson's troops march through Frederick, escaping retribution thanks to Stonewall Jackson's sense of honor.

The Battle of Antietam, or Sharpsburg as the South termed it, saw McClellan's Army of the Potomac and Lee's Army of Northern Virginia massively engaged in a fight on what many call the bloodiest day in American history, September 17, 1862. Possessing advantage in numbers, McClellan's men attacked Lee's entrenchments along Antietam Creek. As the Confederates resisted, USA Maj. Gen. Joseph Hooker led a flanking move against their positions. Maj. Gen. Ambrose Burnside's soldiers captured the stone bridge that crossed the shallow creek, and only the prompt arrival of CSA Maj. Gen. A. P. Hill's troops prevented a rout. Lee staked the entire Maryland campaign on this battle, and the Union's victory prompted him to retreat back across the Potomac. Maryland would not leave the Union. A frustrated President Lincoln faulted

Soldiers near a single grave under a tree on the battlefield of Antietam
LIBRARY OF CONGRESS

McClellan's cautious refusal to pursue the retreating Confederates, but the victory gave Lincoln the credibility he needed to announce the fateful Emancipation Proclamation less than a week later. From that point on, slavery—its abolition or preservation—would be the central theme of the war, which meant no foreign power would dare to support the Confederacy's cause.

Longstreet, one of the most important Southern military figures and a close confidante of Lee's, was a West Pointer who fought valiantly in the Mexican-American War and against Indians on the frontier. Born in South Carolina, he joined the CSA when the war broke out. Here, Longstreet recalls the enormity of this consequential battle between two field armies along once-bucolic Antietam Creek.

The field that I have described—the field lying along the Antietam and including in its scope the little town of Sharpsburg—was destined to pass into history as the scene of the bloodiest single day of fighting of the war, and that 17th of September was to become memorable as the day of greatest carnage in the campaigns between the North and South.

Gettysburg was the greatest battle of the war, but it was for three days, and its total of casualties on either side, terrible as it was, should be one-third larger to make the average per diem equal to the losses at Sharpsburg. Viewed by the measure of losses, Antietam was the fourth battle of the war, Spotsylvania and the Wilderness, as well as Gettysburg, exceeding it in number of killed and wounded, but each of these dragged its tragedy through several days.

Taking Confederate losses in killed and wounded as the criterion of magnitude in battles, the Seven Days' Battle (following McClellan's retreat), Gettysburg, and Chickamauga exceeded Sharpsburg, but each of these occupied several days, and on no single day in any one of them was there such carnage as in this fierce struggle.

The Confederates lost in killed and wounded in the Seven Days' Battle 19,739—more, it will be observed, than at Gettysburg (15,298), though the total loss, including 5150 captured or missing, at the latter, brought the figures up to those of the former (20,614), in which the captured or missing were only 875. Our killed and wounded at Chickamauga were 16,986, but that was in two days' battle, while at Chancellorsville in three days the killed and wounded were 10,746. It is impossible to make the comparison with absolute exactness for the Confederate side, for the reason that our losses are given for the entire campaign in Maryland, instead of separately for the single great battle and several minor engagements. Thus computed they were 12,187. But nearly all of these are known to have been losses at Sharpsburg, and, making proper deductions for the casualties in other actions of the campaign, the Confederate loss in this single day's fighting was still in excess of that at the three days' fight at Chancellorsville (10,746), and for the single day far larger proportionally than in the two days at Chickamauga, three days at Gettysburg, or seven days on the bloody Chickahominy.

But the sanguinary character of this battle is most strikingly exhibited by a comparison of the accurate figures of the Federal losses, returned specifically for the day. These show a total killed and wounded of 11,657 (or, including the captured and missing, 12,410), as contrasted with 17,567 killed and wounded in three days at Gettysburg, 16,141 in eight days at Spotsylvania, and 14,283 in the three days at the Wilderness, while the three and two days' fighting respectively at Chancellorsville and Chicka- mauga were actually productive of less loss than this battle of one day. The exceeding losses of this battle are further shown by the fact that of the 11,657 Federals stricken on the field, the great number of 2108 were actually slain—more than two-thirds of the number killed in three days at Gettysburg (3070). And this tremendous tumult of carnage was entirely compassed in the brief hours from dawn to four o'clock in the afternoon.

A word in closing about the chiefs opposed in this great campaign. General Lee and General McClellan were both graduates of the United States Military Academy at West Point. The former took the second honor of the class of 1829, the latter the second honor of the class of 1846. Their service in the United States army was as military engineers. In 1854 they were both selected by Secretary of War Jefferson Davis for promotion to the new cavalry regiments as lieutenant-colonel and cap- tain respectively. Their early opportunities, social and educational, were superior. They studiously improved them in youth, and applied them with diligence in after-life. Aspirations leading to the higher walks of social and professional life seem to have been alike controlling forces in the character and career of each. They were not unmindful that physical development was important in support of mental improvement. In moral tone and habits they may be called exemplars. In his service, General Lee's pride was duty to his government and to the army under his com- mand. He loved admiration of the outside world, but these duties better. General McClellan's ambition was not so limited.

In stature General Lee stood five feet ten inches, was of well- developed muscular figure, as trim as a youth, and weighed one hundred and seventy pounds. In features he was a model of manly beauty. His teeth were of ivory whiteness; his mouth handsome and expressive of frankness, kindness, and generosity. His nose and chin were full, regu- lar, strong, and gave his face force and character. 'Twas seldom that he allowed his mind to wander to the days of his childhood, and talk of his father and his early associates, but when he did, he was far more charm- ing than he thought. As a commander he was much of the Wellington

"Up-and-at-'em" style. He found it hard, the enemy in sight, to withhold his blows. With McClellan it was more difficult to strike than to march for the enemy.

General McClellan was of short, stout figure, but was of soldierly presence, graceful, and handsome-featured.

In their mounts neither of the great commanders lost anything of his admirable presence. Both were masters of the science but not of the art of war. Lee was successful in Virginia; McClellan in Maryland.

Unjust criticism has been passed upon the Confederate soldiers in the Maryland campaign, based principally upon the great number of absentees. To those who have spent their lives near the ranks of soldiers and learned from experience that there is a limit to physical endurance, explanation is not called for; to those who look upon the soldier as a machine, not even needing oil to facilitate motive power, I will say, try to put yourselves in the soldiers' places. Another point to be noted was, that in the Confederate ranks there were thousands of soldiers who had been wounded once, twice, and in some instances three times, who in any other service would have been on the pension-rolls at their comfortable homes.

Sickness and weakness that creep into an army from irregular food, collected in the stress of march, were no trifling impediments to the maintenance of our ranks in vigorous form.

When, in mature judgment, the historian builds monuments of words for the leaders of the campaign in Maryland, there will be flowers left for the private soldiers, and for the private soldiers' graves.

The full significance of Sharpsburg to the Federal authorities lay in the fact that they needed a victory on which to issue the Emancipation Proclamation, which President Lincoln had prepared two months before and had held in abeyance under advice of members of his Cabinet until the Union arms should win a success. Although this battle was by no means so complete a victory as the President wished, and he was sorely vexed with General McClellan for not pushing it to completion, it was made the most of as a victory, and his Emancipation Proclamation was issued on the 22d of September, five days after the battle. This was one of the decisive political events of the war, and at once put the great struggle outwardly and openly upon the basis where it had before only rested by tacit and covert understanding. If the Southern army had been carefully held in hand, refreshed by easy marches and comfortable supplies, the proclamation could not have found its place in history.

Source: James Longstreet, *From Manassas to Appomattox: Memoirs of the Civil War in America* (Philadelphia: J. B. Lippincott Company, 1896; Project Gutenberg, 2011), chap. 18, http://www.gutenberg.org/ebooks/38418.

BATTLE OF FREDERICKSBURG

DECEMBER 11-15, 1862
GEN. JAMES LONGSTREET, CSA

Burnside's advance across the stone bridge at Antietam Creek seemed to epitomize the fighting vim Lincoln longed to see imbued into the Army of the Potomac. The president promoted the bewhiskered Burnside, who promptly set about planning a decisive battle to break Lee's Army of Northern Virginia and win the war in short order—by Christmas 1862, in fact. The engagement, at Fredericksburg, Virginia, took place December 11–15, 1862, and resulted in a complete Confederate victory. The overoptimistic Burnside's plan was straightforward: to ford the Rappahannock River and dash to Richmond before Lee could set up defenses there. But logistical problems, especially a shortage of pontoon bridges, made the river crossing an extended affair, and by the time Burnside's men made it, Lee had his army in strongly fortified positions along Marye's Heights, a ridge on Fredericksburg's western approaches, blocking the road to the Confederacy's capital. Longstreet commanded soldiers atop these heights, and his troops fired down at attacking Union forces with everything they had. Repeated assaults came to naught; the Union dead piled up. By December 15, Burnside was forced to admit the failure of his plan, and his defeated Army of the Potomac painfully retreated to northern lines. Once again, "On to Richmond!" proved an illusory battle cry. Longstreet describes here what many would term the "butchery" that felled so many blue-clad soldiers.

Building pontoon bridges at Fredericksburg
LIBRARY OF CONGRESS

Under a strong artillery combat Meade marched forward, with Gibbon's division in close support on his right, and Doubleday's farther off on his left. The line encountered Lane's brigade front in a steady, hard fight, and, developing against Archer's left, broke through, forcing the brigades back, encountered Thomas's and Gregg's brigades, threw the latter into confusion, and killed General Gregg. Brockenbrough's and Pender's brigades turned against the penetrating columns and were forced back. Under skillful handling the brigades finally brought the battle to steady work, but Meade's impetuous onward march was bravely made and pressed until three brigades of Early's division were advanced and thrown into action, commanded by Colonels Atkinson, Walker, and Hoke. These, with the combined fire of Hill's broken lines, forced Meade back. Two regiments of Berry's brigade of the Third Corps came to the relief of Meade and were driven back, when Gibbon's division which followed was met, and after severe battle was repulsed. The Confederates made a partial following of the success, beyond the railroad, and until they encountered the fire of the relieving divisions under Birney and Sickles and the reserve batteries. Doubleday's division protected Meade's left as Jackson's right under Taliaferro partially engaged against them; both encountered loss. Hood got one of his brigades in in time to follow the troops as they retired towards their reserve line. At the first moment of the break on Jackson's lines Pickett rode to Hood and urged that the opportunity anticipated was at hand, but Hood failed to see it in time for effective work. About two P.M. the battle quieted into defensive practice of artillery and sharp-shooters.

The opening against the Confederate left, before referred to, was led by French's division of the Second Corps, about 10.30. The Eighteenth and Twenty-fourth Georgia Regiments, Cobb's Georgia Legion, and the Twenty-fourth North Carolina Regiment were in the sunken road, the salient point. On Marye's Hill, back and above, was the Washington Artillery, with nine guns, Ransom's and Cooke's North Carolina brigade in open field, the guns under partial cover, pitted. Other batteries on Taylor's and Lee's Hills posted to this defence as many as twenty guns, holding under range by direct and cross fire the avenues of approach and the open field along Cobb's front.

French's division came in gallant style, but somewhat hurried. He gathered his ranks behind the swell of ground near the canal and moved to the assault. An intervening plank fence gave the troops some trouble in crossing under fire, so that his ranks were not firm after passing it to the attack. Hancock, coming speedily with his division, was better organized and in time to take up the fight as French was obliged to retire. This advance was handsomely maintained, but the galling fire they encountered forced them to open fire. Under this delay their ranks were cut up as rapidly as they had collected at the canal, and when within a hundred yards of the stone wall they were so thinned that they could do nothing but surrender, even if they could leap to the road-bed. But they turned, and the fire naturally slackened, as their hurried steps took them away to their partial cover. The troops behind the stone wall were reinforced during this engagement by two of Cooke's regiments from the hill-top, ordered by General Ransom, and General McLaws ordered part of Kershaw's brigade in on their right.

After Hancock's engagement some minutes passed before arrangements were made for the next. Howard's division had been feeling for a way to get by Cobb's left, when he was called to the front attack, and ordered over the same ground. He arranged his forces with care, and advanced in desperate fight. Under the severe fire of the Confederates his troops were provoked to return fire, and during the delay thus caused his ranks were so speedily decimated that they in turn were obliged to return to cover. The Confederate commander, General Cobb, was killed. General Kershaw, with the other regiments of his brigade, was ordered to the front. The Washington Artillery, exhausted of ammunition, was relieved by guns of Alexander's battalion. The change of batteries seemed to give new hope to the assaulting forces. They cheered and put in their best practice of sharp-shooters and artillery. The greater part of Alexander's loss occurred while galloping up to his position. General Ransom advanced the other regiments of his brigade to the crest of the hill. At the suggestion of General Lee the brigades of Jenkins and Kemper of Pickett's division were called up and assigned, the former to General McLaws and the latter to General Ransom. A supply of ammunition was sent down to the troops in the road in time to meet the next attack, by Sturgis's division of the Ninth Corps, which made the usual brave fight, and encountered the same damaging results. Getty's division of the Ninth Corps came to his support on the left, but did not engage fiercely, losing less than eight hundred men. Carroll's brigade of Whipple's division, Third Corps, came in on Sturgis's left, but only to brace that part of the fight.

As the troops hurried forward from the streets of the city for the Telegraph road, they came at once under the fire of the long-range guns on Lee's Hill. The thirty-pound Parrotts were particularly effective in having the range and dropping their shells in the midst of the columns as they dashed forward. Frequently commands were broken up by this fire and that of other long-range guns, and sought shelter, as they thought, in the railroad cut, but that point was well marked, and the shots were dropped in, in enfilade fire, with precision, often making wide gaps in their ranks.

The siege guns of Stafford Heights gave their especial attention to our heavy guns and put their shots over the parapets very often.

One shell buried itself close under the parapet at General Lee's side, as he sat among the officers of his staff, but it failed to explode. Soon after this our big Parrott gun burst into many fragments. It was closely surrounded by General Lee and staff, officers of the First Corps headquarters, and officers and gunners of the battery, but the explosion caused no other damage than the loss of the gun.

Griffin's division was next ordered to attack, and made the usual desperate struggle. The Confederates meanwhile had accumulated such force in the road that a single division, had it reached that point, would have found its equal in numbers, and of greater vigor, with Ransom at the top of the hill prepared to rush down and join in the mêlée. At that hour we could have safely invited one division into our midst, if assured it was to be the last.

The next attack was made by Humphreys's division. Its commander was a man of superior attainments and accomplishments in the walks of civil as well as military life. He measured justly the situation, and arranged his battle in the only order by which success could have been made possible, but he had only two brigades with which to take a position not assailable and held by more than three brigades of superior troops. His troops were new, so that he felt called to personal example as well as skilful handling. He ordered the attack with empty muskets, and led with his brigade commanders, but half-way up towards the goal his men stopped to load and open fire, which neither he nor his officers could prevent, so they were driven back. Then he made a like effort with his other brigade, under special orders from Generals Burnside and Hooker that the point must be carried before night,—and the dew was then falling. (Just then our second big Parrott gun went into fragments, but without damage to the men.) The troops that had been driven back from previous attacks joined in trying to persuade Humphreys's men not to go forward. Notwithstanding the discouraging surroundings, he led his men on, encountered the same terrific and death-dealing opposition, and his men retired in greater confusion, going beyond his control to the vicinity of the city before he could get them again in ranks. His account of the last effort is interesting:

"The stone wall was a sheet of flame that enveloped the head and flanks of the column. Officers and men were falling rapidly, and the head of the column was at length brought to a stand when close up to the wall. Up to this time not a shot had been fired by the column, but now some firing began. It lasted but a minute, when, in spite of all our efforts, the column turned and began to retire slowly. I attempted to rally the brigade behind the natural embankment so often mentioned, but the united efforts of General Tyler, myself, our staff, and other officers could not arrest the retiring mass."

At that time there were three brigades behind the stone wall and one regiment of Ransom's brigade. The ranks were four or five deep—the rear files loading and passing their guns to the front ranks, so that the volleys by brigade were almost incessant pourings of solid sheets of lead.

Two brigades of Sykes's division, First and Second Regulars, were sent to the front to guard the line. It was some time after nightfall, so that their line could only be distinguished by the blaze of their fire. Some of the batteries and infantry engaged against their fire till night was well advanced.

General Jackson thought to advance against the enemy's left late in the afternoon, but found it so well posted and guarded that he concluded the venture would be too hazardous. He lost his opportunity, failing to follow close upon the repulse of Meade's and Gibbon's divisions. His command was massed and well in hand, with an open field for infantry and artillery. He had, including the divisions of Hood and Pickett—ordered to work with him—about fifty thousand men. Franklin had, including troops of the Centre Grand Division, about equal force.

The charge of Meade's division has been compared with that of Pickett's, Pettigrew's, and Trimble's at Gettysburg, giving credit of better conduct to the former. The circumstances do not justify the comparison.

When the fog lifted over Meade's advance he was within musket-range of A. P. Hill's division, closely supported on his right by Gibbon's, and guarded on his left by Doubleday's division. On Hill's right was a fourteen-gun battery, on his left eight guns. Meade broke through Hill's division, and with the support of Gibbon forced his way till he encountered part of Ewell's division, when he was forced back in some confusion. Two fresh divisions of the Third Corps came to their relief, and there were as many as fifty thousand men at hand who could have been thrown into the fight. Meade's march to meet his adversary was half a mile—the troops of both sides fresh and vigorous.

Of the assaulting columns of Pickett, Pettigrew, and Trimble, only four thousand seven hundred under Pickett were fresh; the entire force of these divisions was only fifteen thousand strong. They had a mile to march over open field before reaching the enemy's line, strengthened by field-works and manned by thrice their numbers. The Confederates at Gettysburg had been fought to exhaustion of men and munitions. They lost about sixty per cent. of the assaulting forces—Meade about forty. The latter had fresh troops behind him, and more than two hundred guns to cover his rallying lines. The Confederates had nothing behind them but field batteries almost exhausted of ammunition. That Meade made a brave, good fight is beyond question, but he had superior numbers and appointments. At Gettysburg the Confederate assault was made against intrenched lines of artillery and infantry, where stood fifty thousand men.

A series of braver, more desperate charges than those hurled against the troops in the sunken road was never known, and the piles and cross-piles of dead marked a field such as I never saw before or since.

Between 1.30 and 2.30 of the afternoon several orders and messages were sent by General Burnside calling on General Franklin to renew the battle of the left. Before 2.30 he received from General Burnside, through his aide-de-camp, Captain Goddard, this despatch: "Tell General Franklin, with my compliments, that I wish him to make a vigorous attack with his whole force. Our right is hard pressed."

Under ordinary circumstances this would be regarded as a strong order, but Franklin had gone far enough in his first battle to be convinced that an attack by his "whole force," the other end of the army "hard pressed," would be extremely hazardous. If undertaken and proved disastrous, he could have been made to shoulder the whole responsibility, for a "wish" implies discretion. It is not just to the subordinate to use such language if orders are intended to be imperative. Men bred as soldiers have no fancy for orders that carry want of faith on their face.

Source: James Longstreet, *From Manassas to Appomattox: Memoirs of the Civil War in America* (Philadelphia: J. B. Lippincott Company, 1896; Project Gutenberg, 2011), chap. 23, http://www.gutenberg.org/ebooks/38418.

Artist's rendering of the Battle of Stones River, or Murfreesboro

DR. C. LENKER DESCRIBES
BATTLE OF STONES RIVER

DECEMBER 31, 1962-JANUARY 2, 1863
SGT. CHRISTIAN LENKER, USA

Christian Lenker was born in Pennsylvania, but when the war broke out he had begun his medical studies as a student at Mount Union College in Ohio. He enlisted, serving in the 19th Ohio Volunteers. Lenker remained with this regiment for over four years, fighting in many battles and keeping a diary in which he recorded his experiences. After the war, he became a physician. In this excerpt, Lenker recounts the Battle of Stones River, also known as Second Murfreesboro, a major engagement in the western theater.

The Battle of Stones River occurred at a critical time, from late December 1862 to early January 1863. The Emancipation Proclamation had just taken effect, enraging and alarming the Southern states, which recognized that it meant the loss of their hopes for foreign diplomatic intervention since it elevated slavery over secession as the war's rationale. Union moods were gloomy due to the defeat at Fredericksburg. Stones River was a notably bloody battle: its casualty rate of 31.4 percent was the highest of all major Civil War engagements. It occurred at a time when both sides were sensitive about the war's progress. The battle saw USA Maj. Gen. William S. Rosecrans's Army of the Cumberland in possession of Nashville, the state capital and a major federal supply center. Rosecrans's men moved out to face CSA Gen. Braxton Bragg's Army of Tennessee at the town of Murfreesboro. The Union advance drew

Confederate counterattacks led by CSA generals William J. Hardee and Leonidas Polk, whose troops plunged in with zeal. The butternuts might have won the engagement early but for a dogged defense led by USA Brig. Gen. Philip Sheridan. Sheridan's men stabilized Union positions, and the federals set about defending the road to Nashville. Fighting climaxed on January 2, when Bragg's men failed to conquer Union troops in command of the heights above the Stones River. Northern artillery forced the Southerners to turn back, and Bragg withdrew. The news of his retreat bolstered Union morale and again drew favorable attention to the success of government forces in the western campaign. Lincoln congratulated Rosecrans, Nashville was secured for the Union, and Middle Tennessee and Kentucky were lost forever to the Confederacy.

After Rosecrans has ordered Major Manderson to take the regiment back to a better position, and we were going towards the rear leisurely, and in good order, the Rebels kept up an annoying fire upon us, wounding men and officers; before we were ordered back, they had run out a field battery, on the right of our regiment, and gave us a destructive enfilading fire. We became tired of this annoying fire by their skirmishers and sharpshooters, while on this short retreat, so John Blyth and I dropped out of the ranks, to take a few shots at them. After I had brought my guns to aim, upon an approaching regiment, Blyth pushed it up and said, "You are excited, you are going to fire upon our men." I replied, "Am I John?" Wait till the smoke clears, then look at the old flag. Has our only three stripes?" "Egad! you are right" was his response. We gave them a few rounds; to avoid capture, we ran after the regiment, and took our place in line. The enemy's fire became more annoying by this time, our division commander and other officers had been wounded, so a staff officer came riding alongside our regiment, and when he came to our company, he said, "Boys, why don't you let them have a few rounds?" Of course we had no orders from the major or captain to do so, but we took the hint. We halted, fronted and gave them one good volley from the company. That settled them and they did not seek any closer and further acquaintance, with the 19th Ohio that afternoon.

At night, after the fighting had ceased, the company commander asked for volunteers to go and bring our knapsacks from the place, where we had left them under a guard. Only one besides myself responded. All were tired and exhausted, by the day's marching and fighting. The moon had risen and lighted the field, by this time. We passed many of the dead, and they left an imperishable picture upon my mind. One thing was peculiar. Nearly all lay on their backs, stretched out straight as if some undertaker had prepared them for burial. I can not recall that I saw any lie on their faces or doubled up. Some kind comrades or friends had gently and lovingly covered their faces with the overcoat capes of the dead. In the morning, all lay cold and stiff, as they fell, covered with a heavy coat of hoarfrost.

On January 2nd., there had been very little fighting, except skirmishing, in front of our line, so I told my partner that I did not believe that there would be any more fighting, that day and as it was drawing pretty well towards evening, I said he should pound the coffee. We drew it unground, and generally crushed it with the blunt end of a bayonet in the tin cups. I emptied the water, which was in my canteen, into a small coffee pot and started for the river and on my return, just as I approached the regiment, the battle broke out with the suddenness of a thunder crash, and rolled rapidly towards us; we were on the reserve. Blyth, my partner, said, "Here is your gun." I took it, and in a few minutes, we were in that hand-to-hand struggle, which General Manderson described so graphically.

On account of an impenetrable brier patch, a part of our company became separated from the others and, when the Rebels turned our right flank, we did not know that the other part of the regiment was falling back and we stood fighting, and immediately the Johnnies were all around us. One of them said to me, "Surrender you Yankee s-n of b-h." I simply remarked, "Not today," and plunged through the confused mass and started for the river, at a gait, which would have done honor to Tam O'Shanter's mare.

Blyth and I had vowed to each other to stay together, during the battle and not separate, under any circumstance. We had done this so far, in the previous fighting, also, we had resolved not to be taken prisoners, unless wounded. I could not imagine how many bullets flew around me on the way to the river, none touched me, but poor Blyth was fated. He was found that night dead, with seven bullet holes in his body. I never saw a braver or cooler boy in my life, companionable and honorable, and yet he was an infidel and did not believe in the Bible, and the boys used to say wait till he gets in the face of Death, and he will change his opinion or belief but no one fought a braver fight or died a braver death. I was told that he had been wounded, and refused to surrender, and then was riddled with bullets. We had become separated in the melee. Our chaplain was absent, for some time, and one, belonging to a neighboring regiment, used to preach to us on Sundays, patriotic sermons, and telling us to be Christians, and live a Christian life, and, when battle or death came, we would not be afraid to meet them. Many of the boys had given him their watches and money, on the day before the battle, and asked me why I didn't. I said if I get killed, I do not need my watch or money, and if I don't, I need both. On the first day's fight, when it looked like that our army would be destroyed or captured, the chaplain mounted a horse and rode away like an Arab of the desert, to Nashville thirty miles distant. He did not return to preach Christianity or courage to us again, and some of the owners of the watches and money heaped many curses and maledictions upon his head. They finally got their property. This does not prove that infidelity makes a patriot, or religion a coward, because many of our boys led exemplary religious lives, and were respected and honored by all.

After I had ran to the river, I found it was too deep to wade, and the opposite side rose in perpendicular rocks. The Rebels now came swooping right behind me, towards the river by thousands, and being driven in the deep water or captured, seemed to be my only alternative, but I took a desperate chance, and ran the gauntlet right in front of the Confederates fully seventy-five yards to the shallow ford above where we had crossed. Most of our men had retreated back from the river, after crossing.

The Rebel Calvary had swept around our flanks to the rear of the army, and destroyed our provision trains, with their contents. On this account we had been notified that whatever provisions were in our haversacks, had to last till the end of the battle, no matter how many days it lasted. My haversack contained a large chunk of fine bacon, and a good many crackers, but my absence for water, and the suddenness of the attack, did not give me time to sling on my haversack and when the Rebels pushed us back, they ran over our bivouac, where I had left the haversack. The thought that some hungry Johnny Rebel should feast upon my grub, which I had saved for an emergency, should one occur, and had not eaten breakfast, dinner or supper, made me feel fighting mad, and I stopped on the river bank, and began to fire into the mass, right across the stream shouting and yelling, waving scores of Rebel flags triumphantly, and getting ready to cross. I kept shooting until the cartridges in the upper apartment of the box were exhausted, then I stepped behind a large oak, near-by, to fill the upper space of the box, with those in the lower. Our regiment was noted for being good fighters on the skirmish line, and we had been taught that when on the skirmish line, we should drive the enemy as far as we could, then secure shelter behind any object, which should protect our bodies, stump, tree, rock, depression or elevation of ground or anything, then 'stick,' hold on to it, and load and fire. I was justifiable in getting behind the tree, from a standpoint of good judgment and teaching, but some invisible and inexplicable power inaudibly said to me, "Step out in the open, and fight, or die like a man." I moved out about five steps and began firing, I here came near Lieutenant Southerland of our company and Lieutenant Reefy of our regiment. Our color bearer and all the color guards had been struck down. Reefy had taken the flag and had it now, and was going to cross the river, right in the face of the horde of Confederates, and I remember that Southerland said, "For God's sake, wait till the regiment rallies, before you cross with that flag, or the Rebels will capture it."

Just about that time, a twelve pound solid shot came from a Rebel battery, across the river, and struck the oak tree, behind which I had been standing, about three feet above the ground, and knocked the trunk to pieces. A large splinter struck the Lieutenant, and knocked him over. I was just going to pick him up, and carry him behind the hill out of bullet range, when he got up and limped back himself. By this time Major Mendenhall opened, point blank, his 52 or 58 pieces of artillery, and sent their destructive missiles, at close range, double-shotted into the Confederate mass. They fell in great numbers, and in a short time, were in full retreat. Miller's Division was coming up from the reserve, but before they reached us, we crossed the river and I got my haversack, pork and crackers untouched. Reefy planted our flag on one of two guns, captured from the famous Rebel Washington Battery.

By this time, on one part of the line, many of the men, who had retreated slowly and reluctantly, as far as the opposite river bank, had rallied and followed the now retreating enemy, bushwhacker style, that is we stood behind a tree and loaded, then followed the enemy and fired, in this manner we ran them back, far beyond their original line that morning, till we saw the tents in their camp, only across a field. We had now formed a regular line in the field, and were going to charge a battery, which opened upon us. This remnant of our routed brigades had the flag of almost every regiment in this line, and they were as close and numerous as a row of sunflowers, in a cornfield. We had no general or regimental officers commanding us. We were doing things on our own hook, but a staff officer came, and ordered us back.

That night, after the battle, I found that out of six, who were near me, in the hand-to-hand clash, Blyth was dead, having been struck by seven bullets. Maurer had been struck upon his U.S. plate, by a rifle ball, and was doubled up for a short time. Paramore had a bayonet wound; Elson and Hetzel were prisoners. They were all of my most close and intimate friends. I did not know what had become of some of them, as we could not find them anywhere, and I believed likely some had been shot in the river, and lay under its waters. I felt so extremely sad and disconsolate that I positively wished that I were sleeping beneath the water. Right around lay 1,500 dead and wounded, Federal and Confederate promiscuously mixed. The battle was over so far as we were concerned in our division. Night after night for nearly a week, in my dreams and night visions, I fought that battle over again. I could see as plainly as I ever saw in day time, that terrible rout on the 31st., masses of men in blue uniforms, coming out of the cedars, followed by lines in gray, with waving banners. I could distinctly hear the roar of cannon, and rolls of musketry. It was a magic picture show. Who can explain the drama? Who can explain the mental philosophy and relations or connections, between our night dreams or during sleep and the daydreams of our imagination? We lost in our regiment in two day's fighting 213 men, being 43 per cent of the number engaged—killed, wounded and missing.

Source: Christian Lenker, *The Civil War Memoir of Sgt. Christian Lenker, 19th Ohio Volunteers*, ed. Michael Barton and Judith Kennedy (Xlibris, 2014; originally published as 174 articles in the *Pottsville (PA) Evening Chronicle*, February 24, 1912, to June 19, 1915), chap. 24.

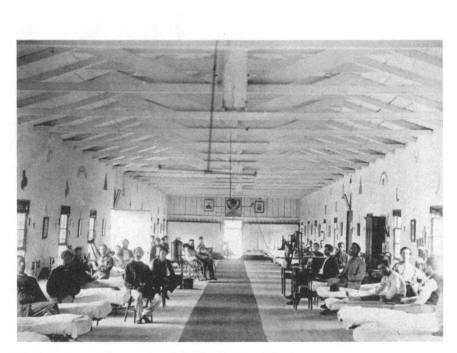

Ward K, Armory Square Hospital, Washington, DC
LIBRARY OF CONGRESS

EVERYDAY LIFE IN THE HOSPITAL

When the Civil War began, military medicine was hard-pressed to keep up with technological advances that made casualties plentiful and treatment difficult. Rifles firing minié balls were more accurate than muskets, improvements in food preservation made feeding large armies feasible, and railroads allowed for transporting ever-larger numbers of soldiers. The upshot was greater casualties as more men than ever before fought each other at close quarters using better weapons. Meanwhile, medical knowledge did not understand the process of infection: Sir Joseph Lister's pioneering improvements in antiseptic operations were a generation away. Even minor wounds or successful amputations were quite likely to result in fatal infections, and hospitals were full of dying patients. Also, germ theory was not yet known, so the pathway of disease meant that crowded conditions provided breeding grounds for typhoid fever, dysentery, cholera, malaria, and a host of other contagious illnesses. Logistical planning for the effective treatment of wounded and sick soldiers lagged on both sides. Especially in the early war years, hospitals were fearful places indeed.

Yet necessity is mother to invention, and the need to save fighting men and return them to the fray made progress in combat medicine vital. In the North, superior organization showed itself in the establishment of systematization of the surgical corps. Surgeon General William A. Hammond upgraded the Army Medical Corps, and nurses were trained and attached to regiments. Meanwhile, the United States Army Medical Department, the United States

Sanitary Commission, and a slew of other agencies improved treatment methods for the wounded and sick as well as cleanup operations on the battlefield. Frederick Law Olmsted, the noted landscape architect, led the way at the Sanitary Commission. Improvements hardly eradicated the problems of infection and disease, but the Union did develop a system that improved as the war went on. The Confederacy, however, suffered greatly from a relative dearth of specialists and resources. Southern logistics were always problematic, and bureaucratic bungling at the beginning of the conflict meant that medical treatment for rebel soldiers was haphazard. Field hospitals emerged, but for many Confederates, the course of treatment involved home furlough, to be taken care of by family members. Medicines and surgical supplies were chronically scarce, and it took enormous resourcefulness on the part of Confederate doctors to care effectively for Southern wounded.

Walt Whitman, one of the greatest American poets and a staunch Union supporter, first came to Washington, DC, to find his brother, George, who fought with federal forces at Fredericksburg. While searching, the poet was stunned by the many wounded men he saw languishing in hospitals in the capital and environs. His deep humanism aroused, Whitman became a nurse. He visited patients, conversed with them, wrote letters to their relatives, or simply listened to what they had to say. This was Whitman's service to the Union cause. He provided wounded soldiers needed comforts, material and emotional, for the remaining years of the war. Here, he recounts his experiences in this excerpt from The Wound-Dresser.

Another celebrated figure who served the Union by aiding its wounded was **Louisa May Alcott**. Author, feminist, and abolitionist, she went to Washington to serve as a nurse in 1862. Already under contract to cover the war for the Atlantic Monthly, Alcott set to work with enthusiasm, only to contract typhus, which nearly killed her. She described her time working in hospitals in an 1863 book, Hospital Sketches, which did much to explain to Americans the situation faced by their wounded sons, brothers, and fathers.

John Bell Hood's Texas Brigade, which earned glory under Stonewall Jackson, was the unit in which **Pvt. William Fletcher, CSA**, *served. The Louisiana native moved to Texas before the war's start and in 1861 signed up at Richmond. Fletcher fought in the Peninsular Campaign at Seven Pines, at Gaines's Mill, and at Second Manassas, where he was wounded. Recovering, he returned to fight at Fredericksburg and Gettysburg. He was wounded again at Chickamauga, an experience he recounts here. After recuperating, Fletcher joined Terry's Texas Rangers, was captured at Murfreesboro, and fought till the end of the war. In later years, he wrote his memoirs,* Rebel Private, Front and Rear, *from which this excerpt is taken.*

Lt. Col. Gilbert C. Kniffin, *grandson of Revolutionary War veterans, grew up in New York State loving the Union. He lived in Kentucky as the war began, and committed himself to keeping that border slave state from seceding. Attracting army attention for his energetic recruiting of Union supporters in divided Kentucky, Kniffin was commissioned and quickly revealed his organizational genius as Assistant Chief Commissary of Subsistence for the Army of the Cumberland. Gen. William S. Rosecrans, USA, praised his logistical skill and patriotism. Kniffin became a journalist after the war. Here, he recapitulates the violence at the bloody Battle of Stones River.*

THE GREAT ARMY OF THE WOUNDED

WALT WHITMAN, USA

The military hospitals, convalescent camps, etc., in Washington and its neighborhood, sometimes contain over fifty thousand sick and wounded men. Every form of wound (the mere sight of some of them having been known to make a tolerably hardy visitor faint away), every kind of malady, like a long procession, with typhoid fever and diarrhœa at the head as leaders, are here in steady motion. The soldier's hospital! how many sleepless nights, how many women's tears, how many long and waking hours and days of suspense, from every one of the Middle, Eastern, and Western States, have concentrated here! Our own New York, in the form of hundreds and thousands of her young men, may consider herself here—Pennsylvania, Ohio, Indiana, and all the West and Northwest the same—and all the New England States the same.

Upon a few of these hospitals I have been almost daily calling as a missionary, on my own account, for the sustenance and consolation of some of the most needy cases of sick and dying men, for the last two months. One has much to learn to do good in these places. Great tact is required. These are not like other hospitals. By far the greatest proportion (I should say five sixths) of the patients are American young men, intelligent, of independent spirit, tender feelings, used to a hardy and healthy life; largely the farmers are represented by their sons—largely the mechanics and workingmen of the cities. Then they are soldiers. All these points must be borne in mind.

People through our Northern cities have little or no idea of the great and prominent feature which these military hospitals and convalescent camps make in and around Washington. There are not merely two or three or a dozen, but some fifty of them, of different degrees of capacity. Some have a thousand and more patients. The newspapers here find it necessary to print every day a directory of the hospitals—a long list, something like what a directory of the churches would be in New York, Philadelphia, or Boston.

The Government (which really tries, I think, to do the best and quickest it can for these sad necessities) is gradually settling down to adopt the plan of placing the hospitals in clusters of one-story wooden barracks, with their accompanying tents and sheds for cooking and all needed purposes. Taking all things into consideration, no doubt these are best adapted to the purpose; better than using churches and large public buildings like the Patent office. These sheds now adopted are long, one-story edifices, sometimes ranged along in a row, with their heads to the street, and numbered either alphabetically, Wards A or B, C, D, and so on; or Wards 1, 2, 3, etc. The middle one will be marked by a flagstaff, and is the office of the establishment, with rooms for the ward surgeons, etc. One of these sheds, or wards, will contain sixty cots; sometimes, on an emergency, they move them close together, and crowd in more. Some of the barracks are larger, with, of course, more inmates. Frequently there are tents, more comfortable here than one might think, whatever they may be down in the army.

Each ward has a ward-master, and generally a nurse for every ten or twelve men. A ward surgeon has, generally, two wards—although this varies. Some of the wards have a woman nurse; the Armory-square wards have some very good ones. The one in Ward E is one of the best.

A few weeks ago the vast area of the second story of that noblest of Washington buildings, the Patent office, was crowded close with rows of sick, badly wounded, and dying soldiers. They were placed in three very large apartments. I went there several times. It was a strange, solemn, and, with all its features of suffering and death, a sort of fascinating sight. I went sometimes at night to soothe and relieve particular cases; some, I found, needed a little cheering up and friendly consolation at that time, for they went to sleep better afterwards. Two of the immense apartments are filled with high and ponderous glass cases crowded with models in miniature of every kind of utensil, machine, or invention it ever entered into the mind of man to conceive, and with curiosities and foreign presents. Between these cases were lateral openings, perhaps eight feet wide, and quite deep, and in these were placed many of the sick; besides a great long double row of them up and down through the middle of the hall. Many of them were very bad cases, wounds and amputations. Then there was a gallery running above the hall, in which there were beds also. It was, indeed, a curious scene at night when lit up. The glass cases, the beds, the sick, the gallery above and the marble pavement under foot; the suffering, and the fortitude to bear it in the various degrees; occasionally, from some, the groan that could not be repressed; sometimes a poor fellow dying, with emaciated face and glassy eyes, the nurse by his side, the doctor also there, but no friend, no relative—such were the sights but lately in the Patent office. The wounded have since been removed from there, and it is now vacant again.

Of course there are among these thousands of prostrated soldiers in hospital here all sorts of individual cases. On recurring to my note-book, I am puzzled which cases to select to illustrate the average of these young men and their experiences. I may here say, too, in general terms, that I could not wish for more candor and manliness, among all their sufferings, than I find among them.

Take this case in Ward 6, Campbell hospital: a young man from Plymouth county, Massachusetts; a farmer's son, aged about twenty or twenty-one; a soldierly, American young fellow, but with sensitive and tender feelings. Most of December and January last he lay very low, and for quite a while I never expected he would recover. He had become prostrated with an obstinate diarrhœa: his stomach would hardly keep the least thing down; he was vomiting half the time. But that was hardly the worst of it. Let me tell his story—it is but one of thousands.

He had been some time sick with his regiment in the field, in front, but did his duty as long as he could; was in the battle of Fredericksburg; soon after was put in the regimental hospital. He kept getting worse—could not eat anything they had there; the doctor told him nothing could be done for him there. The poor fellow had fever also; received (perhaps it could not be helped) little or no attention; lay on the ground, getting worse. Toward the latter part of December, very much enfeebled, he was sent up from the front, from Falmouth station, in an open platform car (such as hogs are transported upon North), and dumped with a crowd of others on the boat at Aquia creek, falling down like a rag where they deposited him, too weak and sick to sit up or help himself at all. No one spoke to him or assisted him; he had nothing to eat or drink; was used (amid the great crowds of sick) either with perfect indifference, or, as in two or three instances, with heartless brutality.

On the boat, when night came and when the air grew chilly, he tried a long time to undo the blankets he had in his knapsack, but was too feeble. He asked one of the employees, who was moving around deck, for a moment's assistance to get the blankets. The man asked him back if he could not get them himself. He answered, no, he had been trying for more than half an hour, and found himself too weak. The man rejoined, he might then go without them, and walked off. So H. lay chilled and damp on deck all night, without anything under or over him, while two good blankets were within reach. It caused him a great injury—nearly cost him his life.

Arrived at Washington, he was brought ashore and again left on the wharf, or above it, amid the great crowds, as before, without any nourishment—not a drink for his parched mouth; no kind hand had offered to cover his face from the forenoon sun. Conveyed at last some two miles by the ambulance to the hospital, and assigned a bed (Bed 49, Ward 6, Campbell hospital, January and February, 1863), he fell down exhausted upon the bed. But the ward-master (he has since been changed) came to him with a growling order to get up: the rules, he said, permitted no man to lie down in that way with his own clothes on; he must sit up—must first go to the bath-room, be washed, and have his clothes completely changed. (A very good rule, properly applied.) He was taken to the bath-room and scrubbed well with cold water. The attendants, callous for a while, were soon alarmed, for suddenly the half-frozen and lifeless body fell limpsy in their hands, and they hurried it back to the cot, plainly insensible, perhaps dying.

Poor boy! the long train of exhaustion, deprivation, rudeness, no food, no friendly word or deed, but all kinds of upstart airs and impudent, unfeeling speeches and deeds, from all kinds of small officials (and some big ones), cutting like razors into that sensitive heart, had at last done the job. He now lay, at times out of his head but quite silent, asking nothing of any one, for some days, with death getting a closer and a surer grip upon him; he cared not, or rather he welcomed death. His heart was broken. He felt the struggle to keep up any longer to be useless. God, the world, humanity—all had abandoned him. It would feel so good to shut his eyes forever on the cruel things around him and toward him.

As luck would have it, at this time I found him. I was passing down Ward No. 6 one day about dusk (4th January, I think), and noticed his glassy eyes, with a look of despair and hopelessness, sunk low in his thin, pallid-brown young face. One learns to divine quickly in the hospital, and as I stopped by him and spoke some commonplace remark (to which he made no reply), I saw as I looked that it was a case for ministering to the affection first, and other nourishment and medicines afterward. I sat down by him without any fuss; talked a little; soon saw that it did him good; led him to talk a little himself; got him somewhat interested; wrote a letter for him to his folks in Massachusetts (to L. H. Campbell, Plymouth county); soothed him down as I saw he was getting a little too much agitated, and tears in his eyes; gave him some small gifts, and told him I should come again soon. (He has told me since that this little visit, at that hour, just saved him; a day more, and it would have been perhaps too late.)

Of course I did not forget him, for he was a young fellow to interest any one. He remained very sick—vomiting much every day, frequent diarrhœa, and also something like bronchitis, the doctor said. For a while I visited him almost every day, cheered him up, took him some little gifts, and gave him small sums of money (he relished a drink of new milk, when it was brought through the ward for sale). For a couple of weeks his condition was uncertain—sometimes I thought there was no chance for him at all; but of late he is doing better—is up and dressed, and goes around more and more (February 21) every day. He will not die, but will recover.

The other evening, passing through the ward, he called me—he wanted to say a few words, particular. I sat down by his side on the cot in the dimness of the long ward, with the wounded soldiers there in their beds, ranging up and down. H. told me I had saved his life. He was in the deepest earnest about it. It was one of those things that repay a soldiers' hospital missionary a thousandfold—one of the hours he never forgets.

A benevolent person, with the right qualities and tact, cannot, perhaps, make a better investment of himself, at present, anywhere upon the varied surface of the whole of this big world, than in these military hospitals, among such thousands of most interesting young men. The army is very young—and so much more American than I supposed. Reader, how can I describe to you the mute appealing look that rolls and moves from many a manly eye, from many a sick cot, following you as you walk slowly down one of these wards? To see these, and to be incapable of responding to them, except in a few cases (so very few compared to the whole of the suffering men), is enough to make one's heart crack. I go through in some cases, cheering up the men, distributing now and then little sums of money—and, regularly, letter-paper and envelopes, oranges, tobacco, jellies, etc., etc.

Many things invite comment, and some of them sharp criticism, in these hospitals. The Government, as I said, is anxious and liberal in its practice toward its sick; but the work has to be left, in its personal application to the men, to hundreds of officials of one grade or another about the hospitals, who are sometimes entirely lacking in the right qualities. There are tyrants and shysters in all positions, and especially those dressed in subordinate authority. Some of the ward doctors are careless, rude, capricious, needlessly strict. One I found who prohibited the men from all enlivening amusements; I found him sending men to the guard-house for the most trifling offence. In general, perhaps, the officials—especially the new ones, with their straps or badges—put on too many airs. Of all places in the world, the hospitals of American young men and soldiers, wounded in the volunteer service of their country, ought to be exempt from mere conventional military airs and etiquette of shoulder-straps. But they are not exempt.

W. W.

Source: Walt Whitman, *The Wound Dresser: A Series of Letters Written from the Hospitals in Washington During the War of the Rebellion,* ed. Richard Maurice Bucke (Small, Maynard & Company, 1897; Project Gutenberg, 2011), chap. 1, http://www.gutenberg.org/ebooks/35725.

Louisa May Alcott in a portrait taken after the war, in 1870

HOSPITAL SKETCHES

LOUISA MAY ALCOTT, USA

All having eaten, drank, and rested, the surgeons began their rounds; and I took my first lesson in the art of dressing wounds. It wasn't a festive scene, by any means; for Dr. P., whose Aid I constituted myself, fell to work with a vigor which soon convinced me that I was a weaker vessel, though nothing would have induced me to confess it then. He had served in the Crimea, and seemed to regard a dilapidated body very much as I should have regarded a damaged garment; and, turning up his cuffs, whipped out a very unpleasant looking housewife, cutting, sawing, patching and piecing, with the enthusiasm of an accomplished surgical seamstress; explaining the process, in scientific terms, to the patient, meantime; which, of course, was immensely cheering and comfortable. There was an uncanny sort of fascination in watching him, as he peered and probed into the mechanism of those wonderful bodies, whose mysteries he understood so well. The more intricate the wound, the better he liked it. A poor private, with both legs off, and shot through the lungs, possessed more attractions for him than a dozen generals, slightly scratched in some "masterly retreat;" and had any one appeared in small pieces, requesting to be put together again, he would have considered it a special dispensation. The amputations were reserved till the morrow, and the merciful magic of ether was not thought necessary that day, so the poor souls had to bear their pains as best they might. It is all very well to talk of the patience of woman; and far be it from me to pluck that feather from her cap, for, heaven knows, she isn't allowed to wear many; but the patient endurance of these men, under trials of the flesh, was truly wonderful; their fortitude seemed contagious, and scarcely a cry escaped them, though

I often longed to groan for them, when pride kept their white lips shut, while great drops stood upon their foreheads, and the bed shook with the irrepressible tremor of their tortured bodies. One or two Irishmen anathematized the doctors with the frankness of their nation, and ordered the Virgin to stand by them, as if she had been the wedded Biddy to whom they could administer the poker, if she didn't; but, as a general thing, the work went on in silence, broken only by some quiet request for roller, instruments, or plaster, a sigh from the patient, or a sympathizing murmur from the nurse.

It was long past noon before these repairs were even partially made; and, having got the bodies of my boys into something like order, the next task was to minister to their minds, by writing letters to the anxious souls at home; answering questions, reading papers, taking possession of money and valuables; for the eighth commandment was reduced to a very fragmentary condition, both by the blacks and whites, who ornamented our hospital with their presence. Pocket books, purses, miniatures, and watches, were sealed up, labelled, and handed over to the matron, till such times as the owners thereof were ready to depart homeward or campward again. The letters dictated to me, and revised by me, that afternoon, would have made an excellent chapter for some future history of the war; for, like that which Thackeray's "Ensign Spooney" wrote his mother just before Waterloo, they were "full of affection, pluck, and bad spelling;" nearly all giving lively accounts of the battle, and ending with a somewhat sudden plunge from patriotism to provender, desiring "Marm," "Mary Ann," or "Aunt Peters," to send along some pies, pickles, sweet stuff, and apples, "to yourn in haste," Joe, Sam, or Ned, as the case might be.

My little Sergeant insisted on trying to scribble something with his left hand, and patiently accomplished some half dozen lines of hieroglyphics, which he gave me to fold and direct, with a boyish blush, that rendered a glimpse of "My Dearest Jane," unnecessary, to assure me that the heroic lad had been more successful in the service of Commander-in-Chief Cupid than that of Gen. Mars; and a charming little romance blossomed instanter in Nurse Periwinkle's romantic fancy, though no further confidences were made that day, for Sergeant fell asleep, and, judging from his tranquil face, visited his absent sweetheart in the pleasant land of dreams.

At five o'clock a great bell rang, and the attendants flew, not to arms, but to their trays, to bring up supper, when a second uproar announced that it was ready. The new comers woke at the sound; and I presently discovered that it took a very bad wound to incapacitate the defenders of the faith for the consumption of their rations; the amount that some of them sequestered was amazing; but when I suggested the probability of a famine hereafter, to the matron, that motherly lady cried out: "Bless their hearts, why shouldn't they eat? It's their only amusement; so fill every one, and, if there's not enough ready to-night, I'll lend my share to the Lord by giving it to the boys." And, whipping up her coffee-pot and plate of toast, she gladdened the eyes and stomachs of two or three dissatisfied heroes, by serving them with a liberal hand; and I haven't the slightest doubt that, having cast her bread upon the waters, it came back buttered, as another large-hearted old lady was wont to say.

Then came the doctor's evening visit; the administration of medicines; washing feverish faces; smoothing tumbled beds; wetting wounds; singing lullabies; and preparations for the night. By eleven, the last labor of love was done; the last "good night" spoken; and, if any needed a reward for that day's work, they surely received it, in the silent eloquence of those long lines of faces, showing pale and peaceful in the shaded rooms, as we quitted them, followed by grateful glances that lighted us to bed, where rest, the sweetest, made our pillows soft, while Night and Nature took our places, filling that great house of pain with the healing miracles of Sleep, and his diviner brother, Death.

Source: L. M. Alcott, *Hospital Sketches* (Boston: James Redpath, 1863; Project Gutenberg, 2003), chap. 3, http://www.gutenberg.org/ebooks/3837.

WOUNDED AT CHICKAMAUGA

PVT. WILLIAM FLETCHER, CSA

From this point I will take the reader to Chickamauga. It was reported that Longstreet's corps was reinforcing Johnson. When we left the train we were marched a few miles and thrown in line of battle and forward no great distance until we were near the enemy and were ordered to lie down. While lying here, to our right the battle was raging and a few bullets being sent from our front that were coming uncomfortably close, under the nervous strain. I fell asleep as I had often done before, under like conditions, and there was, from what I could learn, a small percentage who would take the same. Sleep always has a quieting effect, if only for a few minutes, and I have often remarked that if a fellow wanted a fight out of me, I would advise him not to wake me up to get it, for I would be cocked and primed for the fray. I was shaken and ordered to rise, for just then the enemy raised a yell and charged, throwing a hail of bullets our way. We were ordered to charge, so we plunged forward with a yell, firing as we went. When near, the enemy broke and with but little effort at returning fire, so things were going fast our way. A short distance to the enemy's rear where they started the charge was a high well-built worm rail fence, and as I suppose it was the least of their thoughts of having to return that way, or they would have had it torn down to clear their rear. At this point we were crowding them so close that they had no time to push down the fence or to climb it. My position in line put the corner of the fence about fifty yards to the left in passing to the front and about sixty yards from the corner stood a house about ten feet from the fence; and on the opposite end of the house was a dirt chimney. This I would pass near, going to the front, the enemy who were to my front and right were running over a hundred yards off. A great number of the enemy who were running down the fence and turning the corner attracted my attention from my immediate front. Between the house and fence there was a block that extended nearly back to the corner of the fence—a great majority of them were in a pushing motion and jammed and at close range. I got two shots and thought—oh, for a shotgun loaded with buckshot! I saw I could not get loaded in time to get a third shot before the jamb would be broken, so I struck a long trot and was loading to get a shot just as I would clear the far corner of the house.

I was passing the end of the house about twenty feet to my left when something struck my left foot as I had it up and thrown forward. As I came down on it I fell forward, striking the edge of the hole that was made in removing dirt for the chimney; so in rolling into the hole I landed on my back, stretched full length. Instantly I saw I was well protected, and from sounds, I supposed a piece of flying shell had hit hard enough to trip me. There had been no pain up to this time, so the idea struck me that I was not wounded and had a coward's position, and I was liable to be seen in it. I raised my head to get up, and as I cast my eyes to my feet, I saw the leather on the left shoe torn near center on inside. I turned my foot and saw rent on the outside near the heel; I quickly removed the shoe and found I had a bad foot wound made by a bullet. The hole, when lying down, was all one could wish to protect; but fear of capture put me at once hopping. As I was passing back about seventy-five yards, I was near an oak tree about twenty inches in diameter; there was a wounded Yank sitting down, leaning against it. This gave him protection from the bullets of his own men. Pain here struck me and I felt faint, so with a hop or two I was at the Yank's side, and as there was not room enough for two, I gave him a shove, saying: "The day is ours." He fell over in a doubled position on his side, made no attempt to move, but was groaning. I was not more than well seated with back resting against the tree, when the sound of volley firing rang out and bullets flying thick, and the Texas yell raised. I know boys were charging. I instantly threw myself far enough around the tree to see the front. There were our boys charging in scattered battle line and the enemy firing from solid column. I knew the enemy were doing but little harm as their bullets were flying high, but I thought discretion was the better part of valor and that I would hop on; so I started and would become blind and fall about every hundred feet, but had no more than hit the ground full length before I was scrambling up and off. This falling continued for some distance, but all the time I had an eye for a dead Yankee to prowl; so I soon was near one and stopped, kneeling and went through him, as it was called. He was a poor corpse and it was a poor haul—his knapsack was good but was light and as I did not have tune to make an honorable exchange, I had it off and on my shoulders, over mine, in quick time. I picked up a gun and tried to use as a crutch, but soon dropped it, as I found I could make faster time hopping and speed was what I was after. I struck a "hide-out" and he offered help. I told him he should be at the front; that I was making good time. He said he was going no further; and I said: "You can help me then, and in that way be doing something for your country." He was quickly by my side and I was resting my hand on his shoulder but saw it retarded my speed. I became blinded and fell. He helped me up, asking if I was shot again. I replied: "No, and will not need your services." Our reserve was standing just in front. He pushed on through, a few yards ahead of me; was asked how the front was, and replied that they were killing lots of our men. As I came up, they opened ranks and let me through, asking me how the front was. I replied: "We are giving them hell, boys." There was a chorus of voices: "He has been there, you bet," and such like.

A few hundred yards to the rear of the reserve I found an ambulance. This was my second wound and I never got aid from better bearers and only saw the two men at Manassas, so I guess I always got out early in the game. At an opportune time I examined my knapsack, found several well written sweet letters and from the wording, that fellow sure had some sweet girl stuck on him for she was anticipating a happy meeting and fulfillment of vows, when the "Rebs" were whipped and the cruel war was over. Letters did not arouse any sympathy in me, nor have I felt one pang of regret for being a party to breaking up that match. She wanted me whipped—she got that; I wanted dead Yankees—I got that. So both at least got part of their wants satisfied.

When I arrived at the field infirmary it was dark and there was straw for bedding. I was put in about fifty feet from operating table, with a few others between me and it. I lay there all night, bleeding slowly, as my wound was not of a nature that required immediate attention. Near the table, but not in line, was a stout young man who was shot through the head. From the sides the brain could be seen oozing out. He seemed to be suffering greatly and would rise, make a step or two, and fall. He repeated this time and time again for quite a while after daylight. I don't know at what hour he was brought in, but I thought how brutal human custom was in this particular, and wondered if it was handed down from barbarism and why it was that doctor or friend could not end one's misery, even if done with the best method at hand and that was only a rock or club. With brutes we sympathize and aid—with man we do not, for death is the only relief. I have often heard the remark: "Poor fellow; he had better ten thousand times be dead." I look upon it as cowardice in time of great need, for true friendship is he who comes in when the world goes out. During the night there had been a great number of wounded brought to this point. The doctors looked worn. You would often hear at such times that they drank too much, but it must take a good nerve to stand it and the best remedy to prevent breaking down to go through, as I have seen it, the long hours that their duty calls. Some say that it is not necessary, or other preventatives would do as well. When such remarks are heard by me, I say, "your opinion is not worthy of weight, as you have not been tried."

As I lay on my pallet that morning and heard the continuous roar of battle to the front, I gave the different parts of the line the closest attention from the rifle roar. If I detected the least change in sound on any part of the line it was figured as far as my reason could in shaping the lay of the line of battle, and as the roar went on at times I would mark out in mind some quick change, some parts apparently at a standstill. At one time I had our left center giving, and remarked that if it did not stop soon I would start for the depot, which was several miles off. One of the "F" boys standing near, said: "Bill, how foolish; you would drop on the wayside long before you reached the point." My reply was: "I can hop as fast as I can walk, and it does not tire me much more than walking." Finally there was a perceptible decrease of sound on the entire line, and I felt much relieved. Slowly but surely our whole line was moving to the front and it was only a short time before one could not picture the shape of the battle line as the distance was so great that there was no distinction in the roar. One of "F" boys had received a shot in the side of his face and through the nose and was passing through, seeing what there was to be seen. He looked so disfigured by the shot and swelling that he looked funny. When he saw me he came nearer and we each explained the nature of our wounds and about the point we had received them. I then commenced joking him, telling him he would make better success courting when he got back, with his back to the girls. When I got through, he said: "That will be better than you; as you can't turn any way to hide your wooden leg." I said: "Yes, if I had one." I was debating in my mind on what the doctors would decide when I went on the operating table and was chloroformed for probing examination, so his joke struck me in a tender point that was hurting before he spoke. He said: "Don't you see that man up there (calling his name); he will come first, and you watch and see what they will do for him, for when I was at the table, Doctor Roberts (who was the regiment surgeon) told me that from what he could see, passing, the man mentioned and you would lose a foot." By this time I was well worked up and said: "You are a DL, Frank." He said: "Bill, watch," and walked on. His words sounded as one talking badly through his nose, and were laughable—when one was in humor for it. So I lay and watched. The man mentioned was soon on the table, examined, and foot cast in scrap heap. Just before operation was complete, or rather the binding was complete, Dr. Roberts started my way. He halted when at my feet, and said: "Fletcher, I want to examine your wound," and in a stooping position, had partly got his finger in the wound, before I realized what his mode of examination would be. Under the pain caused and the impulse of the moment, my right foot was quickly against his left shoulder, and as his head was toward me, with a quick shove, I sent him backwards, but not hard enough but what he could keep from falling. His face was flushed when he steadied himself, and he said: "I will leave you alone, without treatment." My reply was: "Doc, that is what I want, and the fellow that I considered most to blame would make the mistake of his life if treated without my sanction, as that man (calling his name) has been treated— put under influence of something and when he comes to, his foot gone."

That evening I was hauled to the station and put aboard car and was off, not knowing where. Was taken off to Augusta, Georgia, and I thought the doctor had sent me to the limit of distance. I was quartered in a good size church, bunked in a pew, with space filled in. I lay there with my head to the wall and feet to the aisle so my wound was convenient to dress, which was once in twenty-four hours. I attended to wetting cloth from time to time. The most of the dressing was done by Sisters of Charity— it was my first experience and I was in love with the women and the uniform at once and have not gotten over it yet; for there is a feeling of gratitude uppermost when and where my eyes behold them. I have often thought: was that branch of the human family, as it were, the mother of the Red Cross Society. My early education, but I am proud to say not at home, however, was far different. It came from the Methodist and Baptist pulpits, as they were the only denominations that I had heard preach, and I was reared under their influence until seventeen years old. Nearly all of the old grandmothers, both white and black, caught on and there was no place in heaven for a catholic; but my opinion changed, after falling in love and my religion's efforts ceased feeling if there was a God "He was a just one," and if He in justice consigned the sisters to hell, there was no use of me trying, as I had already done enough to be on the unpardonable list. I am thankful, however, expressions have changed, if opinion has not, for the old soldiers would have been scrapping to this day. Don't discredit me, however, as throwing discredit at the people of Augusta, as one could not be more fortunate than to be allotted as I and quite a number were, but the sisters were on to their job and were thrown more in a motherly contact with the boys when the most of them were longing for a mother's or sister's care. I was soon furnished with a strip of bandage by a sister, long enough to swing my foot to the shoulder, and I sure did play the act of expert hopper in town, as I was free to go and come at will, and distance had no terror for me. I would nearly every day take a long jaunt through different parts of the town trying, however, daily to get a pair of crutches. I made repeated applications at the hospital and shop, but it was some time before I obtained a pair. The shop men got to telling me that I was at the bottom of the list. I attracted some attention on my hopping rounds, and was often remarked about. The crutches finally came and I was proud of them, not as I was tired, but wanted a change. Gangrene had started among the wounded and there was an appeal notice published asking the citizens to take care of all the wounded possible, as it was contagious. A Mrs. McKinnon called in a buggy for one. I was hustled in and my treatment at the McKinnon home was royal; but it was of short duration. Gangrene in a few days set in where the bullet entered and I was returned to the hospital for treatment. Here they burned the wound with acid and it was very painful. The first three applications nearly gave me the horrors and especially the first. If I had been a drunkard I would probably have thought I at least was threatened with delirium tremens, as the worn or snakey feeling would start at the mouth of wound and make a hurried zig-zag run up near the knee, then would return as though backing out, and running out of the wound. The relief was instantaneous when the sensation had passed out, but was repeated at short intervals for two hours for the first time, the others of less duration. By the time it was through, I was nearly exhausted. This treatment, if I remember correctly, was kept up for seven days, burning each day. After the distressing muscular sensation had passed off, the mind dread was well rooted and all the unfortunates would look forward to the coming day with dread. The hospital medical attendants through their ignorance caused untold suffering. I suppose the disease was new to them. There finally arrived a doctor who was said to be a hospital inspector. He stopped the burning treatment and had warm poultice applied. Soon after the poultice application there was a great expression of relief and joy, both by patient and nurse. In a few days the wounds had sloughed and were healing nicely.

My foot was gradually straightening or turning down, which would have caused me to walk on my toes. This had gone so far that the doctors who examined it left it to me, saying they would break it if I wished, but advised against it, as I would not have one chance in ten of saving it. I said I would prefer life with a crooked leg and walking on toes, to an artificial foot; so they said they would consider it no more. Near the front of the hospital, in the center of the street, was a public well where I would go in the morning to wash my face. I would jump on the platform, which was about eighteen inches high, lean my crutch against the pump barrel and rest my knee on it to steady myself, make a few strokes and wash as water was running out of the spout. The Catholic church was only a short distance from the pump, on the same side of the street as the hospital. There was some order of service of unusual attendance one morning, and while I was washing there were a number of women and girls who came pouring out at the front entrance. I knew there would be quite a lot pass my way, so I was in a hurry to get through before they commenced passing. My knee slipped down the crutch until my toes touched the floor. The pain was sharp and from some cause I fell forward and heard the tearing loose or breaking at or near my ankle. I rolled off the platform in the dust, but was up instantly with crutches under my arm making fast time for the hospital, struck my bunk and sent a fast runner for doctors. They responded promptly, made an examination and said I had done what they were afraid to do, but would do their best to save my foot. The pain was intense. In about forty-eight hours the doctors reported it safe and instructed working ankle joint and dressing it back often, hurt or no hurt, and when it got well I would have a serviceable foot. I followed instructions, and came out all O. K.

Soon I was transferred some distance with others to a small town and remained there until I reported for duty. This place fed different from the Augusta hospital. They had the table set and the food allowance at each place. So, near meal time there was quite a crowd jammed against and near the dining room door, and when the door was opened, there was a scramble and rush to get the best place. The best place was the one the fellow thought as he passed the side of the table that had the most food at it; but it was like picking apples out of an assorted pile. Men in our condition were generally hoggish, so there was quite a murmur of complaint about being half fed, and I was one of the chronic grumblers, as I could not see how we could get able for duty, being half fed. One day I was crutching it out in town and seeing a pair of scales in a store, the idea struck me to weigh. I went in, asked permission to weigh and was granted; so I hopped on the platform, leaned my crutch against the scale and tipped the beam at one hundred and eighty-two pounds. I tried weights back and forth on beam and found that they were in working order. The store man was watching nearby. I asked him if the scales were right and he replied: "Yes." I asked for both buyer and seller. He said: "Why do you ask?" Answer:

"Because I weigh one hundred and eighty-two pounds and I am not get-ting half fed at the hospital—and one hundred and sixty-five pounds is the most I ever weighed, well fed." He laughed heartily, and said: "Young man, it is not the amount of food you eat that you do best on. It is on natural requirements. Appetite is often greedy and should be guarded." I thanked him and returned to the hospital, thinking he had read O. S. Fowler's books. I told the boys in my room my experience, and said: "Boys, let's quit grumbling for I guess these fellows are on to their job and are fattening us up so we will be able to live a while by sucking our paw when they return us for duty."

Source: W. A. Fletcher, *Rebel Private, Front and Rear: Experiences and Observations from the Early Fifties through the Civil War* (Beaumont, TX: Press of the Greer Print, 1908), https://archive.org/details/rebelprivatefron00flet.

THE THIRD DAY AT STONES RIVER

LT. COL. GILBERT C. KNIFFIN, USA

Darkness covered the battlefield. The roar of artillery, the rattle of musketry, the hoarse shouts of command had ceased, and in the silence that followed there fell upon the ears of the soldiers on picket the groans of men in mortal agony lying within the space that separated the lines. In rear of the pickets men sank upon the ground where they stood and shivered through the night without fires, for the faintest flash of light on either side became a target for alert artillerists. A cup of hot coffee, that *Dominus donari* to the weary soldier, on this night of all nights when he needed it most, was denied him. All through the night the ambulances passed to and fro on the road to the hospitals, where further torture awaited the wounded, unless the angel of death kindly relieved them of the ministrations of the surgeons. A space twenty yards in front of the White House, near Overall's Creek, was covered with the mangled forms of men awaiting their turn upon the operating tables. Inside were groups of surgeons with sleeves rolled up to the elbows, their brawny arms red with blood, one handling the saw, another the knife, another the probe, while others bound up the bleeding stumps and turned the patient, henceforth the Nation's ward, over to nurses, who bore them tenderly away. In a corner lay a ghastly heap of arms and legs and hands and feet, useless forevermore. The busy fingers which had indented the last fond message to the anxious wife or mother would never caress them more. Does this horrible recital grate upon the ear? It is as much a part of the history of a battle as is the furious charge and repulse from which it resulted. Forty years have passed since that awful scene was witnessed. The stalwart young men left upon the firing line are old men now, and, in the judgment of some chiefs of bureaus, too old to longer serve the Government.

Source: Gilbert C. Kniffin, *The Third Day at Stone's River* (Washington, DC: Military Order of the Loyal Legion of the United States War Papers 69, 1907; Project Gutenberg, 2010), http://www.gutenberg.org/ebooks/32039.

1863

Trees shattered by artillery fire, Chancellorsville battlefield
LIBRARY OF CONGRESS

CHANCELLORSVILLE

MAY 1-4, 1863
BRIG. GEN. ABNER DOUBLEDAY, USA

At Chancellorsville, in Virginia's Spotsylvania County, Robert E. Lee led what many believe to be his most brilliant battle, against Union forces headed by USA Maj. Gen. Joseph A. Hooker. Outnumbered nearly two to one, Lee took the highly unorthodox risk of repeatedly dividing his army, harrying Union flanks and stymieing Hooker's aspirations to envelop the Confederates. Hooker's best chances occurred early in the battle, but—with some justification—"Fightin' Joe" feared that Lee was preparing to spring an unwelcome surprise. Cavalry under CSA Maj. Gen. J. E. B. Stuart screened Stonewall Jackson's advance along the Union flank, which further complicated Hooker's task. Instead of maintaining the offensive, Hooker adopted a defensive posture, much to the dismay of his staff. Fighting was brutal, chaotic, and confusing, with heavy casualties on both sides. Chancellorsville was a Confederate triumph, but the victory had Pyrrhic elements for Lee. First of all, the Army of Northern Virginia could ill afford such high losses. Also, numbered amongst the slain was none other than Jackson himself, shot in the dark by his own troops, who feared a Yankee ruse. After Chancellorsville, Lee sorely missed the presence of his most fearsome officer. Here, USA Brig. Gen. Abner Doubleday recaps the swirl of battle that made Chancellorsville such a costly ordeal for the vanquished—and the victors.

The close of the battle of Chancellorsville found the Union army still strong in numbers, defeated, but not disheartened, and ready, as soon as reinforcements and supplies arrived, and a brief period of rest and recuperation ensued, to take the field again. To resist the effects of this defeat and recruit our armies required, however, great determination and serious effort on the part of the Administration; for a large and powerful party still clogged and impeded its efforts, and were allowed full liberty to chill the patriotism of the masses, and oppose, with tongue and pen and every species of indirection, all efficient action which looked to national defense. This opposition was so strong and active that the President almost preferred the risk of losing another battle to the commotion which would be excited by attempts to enforce the draft; for hitherto we had relied entirely on voluntary enlistments to increase our strength in the field. Men are chilled by disaster and do not readily enlist after a defeat; yet the terms of service of thirty thousand of the two years' and nine months' men were expiring, and something had to be done. Our army, however, at the end of May was still formidable in numbers, and too strongly posted to be effectually assailed; especially as it had full and free communication with Washington and the North, and could be assisted in case of need by the loyal militia of the free States.

The rebels had obtained a triumph, rather than a substantial victory, at Chancellorsville. It was gained, too, at a ruinous expense of life, and when the battle was over they found themselves too weak to follow up our retreating forces. While the whole South was exulting, their great commander, General Lee, was profoundly depressed. The resources of the Davis Government in men and means were limited, and it was evident that without a foreign alliance, prolonged defensive warfare by an army so far from its base, would ultimately exhaust the seceding States, without accomplishing their independence. It became necessary, therefore, for General Lee to choose one of two plans of campaign: Either to fall back on the center of his supplies at Richmond, and stand a siege there, or to invade the North. By retiring on Richmond he would save the great labor of transporting food and war material to the frontier, and would remove the Northern army still further from its sources of supply and its principal depots. One circumstance, however, would probably in any event, have impelled him to take the bolder course. The situation in Vicksburg was becoming alarming. It was evident the town must fall and with its surrender the Federal fleet would soon regain possession of the Mississippi. The fall of Vicksburg, supplemented by the retreat of Lee's army on Richmond, would dishearten the Southern people, and stimulate the North to renewed efforts. It was essential, therefore, to counterbalance the impending disaster in the West by some brilliant exploit in the East.

There was perhaps another reason for this great forward movement, founded on the relation of the Confederacy to the principal European powers. England still made a pretense of neutrality, but the aristocracy and ruling classes sided with the South, and a large association of their most influential men was established at Manchester to aid the slaveholding oligarchy. The rebels were fighting us with English guns and war material, furnished by blockade runners; while English Shenandoahs and Alabamas, manned by British seamen, under the Confederate flag, burned our merchant vessels and swept our commercial marine from the ocean. The French Government was equally hostile to us, and there was hardly a kingdom in Europe which did not sympathize with the South, allied as they were by their feudal customs to the deplorable system of Southern slavery. Russia alone favored our cause, and stood ready, if need be, to assist us with her fleet; probably more from antagonism to England and France, than from any other motive. The agents of the Confederate Government stated in their official despatches that if General Lee could establish his army firmly on Northern soil England would at once acknowledge the independence of the South; in which case ample loans could not only be obtained on Southern securities, but a foreign alliance might be formed, and perhaps a fleet furnished to re-open the Southern ports.

While thus elated by hopes of foreign intervention, the Confederate spies and sympathizers who thronged the North greatly encouraged the Davis Government by their glowing accounts of the disaffection there, in consequence of the heavy taxation, rendered necessary by the war, and by the unpopularity of the draft, which would soon have to be enforced as a defensive measure. They overrated the influence of the *Copperhead* or anti-war party, and prophesied that a rebel invasion would be followed by outbreaks in the principal cities, which would paralyze every effort to reinforce the Federal forces in the field.

These reasons would have been quite sufficient of themselves to induce Lee to make the movement, but he himself gives an additional one. He hoped by this advance to draw Hooker out, where he could strike him a decisive blow, and thus ensure the permanent triumph of the Confederacy. He was weary of all this marching, campaigning, and bloodshed, and was strongly desirous of settling the whole matter at once. Having been reinforced after the battle of Chancellorsville by Longstreet's two divisions and a large body of conscripts, he determined to advance. On May 31st, his force, according to rebel statements, amounted to 88,754, of which 68,352 were ready for duty. Recruits, too, were constantly coming in from the draft, which was rigidly enforced in the Southern States.

Source: Abner Doubleday, *Chancellorsville and Gettysburg Campaigns of the Civil War* (New York: Charles Scribner's Sons, 1882; Project Gutenberg, 2007), chap. 9, http://www.gutenberg.org/ebooks/20762.

SIEGE OF VICKSBURG

MAY 18-JULY 4, 1863
GEN. ULYSSES S. GRANT, USA

Vicksburg was one of the most important Union victories of the war. It gave navigable control of the Mississippi River to the Union, split the Confederacy into two disconnected portions, and assured that, as a thankful President Lincoln put it when he received the message of triumph from General Grant, "The Father of Waters again goes unvexed to the sea." A fortified city atop commanding bluffs on the river's eastern shore, Vicksburg was the final Confederate strong-point along the Mississippi River. Its guns menaced river shipping, which made it so strategic. Grant successfully besieged it, cutting off CSA Lt. Gen. John C. Pemberton's forces within. The merciless siege grew tighter and tighter, making life under bombardment increasingly trying for defenders and civilians alike. Naval elements under Rear Adm. David D. Porter played a valuable part in the victory. Union determination never waned, even when assaults were fended off by Confederates increasingly desperate to obey Jefferson Davis's order to hold out at all costs. Grant displayed brilliant generalship, aided by highly competent corps commanders, including Maj. Gen. William Tecumseh Sherman. A message by Pemberton to Grant seeking terms was met by the demand for unconditional surrender, delighting Northerners hungry for good news and giving new meaning to "U.S. Grant." Nevertheless, the Union general magnanimously granted Confederate prisoners their parole. When many returned to Confederate fighting ranks, formal prisoner exchanges came to an end. Bitterness now colored every phase of the conflict.

Vicksburg's capture, on July 4, 1863, caused Southern despair and put Grant squarely in the spotlight. Lincoln decided this was the general to come eastward and finally put an end to the depredations of Lee's Army of Northern Virginia. The war would thenceforth be fought along very different lines. Here, Grant's memoirs detail this culminating battle of the Trans-Mississippi theater.

I now determined upon a regular siege—to "out-camp the enemy," as it were, and to incur no more losses. The experience of the 22d convinced officers and men that this was best, and they went to work on the defences and approaches with a will. With the navy holding the river, the investment of Vicksburg was complete. As long as we could hold our position the enemy was limited in supplies of food, men and munitions of war to what they had on hand. These could not last always.

The crossing of troops at Bruinsburg commenced April 30th. On the 18th of May the army was in rear of Vicksburg. On the 19th, just twenty days after the crossing, the city was completely invested and an assault had been made: five distinct battles (besides continuous skirmishing) had been fought and won by the Union forces; the capital of the State had fallen and its arsenals, military manufactories and everything useful for military purposes had been destroyed; an average of about one hundred and eighty miles had been marched by the troops engaged; but five days' rations had been issued, and no forage; over six thousand prisoners had been captured, and as many more of the enemy had been killed or wounded; twenty-seven heavy cannon and sixty-one field-pieces had fallen into our hands; and four hundred miles of the river, from Vicksburg to Port Hudson, had become ours. The Union force that had crossed the Mississippi River up to this time was less than forty-three thousand men. One division of these, Blair's, only arrived in time to take part in the battle of Champion's Hill, but was not engaged there; and one brigade, Ransom's of McPherson's corps, reached the field after the battle. The enemy had at Vicksburg, Grand Gulf, Jackson, and on the roads between these places, over sixty thousand men. They were in their own country, where no rear guards were necessary. The country is admirable for defense, but difficult for the conduct of an offensive campaign. All their troops had to be met. We were fortunate, to say the least, in meeting them in detail: at Port Gibson seven or eight thousand; at Raymond, five thousand; at Jackson, from eight to eleven thousand; at Champion's Hill, twenty-five thousand; at the Big Black, four thousand. A part of those met at Jackson were all that was left of those encountered at Raymond. They were beaten in detail by a force smaller than their own, upon their own ground. Our loss up to this time was:

	KILLED	WOUNDED	MISSING
Port Gibson	131	719	25
South Fork Bayou Pierre		1	
Skirmishes, May 3	1	9	
Fourteen Mile Creek	6	24	
Raymond	66	339	39
Jackson	42	251	7
Champion's Hill	410	1,844	187
Big Black	39	237	3
Bridgeport		1	
Total	695	3,425	259

Of the wounded many were but slightly so, and continued on duty. Not half of them were disabled for any length of time.

After the unsuccessful assault of the 22d the work of the regular siege began. Sherman occupied the right starting from the river above Vicksburg, McPherson the centre (McArthur's division now with him) and McClernand the left, holding the road south to Warrenton. Lauman's division arrived at this time and was placed on the extreme left of the line.

In the interval between the assaults of the 19th and 22d, roads had been completed from the Yazoo River and Chickasaw Bayou, around the rear of the army, to enable us to bring up supplies of food and ammunition; ground had been selected and cleared on which the troops were to be encamped, and tents and cooking utensils were brought up. The troops had been without these from the time of crossing the Mississippi up to this time. All was now ready for the pick and spade. Prentiss and Hurlbut were ordered to send forward every man that could be spared. Cavalry especially was wanted to watch the fords along the Big Black, and to observe Johnston. I knew that Johnston was receiving reinforcements from Bragg, who was confronting Rosecrans in Tennessee. Vicksburg was so important to the enemy that I believed he would make the most strenuous efforts to raise the siege, even at the risk of losing ground elsewhere.

My line was more than fifteen miles long, extending from Haines' Bluff to Vicksburg, thence to Warrenton. The line of the enemy was about seven. In addition to this, having an enemy at Canton and Jackson, in our rear, who was being constantly reinforced, we required a second line of defence facing the other way. I had not troops enough under my command to man these. General Halleck appreciated the situation and, without being asked, forwarded reinforcements with all possible dispatch.

The ground about Vicksburg is admirable for defense. On the north it is about two hundred feet above the Mississippi River at the highest point and very much cut up by the washing rains; the ravines were grown up with cane and underbrush, while the sides and tops were covered with a dense forest. Farther south the ground flattens out somewhat, and was in cultivation. But here, too, it was cut up by ravines and small streams. The enemy's line of defense followed the crest of a ridge from the river north of the city eastward, then southerly around to the Jackson road, full three miles back of the city; thence in a southwesterly direction to the river. Deep ravines of the description given lay in front of these defenses. As there is a succession of gullies, cut out by rains along the side of the ridge, the line was necessarily very irregular. To follow each of these spurs with entrenchments, so as to command the slopes on either side, would have lengthened their line very much. Generally therefore, or in many places, their line would run from near the head of one gully nearly straight to the head of another, and an outer work triangular in shape, generally open in the rear, was thrown up on the point; with a few men in this outer work they commanded the approaches to the main line completely.

The work to be done, to make our position as strong against the enemy as his was against us, was very great. The problem was also complicated by our wanting our line as near that of the enemy as possible. We had but four engineer officers with us. Captain Prime, of the Engineer Corps, was the chief, and the work at the beginning was mainly directed by him. His health soon gave out, when he was succeeded by Captain Comstock, also of the Engineer Corps. To provide assistants on such a long line I directed that all officers who had graduated at West Point, where they had necessarily to study military engineering, should in addition to their other duties assist in the work.

The chief quartermaster and the chief commissary were graduates. The chief commissary, now the Commissary-General of the Army, begged off, however, saying that there was nothing in engineering that he was good for unless he would do for a sap-roller. As soldiers require rations while working in the ditches as well as when marching and fighting, and as we would be sure to lose him if he was used as a sap-roller, I let him off. The general is a large man; weighs two hundred and twenty pounds, and is not tall.

We had no siege guns except six thirty-two pounders, and there were none at the West to draw from. Admiral Porter, however, supplied us with a battery of navy-guns of large calibre, and with these, and the field artillery used in the campaign, the siege began. The first thing to do was to get the artillery in batteries where they would occupy commanding positions; then establish the camps, under cover from the fire of the enemy but as near up as possible; and then construct rifle-pits and covered ways, to connect the entire command by the shortest route. The enemy did not harass us much while we were constructing our batteries. Probably their artillery ammunition was short; and their infantry was kept down by our sharpshooters, who were always on the alert and ready to fire at a head whenever it showed itself above the rebel works.

In no place were our lines more than six hundred yards from the enemy. It was necessary, therefore, to cover our men by something more than the ordinary parapet. To give additional protection sand bags, bullet-proof, were placed along the tops of the parapets far enough apart to make loop-holes for musketry. On top of these, logs were put. By these means the men were enabled to walk about erect when off duty, without fear of annoyance from sharpshooters. The enemy used in their defense explosive musket-balls, no doubt thinking that, bursting over our men in the trenches, they would do some execution; but I do not remember a single case where a man was injured by a piece of one of these shells. When they were hit and the ball exploded, the wound was terrible. In these cases a solid ball would have hit as well. Their use is barbarous, because they produce increased suffering without any corresponding advantage to those using them.

The enemy could not resort to our method to protect their men, because we had an inexhaustible supply of ammunition to draw upon and used it freely. Splinters from the timber would have made havoc among the men behind.

There were no mortars with the besiegers, except what the navy had in front of the city; but wooden ones were made by taking logs of the toughest wood that could be found, boring them out for six or twelve pound shells and binding them with strong iron bands. These answered as cochorns, and shells were successfully thrown from them into the trenches of the enemy.

The labor of building the batteries and entrenching was largely done by the pioneers, assisted by negroes who came within our lines and who were paid for their work; but details from the troops had often to be made. The work was pushed forward as rapidly as possible, and when an advanced position was secured and covered from the fire of the enemy the batteries were advanced. By the 30th of June there were two hundred and twenty guns in position, mostly light field-pieces, besides a battery of heavy guns belonging to, manned and commanded by the navy. We were now as strong for defence against the garrison of Vicksburg as they were against us; but I knew that Johnston was in our rear, and was receiving constant reinforcements from the east. He had at this time a larger force than I had had at any time prior to the battle of Champion's Hill.

As soon as the news of the arrival of the Union army behind Vicksburg reached the North, floods of visitors began to pour in. Some came to gratify curiosity; some to see sons or brothers who had passed through the terrible ordeal; members of the Christian and Sanitary Associations came to minister to the wants of the sick and the wounded. Often those coming to see a son or brother would bring a dozen or two of poultry. They did not know how little the gift would be appreciated. Many of the soldiers had lived so much on chickens, ducks and turkeys without bread during the march, that the sight of poultry, if they could get bacon, almost took away their appetite. But the intention was good.

Among the earliest arrivals was the Governor of Illinois, with most of the State officers. I naturally wanted to show them what there was of most interest. In Sherman's front the ground was the most broken and most wooded, and more was to be seen without exposure. I therefore took them to Sherman's headquarters and presented them. Before starting out to look at the lines—possibly while Sherman's horse was being saddled—there were many questions asked about the late campaign, about which the North had been so imperfectly informed. There was a little knot around Sherman and another around me, and I heard Sherman repeating, in the most animated manner, what he had said to me when we first looked down from Walnut Hills upon the land below on the 18th of May, adding: "Grant is entitled to every bit of the credit for the campaign; I opposed it. I wrote him a letter about it." But for this speech it is not likely that Sherman's opposition would have ever been heard of. His untiring energy and great efficiency during the campaign entitle him to a full share of all the credit due for its success. He could not have done more if the plan had been his own.

When General Sherman first learned of the move I proposed to make, he called to see me about it. I recollect that I had transferred my headquarters from a boat in the river to a house a short distance back from the levee. I was seated on the piazza engaged in conversation with my staff when Sherman came up. After a few moments' conversation he said that he would like to see me alone. We passed into the house together and shut the door after us. Sherman then expressed his alarm at the move I had ordered, saying that I was putting myself in a position voluntarily which an enemy would be glad to manoeuvre a year—or a long time—to get me in. I was going into the enemy's country, with a large river behind me and the enemy holding points strongly fortified above and below. He said that it was an axiom in war that when any great body of troops moved against an enemy they should do so from a base of supplies, which they would guard as they would the apple of the eye, etc. He pointed out all the difficulties that might be encountered in the campaign proposed, and stated in turn what would be the true campaign to make. This was, in substance, to go back until high ground could be reached on the east bank of the river; fortify there and establish a depot of supplies, and move from there, being always prepared to fall back upon it in case of disaster. I said this would take us back to Memphis. Sherman then said that was the very place he would go to, and would move by railroad from Memphis to Grenada, repairing the road as we advanced. To this I replied, the country is already disheartened over the lack of success on the part of our armies; the last election went against the vigorous prosecution of the war, voluntary enlistments had ceased throughout most of the North and conscription was already resorted to, and if we went back so far as Memphis it would discourage the people so much that bases of supplies would be of no use: neither men to hold them nor supplies to put in them would be furnished. The problem for us was to move forward to a decisive victory, or our cause was lost. No progress was being made in any other field, and we had to go on. Sherman wrote to my adjutant general, Colonel J. A. Rawlins, embodying his views of the campaign that should be made, and asking him to advise me to at least get the views of my generals upon the subject. Colonel Rawlins showed me the letter, but I did not see any reason for changing my plans. The letter was not answered and the subject was not subsequently mentioned between Sherman and myself to the end of the war, that I remember of. I did not regard the letter as official, and consequently did not preserve it. General Sherman furnished a copy himself to General Badeau, who printed it in his history of my campaigns. I did not regard either the conversation between us or the letter to my adjutant-general as protests, but simply friendly advice which the relations between us fully justified. Sherman gave the same energy to make the campaign a success that he would or could have done if it had been ordered by himself. I make this statement here to correct an impression which was circulated at the close of the war to Sherman's prejudice, and for which there was no fair foundation.

On the 26th of May I sent Blair's division up the Yazoo to drive out a force of the enemy supposed to be between the Big Black and the Yazoo. The country was rich and full of supplies of both food and forage. Blair was instructed to take all of it. The cattle were to be driven in for the use of our army, and the food and forage to be consumed by our troops or destroyed by fire; all bridges were to be destroyed, and the roads rendered as nearly impassable as possible. Blair went forty-five miles and was gone almost a week. His work was effectually done. I requested Porter at this time to send the marine brigade, a floating nondescript force which had been assigned to his command and which proved very useful, up to Haines' Bluff to hold it until reinforcements could be sent.

On the 26th I also received a letter from Banks, asking me to reinforce him with ten thousand men at Port Hudson. Of course I could not comply with his request, nor did I think he needed them. He was in no danger of an attack by the garrison in his front, and there was no army organizing in his rear to raise the siege.

On the 3d of June a brigade from Hurlbut's command arrived, General Kimball commanding. It was sent to Mechanicsburg, some miles north-east of Haines' Bluff and about midway between the Big Black and the Yazoo. A brigade of Blair's division and twelve hundred cavalry had already, on Blair's return from the Yazoo, been sent to the same place with instructions to watch the crossings of the Big Black River, to destroy the roads in his (Blair's) front, and to gather or destroy all supplies.

On the 7th of June our little force of colored and white troops across the Mississippi, at Milliken's Bend, were attacked by about 3,000 men from Richard Taylor's trans-Mississippi command. With the aid of the gunboats they were speedily repelled. I sent Mower's brigade over with instructions to drive the enemy beyond the Tensas Bayou; and we had no further trouble in that quarter during the siege. This was the first important engagement of the war in which colored troops were under fire. These men were very raw, having all been enlisted since the beginning of the siege, but they behaved well.

On the 8th of June a full division arrived from Hurlbut's command, under General Sooy Smith. It was sent immediately to Haines' Bluff, and General C. C. Washburn was assigned to the general command at that point.

On the 11th a strong division arrived from the Department of the Missouri under General Herron, which was placed on our left. This cut off the last possible chance of communication between Pemberton and Johnston, as it enabled Lauman to close up on McClernand's left while Herron entrenched from Lauman to the water's edge. At this point the water recedes a few hundred yards from the high land. Through this opening no doubt the Confederate commanders had been able to get messengers under cover of night.

On the 14th General Parke arrived with two divisions of Burnside's corps, and was immediately dispatched to Haines' Bluff. These latter troops—Herron's and Parke's—were the reinforcements already spoken of sent by Halleck in anticipation of their being needed. They arrived none too soon.

I now had about seventy-one thousand men. More than half were disposed across the peninsula, between the Yazoo at Haines' Bluff and the Big Black, with the division of Osterhaus watching the crossings of the latter river farther south and west from the crossing of the Jackson road to Baldwin's ferry and below.

There were eight roads leading into Vicksburg, along which and their immediate sides, our work was specially pushed and batteries advanced; but no commanding point within range of the enemy was neglected.

On the 17th I received a letter from General Sherman and one on the 18th from General McPherson, saying that their respective commands had complained to them of a fulsome, congratulatory order published by General McClernand to the 13th corps, which did great injustice to the other troops engaged in the campaign. This order had been sent North and published, and now papers containing it had reached our camps. The order had not been heard of by me, and certainly not by troops outside of McClernand's command until brought in this way. I at once wrote to McClernand, directing him to send me a copy of this order. He did so, and I at once relieved him from the command of the 13th army corps and ordered him back to Springfield, Illinois. The publication of his order in the press was in violation of War Department orders and also of mine. . . .

On July 1st Pemberton, seeing no hope of outside relief, addressed the following letter to each of his four division commanders:

"Unless the siege of Vicksburg is raised, or supplies are thrown in, it will become necessary very shortly to evacuate the place. I see no prospect of the former, and there are many great, if not insuperable obstacles in the way of the latter. You are, therefore, requested to inform me with as little delay as possible, as to the condition of your troops and their ability to make the marches and undergo the fatigues necessary to accomplish a successful evacuation."

Two of his generals suggested surrender, and the other two practically did the same. They expressed the opinion that an attempt to evacuate would fail. Pemberton had previously got a message to Johnston suggesting that he should try to negotiate with me for a release of the garrison with their arms. Johnston replied that it would be a confession of weakness for him to do so; but he authorized Pemberton to use his name in making such an arrangement.

On the 3d about ten o'clock A.M. white flags appeared on a portion of the rebel works. Hostilities along that part of the line ceased at once. Soon two persons were seen coming towards our lines bearing a white flag. They proved to be General Bowen, a division commander, and Colonel Montgomery, aide-de-camp to Pemberton, bearing the following letter to me:

"I have the honor to propose an armistice for—hours, with the view to arranging terms for the capitulation of Vicksburg. To this end, if agreeable to you, I will appoint three commissioners, to meet a like number to be named by yourself at such place and hour to-day as you may find convenient. I make this proposition to save the further effusion of blood, which must otherwise be shed to a frightful extent, feeling myself fully able to maintain my position for a yet indefinite period. This communication will be handed you under a flag of truce, by Major-General John S. Bowen."

It was a glorious sight to officers and soldiers on the line where these white flags were visible, and the news soon spread to all parts of the command. The troops felt that their long and weary marches, hard fighting, ceaseless watching by night and day, in a hot climate, exposure to all sorts of weather, to diseases and, worst of all, to the gibes of many Northern papers that came to them saying all their suffering was in vain, that Vicksburg would never be taken, were at last at an end and the Union sure to be saved.

Source: Ulysses S. Grant, *Personal Memoirs of U. S. Grant* (New York: Charles L. Webster & Company, 1885; Project Gutenberg, 2004), vol. 1, pt. 3, chap. 37, http://www.gutenberg .org/ebooks/5862.

FALL OF A SHELL AT THE
CORNER OF MY CAVE

JUNE 1863
MARY ANN LOUGHBOROUGH, CSA

There is irony in the fact that Mary Ann Webster Loughborough provides the finest firsthand account of the harrowing conditions within Vicksburg, because this nominal southern belle was actually born in New York. Her husband was a Southern-leaning Kentuckian, and together they lived in St. Louis before the war, where their Confederate sympathies became firm. Husband James Loughborough served as a CSA major, while Mary Ann followed him, attempting to reside close to wherever he served. Her daughter in tow, she arrived in Vicksburg on April 15, 1863, just in time to experience the results of Grant's masterful campaign. The Union trap snapped shut. Her diary formed the basis for her later memoir, which gripped readers North and South. Here, she remembers how direly civilians trapped in the city suffered alongside its gray-clad defenders. The deprivations of the siege—hunger, fear, danger, death—did not discriminate between civilian and combatant.

I was sitting near the entrance, about five o'clock, thinking of the pleasant change—oh, bless me!—that to-morrow would bring, when the bombardment commenced more furiously than usual, the shells falling thickly around us, causing vast columns of earth to fly upward, mingled with smoke. As usual, I was uncertain whether to remain within or run out. As the rocking and trembling of the earth was very distinctly felt, and the explosions alarmingly near, I stood within the mouth of the cave ready to make my escape, should one chance to fall above our domicile. In my anxiety I was startled by the shouts of the servants and a most fearful jar and rocking of the earth, followed by a deafening explosion, such as I had never heard before. The cave filled instantly with powder smoke and dust. I stood with a tingling, prickling sensation in my head, hands, and feet, and with a confused brain. Yet alive!—was the first glad thought that came to me;—child, servants, all here, and saved!—from some great danger, I felt. I stepped out, to find a group of persons before my cave, looking anxiously for me; and lying all around, freshly torn, rose bushes, arbor-vitæ trees, large clods of earth, splinters, pieces of plank, wood, &c. A mortar shell had struck the corner of the cave, fortunately so near the brow of the hill, that it had gone obliquely into the earth, exploding as it went, breaking large masses from the side of the hill—tearing away the fence, the shrubbery and flowers—sweeping all, like an avalanche, down near the entrance of my good refuge.

I stood dismayed, and surveyed the havoc that had been made around me, while our little family under it all had been mercifully preserved. Though many of the neighboring servants had been standing near at the time, not one had been injured in the slightest degree; yet, pieces of plank, fragments of earth, and splinters had fallen in all directions. A portion of earth from the roof of my cave had been dislodged and fallen. Saving this, it remained intact.

That evening some friends sat with me: one took up my guitar and played some pretty little airs for us; yet, the noise of the shells threw a discord among the harmonies. To me it seemed like the crushing and bitter spirit of hate near the light and grace of happiness. How could we sing and laugh amid our suffering fellow beings—amid the shriek of death itself?

This, only breaking the daily monotony of our lives!—this thrilling knowledge of sudden and horrible death occurring near us, told to-night and forgotten in to-morrow's renewal!—this sad news of a Vicksburg day! A little negro child, playing in the yard, had found a shell; in rolling and turning it, had innocently pounded the fuse; the terrible explosion followed, showing, as the white cloud of smoke floated away, the mangled remains of a life that to the mother's heart had possessed all of beauty and joy.

A young girl, becoming weary in the confinement of the cave, hastily ran to the house in the interval that elapsed between the slowly falling shells. On returning, an explosion sounded near her—one wild scream, and she ran into her mother's presence, sinking like a wounded dove, the life blood flowing over the light summer dress in crimson ripples from a death-wound in her side, caused by the shell fragment.

A fragment had also struck and broken the arm of a little boy playing near the mouth of his mother's cave. This was one day's account.

I told of my little girl's great distress when the shells fell thickly near us—how she ran to me breathless, hiding her head in my dress without a word; then cautiously looking out, with her anxious face questioning, would say: "Oh! mamma, was it a mortar tell?" Poor children, that their little hearts should suffer and quail amid these daily horrors of war!

The next evening, about four o'clock, M——'s dear face appeared. He told us that he had heard of all the danger through which we had passed, and was extremely anxious to have us out of reach of the mortar shells, and near him; he also thought we would find our new home on the battle field far superior to this; he wished us to go out as soon as possible. As at this hour in the evening, for the last week, the Federal guns had been quiet until almost sundown, he urged me to be ready in the shortest time possible; so I hastened our arrangements, and we soon were in the ambulance, driving with great speed toward the rifle pits.

O the beautiful sunlight and the fresh evening air! How glowing and delightful it all seemed after my incarceration under the earth! I turned to look again and again at the setting sun and the brilliant crimson glow that suffused the atmosphere. All seemed glad and radiant: the sky—the flowers and trees along our drive—the cool and fragrant breeze—all, save now and then the sullen boom of the mortar, as it slowly cast its death-dealing shell over the life we were leaving behind us.

Were it not for the poor souls still within, I could have clapped my hands in a glad, defiant jubilee as I heard the reports, for I thought I was leaving my greatest fear of our old enemy in the desolate cave of which I had taken my last contemptuous glance; yet, the fear returned forcibly to me afterward.

Source: Mary Ann Loughborough, *My Cave Life in Vicksburg, With Letters of Trial and Travel* (New York: D. Appleton and Company, 1864; Project Gutenberg, 2011), chap. 16, http://www.gutenberg.org/ebooks/35700.

REPORT OF GEN. ROBERT E. LEE

GETTYSBURG, JULY 4, 1863

The invasion of Pennsylvania was even more ambitious than the Maryland campaign of the previous year. Again, the notion was to carry the shock of war northward. This time, Lee's goal was to draw out the main body of the Army of the Potomac and smash it in battle. The objective was destruction of the Union's capacity to prevail, and the shattering of its will to fight on. Such a Southern victory might well embolden Northern politicians of shaky will, and result in a settlement acknowledging Southern independence in exchange for peace. When his Army of Northern Virginia started marching in late June, optimism among the troops was unbounded. They had prevailed at Chancellorsville that May and would now move the fighting away from sorely ravaged Virginia and into the enemy's own lands. Let the Yankees experience the ravages of war: their homes wrecked, their crops burned, their civilians terrorized.

On the Northern side, there was pressure to stop Lee from reaching the rail junctions at Harrisburg, which would disrupt internal lines of communications and transport. But merely halting the invasion was not enough: Lincoln wanted to see Lee dealt a blow that would give the initiative to the Union and strip Lee of his mythic aura of invincibility. That image—the Marble Man, the man of unblemished integrity and unrivaled military genius who loved his state above anything else—was perhaps the Confederacy's greatest strategic asset. To put an end to it, Lincoln made a sudden decision. Less than a week before the two armies met on July 1, 1863, at a small crossroads town in south-central Pennsylvania

Union entrenchments on Little Round Top, with Big Round Top in the background

called Gettysburg, the commander in chief relieved Hooker and replaced him with Maj. Gen. George Meade. On the new general's shoulders fell the heavy responsibility of stopping the Confederates and the heretofore indomitable Lee.

The battle that raged at Gettysburg from July 1 to July 3 is widely conceded to be the turning point of the Civil War. The very names of the engagements which the battle comprised—Buford's seizure of the high ground at Herr, McPherson, and Seminary ridges on day one; Little Round Top and Chamberlain's left-wheel attack down the hill, the Wheatfield, Devil's Den, the Peach Orchard, Culp's Hill, and Cemetery Hill on day two; Pickett's Charge on day three; Lee's painful retreat and Meade's decision not to pursue after the Union victory—individually entered the lexicon of Civil War and United States military history. Altogether, they chronicle the war's culminating point. The end was not near; almost two long years of fighting still remained. But after Gettysburg, nothing looked the same. The war would continue solely on Southern grounds. The Union, initiative seized, would decide where and when. And, despite his victory, Meade eventually found himself replaced by the winner from the west: Ulysses S. Grant.

In the first selection, General Lee—who felt his defeat keenly, despite the protestations of continued loyalty from his devoted subordinates—reports on the battle, never shying away from the decisions he made that did not bring his army the victory he sought so desperately.

Mr. President:

After the rear of the army had crossed the Potomac, the leading corps, under General Ewell, pushed on to Carlisle and York, passing through Chambersburg. The other two corps closed up at the latter place, and soon afterward intelligence was received that the army of General Hooker was advancing. Our whole force was directed to concentrate at Gettysburg, and the corps of Generals Ewell and A. P. Hill reached that place on the 1st July, the former advancing from Carlisle and the latter from Chambersburg.

The two leading divisions of these corps, upon reaching the vicinity of Gettysburg, found the enemy, and attacked him, driving him from the town, which was occupied by our troops. The enemy's loss was heavy, including more than 4,000 prisoners. He took up a strong position in rear of the town, which he immediately began to fortify, and where his re-enforcements joined him.

On the 2d July, Longstreet's corps, with the exception of one division, having arrived, we attempted to dislodge the enemy, and, though we gained some ground, we were unable to get possession of his position. The next day, the third division of General Longstreet having come up, a more extensive attack was made. The works on the enemy's extreme right and left were taken, but his numbers were so great and his position so commanding, that our troops were compelled to relinquish their advantage and retire.

It is believed that the enemy suffered severely in these operations, but our own loss has not been light.

General Barksdale is killed. Generals Garnett and Armistead are missing, and it is feared that the former is killed and the latter wounded and a prisoner. Generals Pender and Trimble are wounded in the leg, General Hood in the arm, and General Heth slightly in the head. General Kemper, it is feared, is mortally wounded. Our losses embrace many other valuable officers and men.

General Wade Hampton was severely wounded in a different action in which the cavalry was engaged yesterday.

Very respectfully, your obedient servant,

R E. Lee,
General

His Excellency President Davis
Richmond

Source: Report of Gen. Robert E. Lee, Headquarters, Army of Northern Virginia, near Gettysburg, PA, July 4, 1863, The Civil War Home Page, www.civil-war.net.

REPORT OF COL. JOSHUA L. CHAMBERLAIN

GETTYSBURG, JULY 6, 1863

Because of his writing and elocution gifts, Chamberlain would gain a reputation as one of the ablest and most convincing explicators of the Union's cause. A professor at Bowdoin College in his home state of Maine, Chamberlain joined the army when war broke out. Commissioned as lieutenant, he rose rapidly, compiling a record of courage and commitment until he gained command of his 20th Maine Volunteer Infantry Regiment in June 1863. This put him in place to lead his men at Gettysburg. The newly minted colonel and his unit gained immortal honor during the battle, especially on the last day, when desperate Confederates spied them up Little Round Top, at the very end of the Union line. The Maine men were the extreme left flank of the entire Union army in the field—the end of the blue line. If 15th Alabama could only dislodge them, Southern forces could still prevail by rolling up that exposed flank. Instead, Chamberlain rallied his exhausted troops, explaining the strategic situation and leading them downhill in a tactically complicated left-wheel/frontal assault. He hit the Alabamians on the flank as well as head-on, saving the day, the battle, and perhaps the war for the Union. For his heroism, Chamberlain won the Congressional Medal of Honor. Wounded later at Petersburg, promoted to brigadier general, he fought at Five Forks and was honored with command of Union forces present at Lee's Appomattox surrender. When peace came, Chamberlain went into politics, eventually becoming governor of Maine as well as Bowdoin's president. This selection comes from his official battlefield report.

Sir:

In compliance with the request of the colonel commanding the brigade, I have the honor to submit a somewhat detailed report of the operations of the Twentieth Regiment Maine Volunteers in the battle of Gettysburg, on the 2d and 3d instant.

Having acted as the advance guard, made necessary by the proximity of the enemy's cavalry, on the march of the clay before, my command on reaching Hanover, Pa., just before sunset on that day, were much worn, and lost no time in getting ready for an expected bivouac. Rations were scarcely issued, and the men about preparing supper, when rumors that the enemy had been encountered that day near Gettysburg absorbed every other interest, and very soon orders came to march forthwith to Gettysburg.

My men moved out with a promptitude and spirit extraordinary, the cheers and welcome they received on the road adding to their enthusiasm. After an hour or two of sleep by the roadside just before daybreak, we reached the heights southeasterly of Gettysburg at about 7 am, July 2.

Massed at first with the rest of the division on the right of the road, we were moved several times farther toward the left. Although expecting every moment to be put into action and held strictly in line of battle, yet the men were able to take some rest and make the most of their rations.

Somewhere near 4 p.m. a sharp cannonade, at some distance to our left and front, was the signal for a sudden and rapid movement of our whole division in the direction of this firing, which grew warmer as we approached. Passing an open field in the hollow ground in which some of our batteries were going into position, our brigade reached the skirt of a piece of woods, in the farther edge of which there was a heavy musketry fire, and when about to go forward into line we received from Colonel Vincent, commanding the brigade, orders to move to the left at the double-quick, when we took a farm road crossing Plum Run in order to gain a rugged mountain spur called Granite Spur, or Little Round Top.

The enemy's artillery got range of our column as we were climbing the spur, and the crashing of the shells among the rocks and the tree tops made us move lively along the crest. One or two shells burst in our ranks.

Passing to the southern slope of Little Round Top, Colonel Vincent indicated to me the ground my regiment was to occupy, informing me that this was the extreme left of our general line, and that a desperate attack was expected in order to turn that position, concluding by telling me I was to "hold that ground at all hazards." This was the last word I heard from him.

In order to commence by making my right firm, I formed my regiment on the right into line, giving such direction to the line as should best secure the advantage of the rough, rocky, and straggling wooded ground.

The line faced generally toward a more conspicuous eminence southwest of ours, which is known as Sugar Loaf, or Round Top. Between this and my position intervened a smooth and thinly wooded hollow. My line formed, I immediately detached Company B, Captain Morrill commanding, to extend from my left flank across this hollow as a line of skirmishers, with directions to act as occasion might dictate, to prevent a surprise on my exposed flank and rear.

The artillery fire on our position had meanwhile been constant and heavy, but my formation was scarcely complete when the artillery was replaced by a vigorous infantry assault upon the center of our brigade to my right, but it very soon involved the right of my regiment and gradually extended along my entire front. The action was quite sharp and at close quarters.

In the midst of this, an officer from my center informed me that some important movement of the enemy was going on in his front, beyond that of the line with which we were engaged. Mounting a large rock, I was able to see a considerable body of the enemy moving by the flank in rear of their line engaged, and passing from the direction of the foot of Great Round Top through the valley toward the front of my left. The close engagement not allowing any change of front, I immediately stretched my regiment to the left, by taking intervals by the left flank, and at the same time "refusing" my left wing, so that it was nearly at right angles with my right, thus occupying about twice the extent of our ordinary front, some of the companies being brought into single rank when the nature of the ground gave sufficient strength or shelter. My officers and men understood wishes so well that this movement was executed under fire, the right wing keeping up fire, without giving the enemy any occasion to seize or even to suspect their advantage. But we were not a moment too soon; the enemy's flanking column having gained their desired direction, burst upon my left, where they evidently had expected an unguarded flank, with great demonstration.

We opened a brisk fire at close range, which was so sudden and effective that they soon fell back among the rocks and low trees in the valley, only to burst forth again with a shout, and rapidly advanced, firing as they came. They pushed up to within a dozen yards of us before the terrible effectiveness of our fire compelled them to break and take shelter.

They renewed the assault on our whole front, and for an hour the fighting was severe. Squads of the enemy broke through our line in several places, and the fight was literally hand-to-hand. The edge of the fight rolled backward and forward like a wave. The dead and wounded were now in our front and then in our rear. Forced from our position, we desperately recovered it, and pushed the enemy down to the foot of the slope. The intervals of the struggle were seized to remove our wounded (and those of the enemy also), to gather ammunition from the cartridge boxes of disabled friend or foe on the field, and even to secure better muskets than the Enfields, which we found did not stand service well. Rude shelters were thrown up of the loose rocks that covered the ground.

Captain Woodward, commanding the Eighty-third Pennsylvania Volunteers, on my right, gallantly maintaining his fight, judiciously and with hearty co-operation made his movements conform to my necessities, so that my right was at no time exposed to a flank attack.

The enemy seemed to have gathered all their energies for their final assault. We had gotten our thin line into as good a shape as possible, when a strong force emerged from the scrub wood in the valley, as well as I could judge, in two lines in echelon by the right, and, opening a heavy fire, the first line came on as if they meant to sweep everything before them. We opened on them as well as we could with our scanty ammunition snatched from the field.

It did not seem possible to withstand another shock like this now coming on. Our loss had been severe. One-half of my left wing had fallen, and a third of my regiment lay just behind us, dead or badly wounded. At this moment my anxiety was increased by a great roar of musketry in my rear, on the farther or northerly slope of Little Round Top, apparently on the flank of the regular brigade, which was in support of Hazlett's battery on the crest behind us. The bullets from this attack struck into my left rear, and I feared that the enemy might have nearly surrounded the Little Round Top, and only a desperate chance was left for us. My ammunition was soon exhausted. My men were firing their last shot and getting ready to club their muskets.

It was imperative to strike before we were struck by this overwhelming force in a hand-to-hand fight, which we could not probably have withstood or survived. At that crisis, I ordered the bayonet. The word was enough. It ran like fire along the line, from man to man, and rose into a shout, with which they sprang forward upon the enemy, now not 30 yards away. The effect was surprising; many of the enemy's first line threw down their arms and surrendered. An officer fired his pistol at my head with one hand, while he handed me his sword with the other. Holding fast by our right, and swinging forward our left, we made an extended right wheel, before which the enemy's second line broke and fell back, fighting from tree to tree, many being captured, until we had swept the valley and cleared the front of nearly our entire brigade.

Meantime Captain Morrill with his skirmishers sent out from my left flank, with some dozen or fifteen of the U.S. Sharpshooters who had put themselves under his direction, fell upon the enemy as they were breaking, and by his demonstrations, as well as his well-directed fire, added much to the effect of the charge.

Having thus cleared the valley and driven the enemy up the western slope of the Great Round Top, not wishing to press so far out as to hazard the ground I was to hold by leaving it exposed to a sudden rush of the enemy, I succeeded (although with some effort to stop my men, who declared they were "on the road to Richmond") in getting the regiment into good order and resuming our original position.

Four hundred prisoners, including two field and several line officers, were sent to the rear. These were mainly from the Fifteenth and Forty-seventh Alabama Regiments, with some of the Fourth and Fifth Texas. One hundred and fifty of the enemy were found killed and wounded in our front.

At dusk, Colonel Rice informed me of the fall of Colonel Vincent, which had devolved the command of the brigade on him, and that Colonel Fisher had come up with a brigade to our support. These troops were massed in our rear. It was the understanding, as Colonel Rice informed me, that Colonel Fisher's brigade was to advance and seize the western slope of Great Round Top, where the enemy had shortly before been driven. But, after considerable delay, this intention for some reason was not carried into execution.

We were apprehensive that if the enemy were allowed to strengthen himself in that position, he would have a great advantage in renewing the attack on us at daylight or before. Colonel Rice then directed me to make the movement to seize that crest.

It was now 9 p.m. Without waiting to get ammunition, but trusting in part to the very circumstance of not exposing our movement or our small front by firing, and with bayonets fixed, the little handful of 200 men pressed up the mountainside in very extended order, as the steep and jagged surface of the ground compelled. We heard squads of the enemy failing back before us, and, when near the crest, we met a scattering and uncertain fire, which caused us the great loss of the gallant Lieutenant Linscott, who fell, mortally wounded. In the silent advance in the darkness we laid hold of 25 prisoners, among them a staff officer of General Law, commanding the brigade immediately opposed to us during the fight. Reaching the crest, and reconnoitering the ground, I placed the men in a strong position among the rocks, and informed Colonel Rice, requesting also ammunition and some support to our right, which was very near the enemy, their movements and words even being now distinctly heard by us.

Some confusion soon after resulted from the attempt of some regiment of Colonel Fisher's brigade to come to our support. They had found a wood road up the mountain, which brought them on my right flank, and also in proximity to the enemy, massed a little below. Hearing their approach, and thinking a movement from that quarter could only be from the enemy, I made disposition to receive them as such. In the confusion which attended the attempt to form them in support of my right, the enemy opened a brisk fire, which disconcerted my efforts to form them and disheartened the supports themselves, so that I saw no more of them that night.

Feeling somewhat insecure in this isolated position, I sent in for the Eighty-third Pennsylvania, which came speedily, followed by the Forty-fourth New York, and, having seen these well posted, I sent a strong picket to the front, with instructions to report to me every half hour during the night, and allowed the rest of my men to sleep on their arms.

At some time about midnight, two regiments of Colonel Fisher's brigade came up the mountain beyond my left, and took position near the summit; but as the enemy did not threaten from that direction, I made no effort to connect with them.

We went into the fight with 386, all told 358 guns. Every pioneer and musician who could carry a musket went into the ranks. Even the sick and foot-sore, who could not keep up in the march, came up as soon as they could find their regiments, and took their places in line of battle, while it was battle, indeed. Some prisoners I had under guard, under sentence of court-martial, I was obliged to put into the fight, and they bore their part well, for which I shall recommend a commutation of their sentence.

The loss, so far as I can ascertain it, is 136—30 of whom were killed, and among the wounded are many mortally.

Captain Billings, Lieutenant Kendall, and Lieutenant Linscott are officers whose loss we deeply mourn—efficient soldiers, and pure and high-minded men.

In such an engagement there were many incidents of heroism and noble character which should have place even in an official report; but, under present circumstances, I am unable to do justice to them. I will say of that regiment that the resolution, courage, and heroic fortitude which enabled us to withstand so formidable an attack have happily led to so conspicuous a result that they may safely trust to history to record their merits.

About noon on the 3d of July, we were withdrawn, and formed on the right of the brigade, in the front edge of a piece of woods near the left center of our main line of battle, where we were held in readiness to support our troops, then receiving the severe attack of the afternoon of that day.

On the 4th, we made a reconnaissance to the front, to ascertain the movements of the enemy, but finding that they had retired, at least beyond Willoughby's Run, we returned to Little Round Top, where we buried our dead in the place where we had laid them during the fight, marking each grave by a head-board made of ammunition boxes, with each dead soldiers name cut upon it. We also buried 50 of the enemy's dead in front of our position of July 2. We then looked after our wounded, whom I had taken the responsibility of putting into the houses of citizens in the vicinity of Little Round Top, and, on the morning of the 5th, took up our march on the Emmitsburg road.

I have the honor to be, your obedient servant,

Joshua L. Chamberlain,
Colonel, Commanding Twentieth Maine Volunteers.

Lieut. George B. Herendeen,
A. A. A. G., Third Brig., First Div., Fifth Army Corps.

Source: Report of Col. Joshua L. Chamberlain, Twentieth Maine Infantry, Near Emmitsburg, July 6, 1863, The Civil War Home Page, www.civil-war.net.

GETTYSBURG: THIRD DAY

JULY 3, 1863
GEN. JAMES LONGSTREET, CSA

Lee considered fellow West Pointer James Longstreet so valuable that the otherwise straitlaced general called his corps commander "The Old War Horse." Longstreet served Lee, and the Confederacy, from First Bull Run / Manassas to Appomattox. After the war, he became friends with Grant, joined the Republicans, and served as United States ambassador to the Ottoman Empire's Sublime Porte. Later, he was US commissioner of railroads and also a US marshal. His willingness to recommit to the United States set Longstreet at odds with former peers who nurtured the pro-Southern, Lost Cause myth. He never pretended that slavery was not a central factor leading to the war, either, which further accentuated his reputation as a scalawag. Consequently, Longstreet was disparaged in many Southern-authored Civil War histories, and even blamed for the defeat at Gettysburg. After all, blaming Lee was hardly an option for these custodians of Lee's reputation and the South's blamelessness. But Longstreet never shied from a fight, even on the literary front, and his From Manassas to Appomattox: Memoirs of the Civil War in America *does a masterful job of allowing readers to see why none other than Lee himself considered Longstreet such an able and percipient general. It is from Longstreet's memoirs that this portion about Gettysburg is taken.*

General Lee has reported of arrangements for the day,

"The general plan was unchanged. Longstreet, reinforced by Pickett's three brigades, which arrived near the battle-field during the afternoon of the 2d, was ordered to attack the next morning, and General Ewell was ordered to attack the enemy's right at the same time. The latter during the night reinforced General Johnson with two brigades from Rodes's and one from Early's division."

This is disingenuous. He did not give or send me orders for the morning of the third day, nor did he reinforce me by Pickett's brigades for morning attack. As his head-quarters were about four miles from the command, I did not ride over, but sent, to report the work of the second day. In the absence of orders, I had scouting parties out during the night in search of a way by which we might strike the enemy's left, and push it down towards his centre. I found a way that gave some promise of results, and was about to move the command, when he rode over after sunrise and gave his orders. His plan was to assault the enemy's left center by a column to be composed of McLaws's and Hood's divisions reinforced by Pickett's brigades. I thought that it would not do; that the point had been fully tested the day before, by more men, when all were fresh; that the enemy was there looking for us, as we heard him during the night putting up his defenses; that the divisions of McLaws and Hood were holding a mile along the right of my line against twenty thousand men, who would follow their withdrawal, strike the flank of the assaulting column, crush it, and get on our rear towards the Potomac River; that thirty thousand men was the minimum of force necessary for the work; that even such force would need close co-operation on other parts of the line; that the column as he proposed to organize it would have only about thirteen thousand men (the divisions having lost a third of their numbers the day before); that the column would have to march a mile under concentrating battery fire, and a thousand yards under long-range musketry; that the conditions were different from those in the days of Napoleon, when field batteries had a range of six hundred yards and musketry about sixty yards.

He said the distance was not more than fourteen hundred yards. General Meade's estimate was a mile or a mile and a half (Captain Long, the guide of the field of Gettysburg in 1888, stated that it was a trifle over a mile). He then concluded that the divisions of McLaws and Hood could remain on the defensive line; that he would reinforce by divisions of the Third Corps and Pickett's brigades, and stated the point to which the march should be directed. I asked the strength of the column. He stated fifteen thousand. Opinion was then expressed that the fifteen thousand men who could make successful assault over that field had never been arrayed for battle; but he was impatient of listening, and tired of talking, and nothing was left but to proceed. General Alexander was ordered to arrange the batteries of the front of the First and Third Corps, those of the Second were supposed to be in position; Colonel Walton was ordered to see that the batteries of the First were supplied with ammunition, and to prepare to give the signal-guns for the opening combat. The infantry of the Third Corps to be assigned were Heth's and Pettigrew's divisions and Wilcox's brigade.

At the time of the conversation and arrangement of the assault by the Confederate right, artillery fire was heard on our extreme left. It seems that General Lee had sent orders to General Ewell to renew his battle in the morning, which was intended, and directed, as a co-operation of the attack he intended to order on his right, but General Ruger, anticipating, opened his batteries against Ewell at daylight. The Union divisions—Ruger's and Gary's—were on broken lines, open towards the trenches held by the Confederates, so that assault by our line would expose the force to fire from the enemy's other line. Ruger had occupied the trenches left vacant on his right, and Gary reached to his left under Greene, who held his line against the attack of the day before. It seems that the Confederates failed to bring artillery up to their trenches, and must make their fight with infantry, while on the Union side there were some fifteen or twenty guns playing, and many more at hand if needed.

As the Union batteries opened, Johnson advanced and assaulted the enemy's works on his right towards the center and the adjacent front of the new line, and held to that attack with resolution, putting in fresh troops to help it from time to time. Ruger put two regiments forward to feel the way towards Johnson's left. They got into hot engagement and were repulsed; Johnson tried to follow, but was in turn forced back. He renewed his main attack again, but unsuccessfully, and finally drew back to the trenches. Ruger threw a regiment forward from his left that gained the stone wall; his division was then advanced, and it recovered the entire line of trenches.

The assault were marching and finding positions under the crest of the ridge, where they could be covered during the artillery combat. Alexander put a battery of nine guns under the ridge and out of the enemy's fire to be used with the assaulting column.

General Lee said that the attack of his right was not made as early as expected, which he should not have said. He knew that I did not believe that success was possible; that care and time should be taken to give the troops the benefit of positions and the grounds; and he should have put an officer in charge who had more confidence in his plan. Two-thirds of the troops were of other commands, and there was no reason for putting the assaulting forces under my charge. He had confidence in General Early, who advised in favor of that end of the line for battle. Knowing my want of confidence, he should have given the benefit of his presence and his assistance in getting the troops up, posting them, and arranging the batteries; but he gave no orders or suggestions after his early designation of the point for which the column should march. Fitzhugh Lee claims evidence that General Lee did not even appear on that part of the field while the troops were being assigned to position.

As the commands reported, Pickett was assigned on the right, Kemper's and Garnett's brigades to be supported by Armistead's; Wilcox's brigade of the Third Corps in echelon and guarding Pickett's right; Pettigrew's division on Pickett's left, supported by the brigades of Scales and Lane, under command of General Trimble. The brigades of Pettigrew's division were Archer's, Pettigrew's, Brockenbrough's, and Davis's. (General Archer having been taken prisoner on the 1st, his brigade was under command of Colonel Fry; General Scales being wounded on the same day, his brigade was commanded by Colonel Lawrence.) The ridge upon which the commands were formed was not parallel to that upon which the enemy stood, but bending west towards our left, while the enemy's line bore northwest towards his right, so that the left of the assaulting column formed some little distance farther from the enemy's line than the right. To put the troops under the best cover during the artillery combat they were thus posted for the march, but directed to spread their steps as soon as the march opened the field, and to gain places of correct alignment.

Meanwhile, the enemy's artillery on his extreme right was in practice more or less active, but its meaning was not known or reported, and the sharp-shooters of the command on the right had a lively fusillade about eleven o'clock, in which some of the artillery took part. The order was that the right was to make the signal of battle. General Lee reported that his left attacked before due notice to wait for the opening could be given, which was a mistake, inasmuch as the attack on his left was begun by the Federals, which called his left to their work. General Meade was not apprehensive of that part of the field, and only used the two divisions of the Twelfth Corps, Shaler's brigade of the Sixth, and six regiments of the First and Eleventh Corps in recovering the trenches of his right, holding the other six corps for the battle of his center and left. He knew by the Confederate troops on his right just where the strong battle was to be.

The director of artillery was asked to select a position on his line from which he could note the effect of his practice, and to advise General Pickett when the enemy's fire was so disturbed as to call for the assault. General Pickett's was the division of direction, and he was ordered to have a staff-officer or courier with the artillery director to bear notice of the moment to advance.

The little affair between the skirmish lines quieted in a short time, and also the noise on our extreme left. The quiet filing of one or two of our batteries into position emphasized the profound silence that prevailed during our wait for final orders. Strong battle was in the air, and the veterans of both sides swelled their breasts to gather nerve and strength to meet it. Division commanders were asked to go to the crest of the ridge and take a careful view of the field, and to have their officers there to tell their men of it, and to prepare them for the sight that was to burst upon them as they mounted the crest.

Just then a squadron of Union cavalry rode through detachments of infantry posted at intervals in rear of my right division. It was called a charge, but was probably a reconnaissance.

Colonel Black had reported with a hundred of the First South Carolina Cavalry, not all mounted, and a battery of horse artillery, and was put across the Emmitsburg road, supported by infantry, in front of Merritt's brigade of cavalry.

When satisfied that the work of preparation was all that it could be with the means at hand, I wrote Colonel Walton, of the Washington Artillery,

"HEAD-QUARTERS, July 3, 1863.

"COLONEL—Let the batteries open. Order great care and precision in firing. When the batteries at the Peach Orchard cannot be used against the point we intend to attack, let them open on the enemy's on the rocky hill.

"Most respectfully,

"JAMES LONGSTREET,

"*Lieutenant-General, Commanding.*"

At the same time a note to Alexander directed that Pickett should not be called until the artillery practice indicated fair opportunity. Then I rode to a woodland hard by, to lie down and study for some new thought that might aid the assaulting column. In a few minutes report came from Alexander that he would only be able to judge of the effect of his fire by the return of that of the enemy, as his infantry was not exposed to view, and the smoke of the batteries would soon cover the field. He asked, if there was an alternative, that it be carefully considered before the batteries opened, as there was not enough artillery ammunition for this and another trial if this should not prove favorable.

He was informed that there was no alternative; that I could find no way out of it; that General Lee had considered and would listen to nothing else; that orders had gone for the guns to give signal for the batteries; that he should call the troops at the first opportunity or lull in the enemy's fire.

The signal-guns broke the silence, the blaze of the second gun mingling in the smoke of the first, and salvoes rolled to the left and repeated themselves, the enemy's fine metal spreading its fire to the converging lines, ploughing the trembling ground, plunging through the line of batteries, and clouding the heavy air. The two or three hundred guns seemed proud of their undivided honors and organized confusion. The Confederates had the benefit of converging fire into the enemy's massed position, but the superior metal of the enemy neutralized the advantage of position. The brave and steady work progressed.

Before this the Confederates of the left were driven from their captured trenches, and hope of their effective co-operation with the battle of the right was lost, but no notice of it was sent to the right of the battle. They made some further demonstrations, but they were of little effect. Merritt's brigade of cavalry was in rear of my right, threatening on the Emmitsburg road. Farnsworth's brigade took position between Merritt's and close on my right rear. Infantry regiments and batteries were broken off from my front line and posted to guard on that flank and rear.

Not informed of the failure of the Confederates on the left and the loss of their vantage-ground, we looked with confidence for them to follow the orders of battle.

General Pickett rode to confer with Alexander, then to the ground upon which I was resting, where he was soon handed a slip of paper. After reading it he handed it to me. It read:

"If you are coming at all, come at once, or I cannot give you proper support, but the enemy's fire has not slackened at all. At least eighteen guns are still firing from the cemetery itself.

ALEXANDER."

Pickett said, "General, shall I advance?"

The effort to speak the order failed, and I could only indicate it by an affirmative bow. He accepted the duty with seeming confidence of success, leaped on his horse, and rode gaily to his command. I mounted and spurred for Alexander's post. He reported that the batteries he had reserved for the charge with the infantry had been spirited away by General Lee's chief of artillery; that the ammunition of the batteries of position was so reduced that he could not use them in proper support of the infantry. He was ordered to stop the march at once and fill up his ammunition-chests. But, alas! there was no more ammunition to be had.

The order was imperative. The Confederate commander had fixed his heart upon the work. Just then a number of the enemy's batteries hitched up and hauled off, which gave a glimpse of unexpected hope. Encouraging messages were sent for the columns to hurry on, and they were then on elastic springing step. The officers saluted as they passed, their stern smiles expressing confidence. General Pickett, a graceful horseman, sat lightly in the saddle, his brown locks flowing quite over his shoulders. Pettigrew's division spread their steps and quickly rectified the alignment, and the grand march moved bravely on. As soon as the leading columns opened the way, the supports sprang to their alignments. General Trimble mounted, adjusting his seat and reins with an air and grace as if setting out on a pleasant afternoon ride. When aligned to their places solid march was made down the slope and past our batteries of position.

Confederate batteries put their fire over the heads of the men as they moved down the slope, and continued to draw the fire of the enemy until the smoke lifted and drifted to the rear, when every gun was turned upon the infantry columns. The batteries that had been drawn off were replaced by others that were fresh. Soldiers and officers began to fall, some to rise no more, others to find their way to the hospital tents. Single files were cut here and there, then the gaps increased, and an occasional shot tore wider openings, but, closing the gaps as quickly as made, the march moved on. The divisions of McLaws and Hood were ordered to move to closer lines for the enemy on their front, to spring to the charge as soon as the breach at the center could be made. The enemy's right overreached my left and gave serious trouble. Brockenbrough's brigade went down and Davis's in impetuous charge. The general order required further assistance from the Third Corps if needed, but no support appeared. General Lee and the corps commander were there, but failed to order help.

Colonel Latrobe was sent to General Trimble to have his men fill the line of the broken brigades, and bravely they repaired the damage. The enemy moved out against the supporting brigade in Pickett's rear. Colonel Sorrel was sent to have that move guarded, and Pickett was drawn back to that contention. McLaws was ordered to press his left forward, but the direct fire of infantry and crossfire of artillery was telling fearfully on the front. Colonel Fremantle ran up to offer congratulations on the apparent success, but the big gaps in the ranks grew until the lines were reduced to half their length. I called his attention to the broken, struggling ranks. Trimble mended the battle of the left in handsome style, but on the right the massing of the enemy grew stronger and stronger. Brigadier Garnett was killed, Kemper and Trimble were desperately wounded;

Generals Hancock and Gibbon were wounded. General Lane succeeded Trimble, and with Pettigrew held the battle of the left in steady ranks.

Pickett's lines being nearer, the impact was heaviest upon them. Most of the field officers were killed or wounded. Colonel Whittle, of Armistead's brigade, who had been shot through the right leg at Williamsburg and lost his left arm at Malvern Hill, was shot through the right arm, then brought down by a shot through his left leg.

General Armistead, of the second line, spread his steps to supply the places of fallen comrades. His colors cut down, with a volley against the bristling line of bayonets, he put his cap on his sword to guide the storm. The enemy's massing, enveloping numbers held the struggle until the noble Armistead fell beside the wheels of the enemy's battery. Pettigrew was wounded, but held his command.

General Pickett, finding the battle broken, while the enemy was still reinforcing, called the troops off. There was no indication of panic. The broken files marched back in steady step. The effort was nobly made, and failed from blows that could not be fended. Some of the files were cut off from retreat by fire that swept the field in their rear. Officers of my staff, sent forward with orders, came back with their saddles and bridles in their arms. Latrobe's horse was twice shot.

Looking confidently for advance of the enemy through our open field, I rode to the line of batteries, resolved to hold it until the last gun was lost. As I rode, the shells screaming over my head and ploughing the ground under my horse, an involuntary appeal went up that one of them might take me from scenes of such awful responsibility; but the storm to be met left no time to think of one's self. The battery officers were prepared to meet the crisis, no move had been made for leaving the field. My old acquaintance of Sharpsburg experience, Captain Miller, was walking up and down behind his guns, smoking his pipe, directing his fire over the heads of our men as fast as they were inside of the danger-line; the other officers equally firm and ready to defend to the last. A body of skirmishers put out from the enemy's lines and advanced some distance, but the batteries opened severe fire and drove it back. Our men passed the batteries in quiet walk, and would rally, I knew, when they reached the ridge from which they started.

General Lee was soon with us, and with staff-officers and others assisted in encouraging the men and getting them together.

As the attack failed, General Kilpatrick put his cavalry brigade under General Farnsworth on the charge through the infantry detachment in rear of my right division. The regiments of G. T. Anderson's brigade had been posted at points in rear as guards against cavalry, and the First Texas, Fourth and Fifteenth Alabama, and Bachman's and Reilly's batteries were looking for that adventure. Farnsworth had a rough ride over rocks and stone fences, but bore on in spite of all, cutting and slashing when he could get at the skirmishers or detachments. He made a gallant ride along the rear of our right, but was obliged to come under the infantry and artillery fire at several points. He fell, pierced, it is said, by five mortal wounds. Calls for him to surrender were made, but the cavalry were not riding for that. The command lost heavily, but claimed captives equal to their loss.

Kilpatrick's mistake was in not putting Farnsworth in on Merritt's left, where he would have had an open ride, and made more trouble than was ever made by a cavalry brigade. Had the ride been followed by prompt advance of the enemy's infantry in line beyond our right and pushed with vigor, they could have reached our line of retreat. General Meade ordered his left, but delay in getting the orders and preparing to get through the rough grounds consumed time, and the move was abandoned. The Fifth and Sixth Corps were in convenient position, and would have had good ground for marching after getting out of the rocky fastnesses of Round Top.

As we had no cavalry on our right, the Union cavalry was held on their right to observe the Confederates under Stuart, except Kilpatrick's division (and Custer's brigade of that division was retained on their right). A little while after the repulse of our infantry column, Stuart's cavalry advanced and was met by Gregg's, and made one of the severest and most stubborn fights of cavalry on record. General Wade Hampton was severely wounded. The Union forces held the field.

When affairs had quieted a little, and apprehension of immediate counter-attack had passed, orders were sent the divisions of McLaws and Hood to draw back and occupy the lines from which they had advanced to engage the battle of the second. Orders sent Benning's brigade by the division staff were not understood, and Benning, under the impression that he was to relieve part of McLaws's division, which he thought was to be sent on other service, ordered the Fifteenth Georgia Regiment to occupy that position. When he received the second order he sent for his detached regiment. Meanwhile, the enemy was feeling the way to his front, and before Colonel DuBose received his second order, the enemy was on his front and had passed his right and left flanks. The moment he received the final order, Colonel DuBose made a running fight and escaped with something more than half his men.

In regard to this, as to other battles in which the First Corps was concerned, the knights of peaceful later days have been busy in search of points on which to lay charges or make innuendoes of want of conduct of that corps. General Early has been a picturesque figure in the combination, ready to champion any reports that could throw a shadow over its record, but the charge most pleasing to him was that of *treason* on the part of its commander. The subject was lasting, piquant, and so consoling that one is almost inclined to envy the comfort it gave him in his latter days.

Colonel Taylor and members of the staff claim that General Lee ordered that the divisions of McLaws and Hood should be a part of the assaulting column. Of this General Lee says,

"General Longstreet was delayed by a force occupying the high, rocky reverse as they advanced. His operations had been embarrassed the day previously from the same cause, and he now deemed it necessary to defend his flank and rear with the divisions of Hood and McLaws. He was therefore reinforced by Heth's division and two brigades of Pender's, to the command of which Major-General Trimble was assigned. General Hill was directed to hold his line with the rest of the command, to afford General Longstreet further assistance if required, and to avail himself of any success that might be gained."

Colonel Taylor says,

"As our extreme right was comparatively safe, being well posted, and not at all threatened, one of the divisions of Hood and McLaws, and a greater part of the other, could be moved out of the lines and be made to take part in the attack."

On this point I offer the evidence of General Warren before the Committee of Investigation:

"General Meade had so arranged his troops on our left during the third day that nearly one-half of our army was in reserve in that position. It was a good, sheltered position, and a convenient one from which to reinforce other points of the line, and when the repulse of the enemy took place on that day, General Meade intended to move forward all the forces he could get in hand and assault the enemy in line. He ordered the advance of the Fifth Corps, but it was carried so slowly that it did not amount to much, if anything." General Hancock's evidence on that point is: "General Meade told me before the fight that if the enemy attacked me, he intended to put the Fifth and Sixth Corps on the enemy's flank."

From which it is evident that the withdrawal of the divisions of my right, to be put in the column of assault, would have been followed by those corps swinging around and enveloping the assaulting columns and gaining Lee's line of retreat.

Colonel Venable thinks it a mistake to have put Heth's division in the assaulting column. He says, "They were terribly mistaken about Heth's division in this planning. It had not recuperated, having suffered more than was reported on the first day."

But to accept for the moment Colonel Taylor's premises, the two divisions referred to would have swelled the columns of assault to twenty-three thousand men. We were alone in the battle as on the day before. The enemy had seventy-five thousand men on strong ground, with well-constructed defences. The Confederates would have had to march a mile through the blaze of direct and cross fire and break up an army of seventy-five thousand well-seasoned troops, well defended by field-works!

A rough sketch of the positions of the forces about my right and rear will help to show if it "was comparatively safe, and not at all threatened."

General Gibbon's testimony in regard to the assaulting columns of the 3d:

"I was wounded about the time I suppose the enemy's second line got the result, I think, will carry out my idea in regard to it, because the enemy broke through, forced back my weakest brigade under General each side were using their pistols on each other, and the men frequently clubbed their muskets, and the clothes of men on both sides were burned by the powder of exploding cartridges. An officer of my staff, Lieutenant

Haskell, had been sent by me, just previously to the attack, to General Meade with a message that the enemy were coming. He got back on the top of the hill hunting for me, and was there when this brigade was forced back, and, without waiting orders from me, he rode off to the left and ordered all the troops of the division there to the right. As they came up helter-skelter, everybody for himself, with their officers among them, they commenced firing upon these rebels as they were coming into our lines."

Had the column been augmented by the divisions of my right, it is probable that its brave men would have penetrated far enough to reach Johnson's Island as prisoners; hardly possible that it could have returned to General Lee by any other route.

When engaged collecting the broken files after the repulse, General Lee said to an officer who was assisting, "It is all my fault."

A letter from Colonel W. M. Owen assures me that General Lee repeated this remark at a roadside fire of the Washington Artillery on the 5th of July. A letter from General Lee during the winter of 1863-64 repeated it in substance.

And here is what Colonel T. J. Goree, of Texas, has to say upon the subject:

"I was present, however, just after Pickett's repulse, when General Lee so magnanimously took all the blame of the disaster upon himself. Another important circumstance, which I distinctly remember, was in the winter of 1863-64, when you sent me from East Tennessee to Orange Court-House with some dispatches to General Lee. Upon my arrival there, General Lee asked me into his tent, where he was alone, with two or three Northern papers on the table. He remarked that he had just been reading the Northern reports of the battle of Gettysburg; that he had become satisfied from reading those reports *that if he had permitted you to carry out your plan, instead of making the attack on Cemetery Hill, he would have been successful.*"

Further testimony to this effect comes from another source:

"In East Tennessee, during the winter of 1863-64, you called me into your quarters, and asked me to read a letter just received from General Lee in which he used the following words: 'Oh, general, *had I but followed your advice, instead of pursuing the course that I did, how different all would have been!*' You wished me to bear this language in mind as your correspondence might be lost.

"ERASMUS TAYLOR.

"ORANGE COUNTY, VA."

A contributor to *Blackwood's Magazine* reported,

"But Lee's inaction after Fredericksburg was, as we have called it, an unhappy or negative blunder. Undoubtedly the greatest positive blunder of which he was ever guilty was the unnecessary onslaught which he gratuitously made against the strong position into which, by accident, General Meade fell back at Gettysburg. We have good reason for saying that during the five years of calm reflection which General Lee passed at Lexington, after the conclusion of the American war his maladroit manipulation of the Confederate army during the Gettysburg campaign was to him a matter of ceaseless self reproach. "'If,' said he, on many occasions, 'I had taken General Longstreet's advice on the eve of the second day of the battle of Gettysburg, and filed off the left corps of my army behind the right corps, in the direction of Washington and Baltimore, along the Emmitsburg road, the Confederates would to-day be a free people.'"

It should be stated that kindest relations were maintained between General Lee and myself until interrupted by politics in 1867.

It is difficult to reconcile these facts with the reports put out after his death by members of his family and of his staff, and *post-bellum* champions, that indicate his later efforts to find points by which to so work up public opinion as to shift the disaster to my shoulders.

Some of the statements of the members of the staff have been referred to. General Fitzhugh Lee claims evidence that General Lee said that he would have gained the battle if he had had General Jackson with him. But he had Jackson in the Sharpsburg campaign, which was more blundering than that of Gettysburg. In another account Fitzhugh Lee wrote of General Lee, "He told the father of the writer, his brother, that he was controlled too far by the great confidence he felt in the fighting qualities of his people, and by assurances of most of his higher officers."

No assurances were made from officers of the First Corps, but rather objections. The only assurances that have come to light, to be identified, are those of General Early, who advised the battle, but *from the other end of the line from his command*, which should have given warning that it did not come from the heart of a true soldier.

And this is the epitome of the Confederate battle. The army when it set out on the campaign was all that could be desired, (except that the arms were not all of the most approved pattern), but it was despoiled of two of its finest brigades, Jenkins's and Corse's of Pickett's division, and was fought out by detail. The greatest number engaged at any one time was on the first day, when twenty-six thousand engaged twenty thousand of the First and part of the Eleventh Corps. On the afternoon of the second day about seventeen thousand were engaged on the right, and at night about seven thousand on the left; then later at night about three thousand near the center. On the third day about twelve thousand were engaged at daylight and until near noon, and in the afternoon fifteen thousand, all of the work of the second and third days against an army of seventy thousand and more of veteran troops in strong position defended by field-works.

General Lee was on the field from about three o'clock of the afternoon of the first day. Every order given the troops of the First Corps on that field up to its march on the forenoon of the 2d was issued in his presence. If the movements were not satisfactory in time and speed of moving, it was his power, duty, and privilege to apply the remedy, but it was not a part of a commander's duty or privilege to witness things that did not suit him, fail to apply the remedy, and go off and grumble with his staff-officers about it. In their efforts to show culpable delay in the movements of the First Corps on the 2d, some of the Virginia writers endeavor to show that General Lee did not even give me a guide to lead the way to the field from which his battle was to be opened. He certainly failed to go and look at it, and assist in selecting the ground and preparing for action.

Fitzhugh Lee says of the second day, "Longstreet was attacking the Marye's Hill of the position." At Fredericksburg, General Burnside attacked at Marye's Hill in six or more successive assaults with some twenty or thirty thousand against three brigades under McLaws and Ransom and the artillery; he had about four hundred yards to march from his covered ways about Fredericksburg to Marye's Hill. When his last attack was repulsed in the evening, he arranged and gave his orders for the attack to be renewed in the morning, giving notice that he would lead it with the Ninth Corps, but upon reports of his officers abandoned it. General Lee's assaulting columns of fifteen or twenty thousand had a march of a mile to attack double their numbers, better defended than were the three brigades of Confederates at Marye's Hill that drove back Burnside. The enemy on Cemetery Hill was in stronger position than the Confederates at Marye's Hill.

Fitzhugh Lee writes in the volume already quoted, "Over the splendid scene of human courage and human sacrifice at Gettysburg there arises in the South an apparition, like Banquo's ghost at Macbeth's banquet, which says the battle was lost to the Confederates because some one blundered."

Call them Banquo, but their name is Legion. Weird spirits keep midnight watch about the great boulders, while unknown comrades stalk in ghostly ranks through the black fastnesses of Devil's Den, wailing the lament, "Someone blundered at Gettysburg! Woe is me, whose duty was to die!"

Fitzhugh Lee makes his plans, orders, and movements to suit his purpose, and claims that they would have given Gettysburg to the Confederates, but he is not likely to convince any one outside of his coterie that over the heights of Gettysburg was to be found honor for the South.

General Meade said that the suggestion to work towards his line of communication was sound "military sense." That utterance has been approved by subsequent fair judgment, and it is that potent fact that draws the spiteful fire of latter-day knights.

Forty thousand men, unsupported as we were, could not have carried the position at Gettysburg. The enemy was there. Officers and men knew their advantage, and were resolved to stay until the hills came down over them. It is simply out of the question for a lesser force to march over broad, open fields and carry a fortified front occupied by a greater force of seasoned troops.

Source: James Longstreet, *From Manassas to Appomattox: Memoirs of the Civil War in America* (Philadelphia: J. B. Lippincott Company, 1896; Project Gutenberg, 2011), chap. 28, http://www.gutenberg.org/ebooks/38418.

A LITTLE OF CHICKAMAUGA

SEPTEMBER 19-20, 1863
LT. AMBROSE BIERCE, USA

The Battle of Chickamauga came about because William Rosecrans wanted his Army of the Cumberland to move into Georgia. There, they encountered their familiar rivals, Braxton Bragg's Army of Tennessee, waiting for them at Chickamauga Creek. The result was a Confederate victory, during which Longstreet—recently detached from the Army of Northern Virginia—took advantage of an accidental gap in Union lines to menace Rosecrans's entire position. The men in blue rallied and contained the attack, escaping destruction and then escaping under cover of night. The battle ended with Bragg's men in possession of the heights surrounding the Tennessee city, while down below, Union generals planned how to resist a siege. Here, Ambrose Bierce, with customary literary flair, explains the narrow margin between a Union defeat and a total debacle.

The history of that awful struggle is well known—I have not the intention to record it here, but only to relate some part of what I saw of it; my purpose not instruction, but entertainment.

I was an officer of the staff of a Federal brigade. Chickamauga was not my first battle by many, for although hardly more than a boy in years, I had served at the front from the beginning of the trouble, and had seen enough of war to give me a fair understanding of it. We knew well enough that there was to be a fight: the fact that we did not want one would have told us that, for Bragg always retired when we wanted to fight and fought when we most desired peace. We had maneuvered him out of

Chickamauga battlefield
LIBRARY OF CONGRESS

Chattanooga, but had not maneuvered our entire army into it, and he fell back so sullenly that those of us who followed, keeping him actually in sight, were a good deal more concerned about effecting a junction with the rest of our army than to push the pursuit. By the time that Rosecrans had got his three scattered corps together we were a long way from Chattanooga, with our line of communication with it so exposed that Bragg turned to seize it. Chickamauga was a fight for possession of a road.

Back along this road raced Crittenden's corps, with those of Thomas and McCook, which had not before traversed it. The whole army was moving by its left.

There was sharp fighting all along and all day, for the forest was so dense that the hostile lines came almost into contact before fighting was possible. One instance was particularly horrible. After some hours of close engagement my brigade, with foul pieces and exhausted cartridge boxes, was relieved and withdrawn to the road to protect several batteries of artillery—probably two dozen pieces—which commanded an open field in the rear of our line. Before our weary and virtually disarmed men had actually reached the guns the line in front gave way, fell back behind the guns and went on, the Lord knows whither. A moment later the field was gray with Confederates in pursuit. Then the guns opened fire with grape and canister and for perhaps five minutes—it seemed an hour—nothing could be heard but the infernal din of their discharge and nothing seen through the smoke but a great ascension of dust from the smitten soil. When all was over, and the dust cloud had lifted, the spectacle was too dreadful to describe. The Confederates were still there—all of them, it seemed—some almost under the muzzles of the guns. But not a man of all these brave fellows was on his feet, and so thickly were all covered with dust that they looked as if they had been reclothed in yellow.

"We bury our dead," said a gunner, grimly, though doubtless all were afterward dug out, for some were partly alive.

To a "day of danger" succeeded a "night of waking." The enemy, everywhere held back from the road, continued to stretch his line northward in the hope to overlap us and put himself between us and Chattanooga. We neither saw nor heard his movement, but any man with half a head would have known that he was making it, and we met by a parallel movement to our left. By morning we had edged along a good way and thrown up rude intrenchments at a little distance from the road, on the threatened side. The day was not very far advanced when we were attacked furiously all along the line, beginning at the left. When repulsed, the enemy came again and again—his persistence was dispiriting. He seemed to be using against us the law of probabilities: for so many efforts one would eventually succeed.

One did, and it was my luck to see it win. I had been sent by my chief, General Hazen, to order up some artillery ammunition and rode away to the right and rear in search of it. Finding an ordnance train I obtained from the officer in charge a few wagons loaded with what I wanted, but he seemed in doubt as to our occupancy of the region across which I proposed to guide them. Although assured that I had just traversed it, and that it lay immediately behind Wood's division, he insisted on riding to the top of the ridge behind which his train lay and overlooking the ground. We did so, when to my astonishment I saw the entire country in front swarming with Confederates; the very earth seemed to be moving toward us! They came on in thousands, and so rapidly that we had barely time to turn tail and gallop down the hill and away, leaving them in possession of the train, many of the wagons being upset by frantic efforts to put them about. By what miracle that officer had sensed the situation I did not learn, for we parted company then and there and I never again saw him.

By a misunderstanding Wood's division had been withdrawn from our line of battle just as the enemy was making an assault. Through the gap of a half a mile the Confederates charged without opposition, cutting our army clean in two. The right divisions were broken up and with General Rosecrans in their midst fled how they could across the country, eventually bringing up in Chattanooga, whence Rosecrans telegraphed to Washington the destruction of the rest of his army. The rest of his army was standing its ground.

A good deal of nonsense used to be talked about the heroism of General Garfield, who, caught in the rout of the right, nevertheless went back and joined the undefeated left under General Thomas. There was no great heroism in it; that is what every man should have done, including the commander of the army. We could hear Thomas's guns going—those of us who had ears for them—and all that was needful was to make a sufficiently wide detour and then move toward the sound. I did so myself, and have never felt that it ought to make me President. Moreover, on my way I met General Negley, and my duties as topographical engineer having given me some knowledge of the lay of the land offered to pilot him back to glory. I am sorry to say my good offices were rejected a little uncivilly, which I charitably attributed to the general's obvious absence of mind. His mind, I think, was in Nashville, behind a breastwork.

Unable to find my brigade, I reported to General Thomas, who directed me to remain with him. He had assumed command of all the forces still intact and was pretty closely beset. The battle was fierce and continuous, the enemy extending his lines farther and farther around our right, toward our line of retreat. We could not meet the extension otherwise than by "refusing" our right flank and letting him enclose us; which but for gallant Gordon Granger he would inevitably have done.

This was the way of it. Looking across the fields in our rear (rather longingly) I had the happy distinction of a discoverer. What I saw was the shimmer of sunlight on metal: lines of troops were coming in behind us! The distance was too great, the atmosphere too hazy to distinguish the color of their uniform, even with a glass. Reporting my momentous "find" I was directed by the general to go and see who they were. Galloping toward them until near enough to see that they were of our kidney I hastened back with the glad tidings and was sent again, to guide them to the general's position.

It was General Granger with two strong brigades of the reserve, moving soldier-like toward the sound of heavy firing. Meeting him and his staff I directed him to Thomas, and unable to think of anything better to do decided to go visiting. I knew I had a brother in that gang—an officer of an Ohio battery. I soon found him near the head of a column, and as we moved forward we had a comfortable chat amongst such of the enemy's bullets as had inconsiderately been fired too high. The incident was a trifle marred by one of them unhorsing another officer of the battery, whom we propped against a tree and left. A few moments later Granger's force was put in on the right and the fighting was terrific!

By accident I now found Hazen's brigade—or what remained of it—which had made a half-mile march to add itself to the unrouted at the memorable Snodgrass Hill. Hazen's first remark to me was an inquiry about that artillery ammunition that he had sent me for.

It was needed badly enough, as were other kinds: for the last hour or two of that interminable day Granger's were the only men that had enough ammunition to make a five minutes' fight. Had the Confederates made one more general attack we should have had to meet them with the bayonet alone. I don't know why they did not; probably they were short of ammunition. I know, though, that while the sun was taking its own time to set we lived through the agony of at least one death each, waiting for them to come on.

At last it grew too dark to fight. Then away to our left and rear some of Bragg's people set up "the rebel yell." It was taken up successively and passed round to our front, along our right and in behind us again, until it seemed almost to have got to the point whence it started. It was the ugliest sound that any mortal ever heard—even a mortal exhausted and unnerved by two days of hard fighting, without sleep, without rest, without food and without hope. There was, however, a space somewhere at the back of us across which that horrible yell did not prolong itself; and through that we finally retired in profound silence and dejection, unmolested.

To those of us who have survived the attacks of both Bragg and Time, and who keep in memory the dear dead comrades whom we left upon that fateful field, the place means much. May it mean something less to the younger men whose tents are now pitched where, with bended heads and clasped hands, God's great angels stood invisible among the heroes in blue and the heroes in gray, sleeping their last sleep in the woods of Chickamauga.

Source: Ambrose Bierce, *The Collected Works of Ambrose Bierce*, vol. 1 (New York: Neale Publishing Company, 1909), https://archive.org/details/collectedworksa04biergoog.

CHATTANOOGA OR LOOKOUT MOUNTAIN AND MISSIONARY RIDGE FROM MOCCASIN POINT

NOVEMBER 25, 1863
CAPT. BRADFORD R. WOOD JR., USA

Union leaders considered Chattanooga the key that would open Georgia and Atlanta to Northern attack. The Tennessee city sat astride rail lines running between Nashville, Knoxville, and Atlanta itself. Nestled between Lookout and Raccoon Mountains, and Missionary and Stringer's Ridges, Chattanooga was also a manufacturing center. Consequently, it was ardently targeted by the Union and just as ardently defended by Confederate forces in several engagements, often called the First and Second Battles of Chattanooga (June 7–8, 1862, and August 21, 1863), culminating in the Chattanooga Campaign (November 23–25, 1863), during which battles at Lookout Mountain and Missionary Ridge decided the outcome.

The final Chattanooga Campaign saw Union troops in the city below gazing up with trepidation at Confederate soldiers on the looming heights that hemmed in the city. Sensing that his men would react well to a replacement, Grant moved out Rosecrans and inserted Maj. Gen. George Henry Thomas. The key, as Thomas and Grant both knew, was keeping their nearly besieged soldiers supplied. This was done through the famous "Cracker Line," along which flowed food and matériel, preserving the viability of plans to break out of Chattanooga and claim the high grounds. This they would do, despite energetic Confederate attempts to prevent them.

Union soldiers and officers at Point Lookout, Tennessee

Hooker captured Lookout Mountain on November 24. Sherman attacked Missionary Ridge on November 25, and Thomas's troops took it the same day. Further fighting consolidated Northern gains, and Bragg's Army of Tennessee was forced to vacate their home state and retreat to Georgia. At Chickamauga, Bragg prevented the federals from gaining entry into that critical state. But after being driven from the mountains above Chattanooga, the Southerners found themselves unable to prevent such a menacing Union achievement. Here, Captain Bradford R. Wood Jr., son of a congressman/diplomat, writing in 1907 for the U.S. Veterans Signal Corps Association, recalls the drama of battling up the mountains surrounding the city below, against an enemy fully aware that if Union troops gained the heights, they would also gain entry into Georgia.

Missionary Ridge rises to a height of between 400 and 500 feet. The trees had been cut down and the slope was rough and uneven, in places rocky and covered with trunks and stumps of trees. There were rifle-pits half way up and just below the crest a strong line of intrenchments. While looking through my telescope at the lower line almost directly in front of Gen. Bragg's headquarters, in less than a minute after they had been taken and before the enemy who were driven out had reached the crest, I saw a few of our men start up the hill in pursuit. The movement extended first to the left and afterwards to the right. I exclaimed, "They are going up the hill, may God help them," and some one standing nearby said, "Amen." We did not expect it and it looked like a forlorn hope. The cannonade was terrific. Sometimes our men would halt for a few seconds until others came up, but none went back. The enthusiasm spread and our men kept advancing, inclining a little to the right, taking advantage of what cover there was or stopping to reload, though there was not much firing on their part. During the assault a caisson on the crest a little to the north of Gen. Bragg's headquarters was struck by a shell, probably from Fort Wood, and exploded with great effect, a column of smoke rising high in the air; and not long after another exploded further to the north in a similar manner. Just before our line of troops appeared on the crest I saw a group of men run a gun from the intrenchment to the top of the ridge, fire it to the south along the line of intrenchments and then turn it around and fire it at the fleeing enemy on the other side of the ridge. Capt. McMahon of the 41st Ohio writes: "His regiment was on the right of the first line of Gen. Hazen's brigade. The right company of the regiment captured a section of artillery on the crest, turned the guns, enfiladed the crest and drove the enemy in Gen. Sheridan's front into a precipitate retreat." In a few moments more the crest of the ridge was occupied all along the front of the army of the Cumberland and Gen. Bragg's center was routed. Gen. Hooker soon after swept the ridge northward from Rossville connecting with Gen. Johnson's right. Gen. Hardee's forces opposite Gen. Sherman alone maintained their position. From Gen. Bragg's own declaration and from the observation of those occupying elevated positions, there is no room to doubt that Gen. Thomas J. Wood's division first reached the summit. Gen. Sheridan's and Gen. Baird's, on the right and left, very soon after gained the crest. Gen. Wood's troops enfiladed the enemy's line to the right and left as soon as they broke through it. Many isolated contests were conducted with spirit by the enemy but the fragments of his line were speedily brushed away.

About 6 p.m. I saw a signal flag on a hill in Chattanooga valley near the ridge calling my station, and answering the call received the following message which I forwarded to the Cameron Hill station.

Gen. Thomas: I think we have got them, but I want a battery.

Very early in the morning of Nov. 26 Gen. Davis was ordered by Gen. Sherman to cross his division on the pontoon bridge at the mouth of the Chickamauga and pursue the enemy, and Gen. Howard was ordered to repair a bridge two miles up the creek and follow. Davis in advance reached Chickamauga Station at 11 a.m., in time to witness the burning of the depot building and the greater portion of the supplies. A short distance beyond, the enemy was found partially intrenched, but was speedily forced to retreat. He was pursued and overtaken at dark, when a sharp conflict ensued, but the darkness covered his escape. In the morning Davis reached Graysville and found himself in the rear of Hooker's command. Gen. Howard advanced through Parker's Gap further east and detached a column to destroy railroad communication between Bragg and Longstreet. These movements terminated the pursuit of the enemy.

Gen. Burnside's condition was very critical and Gen. Grant deemed his relief of more importance than the pursuit of Bragg. He therefore directed Gen. Sherman to give his troops a rest of one day before starting to raise the siege of Knoxville. In addition to his own three divisions Gen. Grant gave him Howard's and Granger's corps and Davis' division of the 14th corps. Gen. Hooker was ordered to remain at Ringgold until Nov. 30, to cover Gen. Sherman's movement towards Knoxville and keep up the semblance of pursuit.

It is probable that Gen. Grant had 60,000 men in action in the battle of Chattanooga, and Gen. Bragg 40,000. The former had thirteen divisions including two detached brigades, and the latter had eight divisions. Gen. Bragg's loss in killed and wounded was between 2500 and 3000 men. He lost by capture 6142 men, forty-two guns, sixty-nine gun carriages, and 7000 stand of small arms. His loss in material was immense, part of which he destroyed in his flight, but a large portion which was uninjured fell to the Union army. The aggregate losses of the armies of the Cumberland and Tennessee were 753 killed, 4722 wounded, and 349 missing, making a total of 5824. These losses were small compared with those of other battles of similar proportions, and very small in view of the fact that the enemy generally fought behind intrenchments.

Chattanooga was a very important position for defense or aggression. Fortified on its outer lines by ranges of mountains, after the battle of Chickamauga it had been made strong by intrenchments, forts and redoubts, and heavy guns. Situated at the confluence of several streams and diverging valleys, and especially as the gateway of Georgia, it was the natural base for an invasion of the Gulf states from the north. This position had been the objective point of the army of the Cumberland for a long time, and as a result of a battle compassing all the elements of the most brilliant warfare, it fell into its possession when the troops reached the crest of Missionary Ridge. The issue of the battle produced a startling surprise throughout the South. Gen. Bragg had said that the Ridge ought to have been held by a skirmish line against an assaulting column, but no skirmish line could have held Missionary Ridge against even a portion of the brave men who dashed up its steep acclivity. The moral forces were with the assaulting columns. The battle had been opened by the splendid charge of Wood's division capturing Orchard Knob, and Lookout Mountain had been wrested from the enemy by Gen. Hooker in such a way as to change the martial tone of each army. Those assaulting Missionary Ridge had Chickamauga to avenge and Lookout Mountain to surpass, and the firm and resolute sweep of the charging column for more than a mile expressed in advance the resistless character of the attack. When fifty battle flags forming the foremost line approached the crest, the Confederate soldiers knew that they would wave over their defenses or those who bore them, and many of the 20,000 men who followed would fall. The men who fled had proved themselves brave on other fields and were perhaps less to blame than their impassive general, who had failed to perceive the ruling conditions of the battle. The loss of more than 20 per cent in the two central divisions in a contest of less than an hour shows that the enemy did not yield his position without a struggle. There was a panic, but its cause was not mere fear but the overwhelming impression that resistance was useless.

The battle of Chickamauga was fought on Sept. 19 and 20, 1863. After the battle of Chattanooga it was found that many of the Union dead were left unburied on the field of Chickamauga, and on Nov. 27 the brigade of Col. Wm. Grose of the 4th corps was detailed to proceed to that field and bury the dead. Col. Grose found that on the left of the line the dead had not been sufficiently covered, that toward the center and right few of our dead were covered at all, and that west of the road from Lee and Gordon's mills to Rossville but few burials had been made of either party. All good clothing had been stripped from the bodies. He buried 400 which had been the prey of animals for more than two months. He had not time to examine the entire field.

Source: Bradford R. Wood Jr., *Chattanooga or Lookout Mountain and Missionary Ridge from Moccasin Point* (U.S. Veteran Signal Corps Association, 1907; Project Gutenberg, 2010), http://www.gutenberg.org/ebooks/34242.

THE VARIETY OF WARRIORS

The Civil War is often regarded by military historians as an early example of "total war." This was no relatively restricted affair fought by professionals. Instead, it was a massive struggle between two sides each fighting for what they considered existential reasons. For the Union, the war would either save or destroy the United States of America, and the institution of slavery. For the South, the war would either validate or nullify the Confederate States of America, and that same peculiar institution. The war was continental in land combat, and also included action far across the oceans. Diplomacy was merely another war theater. The war included career soldiers, conscripts, and irregulars; men from all races and walks of life found reason to take up arms. Civilians were very much a part of the war, much to their dismay. Slaves sought to escape to Northern lines and freedom. Women sought to take advantage of their sex and slip information to either the Confederacy or the Union, depending upon their sympathies. Army units opened up to boys as young as twelve, if they could play a drum or carry a musket. It was a total war, and the variety of warriors was wide.

*In the first excerpt, **Capt. John Wilkinson**, CSN, describes life as a commander of Southern blockade runners. Operation Anaconda was the fitting name given by Winfield Scott to the federal plan to strangle Southern hopes by cutting the Confederacy off from trans-Atlantic trade. King Cotton, meant to be the Confederacy's major strategic economic lever, would have scant power if Southern access to ports across the sea was nil. Every bit of supply brought on the return leg meant a defeat for Union plans to cut off the*

Black soldier guarding Napoleon cannon, City Point, Virginia
LIBRARY OF CONGRESS

Confederacy. Blockade-runners were the fast-sailing vessels that the Confederate States Navy used to evade the Union naval block-ade. They needed to be fast as well as nimble; sneaky as well as powerful. Shipbuilding capacity in the industry-poor South was not advanced, so it was necessary to contract for these ships from Brit-ish shipyards. That was politically sensitive, since the Confederacy had no formal standing to conduct international commerce. There was thus a stealthy and glamorous air about the entire blockade-running business. John Wilkinson was perfect for this type of work. He commanded different ships during the war, including the CSS Robert E. Lee and the CSS Chickamauga. He also arranged deals with shipbuilders that a man of lesser talents might not have been able to pull off. Here, Wilkinson gives a glimpse of the Confed-eracy's war at sea.

In Kansas and Missouri, fighting presaged the war, and dur-ing the war the line between regulars and irregulars was impos-sible to discern. There were rival political contenders, pro-Union and pro-Confederacy, both claiming to represent each state. Like the Civil War in microcosm, Missouri and Kansas was a bitter, no-quarter-given affair, and civilians on the "wrong side" often found themselves treated with contempt or worse. Of all the Confederate raiders, Capt. William Clarke Quantrill was the most notorious. **John McCorkle**, born in Savannah, Missouri, in 1838, joined Quantrill's Raiders and first fought at the Battle of Independence, on August 11, 1862. On August 21, 1863, Quantrill led his Confederate raiders into Lawrence, Kansas, which had already suffered grievously during the Bleeding Kansas days of the prewar decade. At the head of 450 men, Quantrill slashed and burned through the unfortunate town, leaving approximately 180 dead in his wake. Freed blacks received no mercy from the raiders, as this account admits. His service with Quantrill saw McCorkle fight elsewhere in Kansas and also in Kentucky. When Quantrill was finally ambushed and killed in 1865, McCorkle was with him. McCorkle's memoirs, Three Years with Quantrill, is more than a thrilling retrospective. It provides an inner look at what life was like for Confederate guerrillas whose entire war experience was spent raiding, riding, and hiding.

    Sarah Emma Edmonds, born in Canada in 1841, grew up in New Brunswick. Desiring to escape an early marriage, she disguised herself as a man and slipped across the American border. Taking on a male alias, she found work with a Bible sales company based in Connecticut. This intrepid woman continued her life as a man, enlisting in Company F of the 2nd Michigan Infantry, often called the Flint Greys. Serving as an army nurse, she was at both Bull Run battles, Antietam, the Peninsular Campaign—or so she claimed. There is some controversy among later historians as to whether or not she was at every battle she claimed to remember, but few contest the fact that she did serve under McClellan. Another claim she made was a turn as a spy, during which she traveled back and forth across Southern lines, donning varying disguises and stealing Confederate papers, which she returned to Union authorities. Her memoirs are so vivid as to be somewhat picaresque, and if several details are in doubt, it does seem certain that Edmonds did have a *colorful, and secret, Civil War career. Readers thrilled to the adventure aspects of her memoir,* Nurse and Spy in the Union Army, *from which our selection is taken.*

Abolition was a sacred cause for **Thomas Wentworth Higginson**. *This Massachusetts-born Unitarian minister found the enslavement of black Americans so intolerable that he joined John Brown's Secret Six. From Cambridge, he grew up immersed in the antislavery movement. Upon ordination, he urged churchgoers to subvert the Fugitive Slave Act, and also joined the Free Soil Party. John Brown's commitment to action drew his support, and he narrowly courted arrest after Brown's failed Harper's Ferry raid. Instead of fleeing, as others supporters did, he raised money for Brown's defense. Higginson joined the 51st Massachusetts in November 1862, and later became colonel of a black regiment, the 1st South Carolina Volunteers, when Secretary of War Edwin E. Stanton ruled that such units could be raised but must have white officers.* Army Life in a Black Regiment, *Higginson's book, appeared in 1870. In it, he stressed the military capabilities and achievements of his troops, and also the centrality of slavery's future to the war's rationale.*

NARRATIVE OF A BLOCKADE-RUNNER

CAPT. JOHN WILKINSON, CSN

Arriving at Nassau on the 8th, we found many blockade-runners in port, waiting for news from Charleston; and on the 10th, the Owl returned, after an unsuccessful attempt to enter Charleston, during which she received a shot through her bows; and intelligence came also of the capture of the "Stag" and "Charlotte." On the 23d, the "Chicora," which had succeeded in getting into Charleston, arrived with the fatal news of its evacuation, and the progress of General Sherman through Georgia and South Carolina. This sad intelligence put an end to all our hopes, and we were now cut off from all communication with the Confederate Government authorities.

In this dilemma, Maffitt and I consulted with Mr. Heyliger, the Confederate agent at Nassau; and it was decided that the Chameleon should be taken over to England. Whatever might be the course of events, our duty appeared to be to turn our vessels over, either to the agent of the Navy Department in Liverpool, or to the firm of Messrs. Fraser, Trenholm & Co. there. We learned afterwards, indeed, that Captain Pembroke Jones, of the Confederate Navy, was at that time on his way to us via Galveston or Mexico, with orders from the Navy Department. All of us were directed to take in cargoes of provisions to a specified point on the Rappahannock River, under the protection of Confederate artillery to be stationed there in readiness. The steamers were to be burned after landing their cargoes, but Jones could not reach us in time.

The bottom of the Chameleon being quite foul, divers were employed to scrub it preparatory to her long sea voyage. These people are wonderfully expert, remaining under the surface nearly two minutes; and the water in the harbor of Nassau is so clear that they can be distinctly seen even at the keel of a vessel. Our cargo of provisions was landed, and an extra supply of coal taken on board. The vessel being under Confederate colors and liable to capture wherever found, except in neutral waters, it behooved us to be prepared at all times to show our heels to a stranger. Some of our crew who wished their discharge, for the purpose of rejoining their families at the South, were paid off; the rest of them shipped for the voyage to Liverpool via Bermuda. We still lingered for later intelligence which was brought by the mail steamer Corsica from New York. Charleston was evacuated on the 17th of February, and Fort Anderson, the last of the defences at Wilmington, fell on the 19th. General Johnston had assumed command of the broken remnant of the army of the Tennessee in North Carolina, and subsequently offered some resistance to the hitherto unimpeded march of General Sherman; but the latter was now about to effect a junction with General Schofield, who commanded a large force which had landed at Wilmington. It was too evident that the end was near. The speculators in Nassau saw that "the bottom had fallen out," and all of them were in the depths of despair. Some of them, it is true, had risen from the desperately hazardous game with large gains, but the majority had staked their all and lost it; and even the fortunate ones had contracted a thirst for rash ventures, which eventually led to the pecuniary and social ruin of some of them. Even the negro stevedores and laborers bewailed our misfortunes, for they knew that the glory of Nassau had departed forever. My old friend Captain Dick Watkins probably more unselfishly regretted the disasters to our arms than the speculators or even the refugees in Nassau, who had succeeded in evading service in the army by skulking abroad. A recruiting officer might have "conscripted" nearly a brigade of the swaggering blusterers. Captain Dick and I parted with mutual regret; and I sincerely hope, if Providence has been pleased to remove the old fellow's helpmeet to a better sphere, that he has found consolation in a virtuous union with one of those "mighty pretty yaller gals" he so much admired; and that Napoleon Bonaparte may rise to the highest dignities in that particolored community of spongers and "wrackers."

We sailed from Nassau on the 22d of March and arrived at St. George's, Bermuda on the 26th. The harbor was deserted, and the town, in its listless inactivity, presented a striking contrast with its late stir and bustle. "'Twas Greece, but living Greece no more." After coaling, we took our departure for Liverpool on the 26th of March, and arrived there on the 9th of April. It was Palm Sunday, and the chimes were ringing sweetly from the church bells, as we came to anchor.

The contrast between this happy, peaceful, prosperous country and our own desolated, war-distracted land, struck a chill to our saddened hearts. The last act in the bloody drama was about to close on that very day at Appomattox Court House, and before that sun had set, the Confederate Government had become a thing of the past. We, who were abroad, were not unprepared for the final catastrophe; for we had learned on our arrival at Liverpool of General Early's defeat in the valley of the Shenandoah, and the accession to General Grant's already overwhelmingly large forces of General Sheridan's cavalry; and of the junction of General Sherman with General Schofield. To oppose these mighty armies, there were 33,000 half starved, ragged heroes in the trenches around Petersburg, and about 25,000 under General Johnston in North Carolina.

This may not be a proper place to allude to the fearful penalties inflicted upon a people who fought and suffered for what they deemed a holy cause. But it should be proclaimed, in the interest of truth and justice, that the South since the close of the war, has been preyed upon by unprincipled adventurers and renegades who are determined to rule or ruin. But a brighter day will come. Calumny and injustice cannot triumph forever. That distinguished officer Colonel C. C. Chesney of the British army in a volume of "Military Biography" lately published by him, in allusion to General Lee, writes thus: "But though America has learned to pardon, she has yet to attain the full reconciliation for which the dead hero would have sacrificed a hundred lives. Time can only bring this to a land, which in her agony, bled at every pore. Time, the healer of all wounds will bring it yet. The day will come, when the evil passions of the great civil strife will sleep in oblivion, and North and South do justice to each other's motives, and forget each other's wrongs. Then History will speak with clear voice of the deeds done on either side, and the citizens of the whole Union do justice to the memories of the dead." Surely all honest men and true patriots will rejoice to see that day.

Source: J. Wilkinson, *The Narrative of a Blockade-Runner* (New York: Sheldon & Company, 1877; Project Gutenberg, 2007), chap. 15, http://www.gutenberg.org/ebooks/21977.

QUANTRILL'S RAIDERS

PVT. JOHN McCORKLE, CSA

On the morning of the 20th of August, Quantrell [sic] gave the order to break camp and march in a southwesterly direction, and went over on the Big Blue to a point south of Little Santa Fe, a town just on the Kansas line. His entire march until he reached the Kansas line was through smoking ruins and blackened fields. He halted in the woods all day and just about dark he gave the order to mount and crossed into Kansas at a point about ten miles south of Little Santa Fe and turned directly west toward the town of Lawrence, and, riding all night, the town was reached just at daylight.

At the entrance to the town, there were a lot of tents in which were camped a detachment of negro soldiers and a few white men. The command halted here and someone fired a shot. Immediately the negroes and white men rushed out of their tents, the majority of them starting in the direction of the river and some going in the direction of town. The command was given to break ranks, scatter and follow them. A few of the negroes reached the river, plunging into it, but none succeeded in reaching the opposite shore.

The troops then dashed back up into the town, down the main street, shooting at every blue coat that came in sight. Just before entering the town Colonel Quantrell turned to his men and said, "Boys, this is the home of Jim Lane and Jennison; remember that in hunting us they gave no quarter. Shoot every soldier you see, but in no way harm a woman or a child." He dashed ahead of his command down Main Street, firing his pistol twice, dismounted from his horse and went into the hotel, where he was met by the landlord, whom he recognized as an old friend and immediately gave orders for the landlord not to be molested and stayed in the hotel and guarded him.

During all this time, his command was busy hunting men with blue clothes and setting fire to the town. Jim Lane and Jennison were the ones wanted and some of the boys dashed at once to Jim Lane's house, but, unfortunately for the world, did not find him. They found his saber, which was very handsome, the scabbard being heavily gold-plated. In the parlor of Lane's house, there were three pianos and the boys recognized two of them as having belonged to Southern people in Jackson County, and a great many other things belonging to Southern people were found in his house.

Quantrell remained in Lawrence about two hours and when he left, the town was in ashes and 175 Jayhawkers were dead. Lane and Jennison had made desolate the border counties of Missouri, pillaged and burned homes, murdered Southern men, insulted, outraged and murdered the wives and sisters of these men. Quantrell and his command had come to Lawrence to be avenged and they were. In this raid, a few innocent men may have been killed but this was not intentional.

Source: "William Quantrill Raids Lawrence, Kansas, 1863," EyeWitness to History, 2010, www.eyewitnesstohistory.com/quantrill.htm; from O. S. Barton, *Three Years with Quantrell [sic]: A True Story Told by His Scout John McCorkle* (1914; republished 1966).

DISGUISED AS A CONTRABAND

S. EMMA E. EDMONDS, USA

After supper I was left to my own reflections, which were anything but pleasant at that time; for in the short space of three hours I must take up my line of march toward the camp of the enemy. As I sat there considering whether it was best for me to make myself known to Mrs. B. before I started, Dr. E. put his head in at the tent door and said in a hurried manner: "Ned, I want you to black my boots to-night; I shall require them early in the morning." "All right, Massa Doct'r," said I; "I allers blacks de boots over night." After washing up the few articles which had taken the place of dishes, and blacking the Doctor's boots, I went to seek an interview with Mrs. B. I found her alone and told her who I was, but was obliged to give her satisfactory proofs of my identity before she was convinced that I was the identical nurse with whom she had parted three days previously.

My arrangements were soon made, and I was ready to start on my first secret expedition toward the Confederate capital. Mrs. B. was pledged to secrecy with regard to her knowledge of "Ned" and his mysterious disappearance. She was not permitted even to tell Mr. B. or Dr. E., and I believe she kept her pledge faithfully. With a few hard crackers in my pocket, and my revolver loaded and capped, I started on foot, without even a blanket or anything which might create suspicion. At half-past nine o'clock I passed through the outer picket line of the Union army, at twelve o'clock I was within the rebel lines, and had not so much as been halted once by a sentinel. I had passed within less than ten rods of a rebel picket, and he had not seen me. I took this as a favorable omen, and thanked heaven for it.

As soon as I had gone a safe distance from the picket lines I lay down and rested until morning. The night was chilly and the ground cold and damp, and I passed the weary hours in fear and trembling. The first object which met my view in the morning was a party of negroes carrying out hot coffee and provisions to the rebel pickets. This was another fortunate circumstance, for I immediately made their acquaintance, and was rewarded for my promptness by receiving a cup of coffee and a piece of corn bread, which helped very much to chase away the lingering chills of the preceding night. I remained there until the darkies returned, and then marched into Yorktown with them without eliciting the least suspicion.

The negroes went to work immediately on the fortifications after reporting to their overseers, and I was left standing alone, not having quite made up my mind what part to act next. I was saved all further trouble in that direction, for my idleness had attracted the notice of an officer, who stepped forward and began to interrogate me after the following manner: "Who do you belong to, and why are you not at work?" I answered in my best negro dialect: "I dusn't belong to nobody, Massa, I'se free and allers was; I'se gwyne to Richmond to work." But that availed me nothing, for turning to a man who was dressed in citizen's clothes and who seemed to be in charge of the colored department, he said: "Take that black rascal and set him to work, and if he don't work well tie him up and give him twenty lashes, just to impress upon his mind that there's no free niggers here while there's a d—d Yankee left in Virginia."

So saying he rode away, and I was conducted to a breast-work which was in course of erection, where about a hundred negroes were at work. I was soon furnished with a pickaxe, shovel, and a monstrous wheelbarrow, and I commenced forthwith to imitate my companions in bondage. That portion of the parapet upon which I was sent to work was about eight feet high. The gravel was wheeled up in wheelbarrows on single planks, one end of which rested on the brow of the breast-work and the other on the ground. I need not say that this work was exceedingly hard for the strongest man; but few were able to take up their wheelbarrows alone, and I was often helped by some good natured darkie when I was just on the verge of tumbling off the plank. All day long I worked in this manner, until my hands were blistered from my wrists to the finger ends.

The colored men's rations were different from those of the soldiers. They had neither meat nor coffee, while the white men had both. Whiskey was freely distributed to both black and white, but not in sufficient quantity to unfit them for duty. The soldiers seemed to be as much in earnest as the officers, and could curse the Yankees with quite as much vehemence. Notwithstanding the hardships of the day I had had my eyes and ears open, and had gained more than would counterbalance the day's work.

Night came, and I was released from toil. I was free to go where I pleased within the fortifications, and I made good use of my liberty. I made out a brief report of the mounted guns which I saw that night in my ramble round the fort, viz.: fifteen three-inch rifled cannon, eighteen four and a half-inch rifled cannon, twenty-nine thirty-two pounders, twenty-one forty-two pounders, twenty-three eight-inch Columbiads, eleven nine-inch Dahlgrens, thirteen ten-inch Columbiads, fourteen ten-inch mortars, and seven eight-inch siege howitzers. This, together with a rough sketch of the outer works, I put under the inner sole of my contraband shoe and returned to the negro quarters.

Finding my hands would not be in a condition to shovel much earth on the morrow, I began to look round among the negroes to find some one who would exchange places with me whose duty was of a less arduous character. I succeeded in finding a lad of about my own size who was engaged in carrying water to the troops. He said he would take my place the next day, and he thought he could find a friend to do the same the day following, for which brotherly kindness I gave him five dollars in greenbacks; but he declared he could not take so much money—"he neber had so much money in all his life before." So by that operation I escaped the scrutiny of the overseer, which would probably have resulted in the detection of my assumed African complexion.

The second day in the Confederate service was much pleasanter than the first. I had only to supply one brigade with water, which did not require much exertion, for the day was cool and the well was not far distant; consequently I had an opportunity of lounging a little among the soldiers, and of hearing important subjects discussed. In that way I learned the number of reinforcements which had arrived from different places, and also had the pleasure of seeing General Lee, who arrived while I was there. It was whispered among the men that he had been telegraphed to for the purpose of inspecting the Yankee fortifications, as he was the best engineer in the Confederacy, and that he had pronounced it impossible to hold Yorktown after McClellan opened his siege guns upon it. Then, too, General J. E. Johnson [*sic*] was hourly expected with a portion of his command. Including all, the rebels estimated their force at one hundred and fifty thousand at Yorktown and in that vicinity.

When Johnson arrived there was a council of war held, and things began to look gloomy. Then the report began to circulate that the town was to be evacuated. One thing I noticed in the rebel army, that they do not keep their soldiers in the dark as our officers do with regard to the movements and destination of the troops. When an order comes to the Federal army requiring them to make some important movement, no person knows whether they are advancing or retreating until they get to Washington, or in sight of the enemy's guns, excepting two or three of the leading generals.

Having a little spare time I visited my sable friends and carried some water for them. After taking a draught of the cool beverage, one young darkie looked up at me in a puzzled sort of manner, and turning round to one of his companions, said: "Jim, I'll be darned if that feller aint turnin' white; if he aint then I'm no nigger." I felt greatly alarmed at the remark, but said, very carelessly, "Well, gem'in I'se allers 'spected to come white some time; my mudder's a white woman." This had the desired effect, for they all laughed at my simplicity, and made no further remarks upon the subject. As soon as I could conveniently get out of sight I took a look at my complexion by means of a small pocket looking-glass which I carried for that very purpose—and sure enough, as the negro had said, I was really turning white. I was only a dark mulatto color now, whereas two days previous I was as black as Cloe [*sic*]. However, I had a small vial of nitrate of silver in weak solution, which I applied to prevent the remaining color from coming off.

Upon returning to my post with a fresh supply of water, I saw a group of soldiers gathered around some individual who was haranguing them in real Southern style. I went up quietly, put down my cans of water, and of course had to fill the men's canteens, which required considerable time, especially as I was not in any particular hurry just then. I thought the voice sounded familiar, and upon taking a sly look at the speaker I recognized him at once as a peddler who used to come to the Federal camp regularly once every week with newspapers and stationery, and especially at headquarters. He would hang round there, under some pretext or other, for half a day at a time.

There he was, giving the rebels a full description of our camp and forces, and also brought out a map of the entire works of McClellan's position. He wound up his discourse by saying: "They lost a splendid officer through my means since I have been gone this time. It was a pity though to kill such a man if he was a d—d Yankee." Then he went on to tell how he had been at headquarters, and heard "Lieutenant V." say that he was going to visit the picket line at such a time, and he had hastened away and informed the rebel sharpshooters that one of the headquarter officers would be there at a certain time, and if they would charge on that portion of the line they might capture him and obtain some valuable information. Instead of this, however, they watched for his approach, and shot him as soon as he made his appearance.

I thanked God for that information. I would willingly have wrought with those negroes on that parapet for two months, and have worn the skin off my hands half a dozen times, to have gained that single item. He was a fated man from that moment; his life was not worth three cents in Confederate scrip. But fortunately he did not know the feelings that agitated the heart of that little black urchin who sat there so quietly filling those canteens, and it was well that he did not.

On the evening of the third day from the time I entered the camp of the enemy I was sent, in company with the colored men, to carry supper to the outer picket posts on the right wing. This was just what I wished for, and had been making preparations during the day, in view of the possibility of such an event, providing, among other things, a canteen full of whiskey. Some of the men on picket duty were black and some were white. I had a great partiality for those of my own color, so calling out several darkies I spread before them some corn cake, and gave them a little whiskey for dessert. While we were thus engaged the Yankee

Minnie balls were whistling round our heads, for the picket lines of the contending parties were not half a mile distant from each other. The rebel pickets do not remain together in groups of three or four as our men do, but are strung along, one in each place, from three to four rods apart. I proposed to remain a while with the pickets, and the darkies returned to camp without me.

Not long after night an officer came riding along the lines, and seeing me he inquired what I was doing there. One of the darkies replied that I had helped to carry out their supper, and was waiting until the Yankees stopped firing before I started to go back. Turning to me he said, "You come along with me." I did as I was ordered, and he turned and went back the same way he came until we had gone about fifty rods, then halting in front of a petty officer he said, "Put this fellow on the post where that man was shot until I return." I was conducted a few rods farther, and then a rifle was put into my hands, which I was told to use freely in case I should see anything or anybody approaching from the enemy. Then followed the flattering remark, after taking me by the coat-collar and giving me a pretty hard shake, "Now, you black rascal, if you sleep on your post I'll shoot you like a dog." "Oh no, Massa, I'se too feerd to sleep," was my only reply.

Source: S. Emma E. Edmonds, *Nurse and Spy in the Union Army; The Adventures and Experiences of a Woman in Hospitals, Camps, and Battle-Fields* (Hartford, CT: W. S. Williams & Co., 1865; Project Gutenberg, 2012), chap. 8, http://www.gutenberg.org/ebooks/38497.

THE NEGRO AS A SOLDIER

COL. THOMAS WENTWORTH HIGGINSON, USA

There was in our regiment a very young recruit, named Sam Roberts, of whom Trowbridge used to tell this story. Early in the war Trowbridge had been once sent to Amelia Island with a squad of men, under direction of Commodore Goldsborough, to remove the negroes from the island. As the officers stood on the beach, talking to some of the older freedmen, they saw this urchin peeping at them from front and rear in a scrutinizing way, for which his father at last called him to account, as thus:

"Hi! Sammy, what you's doin', chile?"

"Daddy," said the inquisitive youth, "don't you know mas'r tell us Yankee hab tail? I don't see no tail, daddy!"

There were many who went to Port Royal during the war, in civil or military positions, whose previous impressions of the colored race were about as intelligent as Sam's view of themselves. But, for once, I had always had so much to do with fugitive slaves, and had studied the whole subject with such interest, that I found not much to learn or unlearn as to this one point. Their courage I had before seen tested; their docile and lovable qualities I had known; and the only real surprise that experience brought me was in finding them so little demoralized. I had not allowed for the extreme remoteness and seclusion of their lives, especially among the Sea Islands. Many of them had literally spent their whole existence on some lonely island or remote plantation, where the master never came, and the overseer only once or twice a week. With these exceptions, such persons had never seen a white face, and of the excitements or sins of larger communities they had not a conception. My friend Colonel Hallowell, of the Fifty-Fourth Massachusetts, told me that he had among his men some of the worst reprobates of Northern cities. While I had some men who were unprincipled and troublesome, there was not one whom I could call a hardened villain. I was constantly expecting to find male Topsies, with no notions of good and plenty of evil. But I never found one. Among the most ignorant there was very often a childlike absence of vices, which was rather to be classed as inexperience than as innocence, but which had some of the advantages of both.

Apart from this, they were very much like other men. General Saxton, examining with some impatience a long list of questions from some philanthropic Commission at the North, respecting the traits and habits of the freedmen, bade some staff-officer answer them all in two words—"Intensely human." We all admitted that it was a striking and comprehensive description.

For instance, as to courage. So far as I have seen, the mass of men are naturally courageous up to a certain point. A man seldom runs away from danger which he ought to face, unless others run; each is apt to keep with the mass, and colored soldiers have more than usual of this gregariousness. In almost every regiment, black or white, there are a score or two of men who are naturally daring, who really hunger after dangerous adventures, and are happiest when allowed to seek them. Every commander gradually finds out who these men are, and habitually uses them; certainly I had such, and I remember with delight their bearing, their coolness, and their dash. Some of them were negroes, some mulattoes. One of them would have passed for white, with brown hair and blue eyes, while others were so black you could hardly see their features. These picked men varied in other respects too; some were neat and well-drilled soldiers, while others were slovenly, heedless fellows—the despair of their officers at inspection, their pride on a raid. They were the natural scouts and rangers of the regiment; they had the two-o'clock-in-the-morning courage, which Napoleon thought so rare. The mass of the regiment rose to the same level under excitement, and were more excitable, I think, than whites, but neither more nor less courageous.

Perhaps the best proof of a good average of courage among them was in the readiness they always showed for any special enterprise. I do not remember ever to have had the slightest difficulty in obtaining volunteers, but rather in keeping down the number. The previous pages include many illustrations of this, as well as of then: endurance of pain and discomfort. For instance, one of my lieutenants, a very daring Irishman, who had served for eight years as a sergeant of regular artillery in Texas, Utah, and South Carolina, said he had never been engaged in anything so risky as our raid up the St. Mary's. But in truth it seems to me a mere absurdity to deliberately argue the question of courage, as applied to men among whom I waked and slept, day and night, for so many months together. As well might he who has been wandering for years upon the desert, with a Bedouin escort, discuss the courage of the men whose tents have been his shelter and whose spears his guard. We, their officers, did not go there to teach lessons, but to receive them. There were more than a hundred men in the ranks who had voluntarily met more dangers in their escape from slavery than any of my young captains had incurred in all their lives.

There was a family named Wilson, I remember, of which we had several representatives. Three or four brothers had planned an escape from the interior to our lines; they finally decided that the youngest should stay and take care of the old mother; the rest, with their sister and her children, came in a "dug-out" down one of the rivers. They were fired upon, again and again, by the pickets along the banks, until finally every man on board was wounded; and still they got safely through. When the bullets began to fly about them, the woman shed tears, and her little girl of nine said to her, "Don't cry, mother, Jesus will help you," and then the child began praying as the wounded men still urged the boat along. This the mother told me, but I had previously heard it from on officer who was on the gunboat that picked them up,—a big, rough man, whose voice fairly broke as he described their appearance. He said that the mother and child had been hid for nine months in the woods before attempting their escape, and the child would speak to no one—indeed, she hardly would when she came to our camp. She was almost white, and this officer wished to adopt her, but the mother said, "I would do anything but that for *oonah*," this being a sort of Indian formation of the second-person-plural, such as they sometimes use. This same officer afterwards saw a reward offered for this family in a Savannah paper.

I used to think that I should not care to read "Uncle Tom's Cabin" in our camp; it would have seemed tame. Any group of men in a tent would have had more exciting tales to tell. I needed no fiction when I had Fanny Wright, for instance, daily passing to and fro before my tent, with her shy little girl clinging to her skirts. Fanny was a modest little mulatto woman, a soldier's wife, and a company laundress. She had escaped from the mainland in a boat, with that child and another. Her baby was shot dead in her arms, and she reached our lines with one child safe on earth and the other in heaven. I never found it needful to give any elementary instructions in courage to Fanny's husband, you may be sure.

There was another family of brothers in the regiment named Miller. Their grandmother, a fine-looking old woman, nearly seventy, I should think, but erect as a pine-tree, used sometimes to come and visit them. She and her husband had once tried to escape from a plantation near Savannah. They had failed, and had been brought back; the husband had received five hundred lashes, and while the white men on the plantation were viewing the punishment, she was collecting her children and grand-children, to the number of twenty-two, in a neighboring marsh, prepa-ratory to another attempt that night. They found a flat-boat which had been rejected as unseaworthy, got on board,—still under the old woman's orders—and drifted forty miles down the river to our lines. Trowbridge happened to be on board the gunboat which picked them up, and he said that when the "flat" touched the side of the vessel, the grandmother rose to her full height, with her youngest grandchild in her arms, and said only, "My God! are we free?" By one of those coincidences of which life is full, her husband escaped also, after his punishment, and was taken up by the same gunboat.

I hardly need point out that my young lieutenants did not have to teach the principles of courage to this woman's grandchildren.

I often asked myself why it was that, with this capacity of daring and endurance, they had not kept the land in a perpetual flame of insurrec-tion; why, especially since the opening of the war, they had kept so still. The answer was to be found in the peculiar temperament of the races, in their religious faith, and in the habit of patience that centuries had forti-fied. The shrewder men all said substantially the same thing. What was the use of insurrection, where everything was against them? They had no knowledge, no money, no arms, no drill, no organization,—above all, no mutual confidence. It was the tradition among them that all insurrections were always betrayed by somebody. They had no mountain passes to defend like the Maroons of Jamaica—no unpenetrable swamps, like the Maroons of Surinam. Where they had these, even on a small scale, they had used them—as in certain swamps round Savannah and in the everglades of Florida, where they united with the Indians, and would stand fire—so I was told by General Saxton, who had fought them there—when the Indians would retreat.

It always seemed to me that, had I been a slave, my life would have been one long scheme of insurrection. But I learned to respect the patient self-control of those who had waited till the course of events should open a better way. When it came they accepted it. Insurrection on their part would at once have divided the Northern sentiment; and a large part of our army would have joined with the Southern army to hunt them down. By their waiting till we needed them, their freedom was secured.

Two things chiefly surprised me in their feeling toward their former masters—the absence of affection and the absence of revenge. I expected to find a good deal of the patriarchal feeling. It always seemed to me a very ill-applied emotion, as connected with the facts and laws of American slavery—still I expected to find it. I suppose that my men and their families and visitors may have had as much of it as the mass of freed slaves; but certainly they had not a particle. I never could cajole one of them, in his most discontented moment, into regretting "ole mas'r time" for a single instant. I never heard one speak of the masters except as natural enemies. Yet they were perfectly discriminating as to individuals; many of them claimed to have had kind owners, and some expressed great gratitude to them for particular favors received. It was not the individuals, but the ownership, of which they complained. That they saw to be a wrong which no special kindnesses could right. On this, as on all points connected with slavery, they understood the matter as clearly as Garrison or Phillips; the wisest philosophy could teach them nothing as to that, nor could any false philosophy befog them. After all, personal experience is the best logician.

Certainly this indifference did not proceed from any want of personal affection, for they were the most affectionate people among whom I had ever lived. They attached themselves to every officer who deserved love, and to some who did not; and if they failed to show it to their masters, it proved the wrongfulness of the mastery. On the other hand, they rarely showed one gleam of revenge, and I shall never forget the self-control with which one of our best sergeants pointed out to me, at Jacksonville, the very place where one of his brothers had been hanged by the whites for leading a party of fugitive slaves. He spoke of it as a historic matter, without any bearing on the present issue.

But side by side with this faculty of patience, there was a certain tropical element in the men, a sort of fiery ecstasy when aroused, which seemed to link them by blood with the French Turcos, and made them really resemble their natural enemies, the Celts, far more than the Anglo-Saxon temperament. To balance this there were great individual resources when alone—a sort of Indian wiliness and subtlety of resource. Their gregariousness and love of drill made them more easy to keep in hand than white American troops, who rather like to straggle or go in little squads, looking out for themselves, without being bothered with officers. The blacks prefer organization.

The point of inferiority that I always feared, though I never had occasion to prove it, was that they might show less fibre, less tough and dogged resistance, than whites, during a prolonged trial—a long, disastrous march, for instance, or the hopeless defense of a besieged town. I should not be afraid of their mutinying or running away, but of their drooping and dying. It might not turn out so; but I mention it for the sake of fairness, and to avoid overstating the merits of these troops. As to the simple general fact of courage and reliability I think no officer in our camp ever thought of there being any difference between black and white. And certainly the opinions of these officers, who for years risked their lives every moment on the fidelity of their men, were worth more than those of all the world beside.

No doubt there were reasons why this particular war was an especially favorable test of the colored soldiers. They had more to fight for than the whites. Besides the flag and the Union, they had home and wife and child.

They fought with ropes round their necks, and when orders were issued that the officers of colored troops should be put to death on capture, they took a grim satisfaction. It helped their *esprit de corps* immensely. With us, at least, there was to be no play-soldier. Though they had begun with a slight feeling of inferiority to the white troops, this compliment substituted a peculiar sense of self-respect. And even when the new colored regiments began to arrive from the North my men still pointed out this difference—that in case of ultimate defeat, the Northern troops, black or white, would go home, while the First South Carolina must fight it out or be re-enslaved. This was one thing that made the St. John's River so attractive to them and even to me—it was so much nearer the everglades. I used seriously to ponder, during the darker periods of the war, whether I might not end my days as an outlaw—a leader of Maroons.

Meanwhile, I used to try to make some capital for the Northern troops, in their estimate, by pointing out that it was a disinterested thing in these men from the free States, to come down there and fight, that the slaves might be free. But they were apt keenly to reply that many of the white soldiers disavowed this object, and said that that was not the object of the war, nor even likely to be its end. Some of them even repeated Mr. Seward's unfortunate words to Mr. Adams, which some general had been heard to quote. So, on the whole, I took nothing by the motion, as was apt to be the case with those who spoke a good word for our Government, in those vacillating and half proslavery days.

At any rate, this ungenerous discouragement had this good effect, that it touched their pride; they would deserve justice, even if they did not obtain it. This pride was afterwards severely tested during the disgraceful period when the party of repudiation in Congress temporarily deprived them of their promised pay. In my regiment the men never mutinied, nor even threatened mutiny; they seemed to make it a matter of honor to do their part, even if the Government proved a defaulter; but one third of them, including the best men in the regiment, quietly refused to take a dollar's pay, at the reduced price. "We'se gib our sogerin' to de Guv'ment, Gunnel," they said, "but we won't 'spise ourselves so much for take de seben dollar." They even made a contemptuous ballad, of which I once caught a snatch.

"Ten dollar a month! Tree ob dat for clothin'l Go to Washington. Fight for Linkum's darter!"

This "Lincoln's daughter" stood for the Goddess of Liberty, it would seem. They would be true to her, but they would not take the half-pay. This was contrary to my advice, and to that of other officers; but I now think it was wise. Nothing less than this would have called the attention of the American people to this outrageous fraud. The same slow forecast had often marked their action in other ways. One of our ablest sergeants, Henry McIntyre, who had earned two dollars and a half per day as a master-carpenter in Florida, and paid one dollar and a half to his master, told me that he had deliberately refrained from learning to read, because that knowledge exposed the slaves to so much more watching and suspicion. This man and a few others had built on contract the greater part of the town of Micanopy in Florida, and was a thriving man when his accustomed discretion failed for once, and he lost all. He named his child William Lincoln, and it brought upon him such suspicion that he had to make his escape.

I cannot conceive what people at the North mean by speaking of the negroes as a bestial or brutal race. Except in some insensibility to animal pain, I never knew of an act in my regiment which I should call brutal. In reading Kay's "Condition of the English Peasantry" I was constantly struck with the unlikeness of my men to those therein described. This could not proceed from my prejudices as an abolitionist, for they would have led me the other way, and indeed I had once written a little essay to show the brutalizing influences of slavery. I learned to think that we abolitionists had underrated the suffering produced by slavery among the negroes, but had overrated the demoralization. Or rather, we did not know how the religious temperament of the negroes had checked the demoralization. Yet again, it must be admitted that this temperament, born of sorrow and oppression, is far more marked in the slave than in the native African.

Theorize as we may, there was certainly in our camp an average tone of propriety which all visitors noticed, and which was not created, but only preserved by discipline. I was always struck, not merely by the courtesy of the men, but also by a certain sober decency of language. If a man had to report to me any disagreeable fact, for instance, he was sure to do it with gravity and decorum, and not blurt it out in an offensive way. And it certainly was a significant fact that the ladies of our camp, when we were so fortunate as to have such guests, the young wives, especially, of the adjutant and quartermaster, used to go among the tents when the men were off duty, in order to hear their big pupils read and spell, without the slightest fear of annoyance. I do not mean direct annoyance or insult, for no man who valued his life would have ventured that in presence of the others, but I mean the annoyance of accidentally seeing or hearing improprieties not intended for them. They both declared that they would not have moved about with anything like the same freedom in any white camp they had ever entered, and it always roused their indignation to hear the negro race called brutal or depraved.

This came partly from natural good manners, partly from the habit of deference, partly from ignorance of the refined and ingenious evil which is learned in large towns; but a large part came from their strongly religious temperament. Their comparative freedom from swearing, for instance— an abstinence which I fear military life did not strengthen—was partly a matter of principle. Once I heard one of them say to another, in a transport of indignation, "Ha-a-a, boy, s'pose I no be a Christian, I cuss you so!"—which was certainly drawing pretty hard upon the bridle. "Cuss," however, was a generic term for all manner of evil speaking; they would say, "He cuss me fool," or "He cuss me coward," as if the essence of propriety were in harsh and angry speech—which I take to be good ethics. But certainly, if Uncle Toby could have recruited his army in Flanders from our ranks, their swearing would have ceased to be historic.

It used to seem to me that never, since Cromwell's time, had there been soldiers in whom the religious element held such a place. "A religious army," "a gospel army," were their frequent phrases. In their prayer-meetings there was always a mingling, often quaint enough, of the warlike and the pious. "If each one of us was a praying man," said Corporal Thomas Long in a sermon, "it appears to me that we could fight as well with prayers as with bullets—for the Lord has said that if you have faith even as a grain of mustard-seed cut into four parts, you can say to the sycamore-tree, Arise, and it will come up." And though Corporal Long may have got a little perplexed in his botany, his faith proved itself by works, for he volunteered and went many miles on a solitary scouting expedition into the enemy's country in Florida, and got back safe, after I had given him up for lost.

The extremes of religious enthusiasm I did not venture to encourage, for I could not do it honestly; neither did I discourage them, but simply treated them with respect, and let them have their way, so long as they did not interfere with discipline. In general they promoted it. The mischievous little drummer-boys, whose scrapes and quarrels were the torment of my existence, might be seen kneeling together in their tents to say their prayers at night, and I could hope that their slumbers were blessed by some spirit of peace, such as certainly did not rule over their waking. The most reckless and daring fellows in the regiment were perfect fatalists in their confidence that God would watch over them, and that if they died, it would be because their time had come. This almost excessive faith, and the love of freedom and of their families, all co-operated with their pride as soldiers to make them do their duty. I could not have spared any of these incentives. Those of our officers who were personally the least influenced by such considerations, still saw the need of encouraging them among the men.

I am bound to say that this strongly devotional turn was not always accompanied by the practical virtues; but neither was it strikingly divorced from them. A few men, I remember, who belonged to the ancient order of hypocrites, but not many. Old Jim Cushman was our favorite representative scamp. He used to vex his righteous soul over the admission of the unregenerate to prayer-meetings, and went off once shaking his head and muttering, "Too much goat shout wid de sheep." But he who objected to this profane admixture used to get our mess-funds far more hopelessly mixed with his own, when he went out to buy chickens. And I remember that, on being asked by our Major, in that semi-Ethiopian dialect into which we sometimes slid, "How much wife you got, Jim?" the veteran replied, with a sort of penitence for lost opportunities, "On'y but four, Sah!"

Another man of somewhat similar quality went among us by the name of Henry Ward Beecher, from a remarkable resemblance in face and figure to that sturdy divine. I always felt a sort of admiration for this worthy, because of the thoroughness with which he outwitted me, and the sublime impudence in which he culminated. He got a series of passes from me, every week or two, to go and see his wife on a neighboring plantation, and finally, when this resource seemed exhausted, he came boldly for one more pass, that he might go and be married.

We used to quote *him* a good deal, also, as a sample of a certain Shakespearian boldness of personification in which the men sometimes indulged. Once, I remember, his captain had given him a fowling-piece to clean. Henry Ward had left it in the captain's tent, and the latter, finding it, had transferred the job to some one else.

Then came a confession, in this precise form, with many dignified gesticulations:

"Cappen! I took dat gun, and I put bun in Cappen tent. Den I look, and de gun not dar! Den Conscience say, Cappen mus' hab gib dat gun to somebody else for clean. Den I say, Conscience, you reason correck."

Compare Lancelot Gobbo's soliloquy in the "Two Gentlemen of Verona"!

Still, I maintain that, as a whole, the men were remarkably free from inconvenient vices. There was no more lying and stealing than in average white regiments. The surgeon was not much troubled by shamming sickness, and there were not a great many complaints of theft. There was less quarrelling than among white soldiers, and scarcely ever an instance of drunkenness. Perhaps the influence of their officers had something to do with this; for not a ration of whiskey was ever issued to the men, nor did I ever touch it, while in the army, nor approve a requisition for any of the officers, without which it could not easily be obtained. In this respect our surgeons fortunately agreed with me, and we never had reason to regret it. I believe the use of ardent spirits to be as useless and injurious in the army as on board ship, and among the colored troops, especially, who had never been accustomed to it, I think that it did only harm.

The point of greatest laxity in their moral habits—the want of a high standard of chastity—was not one which affected their camp life to any great extent, and it therefore came less under my observation. But I found to my relief that, whatever their deficiency in this respect, it was modified

by the general quality of their temperament, and indicated rather a soft-
ening and relaxation than a hardening and brutalizing of their moral
natures. Any insult or violence in this direction was a thing unknown. I
never heard of an instance. It was not uncommon for men to have two
or three wives in different plantations,—the second, or remoter, partner
being called a "'broad wife,'"—i.e. wife abroad. But the whole tendency
was toward marriage, and this state of things was only regarded as a
bequest from "mas'r time."

I knew a great deal about their marriages, for they often consulted
me, and took my counsel as lovers are wont to do,—that is, when it
pleased their fancy. Sometimes they would consult their captains first,
and then come to me in despairing appeal. "Cap'n Scroby [Trowbridge]
he acvise me not for marry dis lady, 'cause she hab seben chil'en. What for
use? Cap'n Scroby can't lub for me. I mus' lub for myself, and I lub he." I
remember that on this occasion "he" stood by, a most unattractive woman,
jet black, with an old pink muslin dress, torn white cotton gloves, and a
very flowery bonnet, that must have descended through generations of
tawdry mistresses.

I felt myself compelled to reaffirm the decision of the inferior court.
The result was as usual. They were married the next day, and I believe that
she proved an excellent wife, though she had seven children, whose father
was also in the regiment. If she did not, I know many others who did, and
certainly I have never seen more faithful or more happy marriages than
among that people.

The question was often asked, whether the Southern slaves or the
Northern free blacks made the best soldiers. It was a compliment to both
classes that each officer usually preferred those whom he had personally
commanded. I preferred those who had been slaves, for their greater docil-
ity and affectionateness, for the powerful stimulus which their new freedom gave, and for the fact that they were fighting, in a manner, for their
own homes and firesides. Every one of these considerations afforded a
special aid to discipline, and cemented a peculiar tie of sympathy between
them and their officers. They seemed like clansmen, and had a more con-
fiding and filial relation to us than seemed to me to exist in the Northern
colored regiments.

So far as the mere habits of slavery went, they were a poor preparation for military duty. Inexperienced officers often assumed that, because these men had been slaves before enlistment, they would bear to be treated as such afterwards. Experience proved the contrary. The more strongly we marked the difference between the slave and the soldier, the better for the regiment. One half of military duty lies in obedience, the other half in self-respect. A soldier without self-respect is worthless. Consequently there were no regiments in which it was so important to observe the courtesies and proprieties of military life as in these. I had to caution the officers to be more than usually particular in returning the salutations of the men; to be very careful in their dealings with those on picket or guard-duty; and on no account to omit the titles of the non-commissioned officers. So, in dealing out punishments, we had carefully to avoid all that was brutal and arbitrary, all that savored of the overseer. Any such dealing found them as obstinate and contemptuous as was Topsy when Miss Ophelia undertook to chastise her. A system of light punishments, rigidly administered according to the prescribed military forms, had more weight with them than any amount of angry severity. To make them feel as remote as possible from the plantation, this was essential. By adhering to this, and constantly appealing to their pride as soldiers and their sense of duty, we were able to maintain a high standard of discipline—so, at least, the inspecting officers said—and to get rid, almost entirely, of the more degrading class of punishments—standing on barrels, tying up by the thumbs, and the ball and chain.

In all ways we had to educate their self-respect. For instance, at first they disliked to obey their own non-commissioned officers. "I don't want him to play de white man ober me," was a sincere objection. They had been so impressed with a sense of inferiority that the distinction extended to the very principles of honor. "I ain't got colored-man principles," said Corporal London Simmons, indignantly defending himself from some charge before me. "I'se got white-gemman principles. I'se do my best. If Cap'n tell me to take a man, s'pose de man be as big as a house, I'll clam hold on him till I die, inception [excepting] I'm sick."

But it was plain that this feeling was a bequest of slavery, which military life would wear off. We impressed it upon them that they did not obey their officers because they were white, but because they were their officers, just as the Captain must obey me, and I the General; that we were all subject to military law, and protected by it in turn. Then we taught them to take pride in having good material for noncommissioned officers among themselves, and in obeying them. On my arrival there was one white first sergeant, and it was a question whether to appoint others. This I prevented, but left that one, hoping the men themselves would at last petition for his removal, which at length they did. He was at once detailed on other duty. The picturesqueness of the regiment suffered, for he was very tall and fair, and I liked to see him step forward in the centre when the line of first sergeants came together at dress-parade. But it was a help to discipline to eliminate the Saxon, for it recognized a principle.

Afterwards I had excellent battalion-drills without a single white officer, by way of experiment; putting each company under a sergeant, and going through the most difficult movements, such as division-columns and oblique-squares. And as to actual discipline, it is doing no injustice to the line-officers of the regiment to say that none of them received from the men more implicit obedience than Color-Sergeant Rivers. I should have tried to obtain commissions for him and several others before I left the regiment, had their literary education been sufficient; and such an attempt was finally made by Lieutenant-Colonel Trowbridge, my successor in immediate command, but it proved unsuccessful. It always seemed to me an insult to those brave men to have novices put over their heads, on the ground of color alone; and the men felt it the more keenly as they remained longer in service. There were more than seven hundred enlisted men in the regiment, when mustered out after more than three years' service. The ranks had been kept full by enlistment, but there were only fourteen line-officers instead of the full thirty. The men who should have filled those vacancies were doing duty as sergeants in the ranks.

In what respect were the colored troops a source of disappointment? To me in one respect only,—that of health. Their health improved, indeed, as they grew more familiar with military life; but I think that neither their physical nor moral temperament gave them that toughness, that obstinate purpose of living, which sustains the more materialistic Anglo-Saxon. They had not, to be sure, the same predominant diseases, suffering in the pulmonary, not in the digestive organs; but they suffered a good deal. They felt malaria less, but they were more easily choked by dust and made ill by dampness. On the other hand, they submitted more readily to sanitary measures than whites, and, with efficient officers, were more easily kept clean. They were injured throughout the army by an undue share of fatigue duty, which is not only exhausting but demoralizing to a soldier; by the un-suitableness of the rations, which gave them salt meat instead of rice and hominy; and by the lack of good medical attendance. Their childlike constitutions peculiarly needed prompt and efficient surgical care; but almost all the colored troops were enlisted late in the war, when it was hard to get good surgeons for any regiments, and especially for these. In this respect I had nothing to complain of, since there were no surgeons in the army for whom I would have exchanged my own.

And this late arrival on the scene affected not only the medical supervision of the colored troops, but their opportunity for a career. It is not my province to write their history, nor to vindicate them, nor to follow them upon those larger fields compared with which the adventures of my regiment appear but a partisan warfare. Yet this, at least, may be said. The operations on the South Atlantic coast, which long seemed a merely subordinate and incidental part of the great contest, proved to be one of the final pivots on which it turned. All now admit that the fate of the Confederacy was decided by Sherman's march to the sea. Port Royal was the objective point to which he marched, and he found the Department of the South, when he reached it, held almost exclusively by colored troops. Next to the merit of those who made the march was that of those who held open the door. That service will always remain among the laurels of the black regiments.

Source: Thomas Wentworth Higginson, *Army Life in a Black Regiment* (Cambridge, MA: Riverside Press, 1900; Project Gutenberg, 2004), chap. 12, http://www.gutenberg.org/ebooks/6764.

1864

BATTLE OF THE WILDERNESS

MAY 5-7, 1864
GEN. JAMES LONGSTREET, CSA

The Battle of the Wilderness scarred nearly everyone who went through it. This engagement marked the formal start of Grant's Overland Campaign through Virginia. The Army of the Potomac was on the move through the dense woods and underbrush of Spotsylvania County when Lee sent his Army of Northern Virginia to intercept them and halt their advance. What Lee needed was to destroy Grant's army, to whip it and send it slinking back northward. What Grant wanted was to grind down Lee's strength through an attritional campaign the Confederates could ill afford.

Grant's plan to move through the tangled Spotsylvania campaign came to naught. Many of the commanders on both sides were by now well known to their enemies: George Gordon Meade and Winfield Hancock on the Northern side; Longstreet, Richard Ewell, A. P. Hill, John B. Gordon on the Southern. The two sides fought an inconclusive, three-day running battle along the wooded roads and in the forest. The cries of the wounded mingled with the shouts of the combatants, and the result was chaotic. Fires broke out; many bodies were never found, and remain where they fell to this day. Eventually, Grant disengaged rather than directly assault fortified Confederate positions, preferring to maneuver toward better ground and keep edging toward Richmond. In this passage, Longstreet describes the frenetic and frequently confusing Battle of the Wilderness. Even the outcome was uncertain. Usually, the army that disengages can be considered defeated. Certainly, that was

*what happened previously: when Union attacks foundered, the blue
jackets headed forlornly back to safer lines. But this time, Grant
simply continued his advance through Virginia. His men noticed the
difference, and their spirits were high. Lee began to see that his
new rival was different, and the fact must have been disconcerting
in the extreme.*

After reporting the return of my command to service with the Army of
Northern Virginia, I took the earliest opportunity to suggest that the
preliminaries of the campaign should be carefully confined to strategic
manœuvre until we could show better generalship. That accomplished, I
argued, the enemy's forces would lose confidence in the superiority of their
leader's skill and prowess; that both armies were composed of intelligent,
experienced veterans, who were as quick to discover the better handling
of their ranks as trained generals; that by such successful manœuvres the
Confederates would gain confidence and power as the enemy began to
lose prestige; that then we could begin to look for a favorable opportunity
to call the enemy to aggressive work, while immediate aggression from
us against his greater numbers must make our labors heavy and more or
less doubtful; that we should first show that the power of battle is in generalship more than in the number of soldiers, which, properly illustrated,
would make the weaker numbers of the contention the stronger force.

In this connection I refer to the policy of attrition which became a
prominent feature during part of the campaign, and showed that the enemy
put his faith in numbers more than in superior skill and generalship. . . .

At midnight of the 3d of May, 1864, the Army of the Potomac took
its line of march for the lower crossings of the Rapidan River at Germania and Ely's Fords, the Fifth and Sixth Corps for the former, the Second for the latter, Wilson's division of cavalry leading the first, Gregg's the
second column. The cavalry was to secure the crossings and lay bridges for
the columns as they came up. Wilson's cavalry crossed at Germania ford,
drove off the Confederate outpost, and began the construction of a bridge
at daylight. Gregg also was successful, and the bridges were ready when
the solid columns came. Warren's (Fifth Corps) crossed after Wilson's
cavalry, marching westward as far as Wilderness Tavern. Sedgwick's corps

followed and pitched camp near the crossing. Hancock's corps followed Gregg's cavalry, and made camp at Chancellorsville. Generals Grant and Meade went over after Warren's column and established head-quarters near the crossing. General Grant dispatched for Burnside's corps to come and join him by night march. Sheridan was expected to engage Stuart's cavalry at Hamilton's Crossing near Fredericksburg.

General Grant had no fixed plan of campaign beyond the general idea to avoid the strong defensive line occupied by General Lee behind Mine Run, and find a way to draw him out to open battle.

The Wilderness is a forest land of about fifteen miles square, lying between and equidistant from Orange Court-House and Fredericksburg. It is broken occasionally by small farms and abandoned clearings, and two roads—the Orange Plank road and the turnpike, which are cut at right angles by the Germania road—in general course nearly parallel, open ways through it between Fredericksburg and the Court-House. The Germania Ford road joins the Brock road, the strategic line of the military zone, and crosses the turnpike at Wilderness Tavern and the Plank road about two miles south of that point.

Though the march was set on foot at midnight it was soon made known to General Lee, and its full purport was revealed by noon of the 4th, and orders were sent the different commanders for their march to meet the enemy,—the Second Corps (Ewell's), consisting of Rodes's, Johnson's, and Early's divisions, by the Orange Turnpike; in accordance with the general plan of turning the Confederate right without touching our intrenched line along Mine Run, the Army of the Potomac had been put in motion early on the 5th, the Second Corps towards Shady Grove Church by the Todd's Tavern road, the Fifth by the dirt road towards Parker's Store on the Plank road, the Sixth on the right, to follow the Fifth as movements developed. General Warren moved with three divisions, leaving Griffin's on the turnpike. Presently, after taking up his march towards Parker's Store, the Confederates were discovered on the Plank road, and General Meade ordered the corps made ready for battle. The Sixth, except Getty's division, was ordered to make connection on the right of the Fifth by wood roads, and prepare for the battle. Getty's division was ordered to the Plank road at the Brock road crossing, to hold that point at all hazards until the Second Corps could join it, the latter being recalled from Todd's Tavern for that holding and developments there indicated the Third (A. P. Hill's)—R. H. Anderson's, Heth's, and Wilcox's divisions—by the Orange Plank road in accordance with the general plan of turning the Confederate right without touching our entrenched line along Mine Run, the Army of the Potomac had been put in motion early on the 5th, the Second Corps towards Shady Grove Church by the Todd's Tavern road, the Fifth by the dirt road towards Parker's Store on the Plank road, the Sixth on the right, to follow the Fifth as movements developed. General Warren moved with three divisions, leaving Griffin's on the turnpike. Presently, after taking up his march towards Parker's Store, the Confederates were discovered on the Plank road, and General Meade ordered the corps made ready for battle. The Sixth, except Getty's division, was ordered to make connection on the right of the Fifth by wood roads, and prepare for the battle. Getty's division was ordered to the Plank road at the Brock road crossing, to hold that point at all hazards until the Second Corps could join it, the latter being recalled from Todd's Tavern for that holding and developments there indicated.

General Getty was in time to drive back a few of our men who had reached the Brock road in observation, and Hancock's corps joined him at two p.m., fronting his divisions—Birney's, Mott's, Gibbon's, and Barlow's—along the Brock road, on the left of Getty's. His artillery was massed on his left, near Barlow, except a battery nearer the Plank road, and one section at the crossing. He ordered his line entrenched.

As soon as he found his troops in hand at the cross-roads, General Meade ordered them into action. Getty's division, supported by the Second Corps, was to drive Hill back, occupy Parker's Store, and connect with Warren's line. He afterwards learned of the repulse of Warren on the turnpike, but repeated his orders for the advance on the Plank road. At 4.15 Getty's division advanced, and met the divisions of Heth and Wilcox a few hundred yards in advance of their trenches.

In the fierce engagement that followed, Birney's and Mott's divisions were engaged on Getty's left, and later the brigades of Carroll and Owen, of Gibbon's division. Wadsworth's division and Baxter's brigade of the Fifth Corps were put in to aid Getty's right. The combination forced

Heth and Wilcox back about half a mile, when the battle rested for the night. Hancock reinforced his front by Webb's brigade of Gibbon's division, and was diligently employed at his lines during the night putting up field-works.

About eleven o'clock in the night the guide reported from General Lee to conduct my command through the wood across to the Plank road, and at one o'clock the march was resumed. The road was overgrown by the bushes, except the sidetracks made by the draft animals and the ruts of wheels which marked occasional lines in its course. After a time the wood became less dense, and the unused road was more difficult to follow, and presently the guide found that there was no road under him; but no time was lost, as, by ordering the lines of the divisions doubled, they were ready when the trail was found, and the march continued in double line. At daylight we entered the Plank road, and filed down towards the field of strife of the afternoon of the 5th and daylight of the 6th. . . .

Hancock advanced and struck the divisions before sunrise, just as my command reported to General Lee. My line was formed on the right and left of the Plank road, Kershaw on the right, Field on the left. As the line deployed, the divisions of Heth and Wilcox came back upon us in disorder, more and more confused as their steps hurried under Hancock's musketry. As my ranks formed the men broke files to give free passage for their comrades to the rear. The advancing fire was getting brisk, but not a shot was fired in return by my troops until the divisions were ready. Three of Field's brigades, the Texas, Alabama, and Benning's Georgia, were formed in line on the left of the road, and three of Kershaw's on the right. General Lee, appalled at the condition of affairs, thought to lead the Texas brigade alone into desperate charge, before my lines were well formed. The ordeal was trying, but the steady troops, seeing him off his balance, refused to follow, begged him to retire, and presently Colonel Venable, of his staff, reported to me General Lee's efforts to lead the brigade, and suggested that I should try to call him from it. I asked that he would say, with my compliments, that his line would be recovered in an hour if he would permit me to handle the troops, but if my services were not needed, I would like to ride to some place of safety, as it was not quite comfortable where we were.

As full lines of battle could not be handled through the thick wood, I ordered the advance of the six brigades by heavy skirmish lines, to be followed by stronger supporting lines. Hancock's lines, thinned by their push through the wood, and somewhat by the fire of the disordered divisions, weaker than my line of fresh and more lively skirmishers, were checked by our first steady, rolling fire, and after a brisk fusillade were pushed back to their intrenched line, when the fight became steady and very firm, occasionally swinging parts of my line back and compelling the reserves to move forward and recover it. . . .

The Twelfth Virginia Regiment got to the plank road some little time before the other regiments of the brigade, and, viewing the contention on the farther side between Field's and Wadsworth's divisions, dashed across and struck the left of Wadsworth's line. This relieved Field a little, and, under this concentrating push and fire, Wadsworth fell mortally wounded. In a little while followed the general break of the Union battle. The break of his left had relieved Kershaw's troops, and he was waiting for the time to advance, and Jenkins's brigade that had been held in reserve and that part of R. H. Anderson's division not in use were ready and anxious for opportunity to engage, and followed as our battle line pushed forward.

General Smith then came and reported a way across the Brock road that would turn Hancock's extreme left. He was asked to conduct the flanking brigades and handle them as the ranking officer. He was a splendid tactician as well as skillful engineer, and gallant withal. He started, and, not to lose time or distance, moved by inversion, Wofford's left leading, Wofford's favorite manœuvre. As Wofford's left stepped out, the other troops moved down the Plank road, Jenkins's brigade by the road, Kershaw's division alongside. I rode at the head of the column, Jenkins, Kershaw, and the staff with me. After discussing the dispositions of their troops for reopening battle, Jenkins rode closer to offer congratulations, saying, "I am happy; I have felt despair of the cause for some months, but am relieved, and feel assured that we will put the enemy back across the Rapidan before night." Little did he or I think these sanguine words were the last he would utter.

When Wadsworth fell the Union battle broke up in hasty retreat. Field's brigades closed to fresh ranks, the flanking brigades drew into line near the Plank road, and with them the other regiments of Mahone's brigade; but the Twelfth Regiment, some distance in advance of the others, had crossed the road to strike at Wadsworth's left before the other regiments were in sight, and was returning to find its place in line. The order for the flanking brigades to resume march by their left had not moved those brigades of the right. As the Twelfth Regiment marched back to find its place on the other side of the Plank road, it was mistaken, in the wood, for an advance of the enemy, and fire was opened on it from the other regiments of the brigade. The men threw themselves to the ground to let the fire pass. Just then our party of officers was up and rode under the fire. General Jenkins had not finished the expressions of joyful congratulations which I have quoted when he fell mortally wounded.

Captain Doby and the orderly, Bowen, of Kershaw's staff, were killed. General Kershaw turned to quiet the troops, when Jenkins's brigade with leveled guns were in the act of returning the fire of the supposed enemy concealed in the wood, but as Kershaw's clear voice called out "F-r-i-e-n-d-s!" the arms were recovered, without a shot in return, and the men threw themselves down upon their faces.

At the moment that Jenkins fell I received a severe shock from a minie ball passing through my throat and right shoulder. The blow lifted me from the saddle, and my right arm dropped to my side, but I settled back to my seat, and started to ride on, when in a minute the flow of blood admonished me that my work for the day was done. As I turned to ride back, members of the staff, seeing me about to fall, dismounted and lifted me to the ground. . . .

My command, less than ten thousand, had found the battle on the Plank road in retreat, little less than a panic. In a few hours we changed defeat to victory, the broken divisions of the Third Corps rallying in their rear.

As my litter was borne to the rear my hat was placed over my face, and soldiers by the road-side said, "He is dead, and they are telling us he is only wounded." Hearing this repeated from time to time, I raised my hat with my left hand, when the burst of voices and the flying of hats in the air eased my pains somewhat.

Source: James Longstreet, *From Manassas to Appomattox: Memoirs of the Civil War in America* (Philadelphia: J. B. Lippincott Company, 1896; Project Gutenberg, 2011), chap. 38, http://www.gutenberg.org/ebooks/38418.

SPOTSYLVANIA AND THE
DEATH OF JEB STUART

MAY 8-21, 1864
GEN. PHILIP H. SHERIDAN, USA

J. E. B. Stuart was among the most dashing and charismatic Confederate generals. His cavalry exploits frequently did more than defeat Union forces; often, he humiliated his opponents. He understood the martial value that his image enhanced and cultivated it by wearing a plumed hat, cape, and sash. His horsemen were Lee's eyes and ears, and their leader was, by looks and accomplishments, the living embodiment of the Confederate cavalier. Stuart's escapades and victories stretched from Bull Run through the Peninsular and Maryland campaigns, Chancellorsville, Brandy Station, and Gettysburg. As the Overland Campaign developed, this gallant cavalryman was a CSA major general and still one of Lee's most valued associates (despite complaints that, at Gettysburg, Stuart's feat of circumnavigating Union positions did nothing but satisfy his ego and deprive Lee of needed intelligence). Stuart's men fought hard at The Wilderness, and Lee warned his favorite not to wear out the cavalry. At Spotsylvania Court House, Stuart took charge of impeding the ambitious Union cavalry, so ardent now that it was unleashed deep in Virginia.

The Union horse soldiers felt confident because their commander, Sheridan, was perhaps the one Northern general who could match Stuart for hard-charging charisma, battlefield skill, and resolute spirit. At Spotsylvania Court House, Meade and Sheridan

J. E. B. Stuart

squabbled. Sheridan demanded to be turned loose against Stu-art, whom he promised to whip. Grant mediated, pointing out that Sheridan usually backed up his big talk, and the Union horsemen rode out to raid railroads and destroy infrastructure. As Sheridan hoped, Stuart's men rode to meet them, and they met at Yellow Tavern. Stuart fought with his usual vigor, but was felled by a rifle bullet. He lingered long enough to see Jefferson Davis, and pro-nounced his willingness to die for his country, which is precisely what happened. Stuart was thirty-one when he was killed, and, as previously with Stonewall Jackson, Lee found himself deprived of a trusted commander and sustaining casualties he could not afford. Here, Sheridan recounts the battle that cost the Confederacy his most colorful rival.

Headquarters
Army of the Potomac
May 8th, 1864, 1 p.m.

General Sheridan,
Commanding Cavalry Corps

The major-general commanding directs you to immediately concen-trate your available mounted force, and with your ammunition trains and such supply trains as are filled (exclusive of ambulances) proceed against the enemy's cavalry, and when your supplies are exhausted, proceed via New Market and Green Bay to Haxall's Landing on the James River, there communicating with General Butler, procuring supplies and return to this army. Your dismounted men will be left with the train here.

A. A. Humphreys
Major-General, Chief-of-Staff

As soon as the above order was received I issued instructions for the con-centration of the three divisions of cavalry at Aldrich's to prepare for the contemplated expedition. Three days' rations for the men were distributed, and half rations of grain for one day were doled out for the horses. I sent for Gregg, Merritt, and Wilson and communicated the order to them, saying at the same time, "We are going out to fight Stuart's cavalry in consequence of a suggestion from me; we will give him a fair, square fight; we are strong, and I know we can beat him, and in view of my recent representations to General Meade I shall expect nothing but success." I also indicated to my division commanders the line of march I should take—moving in one column around the right flank of Lee's army to get in its rear—and stated at the same time that it was my intention to fight Stuart wherever he presented himself, and if possible go through to Haxall's Landing; but that if Stuart should successfully interpose between us and that point we would swing back to the Army of the Potomac by passing around the enemy's left flank by way of Gordonsville. At first the proposition seemed to surprise the division commanders somewhat, for hitherto even the boldest, mounted expeditions had been confined to a hurried ride through the enemy's country, without purpose of fighting more than enough to escape in case of molestation, and here and there to destroy a bridge. Our move would be a challenge to Stuart for a cavalry duel behind Lee's lines, in his own country, but the advantages which it was reasonable to anticipate from the plan being quickly perceived, each division commander entered into its support unhesitatingly, and at once set about preparing for the march next day . . .

The expedition which resulted in the battle of Yellow Tavern and the death of General Stuart started from the vicinity of Aldrich's toward Fredericksburg early on the morning of May 9, 1864, marching on the plank-road, Merritt's division leading. When the column reached Tabernacle Church it headed almost due east to the telegraph road, and thence down that highway to Thornburg, and from that point through Childsburg to Anderson's crossing of the North Anna River, it being my desire to put my command south of that stream if possible, where it could procure forage before it should be compelled to fight. The corps moved at a walk, three divisions on the same road, making a column nearly thirteen miles in length, and marched around the right flank of the enemy unsuspected until my rear guard had passed Massaponax Church. Although the column was very long, I preferred to move it all on one road rather than to attempt combinations for carrying the divisions to any given point by different routes. Unless the separate commands in an expedition of this nature are very prompt in movement, and each fully equal to overcoming at once any obstacle it may meet, combinations rarely work out as expected; besides, an engagement was at all times imminent, hence it was specially necessary to keep the whole force well together.

As soon as the Ny, Po, and Ta rivers were crossed, each of which streams would have afforded an excellent defensive line to the enemy, all anxiety as to our passing around Lee's army was removed, and our ability to cross the North Anna placed beyond doubt. Meanwhile General Stuart had discovered what we were about, and he set his cavalry in motion, sending General Fitzhugh Lee to follow and attack my rear on the Childsburg road, Stuart himself marching by way of Davenport's bridge, on the North Anna, toward Beaver Dam Station, near which place his whole command was directed to unite the next day.

My column having passed the Ta River, Stuart attacked its rear with considerable vigor, in the hope that he could delay my whole force long enough to permit him to get at least a part of his command in my front; but this scheme was frustrated by Davies's brigade, which I directed to fight as a rear-guard, holding on at one position and then at another along the line of march just enough to deter the enemy from a too rapid advance. Davies performed this responsible and trying duty with tact and good judgment, following the main column steadily as it progressed to the south, and never once permitting Fitzhugh Lee's advance to encroach far enough to compel a halt of my main body. About dark Merritt's division crossed the North Anna at Anderson's ford, while Gregg and Wilson encamped on the north side, having engaged the enemy, who still hung on my rear up to a late hour at night.

After Merritt's division passed the river, Custer's brigade proceeded on to Beaver Dam Station to cut the Virginia Central railroad. Before reaching the station he met a small force of the enemy, but this he speedily drove off, recapturing from it about four hundred Union prisoners, who had been taken recently in the Wilderness and were being conducted to Richmond. Custer also destroyed the station, two locomotives, three trains of cars, ninety wagons, from eight to ten miles of railroad and tele-graph lines, some two hundred thousand pounds of bacon and other sup-plies, amounting in all to about a million and a half of rations, and nearly all they medical stores of General Lee's army, which had been moved from Orange Court House either because Lee wished to have them directly in his rear or because he contemplated falling back to the North Anna . . .

Stuart had hardly united his troops near Beaver Dam when he real-ized that concentrating there was a mistake, so he began making disposi-tions for remedying his error, and while we leisurely took the Negro-foot road toward Richmond, he changed his tactics and hauled off from my rear, urging his horses to the death in order to get in between Richmond and my column. This he affected about 10 o'clock on the morning of the 11th, concentrating at Yellow Tavern, six miles from the city, on the Brook turnpike. His change of tactics left my march on the 10th practi-cally unmolested, and we quietly encamped that night on the south bank of the South Anna, near Ground Squirrel Bridge. Here we procured an abundance of forage, and as the distance traveled that day had been only fifteen to eighteen miles, men and horses were able to obtain a good rest during the night . . .

By forced marches General Stuart succeeded in reaching Yellow Tav-ern ahead of me on May 11; and the presence of his troops, on the Ashland and Richmond road becoming known to Merritt as he was approaching the Brook turnpike, this general pressed forward at once to the attack. Pushing his division to the front, he soon got possession of the turnpike and drove the enemy back several hundred yards to the east of it. This success had the effect of throwing the head of my column to the east of the pike, and I quickly brought up Wilson and one of Gregg's brigades to take advantage of the situation by forming a line of battle on that side or the road. Meanwhile the enemy, desperate but still confident, poured in a heavy fire from his line and from a battery which enfiladed the Brook road, and made Yellow Tavern an uncomfortably hot place. Gibbs's and Devin's brigades, however, held fast there, while Custer, supported by Chapman's brigade, attacked the enemy's left and battery in a mounted charge.

Custer's charge, with Chapman on his flank and the rest of Wilson's division sustaining him, was brilliantly executed. Beginning at a walk, he increased his gait to a trot, and then at full speed rushed at the enemy. At the same moment the dismounted troops along my whole front moved forward, and as Custer went through the battery, capturing two of the guns with their cannoneers and breaking up the enemy's left, Gibbs and Devin drove his center and right from the field. Gregg meanwhile, with equal success, charged the force in his rear-Gordon's brigade and the engagement ended by giving us complete control of the road to Richmond. We captured a number of prisoners, and the casualties on both sides were quite severe, General Stuart himself falling mortally wounded, and General James B. Gordon, one of his brigade commanders, being killed ...

Meanwhile the most intense excitement prevailed in Richmond. The Confederates, supposing that their capital was my objective point, were straining every effort to put it in a state of defense, and had collected between four and five thousand irregular troops, under General Bragg, besides bringing up three brigades of infantry from the force confronting General Butler south of the James River, the alarm being intensified by the retreat, after the defeat at Yellow Tavern, of Stuart's cavalry, now under General Fitzhugh Lee, by way of Ashland to Mechanicsville, on the north side of the Chickahominy, for falling back in that direction, left me between them and Richmond ...

The Confederates advanced from behind their works at Richmond, and attacked Wilson and Gregg. Wilson's troops were driven back in some confusion at first; but Gregg, in anticipation of attack, had hidden a heavy line of dismounted men in a bushy ravine on his front, and when the enemy marched upon it, with much display and under the eye of the President of the Confederacy, this concealed line opened a destructive fire with repeating carbines; and at the same time the batteries of horse-artillery, under Captain Robinson, joining in the contest, belched forth shot and shell with fatal effect. The galling fire caused the enemy to falter, and while still wavering Wilson rallied his men, and turning some of them against the right flank of the Confederates, broke their line, and compelled them to withdraw for security behind the heavy works thrown up for the defense of the city in 1862.

By destroying the Meadow bridge and impeding my column on the Mechanicsville, pike, the enemy thought to corner us completely, for he still maintained the force in Gregg's rear that had pressed it the day before; but the repulse of his infantry ended all his hopes of doing us any serious damage on the limited ground between the defenses of Richmond and the Chickahominy. He felt certain that on account of the recent heavy rains we could not cross the Chickahominy except by the Meadow bridge, and it also seemed clear to him that we could not pass between the river and his intrenchments; therefore he hoped to ruin us, or at least compel us to return by the same route we had taken in coming, in which case we would run into Gordon's brigade, but the signal repulse of Bragg's infantry dispelled these illusions . . .

The chances of seriously injuring us were more favorable to the enemy this time than ever they were afterward, for with the troops from Richmond, comprising three brigades of veterans and about five thousand irregulars on my front and right flank, with Gordon's cavalry in the rear, and Fitzhugh Lee's cavalry on my left flank, holding the Chickahominy and Meadow bridge, I was apparently hemmed in on every side, but relying on the celerity with which mounted troops could be moved, I felt perfectly confident that the seemingly perilous situation could be relieved under circumstances even worse than those then surrounding us. Therefore, instead of endeavoring to get away without a fight, I concluded that there would be little difficulty in withdrawing, even should I be beaten, and none whatever if I defeated the enemy.

In accordance with this view I accepted battle; and the complete repulse of the enemy's infantry, which assailed us from his entrenchments, and of Gordon's cavalry, which pressed Gregg on the Brook road, ended the contest in our favor. The rest of the day we remained on the battle-field undisturbed, and our time was spent in collecting the wounded, burying the dead, grazing the horses, and reading the Richmond journals, two small newsboys with commendable enterprise having come within our lines from the Confederate capital to sell their papers. They were sharp youngsters, and having come well supplied, they did a thrifty business. When their stock in trade was all disposed of they wished to return, but they were so intelligent and observant that I thought their mission involved other purposes than the mere sale of newspapers, so they were held till we crossed the Chickahominy and then turned loose.

After Merritt had crossed the Chickahominy and reached Mechanic-sville, I sent him orders to push on to Gaines's Mills. Near the latter place he fell in with the enemy's cavalry again, and sending me word, about 4 o'clock in the afternoon I crossed the Chickahominy with Wilson and Gregg, but when we overtook Merritt he had already brushed the Confederates away, and my whole command went into camp between Walnut Grove and Gaines's Mills.

The main purposes of the expedition had now been executed. They were "to break up General Lee's railroad communications, destroy such depots of supplies as could be found in his rear, and to defeat General Stuart's cavalry." Many miles of the Virginia Central and of the Richmond and Fredericksburg railroads were broken up, and several of the bridges on each burnt. At Beaver Dam, Ashland, and other places, about two millions of rations had been captured and destroyed. The most important of all, however, was the defeat of Stuart. Since the beginning of the war this general had distinguished himself by his management of the Confederate mounted force. Under him the cavalry of Lee's army had been nurtured, and had acquired such prestige that it thought itself well nigh invincible; indeed, in the early years of the war it had proved to be so. This was now dispelled by the successful march we had made in Lee's rear; and the discomfiture of Stuart at Yellow Tavern had inflicted a blow from which entire recovery was impossible.

In its effect on the Confederate cause the defeat of Stuart was most disheartening, but his death was even a greater calamity, as is evidenced by the words of a Confederate writer (Cooke), who says: "Stuart could be ill spared at this critical moment, and General Lee was plunged into the deepest melancholy at the intelligence of his death. When it reached him he retired from those around him, and remained for some time communing with his own heart and memory. When one of his staff entered and spoke of Stuart, General Lee said: 'I can scarcely think of him without weeping.'"

Source: Philip H. Sheridan, *Personal Memoirs of P. H. Sheridan* (New York: Charles L. Webster & Company, 1888; Project Gutenberg, 2004), vol. 1, chap. 18, http://www .gutenberg.org/ebooks/4362.

THE CRIME AT PICKETT'S MILL;
THE ATLANTA CAMPAIGN

MAY 27, 1864
LT. AMBROSE BIERCE, USA

Just as everyone knew that Richmond was Grant's objective, so too did they understand that Sherman was headed for Atlanta. With increasing desperation, the Confederacy threw its waning resources and exhausted men against this Union menace. But Sherman, like Grant, would not be stopped. Even when Union troops lost a battle, as they did at New Hope Church, Sherman retained the initiative and kept up the pressure. At New Hope Church, Confederates lay in wait for Gen. Oliver O. Howard's expected assault. The attack failed; in the fog of war, expected reinforcements did not show up, and Howard's men were driven off. Among them was Ambrose Bierce, who recounts this defeat. It was a victory that did give Confederate morale a boost, but at best it merely slowed Sherman's inexorable progress.

There is a class of events which by their very nature, and despite any intrinsic interest that they may possess, are foredoomed to oblivion. They are merged in the general story of those greater events of which they were a part, as the thunder of a billow breaking on a distant beach is unnoted in the continuous roar. To how many having knowledge of the battles of our Civil War does the name Pickett's Mill suggest acts of heroism and devotion performed in scenes of awful carnage to accomplish the impossible? Buried in the official reports of the victors there are indeed imperfect accounts of the engagement: the vanquished have not thought it expedient to relate it. It is ignored by General Sherman in his memoirs, yet Sherman ordered it. General Howard wrote an account of the campaign of which it was an incident, and dismissed it in a single sentence; yet General Howard planned it, and it was fought as an isolated and independent action under his eye. Whether it was so trifling an affair as to justify this inattention let the reader judge.

The fight occurred on the 27th of May, 1864, while the armies of Generals Sherman and Johnston confronted each other near Dallas, Georgia, during the memorable "Atlanta campaign." For three weeks we had been pushing the Confederates southward, partly by manoeuvring, partly by fighting, out of Dalton, out of Resaca, through Adairsville, Kingston and Cassville. Each army offered battle everywhere, but would accept it only on its own terms. At Dallas Johnston made another stand and Sherman, facing the hostile line, began his customary manoeuvring for an advantage. General Wood's division of Howard's corps occupied a position opposite the Confederate right. Johnston finding himself on the 26th overlapped by Schofield, still farther to Wood's left, retired his right (Polk) across a creek, whither we followed him into the woods with a deal of desultory bickering, and at nightfall had established the new lines at nearly a right angle with the old—Schofield reaching well around and threatening the Confederate rear.

The civilian reader must not suppose when he reads accounts of military operations in which relative positions of the forces are defined, as in the foregoing passages, that these were matters of general knowledge to those engaged. Such statements are commonly made, even by those high in command, in the light of later disclosures, such as the enemy's official reports. It is seldom, indeed, that a subordinate officer knows anything about the disposition of the enemy's forces—except that it is unaimable—or precisely whom he is fighting. As to the rank and file, they can know nothing more of the matter than the arms they carry. They hardly know what troops are upon their own right or left the length of a regiment away. If it is a cloudy day they are ignorant even of the points of the compass. It may be said, generally, that a soldier's knowledge of what is going on about him is coterminous with his official relation to it and his personal connection with it; what is going on in front of him he does not know at all until he learns it afterward.

At nine o'clock on the morning of the 27th Wood's division was withdrawn and replaced by Stanley's. Supported by Johnson's division, it moved at ten o'clock to the left, in the rear of Schofield, a distance of four miles through a forest, and at two o'clock in the afternoon had reached a position where General Howard believed himself free to move in behind the enemy's forces and attack them in the rear, or at least, striking them in the flank, crush his way along their line in the direction of its length, throw them into confusion and prepare an easy victory for a supporting attack in front. In selecting General Howard for this bold adventure General Sherman was doubtless not unmindful of Chancellorsville, where Stonewall Jackson had executed a similar manoeuvre for Howard's instruction. Experience is a normal school: it teaches how to teach.

There are some differences to be noted. At Chancellorsville it was Jackson who attacked; at Pickett's Mill, Howard. At Chancellorsville it was Howard who was assailed; at Pickett's Mill, Hood. The significance of the first distinction is doubled by that of the second.

The attack, it was understood, was to be made in column of brigades, Hazen's brigade of Wood's division leading. That such was at least Hazen's understanding I learned from his own lips during the movement, as I was an officer of his staff. But after a march of less than a mile an hour and a further delay of three hours at the end of it to acquaint the enemy of our intention to surprise him, our single shrunken brigade of fifteen hundred men was sent forward without support to double up the army of General Johnston. "We will put in Hazen and see what success he has." In these words of General Wood to General Howard we were first apprised of the true nature of the distinction about to be conferred upon us.

General W.B. Hazen, a born fighter, an educated soldier, after the war Chief Signal Officer of the Army and now long dead, was the best hated man that I ever knew, and his very memory is a terror to every unworthy soul in the service. His was a stormy life: he was in trouble all round. Grant, Sherman, Sheridan and a countless multitude of the less eminent luckless had the misfortune, at one time and another, to incur his disfavor, and he tried to punish them all. He was always—after the war—the central figure of a court-martial or a Congressional inquiry, was accused of everything, from stealing to cowardice, was banished to obscure posts, "jumped on" by the press, traduced in public and in private, and always emerged triumphant. While Signal Officer, he went up against the Secretary of War and put him to the controversial sword. He convicted Sheridan of falsehood, Sherman of barbarism, Grant of inefficiency. He was aggressive, arrogant, tyrannical, honorable, truthful, courageous—skillful soldier, a faithful friend and one of the most exasperating of men. Duty was his religion, and like the Moslem he proselyted with the sword. His missionary efforts were directed chiefly against the spiritual darkness of his superiors in rank, though he would turn aside from pursuit of his erring commander to set a chicken-thieving orderly astride a wooden horse, with a heavy stone attached to each foot. "Hazen," said a brother brigadier, "is a synonym of insubordination." For my commander and my friend, my master in the art of war, now unable to answer for himself, let this fact answer: when he heard Wood say they would put him in and see what success he would have in defeating an army—when he saw Howard assent—he uttered never a word, rode to the head of his feeble brigade and patiently awaited the command to go. Only by a look which I knew how to read did he betray his sense of the criminal blunder.

The enemy had now had seven hours in which to learn of the movement and prepare to meet it. General Johnston says:

"The Federal troops extended their entrenched line [we did not entrench] so rapidly to their left that it was found necessary to transfer Cleburne's division to Hardee's corps to our right, where it was formed on the prolongation of Polk's line."

General Hood, commanding the enemy's right corps, says:

"On the morning of the 27th the enemy were known to be rapidly extending their left, attempting to turn my right as they extended. Cleburne was deployed to meet them, and at half-past five P.M. a very stubborn attack was made on this division, extending to the right, where Major-General Wheeler with his cavalry division was engaging them. The assault was continued with great determination upon both Cleburne and Wheeler."

That, then, was the situation: a weak brigade of fifteen hundred men, with masses of idle troops behind in the character of audience, waiting for the word to march a quarter-mile up hill through almost impassable tangles of underwood, along and across precipitous ravines, and attack breastworks constructed at leisure and manned with two divisions of troops as good as themselves. True, we did not know all this, but if any man on that ground besides Wood and Howard expected a "walkover" his must have been a singularly hopeful disposition. As topographical engineer it had been my duty to make a hasty examination of the ground in front. In doing so I had pushed far enough forward through the forest to hear distinctly the murmur of the enemy awaiting us, and this had been duly reported; but from our lines nothing could be heard but the wind among the trees and the songs of birds. Some one said it was a pity to frighten them, but there would necessarily be more or less noise. We laughed at that: men awaiting death on the battlefield laugh easily, though not infectiously.

The brigade was formed in four battalions, two in front and two in rear. This gave us a front of about two hundred yards. The right front battalion was commanded by Colonel R. L. Kimberly of the 41st Ohio, the left by Colonel O. H. Payne of the 124th Ohio, the rear battalions by Colonel J. C. Foy, 23d Kentucky, and Colonel W. W. Berry, 5th Kentucky—all brave and skillful officers, tested by experience on many fields. The whole command (known as the Second Brigade, Third Division, Fourth Corps) consisted of no fewer than nine regiments, reduced by long service to an average of less than two hundred men each. With full ranks and only the necessary details for special duty we should have had some eight thousand rifles in line.

We moved forward. In less than one minute the trim battalions had become simply a swarm of men struggling through the undergrowth of the forest, pushing and crowding. The front was irregularly serrated, the strongest and bravest in advance, the others following in fan-like formations, variable and inconstant, ever defining themselves anew. For the first two hundred yards our course lay along the left bank of a small creek in a deep ravine, our left battalions sweeping along its steep slope. Then we came to the fork of the ravine. A part of us crossed below, the rest above, passing over both branches, the regiments inextricably intermingled, rendering all military formation impossible. The color-bearers kept well to the front with their flags, closely furled, aslant backward over their shoulders. Displayed, they would have been torn to rags by the boughs of the trees. Horses were all sent to the rear; the general and staff and all the field officers toiled along on foot as best they could. "We shall halt and form when we get out of this," said an aide-de-camp.

Suddenly there were a ringing rattle of musketry, the familiar hissing of bullets, and before us the interspaces of the forest were all blue with smoke. Hoarse, fierce yells broke out of a thousand throats. The forward fringe of brave and hardy assailants was arrested in its mutable extensions; the edge of our swarm grew dense and clearly defined as the foremost halted, and the rest pressed forward to align themselves beside them, all firing. The uproar was deafening; the air was sibilant with streams and sheets of missiles. In the steady, unvarying roar of small arms the frequent shock of the cannon was rather felt than heard, but the gusts of grape which they blew into that populous wood were audible enough, screaming among the trees and cracking against their stems and branches. We had, of course, no artillery to reply.

Our brave color-bearers were now all in the forefront of battle in the open, for the enemy had cleared a space in front of his breastworks. They held the colors erect, shook out their glories, waved them forward and back to keep them spread, for there was no wind. From where I stood, at the right of the line—we had "halted and formed," indeed—I could see six of our flags at one time. Occasionally one would go down, only to be instantly lifted by other hands.

I must here quote again from General Johnston's account of this engagement, for nothing could more truly indicate the resolute nature of the attack than the Confederate belief that it was made by the whole Fourth Corps, instead of one weak brigade:

"The Fourth Corps came on in deep order and assailed the Texans with great vigor, receiving their close and accurate fire with the fortitude always exhibited by General Sherman's troops in the actions of this campaign . . . The Federal troops approached within a few yards of the Confederates, but at last were forced to give way by their storm of well-directed bullets, and fell back to the shelter of a hollow near and behind them. They left hundreds of corpses within twenty paces of the Confederate line. When the United States troops paused in their advance within fifteen paces of the Texan front rank one of their color-bearers planted his colors eight or ten feet in front of his regiment, and was instantly shot dead. A soldier sprang forward to his place and fell also as he grasped the color-staff. A second and third followed successively, and each received death as speedily as his predecessors. A fourth, however, seized and bore back the object of soldierly devotion."

Such incidents have occurred in battle from time to time since men began to venerate the symbols of their cause, but they are not commonly related by the enemy. If General Johnston had known that his veteran divisions were throwing their successive lines against fewer than fifteen hundred men his glowing tribute to his enemy's valor could hardly have been more generously expressed. I can attest the truth of his soldierly praise: I saw the occurrence that he relates and regret that I am unable to recall even the name of the regiment whose colors were so gallantly saved.

Early in my military experience I used to ask myself how it was that brave troops could retreat while still their courage was high. As long as a man is not disabled he can go forward; can it be anything but fear that makes him stop and finally retire? Are there signs by which he can infallibly know the struggle to be hopeless? In this engagement, as in others, my doubts were answered as to the fact; the explanation is still obscure. In many instances that have come under my observation, when hostile lines of infantry engage at close range and the assailants afterward retire, there was a "dead-line" beyond which no man advanced but to fall. Not a soul of them ever reached the enemy's front to be bayoneted or captured. It was a matter of the difference of three or four paces—too small a distance to affect the accuracy of aim. In these affairs no aim is taken at individual antagonists; the soldier delivers his fire at the thickest mass in his front. The fire is, of course, as deadly at twenty paces as at fifteen; at fifteen as at ten. Nevertheless, there is the "dead-line," with its well-defined edge of corpses—those of the bravest. Where both lines are fighting without cover—as in a charge met by a counter-charge—each has its "dead-line," and between the two is a clear space—neutral ground, devoid of dead, for the living cannot reach it to fall there.

I observed this phenomenon at Pickett's Mill. Standing at the right of the line I had an unobstructed view of the narrow, open space across which the two lines fought. It was dim with smoke, but not greatly obscured: the smoke rose and spread in sheets among the branches of the trees. Most of our men fought kneeling as they fired, many of them behind trees, stones and whatever cover they could get, but there were considerable groups that stood. Occasionally one of these groups, which had endured the storm of missiles for moments without perceptible reduction, would push forward, moved by a common despair, and wholly detach itself from the line. In a second every man of the group would be down. There had been no visible movement of the enemy, no audible change in the awful, even roar of the firing—yet all were down. Frequently the dim figure of an individual soldier would be seen to spring away from his comrades, advancing alone toward that fateful interspace, with leveled bayonet. He got no farther than the farthest of his predecessors. Of the "hundreds of corpses within twenty paces of the Confederate line," I venture to say that a third were within fifteen paces, and not one within ten.

It is the perception—perhaps unconscious—of this inexplicable phenomenon that causes the still unharmed, still vigorous and still courageous soldier to retire without having come into actual contact with his foe. He sees, or feels, that he *cannot*. His bayonet is a useless weapon for slaughter; its purpose is a moral one. Its mandate exhausted, he sheathes it and trusts to the bullet. That failing, he retreats. He has done all that he could do with such appliances as he has.

No command to fall back was given, none could have been heard. Man by man, the survivors withdrew at will, sifting through the trees into the cover of the ravines, among the wounded who could drag themselves back; among the skulkers whom nothing could have dragged forward. The left of our short line had fought at the corner of a cornfield, the fence along the right side of which was parallel to the direction of our retreat. As the disorganized groups fell back along this fence on the wooded side, they were attacked by a flanking force of the enemy moving through the field in a direction nearly parallel with what had been our front. This force, I infer from General Johnston's account, consisted of the brigade of General Lowry, or two Arkansas regiments under Colonel Baucum. I had been sent by General Hazen to that point and arrived in time to witness this formidable movement. But already our retreating men, in obedience to their officers, their courage and their instinct of self-preservation, had formed along the fence and opened fire. The apparently slight advantage of the imperfect cover and the open range worked its customary miracle: the assault, a singularly spiritless one, considering the advantages it promised and that it was made by an organized and victorious force against a broken and retreating one, was checked. The assailants actually retired, and if they afterward renewed the movement they encountered none but our dead and wounded.

The battle, as a battle, was at an end, but there was still some slaughtering that it was possible to incur before nightfall; and as the wreck of our brigade drifted back through the forest we met the brigade (Gibson's) which, had the attack been made in column, as it should have been, would have been but five minutes behind our heels, with another five minutes behind its own. As it was, just forty-five minutes had elapsed, during which the enemy had destroyed us and was now ready to perform the same kindly office for our successors. Neither Gibson nor the brigade which was sent to his "relief" as tardily as he to ours accomplished, or could have hoped to accomplish, anything whatever. I did not note their movements, having other duties, but Hazen in his "Narrative of Military Service" says:

"I witnessed the attack of the two brigades following my own, and none of these (troops) advanced nearer than one hundred yards of the enemy's works. They went in at a run, and as organizations were broken in less than a minute."

Nevertheless their losses were considerable, including several hundred prisoners taken from a sheltered place whence they did not care to rise and run. The entire loss was about fourteen hundred men, of whom nearly one-half fell killed and wounded in Hazen's brigade in less than thirty minutes of actual fighting.

General Johnston says:

"The Federal dead lying near our line were counted by many persons, officers and soldiers. According to these counts there were seven hundred of them."

This is obviously erroneous, though I have not the means at hand to ascertain the true number. I remember that we were all astonished at the uncommonly large proportion of dead to wounded—a consequence of the uncommonly close range at which most of the fighting was done.

The action took its name from a water-power mill near by. This was on a branch of a stream having, I am sorry to say, the prosaic name of Pumpkin Vine Creek. I have my own reasons for suggesting that the name of that watercourse be altered to Sunday-School Run.

Source: Ambrose Bierce, *The Collected Works of Ambrose Bierce*, vol. 1 (New York: Neale Publishing Company, 1909; Project Gutenberg, 2004), http://www.gutenberg.org/ebooks/13541.

COLD HARBOR AND PETERSBURG

JUNE 1–AUGUST 24, 1864
PVT. WILLIAM A. CANFIELD, USA

Grant never enjoyed those worshipful public relations that shrouded Lee in an aura of infallibility. The Northern general drank whiskey at night, wore a dirty field jacket, smoked cigars, and was plain in speech and manner. But most damning to his critics, Grant was honest and upfront about the attritional strategy he must wage to win the war. The Union outnumbered the Confederacy; its logistics were superior, its supply chain more fruitful. Its advantages grew with each passing day, and time was on the Union's side. The Confederacy, however, grew weaker. He knew these strengths, and Grant was unapologetic about using them to win. His goal was victory, not image-crafting. At Cold Harbor, Grant's grim awareness that his side could sustain losses while Lee's could not nearly went too far, for Northern casualties were extremely high, with no advantage gained.

A mere ten miles from Richmond, Cold Harbor was a crossroads from which Union troops moved against well-fortified Confederate lines. The battle was essentially a series of frontal assaults against the strongly entrenched rebels at various points along a seven-mile line. None of the Northern assaults succeeded, and Grant, who was normally grimly pragmatic about the nature of the war he needed to fight, wrote in his memoirs that he regretted the last assault in particular because "no advantage whatever was gained to compensate for the heavy loss we sustained." He thus revealed in writing that, contrary to his enemies' claims, he did recognize and feel the gravity of battlefield death. There was plenty of death at Cold Harbor: over 12,000 casualties on the Union side, with over 1,800 killed. Confederates lost 5,287, with 788 killed. Union private William Canfield was in the fight and paid the price.

My parents always taught us to reverence the stars and stripes; I loved my country's banner, and when rebel hands were raised to hurl it to the ground, I felt as if I must go and bear a part in the great struggle. My ancestors had fought bravely to establish the glorious liberty I had so long enjoyed. It was hard, very hard, for me to leave those whom I loved so dearly, but still harder to sit with folded hands here at home, while others were dying for the aid I could render. Frequently, when about my work, would my eye fall upon my hands (I have often thought it strange), and they seemed to reproach me every time I looked at them. At last I could bear it no longer; I felt sure it was my duty to go, and go I must.

I enlisted under H. D. Davis, at Manchester, N. H., July 12, 1862, in the Ninth Regiment New Hampshire Volunteers. I went directly to Northfield, to visit my parents and friends before going into camp. It is almost useless for me to speak of the parting scene. I took leave of all my friends except my wife and sister, with her husband. My aged parents were bowed down with sorrow and grief. They had buried their oldest son and two daughters; there were only three of us left—and now to lose me (for they had little hope of ever seeing me again) was almost too much for them to bear.

We went into camp the first of August. Spent the first night in the barracks. I did not sleep much, I assure you, every thing was so strange— so much noise and confusion of tongues. But I soon became accustomed to my surroundings, and found real attractions in camp life.

I had always made it a rule to reprove sin whenever an opportunity offered; but I soon found out what it meant to cast pearls before swine.

Then I adopted another plan; it was this: first, to watch every opportunity of doing a good turn for my comrades. I interested myself in the loved ones they had left at home—in a word, I tried to make them love me; and I succeeded far beyond what I expected. I do not think there was one in our company who would have seen any harm come to me if they could have prevented it. Then, when occasion required, I could reprove sin without being reproached and made to understand it was none of my business.

Our time was mostly occupied in drilling, until the 24th of August, when we were mustered into the United States' service. On the 29th, we struck tents early in the morning and marched to the depot, where we took the cars for the seat of war. It was a sad time with us that morning, as one after another bid farewell to loved ones. Very few of those brave men ever returned. I had previously taken leave of my friends and told them I should return to them again.....

June 1st, 1864. All quiet till about ten o'clock; then the enemy charged on our left and were driven back with heavy loss. They also charged on our right in plain sight. Two lines came up on the double-quick till within two hundred yards. Then you might have seen a line of dusty forms spring up as if by magic, and a sheet of fire burst forth which sent them reeling back to their cover in the woods. They soon rallied again and came on with double the force that had first assailed us. Just then, one of our light batteries, of six guns, was placed in position in the woods, and gave them grape and canister.

On they came regardless of life and fearless as demons; but soon they met a sheet of fire which seemed to consume them; they retreated to the woods for the second time, and made no further attack on that part of our line.

On the 2d, we fell back and moved about five miles to the left. At four o'clock, they came down on us and tried to get in our rear; but all to no purpose. We fought hard during the following day, but rested that night. On the 4th, we moved about four miles, and formed on the right of the line at Coal [Cold] Harbor. Every one knows about this place. It will be sufficient to say that we had work to do, and I think all were glad when the order came to fall back.

Just after dark, on the 11th, we started back and took our breakfast near Whitehouse landing, and continued our march. Our next rest was near the James river, where we remained until the 15th, when we took up our line of march just at dusk, and marched all night and till four o'clock of the following day. Forming on the line of battle near the Weldon rail-road, we went in on a charge, and fought more or less all night.

On the morning of the 17th, we charged all along the line, drove the enemy back, took several pieces of artillery, and more or less prisoners. Advanced about one mile on the 18th, and during the night threw up earth works in an old oat field near a peach orchard. On the 19th, we dug our pit eight feet wide and three deep, throwing all the earth in front. Hard fighting on the left. On the 20th, hard fighting all along the line. I received a slight wound across my left temple.

June 21st ended my term in the field [Petersburg]. I was wounded in the left arm, and had it amputated just above the elbow. Now for the hospital. I was carried to City Point on the 23d. Thanks to the Christian and Sanitary Commissions, which greatly relieved us, not only in furnishing so many good things, but in sending to us those who always had a kind word for us all.

On the 30th, I was carried on board the hospital boat, and arrived at Washington, D. C., on the 1st of July, and was carried to Finley Hospital. I was well cared for here, and my arm healed rapidly, while many others sickened and died.

On the 22d of August, I received a furlough for sixty days. I arrived home on the 24th. I cannot attempt to describe my feelings as I crossed the threshold, and placed this good right arm around the aged form of my beloved mother, who tottered to meet me, and throwing her arms around my neck, kissed me again and again. Not less welcome was the fervent "God bless you, my son," from father. My wife was absent at this time, at the bedside of a sick sister, who died in about two weeks after I got home. Then she returned to me, and entered into the general rejoicing at my safe arrival.

Soon after I came home the stump of my arm began to trouble me very much. Gangrene set in, the stump swelled up and turned black. They carried me to my sister's, Mrs. Smith Hancock, in Franklin, where I was attended by Dr. Knights of that town. For about three weeks my life was despaired of; then I began to gain. Through the kind care of all and the skill of Dr. Knights—but more through the providence of God—I was spared; for what, I do not know. God knows, and he doeth all things well. . . .

My story is told.

Source: William A. Canfield, *A History of the Army Experience of William A. Canfield* (Manchester, NH: C. F. Livingston, 1869; Project Gutenberg, 2010), http://www.gutenberg.org/ebooks/31998.

DEAD ANGLE AND KENNESAW MOUNTAIN

JUNE 27, 1864
CPL. SAM R. WATKINS, CSA

The year 1864 saw the Confederacy at bay on every front. While Grant mercilessly and methodically moved on Richmond, refusing to be turned aside, far to the south Sherman's armies—of the Cumberland, Ohio, and Tennessee—kept on flanking Joe Johnston's Army of Tennessee. Always, Sherman headed for Atlanta. Every Union move meant that the Confederates had to evacuate their protected positions and re-entrench elsewhere. Then, in late June—a summer hot as a Georgia summer can be—there seemed to be no more room for another Sherman end run. There before his men loomed Kennesaw Mountain, the highest ridge near Atlanta. Eschewing previous methods, Sherman ordered direct charges up the mountain. Confederates pushed these back, gaining a tactical victory. But while the ridge fighting raged, USA Maj. Gen. John M. Schofield, at the Union line's southernmost point, its right flank, slipped around Southern positions, threatening to turn the entire Confederate line. Once again, frustrated Southern soldiers had to pull back, while their enemy drew closer to the Chattahoochee River, the last physical barrier between Sherman and Atlanta.

CSA Cpl. Sam R. Watkins was present at one of the most blistering parts of the battle, the so-called Dead Angle. His excerpt here recounts the danger he and his fellow butternuts faced in that exposed position, where they dodged Yankee bullets while firing from behind their own breastworks and abatis. As usual, Watkins narrates danger honestly and realistically, leavening his account with dry humor.

The First and Twenty-seventh Tennessee Regiments will ever remember the battle of "Dead Angle," which was fought June 27th, on the Kennesaw line, near Marietta, Georgia. It was one of the hottest and longest days of the year, and one of the most desperate and determinedly resisted battles fought during the whole war. Our regiment was stationed on an angle, a little spur of the mountain, or rather promontory of a range of hills, extending far out beyond the main line of battle, and was subject to the enfilading fire of forty pieces of artillery of the Federal batteries. It seemed fun for the guns of the whole Yankee army to play upon this point. We would work hard every night to strengthen our breastworks, and the very next day they would be torn down smooth with the ground by solid shots and shells from the guns of the enemy. Even the little trees and bushes which had been left for shade, were cut down as so much stubble. For more than a week this constant firing had been kept up against this salient point. In the meantime, the skirmishing in the valley below resembled the sounds made by ten thousand wood-choppers.

Well, on the fatal morning of June 27th, the sun rose clear and cloudless, the heavens seemed made of brass, and the earth of iron, and as the sun began to mount toward the zenith, everything became quiet, and no sound was heard save a peckerwood on a neighboring tree, tapping on its old trunk, trying to find a worm for his dinner. We all knew it was but the dead calm that precedes the storm. On the distant hills we could plainly see officers dashing about hither and thither, and the Stars and Stripes moving to and fro, and we knew the Federals were making preparations for the mighty contest. We could hear but the rumbling sound of heavy guns, and the distant tread of a marching army, as a faint roar of the coming storm, which was soon to break the ominous silence with the sound of conflict, such as was scarcely ever before heard on this earth. It seemed that the archangel of Death stood and looked on with outstretched wings, while all the earth was silent, when all at once a hundred guns from the Federal line opened upon us, and for more than an hour they poured their solid and chain shot, grape and shrapnel right upon this salient point, defended by our regiment alone, when, all of a sudden, our pickets jumped into our works and reported the Yankees advancing, and almost at the same time a solid line of blue coats came up the hill. I discharged my gun, and happening to look up, there was the beautiful flag of the Stars and Stripes flaunting right in my face, and I heard John Branch, of the Rock City Guards, commanded by Captain W. D. Kelly, who were next Company H, say, "Look at that Yankee flag; shoot that fellow; snatch that flag out of his hand!" My pen is unable to describe the scene of carnage and death that ensued in the next two hours. Column after column of Federal soldiers were crowded upon that line, and by referring to the history of the war you will find they were massed in column forty columns deep; in fact, the whole force of the Yankee army was hurled against this point, but no sooner would a regiment mount our works than they were shot down or surrendered, and soon we had every "gopher hole" full of Yankee prisoners. Yet still the Yankees came. It seemed impossible to check the onslaught, but every man was true to his trust, and seemed to think that at that moment the whole responsibility of the Confederate government was rested upon his shoulders. Talk about other battles, victories, shouts, cheers, and triumphs, but in comparison with this day's fight, all others dwarf into insignificance. The sun beaming down on our uncovered heads, the thermometer being one hundred and ten degrees in the shade, and a solid line of blazing fire right from the muzzles of the Yankee guns being poured right into our very faces, singeing our hair and clothes, the hot blood of our dead and wounded spurting on us, the blinding smoke and stifling atmosphere filling our eyes and mouths, and the awful concussion causing the blood to gush out of our noses and ears, and above all, the roar of battle, made it a perfect pandemonium. Afterward I heard a soldier express himself by saying that he thought "Hell had broke loose in Georgia, sure enough."

I have heard men say that if they ever killed a Yankee during the war they were not aware of it. I am satisfied that on this memorable day, every man in our regiment killed from one score to four score, yea, five score men. I mean from twenty to one hundred each. All that was necessary was to load and shoot. In fact, I will ever think that the reason they did not capture our works was the impossibility of their living men passing over the bodies of their dead. The ground was piled up with one solid mass of dead and wounded Yankees. I learned afterwards from the burying squad that in some places they were piled up like cord wood, twelve deep.

After they were time and time again beaten back, they at last were enabled to fortify a line under the crest of the hill, only thirty yards from us, and they immediately commenced to excavate the earth with the purpose of blowing up our line.

We remained here three days after the battle. In the meantime the woods had taken fire, and during the nights and days of all that time continued to burn, and at all times, every hour of day and night, you could hear the shrieks and screams of the poor fellows who were left on the field, and a stench, so sickening as to nauseate the whole of both armies, arose from the decaying bodies of the dead left lying on the field.

On the third morning the Yankees raised a white flag, asked an armistice to bury their dead, not for any respect either army had for the dead, but to get rid of the sickening stench. I get sick now when I happen to think about it. Long and deep trenches were dug, and hooks made from bayonets crooked for the purpose, and all the dead were dragged and thrown pell-mell into these trenches. Nothing was allowed to be taken off the dead, and finely dressed officers, with gold watch chains dangling over their vests, were thrown into the ditches. During the whole day both armies were hard at work, burying the Federal dead.

Every member of the First and Twenty-seventh Tennessee Regiments deserves a wreath of imperishable fame, and a warm place in the hearts of their countrymen, for their gallant and heroic valor at the battle of Dead Angle. No man distinguished himself above another. All did their duty, and the glory of one is but the glory and just tribute of the others.

After we had abandoned the line, and on coming to a little stream of water, I undressed for the purpose of bathing, and after undressing found my arm all battered and bruised and bloodshot from my wrist to my shoulder, and as sore as a blister. I had shot one hundred and twenty times that day. My gun became so hot that frequently the powder would flash before I could ram home the ball, and I had frequently to exchange my gun for that of a dead comrade.

Colonel H. R. Field was loading and shooting the same as any private in the ranks when he fell off the skid from which he was shooting right over my shoulder, shot through the head. I laid him down in the trench, and he said, "Well, they have got me at last, but I have killed fifteen of them; time about is fair play, I reckon." But Colonel Field was not killed—only wounded, and one side paralyzed. Captain Joe P. Lee, Captain Mack Campbell, Lieutenant T. H. Maney, and other officers of the regiment, threw rocks and beat them in their faces with sticks. The Yankees did the same. The rocks came in upon us like a perfect hailstorm, and the Yankees seemed very obstinate, and in no hurry to get away from our front, and we had to keep up the firing and shooting them down in self-defense. They seemed to walk up and take death as coolly as if they were automatic or wooden men, and our boys did not shoot for the fun of the thing. It was, verily, a life and death grapple, and the least flicker on our part, would have been sure death to all. We could not be reinforced on account of our position, and we had to stand up to the rack, fodder or no fodder. When the Yankees fell back, and the firing ceased, I never saw so many broken down and exhausted men in my life. I was as sick as a horse, and as wet with blood and sweat as I could be, and many of our men were vomiting with excessive fatigue, over-exhaustion, and sunstroke; our tongues were parched and cracked for water, and our faces blackened with powder and smoke, and our dead and wounded were piled indiscriminately in the trenches. There was not a single man in the company who was not wounded, or had holes shot through his hat and clothing. Captain Beasley was killed, and nearly all his company killed and wounded. The Rock City Guards were almost piled in heaps and so was our company. Captain Joe P. Lee was badly wounded. Poor Walter Hood and Jim Brandon were lying there among us, while their spirits were in heaven; also, William A. Hughes, my old messmate and friend, who had clerked with me for S. F. & J. M. Mayes, and who had slept with me for lo! These many years, and a boy who loved me more than any other person on earth has ever done. I had just discharged the contents of my gun into the bosoms of two men, one right behind the other, killing them both, and was re-loading, when a Yankee rushed upon me, having me at a disadvantage, and said, "You have killed my two brothers, and now I've got you." Everything I had ever done rushed through my mind. I heard the roar, and felt the flash of fire, and saw my more than friend, William A. Hughes, grab the muzzle of the gun, receiving the whole contents in his hand and arm, and mortally wounding him. Reader, he died for me. In saving my life, he lost his own. When the infirmary corps carried him off, all mutilated and bleeding he told them to give me "Florence Fleming" (that was the name of his gun, which he had put on it in silver letters), and to give me his blanket and clothing. He gave his life for me, and everything that he had. It was the last time that I ever saw him, but I know that away up yonder, beyond the clouds, blackness, tempest and night, and away above the blue vault of heaven, where the stars keep their ceaseless vigils, away up yonder in the golden city of the New Jerusalem, where God and Jesus Christ, our Savior, ever reign, we will sometime meet at the marriage supper of the Son of God, who gave His life for the redemption of the whole world.

For several nights they made attacks upon our lines, but in every attempt, they were driven back with great slaughter. They would ignite the tape of bombshells, and throw them over in our lines, but, if the shell did not immediately explode, they were thrown back. They had a little shell called "hand grenade," but they would either stop short of us, or go over our heads, and were harmless. . . . That night about midnight, an alarm was given that the Yankees were advancing. They would only have to run about twenty yards before they would be in our works. We were ordered to "shoot." Every man was hallooing at the top of his voice, "Shoot, shoot, tee, shoot, shootee." On the alarm, both the Confederate and Federal lines opened, with both small arms and artillery, and it seemed that the very heavens and earth were in a grand conflagration, as they will be at the final judgment, after the resurrection. I have since learned that this was a false alarm, and that no attack had been meditated.

Previous to the day of attack, the soldiers had cut down all the trees in our immediate front, throwing the tops down hill and sharpening the limbs of the same, thus making, as we thought, an impenetrable abattis of vines and limbs locked together; but nothing stopped or could stop the advance of the Yankee line, but the hot shot and cold steel that we poured into their faces from under our head-logs.

One of the most shameful and cowardly acts of Yankee treachery was committed there that I ever remember to have seen. A wounded Yankee was lying right outside of our works, and begging most piteously for water, when a member of the railroad company (his name was Hog Johnson, and the very man who stood videt with Theodore Sloan and I at the battle of Missionary Ridge, and who killed the three Yankees, one night, from Fort Horsley), got a canteen of water, and gave the dying Yankee a drink, and as he started back, he was killed dead in his tracks by a treacherous Yankee hid behind a tree. It matters not, for somewhere in God's Holy Word, which cannot lie, He says that "He that giveth a cup of cold water in my name, shall not lose his reward." And I have no doubt, reader, in my own mind, that the poor fellow is reaping his reward in Emanuel's land with the good and just. In every instance where we tried to assist their wounded, our men were killed or wounded. A poor wounded and dying boy, not more than sixteen years of age, asked permission to crawl over our works, and when he had crawled to the top, and just as Blair Webster and I reached up to help the poor fellow, he, the Yankee, was killed by his own men. In fact, I have ever thought that is why the slaughter was so great in our front, that nearly, if not as many, Yankees were killed by their own men as by us. The brave ones, who tried to storm and carry our works, were simply between two fires. It is a singular fanaticism, and curious fact, that enters the mind of a soldier, that it is a grand and glorious death to die on a victorious battlefield. . . .

A perfect hail of minnie balls was being continually poured into our head-logs the whole time we remained here. The Yankees would hold up small looking-glasses, so that our strength and breastworks could be seen in the reflection in the glass; and they also had small mirrors on the butts of their guns, so arranged that they could sight up the barrels of their guns by looking through these glasses, while they themselves would not be exposed to our fire, and they kept up this continual firing day and night, whether they could see us or not. Sometimes a glancing shot from our head-logs would wound some one.

Reader mine, I fear that I have wearied you with too long a description of the battle of "Dead Angle"; if so, please pardon me, as this is but a sample of the others which will now follow each other in rapid succession. And, furthermore, in stating the above facts, the half has not been told, but it will give you a faint idea of the hard battles and privations and hardships of the soldiers in that stormy epoch—who died, grandly, gloriously, nobly; dyeing the soil of old mother earth, and enriching the same with their crimson life's blood, while doing what? Only trying to protect their homes and families, their property, their constitution and their laws, that had been guaranteed to them as a heritage forever by their forefathers. They died for the faith that each state was a separate sovereign government, as laid down by the Declaration of Independence and the Constitution of our fathers.

Source: Sam R. Watkins, *"Co. Aytch," Maury Grays, First Tennessee Regiment; or, A Side Show of the Big Show*, 2nd. ed. (self-pub., 1882; Chattanooga: Chattanooga Times, 1900), chap. 12, http://www.fullbooks.com/Co-Aytch-1.html.

BATTLE OF THE CRATER

JULY 30, 1864
CAPT. SUMNER SHEARMAN, USA

The Siege of Petersburg began on June 9, 1864, and would last until March 25, 1865. Its essence was trench warfare, during which Lee's once supremely mobile soldiers manned dugouts trying to protect Petersburg, a valued supply center and railhead and the so-called back door to Richmond, from the menace of Grant's and Meade's armies. By the end of the first month, dreams of breaching the defenses dancing in their imaginations, Union leaders came up with a novel idea to blast a hole through fortified Southern lines. There were, in Maj. Gen. Ambrose Burnside's IX Corps, a number of experienced miners from Pennsylvania. These men knew how to handle explosives, and how to tunnel. They were born sappers. The idea was the brainchild of Lt. Col. Henry Pleasants, commander of the 48th Pennsylvania. He supervised the digging of a tunnel beneath Confederate trenches and filled the position under Elliot's Salient, a fort, with explosives. The plan was nothing if not imaginative: the humongous explosion would rip a gash in the Southern lines, stun the defenders, and offer a brief opening through which waiting Union troops would charge. Burnside was entranced and approved Pleasants's plan.

The Pennsylvanians did build their shaft, removing tons of earth and utilizing all their skills, yet managing to keep the project secret from the enemy. Burnside designated Edward Ferrero's African-American division to lead the ensuing charge but was overruled by Meade. The replacements were less well briefed than the USCT men, and so their conception of the need for precision in the initial onslaught was sketchy. The blast was enormous, disorientingly so. It succeeded not only in blowing the hole in Confederate positions but also in rearranging the entire landscape. Union men rushed into the breach, but unfortunately for Burnside, they headed straight into the newly formed crater, where they were nearly annihilated by Confederates firing from above. Perhaps had they understood their mission better, they would have avoided the headlong rush into newly low ground. As it happened, the Crater would be yet another defeat for Burnside, who was blamed for the fiasco. Meade escaped serious censure. Union casualties were high, especially among Ferrero's black troops. Grant, well aware of a unique chance squandered, termed the Crater "the saddest affair I have witnessed in this war." The general-in-chief later testified before Congress that removing Ferrero's black troops from the vanguard was a mistake that likely cost a Union victory. In this passage, USA Capt. Sumner Shearman, 4th Rhode Island Infantry, recalls this weirdest of all Civil War battles.

I have been asked by the Society under whose auspices we are gathered to-night to tell you something of my personal experiences in the Battle of the Mine, or of the Crater, as it is sometimes called. . . .

At the time of the battle I was captain of Company A, Fourth Rhode Island Volunteers Infantry. The regiment to which I belonged was a portion of the Ninth Army Corps, under the command of General Burnside. The battle was fought on the 30th of July, 1864. But some months previous, as far back as January, 1863, the regiment, as also the corps, had been detached from the Army of the Potomac. Burnside, as you know, succeeded McClellan after the battle of Antietam in command of the Army of the Potomac; but he himself was removed from that command in January, 1863, and taken away from the Army of the Potomac. But the regiment to which I belonged ultimately became separated from the corps, and was on detached duty in the city of Norfolk, Virginia, and afterwards at Point Lookout, Maryland, where we were when the order came for us to rejoin the Ninth Corps, which had been brought back to the Army of the Potomac.

We arrived in front of Petersburg, at a point on the line where the Ninth Army Corps was stationed, on the Fourth of July, 1864. The two lines, our line and the enemy's, were at this point very near each other, from one hundred and fifty to three hundred yards apart, the distance varying according to the line of the works. We were ordered to encamp in some woods in the rear of our line of rifle-pits, and not far from them.

Shots from the enemy were continually coming into our camp, being fired at the men in the breastworks in front. We had to erect a barricade in the camp to protect ourselves, behind which we lived. Men of course strayed more or less away from the barricade, and every now and then some one would be wounded. Every three or four days it became our turn to take our places in the rifle-pits, where we had to stay forty-eight hours, and sometimes longer. We never went into the rifle-pits without some one being killed or wounded.

While we were encamped in this way, we heard of the plan of Lieutenant-Colonel Henry Pleasants, of the Forty-eighth Pennsylvania Infantry, who was a practical miner, and his men were largely men who had worked in the coalmines of Pennsylvania. He conceived the idea of building a mine under a certain portion of the enemy's works, with the purpose of blowing them up. At a certain point in the enemy's line, opposite the point where we were located, was a very strong earthwork, mounting several guns of large caliber, which did very much damage to our fortifications and troops. It was but one hundred and fifty yards from our line to that point. Back of it, on higher ground, was a hill called Cemetery Hill, regarded as a strategic point. If we could capture that hill, it was believed that much would be done to force General Lee out of Richmond. This fort stood in the way. Colonel Pleasants believed that he could remove it by his plan of blowing it up. The idea was that, if the fort could be removed by the explosion, the enemy being taken by surprise, opportunity would be afforded for our troops, already in position, to charge in through the open space thus made, and, taking advantage of the surprise on the part of the enemy, to push on to the crest of Cemetery Hill.

Colonel Pleasants met with no encouragement on the part of General Meade, in command of the Army of the Potomac; nevertheless, as General Burnside, his corps commander, approved of it, he was allowed to undertake it. No assistance whatever was afforded him by the Engineer Corps of the Army. He had to devise such methods as he could to accomplish his purpose, working at a great disadvantage all the time, but he finally accomplished the task. He began the work inside of our lines, under cover of a hill, at a point where the enemy could not perceive what was being done, and carried his tunnel through the earth the whole distance of one hundred and fifty yards, until he reached the fort. It was twenty feet beneath the surface of the ground at the point he reached. From thence he made a branch at right angles on either side, making it in the form of a letter T, as it were, at that point. In these branches he placed large wooden tanks in which powder was to be put. Four tons of powder were placed in these wooden boxes and connected by a fuse at the entrance of the mine.

The 30th of July, 1864, was fixed upon as the time for the explosion to take place. It was intended to have it take place somewhere about three o'clock in the morning. Troops were gotten into position the night before under cover of the darkness, ready to charge as soon as the mine should be exploded.

I had been engaged for some days previous at the headquarters of the Third Division of the Ninth Army Corps, General Potter commanding, as judge advocate in connection with a court-martial. On the evening before the battle, the evening of the 29th, an order came to me to report to my regiment. I did so, and found that it was about to take its place in line of battle, ready to join in the charge on the morning of the next day. I had my supper in camp as usual, and we started to take up our position, carrying with us no food, nor anything in the way of clothing, except the clothes we had on.

The time arrived when the explosion was expected to take place, but no explosion occurred. It was learned that the fuse had gone out. An officer of the Forty-eighth Pennsylvania volunteered to go in and relight the fuse; and, as I remember, it went out a second time, and was relighted. Shortly before five o'clock, just as the sun was rising, a sound as of thunder was distinctly heard, and in a moment the earth at the point where the mine had been constructed was thrown upward, slowly mounting into the air to a height of some two hundred feet, and then, spreading out like a fan, fell back again into the excavation made by the explosion. The soil was of a clayey character, and enormous boulders of clay were thrown up and fell back around the opening, resembling in some respects the crater of a volcano; hence the battle has sometimes been called the Battle of the Crater. The men who were in this fort, and the artillery, and everything pertaining to the fortifications, huge timbers, ammunition, tents, and everything that would be naturally located there, were all thrown heavenward. The men, of course, were either killed or wounded, with hardly an exception. A large number of men were in the fort. It has been estimated by some that there were a thousand.

As soon as the explosion took place, the artillery all along the line on our side, some one hundred and twenty pieces or more, began firing at that point. The firing lasted some moments, and then the troops were directed to charge. It had been the plan of General Burnside to have his division of colored troops lead the advance. There was in the Ninth Corps at that time a division of colored troops. They had been drilled with the idea of taking the advance, but General Meade overruled Burnside's plan, and thought it best that the colored troops should not be put in that position. So General Burnside called together his division commanders, and told them of the change of plan on the very night before the battle, and allowed them to draw lots to see which one should take the lead. The lot fell to General Ledlie, the least efficient of the division commanders in the Ninth Corps.

When the Third Division, to which my regiment belonged, charged over our breastworks and across the space between our line and the enemy's line, they came upon the enemy's works to the right of the crater; but by that time the enemy had recovered from his surprise, and was concentrating a terrible fire upon all that region. The men instinctively sought shelter in the excavation made by the explosion, but when we arrived at that point we found the crater filled with troops of General Ledlie's division. There seemed to be complete chaos reigning there. The lieutenant-colonel of our regiment, who was in command, Colonel Buffum, tried to rally the men, as did officers of other regiments, and to push on to Cemetery Hill; but General Ledlie, who should have been with his command, remained behind in a bomb-proof. I remember seeing him, as we passed the front, secure in a bombproof. His troops had fallen into confusion in the way I have explained, and he was not there to remedy the situation. It seemed impossible for the officers to accomplish anything in the midst of the reigning confusion.

The Fourth Rhode Island, the few of us that were together at that time, followed the colonel and the color bearer out beyond the enemy's works towards Cemetery Hill, but we encountered such a hurricane of shot and shell that it was impossible to face it, and we were driven back again into the shelter of the enemy's works, where we remained. The attempt to capture Cemetery Hill had proved a failure. Many of the men and officers tried to get back to our own line, but the enemy by that time had a raking fire over the space between their line and our own, and it was almost sure death for any person to undertake to cross it. Very few of those who did escaped being killed or wounded. The space between was so covered with the dead and the wounded that it was possible for a person to go from one line to the other without stepping on the earth. I have learned since that an order was issued for the troops in the crater to return to our own lines, but I myself did not hear of such an order, neither did Lieutenant-Colonel Buffum. We remained in the crater. It was on the 30th of July, as I have said, and one of the hottest days of the summer. The enemy had gotten range upon the crater, and were dropping mortar shell into our midst, but we held them at bay until our ammunition gave out. Finally they made a charge, and succeeded in reaching the crater, and were firing directly down upon us. General Bartlett, the highest officer in rank in the crater, a general from Massachusetts, gave the order for us to surrender. An officer of my regiment, a lieutenant of the Fourth Rhode Island, Lieutenant Kibby, tied a white handkerchief on his sword, and held it up in token of surrender. The enemy ceased firing.

I may mention that General Bartlett in a previous battle had lost a leg, and it had been replaced by a wooden one. A shot struck him and his leg was broken, but it proved to be the wooden leg. . . .

Source: Sumner Upham Shearman, *Battle of the Crater and Experiences of Prison Life* (Providence: Rhode Island Soldiers and Sailors Historical Society, 1898; Project Gutenberg, 2014), http://www.gutenberg.org/ebooks/47778.

MISS REBECCA WRIGHT

SEPTEMBER 19, 1864
GEN. PHILIP H. SHERIDAN, USA

In order to win the Shenandoah Valley campaign, Philip Sheridan knew he had to do more than defeat Southern forces in the field. Just as importantly, he had to wage war against the Confederacy's capability to fight. That meant tackling the civilians—farmers, especially—who worked in this fertile Confederate breadbasket. It was their crops that fed the Southern army. For this reason, the Union cavalryman and his troops did not shy away from seizing and burning crops, much to the bitter chagrin of residents. At the same time, they chased the evasive rebel cavalry, which still utilized the hit-and-run tactics demonstrated by now-dead Stonewall Jackson.

Rebecca Wright was a local woman—a Quaker and schoolteacher in Winchester, at the northern head of the valley. Like many of her faith, she considered slavery an abomination. Unlike her neighbors, Wright was staunchly pro-Union. These feelings ran in her family, resulting in her father's arrest and death in prison. Sheridan's intelligence network spotted her as a likely spy, and this brave young woman agreed to provide tactical information to the general. The intelligence she provided helped Sheridan's soldiers catch up with the wily Jubal Early's mounted troopers. In September 1864, Early's army was smashed repeatedly, losing its combat effectiveness and removing the main threat to Sheridan's efforts. The Union general would make Winchester his headquarters from then on. Sheridan was grateful to Wright, but she knew that public thanks would result in her ostracism by vengeful pro-Confederate

An artist's depiction of the battle of Shenandoah Valley, 1864
LIBRARY OF CONGRESS

citizens. After the war, her identity was unmasked and this icy-nerved espionage ace was forced to leave for Washington, DC. Here, Sheridan explains how one woman's intrepid commitment to the Union cause helped his soldiers wrest control of the Shenandoah Valley from Confederate hands.

While occupying the ground between Clifton and Berryville, I felt the need of an efficient body of scouts to collect information regarding the enemy, for the defective intelligence-establishment with which I started out from Harper's Ferry early in August had not proved satisfactory. I therefore began to organize my scouts on a system which I hoped would give better results than had the method hitherto pursued in the department, which was to employ on this service doubtful citizens and Confederate deserters. If these should turn out untrustworthy, the mischief they might do us gave me grave apprehension, and I finally concluded that those of our own soldiers who should volunteer for the delicate and hazardous duty would be the most valuable material, and decided that they should have a battalion organization and be commanded by an officer, Major H. K. Young, of the First Rhode Island Infantry. These men were disguised in Confederate uniforms whenever necessary, were paid from the Secret-Service Fund in proportion to the value of the intelligence they furnished, which often stood us in good stead in checking the forays of Gilmore, Mosby, and other irregulars. Beneficial results came from the plan in many other ways too, and particularly so when in a few days two of my scouts put me in the way of getting news conveyed from Winchester. They had learned that just outside of my lines, near Millwood, there was living an old colored man, who had a permit from the Confederate commander to go into Winchester and return three times a week, for the purpose of selling vegetables to the inhabitants. The scouts had sounded this man, and, finding him both loyal and shrewd, suggested that he might be made useful to us within the enemy's lines; and the proposal struck me as feasible, provided there could be found in Winchester some reliable person who would be willing to co-operate and correspond with me. I asked General Crook, who was acquainted with many of the Union people of Winchester, if he knew of such a person, and he recommended a Miss Rebecca Wright, a young lady whom he had met there before the battle of Kernstown, who, he said, was a member of the Society of Friends and the teacher of a small private school. He knew she was faithful and loyal to the Government, and thought she might be willing to render us assistance, but he could not be certain of this, for on account of her well known loyalty she was under constant surveillance. I hesitated at first, but finally deciding to try it, dispatched the two scouts to the old negro's cabin, and they brought him to my headquarters late that night. I was soon convinced of the negro's fidelity, and asking him if he was acquainted with Miss Rebecca Wright, of Winchester, he replied that he knew her well. Thereupon I told him what I wished to do, and after a little persuasion he agreed to carry a letter to her on his next marketing trip. My message was prepared by writing it on tissue paper, which was then compressed into a small pellet, and protected by wrapping it in tin-foil so that it could be safely carried in the man's mouth. The probability of his being searched when he came to the Confederate picketline was not remote, and in such event he was to swallow the pellet. The letter appealed to Miss Wright's loyalty and patriotism, and requested her to furnish me with information regarding the strength and condition of Early's army. The night before the negro started one of the scouts placed the odd-looking communication in his hands, with renewed injunctions as to secrecy and promptitude. Early the next morning it was delivered to Miss Wright, with an intimation that a letter of importance was enclosed in the tin-foil, the negro telling her at the same time that she might expect him to call for a message in reply before his return home. At first Miss Wright began to open the pellet nervously, but when told to be careful, and to preserve the foil as a wrapping for her answer, she proceeded slowly and carefully, and when the note appeared intact the messenger retired, remarking again that in the evening he would come for an answer.

On reading my communication Miss Wright was much startled by the perils it involved, and hesitatingly consulted her mother, but her devoted loyalty soon silenced every other consideration, and the brave girl resolved to comply with my request, notwithstanding it might jeopardize her life. The evening before a convalescent Confederate officer had visited her mother's house, and in conversation about the war had disclosed the fact that Kershaw's division of infantry and Cutshaw's battalion of artillery had started to rejoin General Lee. At the time Miss Wright heard this she attached little if any importance to it, but now she perceived the value of the intelligence, and, as her first venture, determined to send it to me at once, which she did with a promise that in the future she would with great pleasure continue to transmit information by the negro messenger.

SEPTEMBER 15, 1864

I learn from Major-General Crook that you are a loyal lady, and still love the old flag. Can you inform me of the position of Early's forces, the number of divisions in his army, and the strength of any or all of them, and his probable or reported intentions? Have any more troops arrived from Richmond, or are any more coming, or reported to be coming?

You may trust the bearer.

I am, very respectfully, your most obedient servant,

P. H. SHERIDAN, *Major-General Commanding.*

SEPTEMBER 16, 1864.

I have no communication whatever with the rebels, but will tell you what I know. The division of General Kershaw, and Cutshaw's artillery, twelve guns and men, General Anderson commanding, have been sent away, and no more are expected, as they cannot be spared from Richmond. I do not know how the troops are situated, but the force is much smaller than represented. I will take pleasure hereafter in learning all I can of their strength and position, and the bearer may call again.

Very respectfully yours,

.... *[REBECCA WRIGHT]*

Miss Wright's answer proved of more value to me than she anticipated, for it not only quieted the conflicting reports concerning Anderson's corps, but was most important in showing positively that Kershaw was gone, and this circumstance led, three days later, to the battle of the Opequon, or Winchester as it has been unofficially called. Word to the effect that some of Early's troops were under orders to return to Petersburg, and would start back at the first favorable opportunity, had been communicated to me already from many sources, but we had not been able to ascertain the date for their departure. Now that they had actually started, I decided to wait before offering battle until Kershaw had gone so far as to preclude his return, feeling confident that my prudence would be justified by the improved chances of victory; and then, besides, Mr. Stanton kept reminding me that positive success was necessary to counteract the political dissatisfaction existing in some of the Northern States. This course was advised and approved by General Grant, but even with his powerful backing it was difficult to resist the persistent pressure of those whose judgment, warped by their interests in the Baltimore and Ohio railroad, was often confused and misled by stories of scouts (sent out from Washington), averring that Kershaw and Fitzhugh Lee had returned to Petersburg, Breckenridge to southwestern Virginia, and at one time even maintaining that Early's whole army was east of the Blue Ridge, and its commander himself at Gordonsville.

During the inactivity prevailing in my army for the ten days preceding Miss Wright's communication the infantry was quiet, with the exception of Getty's division, which made a reconnaissance to the Opequon, and developed a heavy force of the enemy at Edwards's Corners. The cavalry, however, was employed a good deal in this interval skirmishing heavily at times to maintain a space about six miles in width between the hostile lines, for I wished to control this ground so that when I was released from the instructions of August 12, I could move my men into position for attack without the knowledge of Early. The most noteworthy of these mounted encounters was that of McIntosh's brigade, which captured the Eighth South Carolina at Abraham's Creek September 13.

It was the evening of the 16th of September that I received from Miss Wright the positive information that Kershaw was in march toward Front Royal on his way by Chester Gap to Richmond. Concluding that this was my opportunity, I at once resolved to throw my whole force into Newtown the next day, but a dispatch from General Grant directing me to meet him at Charlestown, whither he was coming to consult with me, caused me to defer action until after I should see him. In our resulting interview at Charlestown, I went over the situation very thoroughly, and pointed out with so much confidence the chances of a complete victory should I throw my army across the Valley pike near Newtown that he fell in with the plan at once, authorized me to resume the offensive, and to attack Early as soon as I deemed it most propitious to do so; and although before leaving City Point he had outlined certain operations for my army, yet he neither discussed nor disclosed his plans, my knowledge of the situation striking him as being so much more accurate than his own.

Source: Philip H. Sheridan, *Personal Memoirs of P. H. Sheridan* (New York: Charles L. Webster & Company, 1888; Project Gutenberg, 2004), vol. 2, chap. 1, http://www.gutenberg .org/ebooks/4362.

THE MARCH TO THE SEA FROM ATLANTA TO SAVANNAH

NOVEMBER 15-DECEMBER 21,1864
GEN. WILLIAM T. SHERMAN, USA

Just like Sheridan and Grant, Sherman understood that victory for the United States must mean more than a battlefield exercise. To justify the carnage of the war, it would be necessary to settle the secession issue, the slavery issue, and the matter of defeat or victory in the most overwhelmingly obvious way possible. For Sherman, fresh off the capture of Atlanta on September 3, the answer to these challenges was a march to the coastal city of Savannah, which his Army of the Tennessee and Army of Georgia reached and seized on December 21. Willfully, and with meticulous attention, the Union advance epitomized a scorched-earth advance: farms, homes, buildings, warehouses, and the contents therein were burned to the ground. Railroad ties were wrested from the earth. Nothing with even the remotest value for the Confederate war effort was to be left intact. There was no effective Confederate resistance; the Southern reaction consisted mostly of rueful tears and sputtering outrage. But Sherman—and President Lincoln—understood what they were doing. The plan was to signal beyond any conceivable doubt that the Union was intent on total victory, and that the Confederate cause had come to naught. By burning this sixty-mile scar across the Georgia landscape, Sherman left an enduring mark across the Southern psyche. No matter how much Lost Cause romanticizing

Destruction of Confederate ordnance train, Georgia Central Railroad, 1864
LIBRARY OF CONGRESS

the future held, nobody could sensibly claim that the Confederacy was not utterly beaten.

Despite outraged claims, Sherman was no heartless monster. He did not revel in cruelty. Like Grant and Sheridan, he aimed at one overriding objective: total victory. Devoid of false illusions about gallantry and the rules of war, Sherman marched to the sea not just to win the war, but to ensure the future peace between American states.

The skill and success of the men in collecting forage was one of the features of this march. Each brigade commander had authority to detail a company of foragers, usually about fifty men, with one or two commissioned officers selected for their boldness and enterprise. This party would be dispatched before daylight with a knowledge of the intended day's march and camp; would proceed on foot five or six miles from the route traveled by their brigade, and then visit every plantation and farm within range. They would usually procure a wagon or family carriage, load it with bacon, corn-meal, turkeys, chickens, ducks, and every thing that could be used as food or forage, and would then regain the main road, usually in advance of their train. When this came up, they would deliver to the brigade commissary the supplies thus gathered by the way. Often would I pass these foraging-parties at the roadside, waiting for their wagons to come up, and was amused at their strange collections—mules, horses, even cattle, packed with old saddles and loaded with hams, bacon, bags of cornmeal, and poultry of every character and description. Although this foraging was attended with great danger and hard work, there seemed to be a charm about it that attracted the soldiers, and it was a privilege to be detailed on such a party. Daily they returned mounted on all sorts of beasts, which were at once taken from them and appropriated to the general use; but the next day they would start out again on foot, only to repeat the experience of the day before. No doubt, many acts of pillage, robbery, and violence, were committed by these parties of foragers, usually called "bummers;" for I have since heard of jewelry taken from women, and the plunder of articles that never reached the commissary; but these acts were exceptional and incidental. I never heard of any cases of murder or rape; and no army could have carried along sufficient food and forage for a march of three hundred miles; so that foraging in some shape was necessary. The country was sparsely settled, with no magistrates or civil authorities who could respond to requisitions, as is done in all the wars of Europe; so that this system of foraging was simply indispensable to our success. By it our men were well supplied with all the essentials of life and health, while the wagons retained enough in case of unexpected delay, and our animals were well fed. Indeed, when we reached Savannah, the trains were pronounced by experts to be the finest in flesh and appearance ever seen with any army.

Habitually each corps followed some main road, and the foragers, being kept out on the exposed flank, served all the military uses of flank-ers. The main columns gathered, by the roads traveled, much forage and food, chiefly meat, corn, and sweet potatoes, and it was the duty of each division and brigade quartermaster to fill his wagons as fast as the contents were issued to the troops. The wagon trains had the right to the road always, but each wagon was required to keep closed up, so as to leave no gaps in the column. If for any purpose any wagon or group of wagons dropped out of place, they had to wait for the rear. And this was always dreaded, for each brigade commander wanted his train up at camp as soon after reaching it with his men as possible.

I have seen much skill and industry displayed by these quarter-masters on the march, in trying to load their wagons with corn and fodder by the way without losing their place in column. They would, while marching, shift the loads of wagons, so as to have six or ten of them empty. Then, riding well ahead, they would secure possession of certain stacks of fodder near the road, or cribs of corn, leave some men in charge, then open fences and a road back for a couple of miles, return to their trains, divert the empty wagons out of column, and conduct them rapidly to their forage, load up and regain their place in column without losing distance. On one occasion I remember to have seen ten or a dozen wagons thus loaded with corn from two or three full cribs, almost without halting. These cribs were built of logs, and roofed. The train-guard, by a lever, had raised the whole side of the crib a foot or two; the wagons drove close alongside, and the men in the cribs, lying on their backs, kicked out a wagon-load of corn in the time I have taken to describe it.

In a well-ordered and well-disciplined army, these things might be deemed irregular, but I am convinced that the ingenuity of these younger officers accomplished many things far better than I could have ordered, and the marches were thus made, and the distances were accomplished, in the most admirable way. Habitually we started from camp at the earliest break of dawn, and usually reached camp soon after noon. The marches varied from ten to fifteen miles a day, though sometimes on extreme flanks it was necessary to make as much as twenty, but the rate of travel was regulated by the wagons; and, considering the nature of the roads, fifteen miles per day was deemed the limit.

The pontoon-trains were in like manner distributed in about equal proportions to the four corps, giving each a section of about nine hundred feet. The pontoons were of the skeleton pattern, with cotton-canvas covers, each boat, with its proportion of balks and cheeses, constituting a load for one wagon. By uniting two such sections together, we could make a bridge of eighteen hundred feet, enough for any river we had to traverse; but habitually the leading brigade would, out of the abundant timber, improvise a bridge before the pontoon-train could come up, unless in the cases of rivers of considerable magnitude, such as the Ocmulgee, Oconee, Ogeechee, Savannah, etc.

On the 20th of November I was still with the Fourteenth Corps, near Eatonton Factory, waiting to hear of the Twentieth Corps; and on the 21st we camped near the house of a man named Mann; the next day, about 4 p.m., General Davis had halted his head of column on a wooded ridge, overlooking an extensive slope of cultivated country, about ten miles short of Milledgeville, and was deploying his troops for camp when I got up. There was a high, raw wind blowing, and I asked him why he had chosen so cold and bleak a position. He explained that he had accomplished his full distance for the day, and had there an abundance of wood and water. He explained further that his advance-guard was a mile or so ahead; so I rode on, asking him to let his rear division, as it came up, move some distance ahead into the depression or valley beyond. Riding on some distance to the border of a plantation, I turned out of the main road into a cluster of wild-plum bushes, that broke the force of the cold November wind, dismounted, and instructed the staff to pick out the place for our camp.

The afternoon was unusually raw and cold. My orderly was at hand with his invariable saddlebags, which contained a change of under-clothing, my maps, a flask of whiskey, and bunch of cigars. Taking a drink and lighting a cigar, I walked to a row of negro-huts close by, entered one and found a soldier or two warming themselves by a wood-fire. I took their place by the fire, intending to wait there till our wagons had got up, and a camp made for the night. I was talking to the old negro woman, when some one came and explained to me that, if I would come farther down the road, I could find a better place. So I started on foot, and found on the main road a good double-hewed-log house, in one room of which Colonel Poe, Dr. Moore, and others, had started a fire. I sent back orders to the "plum-bushes" to bring our horses and saddles up to this house, and an orderly to conduct our headquarter wagons to the same place. In looking around the room, I saw a small box, like a candle-box, marked "Howell Cobb," and, on inquiring of a negro, found that we were at the plantation of General Howell Cobb, of Georgia, one of the leading rebels of the South, then a general in the Southern army, and who had been Secretary of the United States Treasury in Mr. Buchanan's time. Of course, we confiscated his property, and found it rich in corn, beans, peanuts, and sorghum-molasses. Extensive fields were all round the house; I sent word back to General David to explain whose plantation it was, and instructed him to spare nothing. That night huge bonfires consumed the fence-rails, kept our soldiers warm, and the teamsters and men, as well as the slaves, carried off an immense quantity of corn and provisions of all sorts.

In due season the headquarter wagons came up, and we got supper. After supper I sat on a chair astride, with my back to a good fire, musing, and became conscious that an old negro, with a tallow-candle in his hand, was scanning my face closely. I inquired, "What do you want, old man!" He answered, "Dey say you is Massa Sherman." I answered that such was the case, and inquired what he wanted. He only wanted to look at me, and kept muttering, "Dis nigger can't sleep dis night." I asked him why he trembled so, and he said that he wanted to be sure that we were in fact "Yankees," for on a former occasion some rebel cavalry had put on light-blue overcoats, personating Yankee troops, and many of the negroes were deceived thereby, himself among the number had shown them sympathy, and had in consequence been unmercifully beaten therefor. This time he wanted to be certain before committing himself; so I told him to go out on the porch, from which he could see the whole horizon lit up with camp-fires, and he could then judge whether he had ever seen any thing like it before. The old man became convinced that the "Yankees" had come at last, about whom he had been dreaming all his life; and some of the staff officers gave him a strong drink of whiskey, which set his tongue going. Lieutenant Spelling, who commanded my escort, was a Georgian, and recognized in this old negro a favorite slave of his uncle, who resided about six miles off; but the old slave did not at first recognize his young master in our uniform. One of my staff-officers asked him what had become of his young master, George. He did not know, only that he had gone off to the war, and he supposed him killed, as a matter of course. His attention was then drawn to Spelling's face, when he fell on his knees and thanked God that he had found his young master alive and along with the Yankees. Spelling inquired all about his uncle and the family, asked my permission to go and pay his uncle a visit, which I granted, of course, and the next morning he described to me his visit. The uncle was not cordial, by any means, to find his nephew in the ranks of the host that was desolating the land, and Spelling came back, having exchanged his tired horse for a fresher one out of his uncle's stables, explaining that surely some of the "bummers" would have got the horse had he not.

Source: William T. Sherman, *Personal Memoirs of Gen. W. T. Sherman*, 3rd ed., vol. 1 (New York: Charles L. Webster & Company, 1890), https://archive.org/details/personal memoirso6947sher.

A WOMAN'S WARTIME JOURNAL: AN ACCOUNT OF THE PASSAGE OVER A GEORGIA PLANTATION OF SHERMAN'S ARMY ON THE MARCH TO THE SEA

NOVEMBER 28, 1964
DOLLY SUMNER LUNT, CSA

Of course, to the unwitting civilians whose homes and farms were destroyed, grand strategy was a remote concern. Of immediate import was the fact that their security, their present safety, their possessions, and even their futures were suddenly up in smoke. Their memories of Northern vengefulness made Sherman's name an execration for more than a century after the war. He accepted such hate as the price of his position, and never wavered from the necessity of his campaign. Today, the damage Sherman wrought remains folkloric in those parts. Part of the reason for the long memories must be Dolly Sumner Lunt's gift as a writer. She was an unlikely Southern diehard in some ways: born in Maine in 1817, she was a relative of Charles Sumner—Republican senator from Massachusetts, scourge of Southern interests, and strong abolitionist—but Dolly moved to Georgia to join her sister and work as a schoolteacher. She married Thomas Burge, who died in 1858. Dolly took up the life of a Southern wife, then widow, with real verve. She kept a journal during the war, and as Sherman's men approached her farm, she tried hard to hide her valuables, so as to preserve them from destruction or seizure by the Union. She distributed meat and foodstuffs among her slaves, and hid her mules in the woods. Despite such efforts, Sherman's men set her cotton stores and barn afire, while her slaves happily marched off to jubilee behind the men in blue. Thankfully for Dolly, the fire did not destroy her barn and buildings, and her journal later recounts her postbellum rebuilding. But neither she nor her neighbors forgot or forgave General Sherman.

November 28, 1864

Slept in my clothes last night, as I heard that the Yankees went to neighbor Montgomery's on Thursday night at one o'clock, searched his house, drank his wine, and took his money and valuables. As we were not disturbed, I walked after breakfast, with Sadai, up to Mr. Joe Perry's, my nearest neighbor, where the Yankees were yesterday. Saw Mrs. Laura [Perry] in the road surrounded by her children, seeming to be looking for some one. She said she was looking for her husband, that old Mrs. Perry had just sent her word that the Yankees went to James Perry's the night before, plundered his house, and drove off all his stock, and that she must drive hers into the old fields. Before we were done talking, up came Joe and Jim Perry from their hiding-place. Jim was very much excited. Happening to turn and look behind, as we stood there, I saw some blue-coats coming down the hill. Jim immediately raised his gun, swearing he would kill them anyhow.

"No, don't!" said I, and ran home as fast as I could, with Sadai.

I could hear them cry, "Halt! Halt!" and their guns went off in quick succession. Oh God, the time of trial has come!

A man passed on his way to Covington. I halloed to him, asking him if he did not know the Yankees were coming.

"No—are they?"

"Yes," said I; "they are not three hundred yards from here."

"Sure enough," said he. "Well, I'll not go. I don't want them to get my horse." And although within hearing of their guns, he would stop and look for them. Blissful ignorance! Not knowing, not hearing, he has not suffered the suspense, the fear that I have for the past forty-eight hours. I walked to the gate. There they came filing up.

I hastened back to my frightened servants and told them that they had better hide, and then went back to the gate to claim protection and a guard. But like demons they rush in! My yards are full. To my smoke-house, my dairy, pantry, kitchen, and cellar, like famished wolves they come, breaking locks and whatever is in their way. The thousand pounds of meat in my smoke-house is gone in a twinkling, my flour, my meat, my lard, butter, eggs, pickles of various kinds—both in vinegar and brine—wine, jars, and jugs are all gone. My eighteen fat turkeys, my hens, chickens, and fowls, my young pigs, are shot down in my yard and hunted as if they were rebels themselves. Utterly powerless I ran out and appealed to the guard.

"I cannot help you, Madam; it is orders."

As I stood there, from my lot I saw driven, first, old Dutch, my dear old buggy horse, who has carried my beloved husband so many miles, and who would so quietly wait at the block for him to mount and dismount, and who at last drew him to his grave; then came old Mary, my brood mare, who for years had been too old and stiff for work, with her three-year-old colt, my two-year-old mule, and her last little baby colt. There they go! There go my mules, my sheep, and, worse than all, my boys [slaves]!

Alas! little did I think while trying to save my house from plunder and fire that they were forcing my boys from home at the point of the bayonet. One, Newton, jumped into bed in his cabin, and declared himself sick. Another crawled under the floor—a lame boy he was—but they pulled him out, placed him on a horse, and drove him off. Mid, poor Mid! The last I saw of him, a man had him going around the garden, looking, as I thought, for my sheep, as he was my shepherd. Jack came crying to me, the big tears coursing down his cheeks, saying they were making him go. I said: "Stay in my room."

But a man followed in, cursing him and threatening to shoot him if he did not go; so poor Jack had to yield. James Arnold, in trying to escape from a back window, was captured and marched off. Henry, too, was taken; I know not how or when, but probably when he and Bob went after the mules. I had not believed they would force from their homes the poor, doomed negroes, but such has been the fact here, cursing them and saying that "Jeff Davis wanted to put them in his army, but that they should not fight for him, but for the Union." No! Indeed no! They are not friends to the slave. We have never made the poor, cowardly negro fight, and it is strange, passing strange, that the all-powerful Yankee nation with the whole world to back them, their ports open, their armies filled with soldiers from all nations, should at last take the poor negro to help them out against this little Confederacy which was to have been brought back into the Union in sixty days' time!

My poor boys! My poor boys! What unknown trials are before you! How you have clung to your mistress and assisted her in every way you knew.

Never have I corrected them; a word was sufficient. Never have they known want of any kind. Their parents are with me, and how sadly they lament the loss of their boys. Their cabins are rifled of every valuable, the soldiers swearing that their Sunday clothes were the white people's, and that they never had money to get such things as they had. Poor Frank's chest was broken open, his money and tobacco taken. He has always been a money-making and saving boy; not infrequently has his crop brought him five hundred dollars and more. All of his clothes and Rachel's clothes, which dear Lou gave her before her death and which she had packed away, were stolen from her. Ovens, skillets, coffee-mills, of which we had three, coffee-pots—not one have I left. Sifters all gone!

Seeing that the soldiers could not be restrained, the guard ordered me to have their [of the negroes] remaining possessions brought into my house, which I did, and they all, poor things, huddled together in my room, fearing every movement that the house would be burned.

A Captain Webber from Illinois came into my house. Of him I claimed protection from the vandals who were forcing themselves into my room. He said that he knew my brother Orrington [the late Orrington Lunt, a well-known early settler of Chicago]. At that name I could not restrain my feelings, but, bursting into tears, implored him to see my brother and let him know my destitution. I saw nothing before me but starvation. He promised to do this, and comforted me with the assurance that my dwelling house would not be burned, though my outbuildings might. Poor little Sadai went crying to him as to a friend and told him that they had taken her doll, Nancy. He begged her to come and see him, and he would give her a fine waxen one. [The doll was found later in the yard of a neighbor, where a soldier had thrown it, and was returned to the little girl. Her children later played with it, and it is now the plaything of her granddaughter.]

He felt for me, and I give him and several others the character of gentlemen. I don't believe they would have molested women and children had they had their own way. He seemed surprised that I had not laid away in my house flour and other provisions. I did not suppose I could secure them there, more than where I usually kept them, for in last summer's raid houses were thoroughly searched. In parting with him, I parted as with a friend.

Sherman himself and a greater portion of his army passed my house that day. All day, as the sad moments rolled on, were they passing not only in front of my house, but from behind; they tore down my garden palings, made a road through my back-yard and lot field, driving their stock and riding through, tearing down my fences and desolating my home— wantonly doing it when there was no necessity for it.

Such a day, if I live to the age of Methuselah, may God spare me from ever seeing again!

As night drew its sable curtains around us, the heavens from every point were lit up with flames from burning buildings. Dinnerless and supperless as we were, it was nothing in comparison with the fear of being driven out homeless to the dreary woods. Nothing to eat! I could give my guard no supper, so he left us. I appealed to another, asking him if he had wife, mother, or sister, and how he should feel were they in my situation. A colonel from Vermont left me two men, but they were Dutch, and I could not understand one word they said.

My Heavenly Father alone saved me from the destructive fire. My carriage-house had in it eight bales of cotton, with my carriage, buggy, and harness. On top of the cotton were some carded cotton rolls, a hundred pounds or more. These were thrown out of the blanket in which they were, and a large twist of the rolls taken and set on fire, and thrown into the boat of my carriage, which was close up to the cotton bales. Thanks to my God, the cotton only burned over, and then went out. Shall I ever forget the deliverance?

Tonight, when the greater part of the army had passed, it came up very windy and cold. My room was full, nearly, with the negroes and their bedding. They were afraid to go out, for my women could not step out of the door without an insult from the Yankee soldiers. They lay down on the floor; Sadai got down and under the same cover with Sally, while I sat up all night, watching every moment for the flames to burst out from some of my buildings. The two guards came into my room and laid themselves by my fire for the night. I could not close my eyes, but kept walking to and fro, watching the fires in the distance and dreading the approaching day, which, I feared, as they had not all passed, would be but a continuation of horrors.

Source: Dolly Sumner Lunt (Mrs. Thomas Burge), *A Woman's Wartime Journal: An Account of the Passage Over a Georgia Plantation of Sherman's Army on the March to the Sea, as Recorded in the Diary of Dolly Sumner Lunt* (New York: Century Co., 1918).

THE VARIETY OF CIVIL WAR EXPERIENCE

"Give me that sword, you damn Yankee!" Such was **Capt. Sumner Shearman**'s introduction to Southern manners when he and his men surrendered after the debacle at the Crater. Marched back through Confederate lines to Petersburg, he caught a quick glimpse of General Lee, and then embarked on the prison stay that would mark the rest of his war experience. Prisoners of war endured real horror on both sides during the conflict. This was due to many factors, cruelty among them. But confused logistics, problems with supply management, and ignorance of disease prevention and treatment also played their part. To this day, names like "Andersonville" and "Elmira" provoke grim recognition that being flung in prison camp hardly reduced a soldier's chance of death in uniform. Luckily for Shearman, his trip to Andersonville was forestalled by an exchange, so his recollection of POW life consists of his journey from Virginia to Charleston, South Carolina, and his trip back to Northern control in Maryland.

Death could never be far from the awareness of any soldier, North or South. **Sam Watkins** knew this, and his recounting of the "Presentment of the Wing of the Angel of Death" describes how one of his Confederate fellows handled the mysterious foreknowledge of his own imminent demise by divvying up his possessions before the presumably fatal battle. His belongings dispersed and leaving explicit instructions for communicating with his home kin, Bob Stout marched into battle with Watkins to await his fate.

CSA Maj. Gen. Nathan Bedford Forrest rivaled Jeb Stuart's derring-do. His commitment to the Southern cause was total, and his belief in the racial assumptions that underpinned the peculiar institution was just as absolute. Thus it was that at Fort Pillow, Tennessee, site of an April 12 battle along the Mississippi River, Forrest's men refused the surrender of United States Colored Troops and their white officers who were trying to surrender. Instead, the Confederates massacred the Union soldiers en masse. Investigator **D. W. Gooch** interviewed survivors, who later testified that they had thrown down their weapons, only to be met with cries of "No quarter!" and bayoneted or shot on the spot. Northern outrage at the news was ferocious, going a long way toward tamping down pro–peace settlement rhetoric. Public ire was roused by lurid accounts in local newspapers and national periodicals; cries for revenge ensued. Also ensuing was the question of whether or not Forrest was aware of the situation, or gave the order. Congressional hearings in Washington, DC, investigated and found little reason to excuse the Southern misdeeds at Fort Pillow. Up to 350 federal soldiers were slain, and Grant soon issued orders to USA Gen. Benjamin Butler that, henceforth, black prisoners of war must be treated the same as their white brethren when prisoner exchanges were negotiated. The Union made it known that if prisoners of any color were executed by Confederates, a like number of Southern soldiers would face the same fate in Union hands. Fairly or not, the massacre colored the historical reputation of Forrest, who prior to Fort Pillow, had been known for generally kind treatment of prisoners. The site would be preserved, and Mark Twain noted it acerbically in Life on the Mississippi *as a place demonstrating the vagaries of Anglo-Saxon values.*

Finally, **D. P. Conyngham** tells of a heartbreaking experience on the battlefield.

EXPERIENCES OF PRISON LIFE

CAPT. SUMNER SHEARMAN, USA

When we surrendered, I, in common with others, began clambering out of the excavation, up over the boulders of clay to firm ground, and as I reached the surface, a Confederate soldier confronted me, saying, "Give me that sword, you damn Yankee!" I of course immediately surrendered my sword, giving him sword and belt and pistol. I was walking with the colonel to the rear, under the escort of Confederate soldiers, when another soldier, without any ceremony, took my colonel's hat off his head, and put a much worse one in its place. The colonel wore a felt hat, and they seemed to be desirous of hats of that description. I had on an infantry cap, and my head was not disturbed. We had gone but a few paces when another Confederate soldier took off the hat that the colonel now had, and put on a still worse one. It seemed very strange to me to see my colonel treated with such disrespect, but he endured it without protest.

I felt very weak, and I suppose was not able to walk with my usual steadiness, for I heard one Confederate soldier say to another, pointing to me, "I wish I had the whiskey in me that he has." If I only could have had a little at that time, I think it would have been good for me.

We were taken to the rear of the enemy's line to a field just outside of Petersburg, where we were placed under a Confederate guard, and remained there all that afternoon and all night. It was about two o'clock in the afternoon when we surrendered. A mounted officer rode up during the afternoon to take a view of us, who I was told was General Lee. If it was, it was the only time I ever saw that famous officer.

As I have said, I was completely prostrated, and lay upon the ground, with no desire and scarcely the strength to get up. A fellow-officer brought

Libby Prison, Richmond, Virginia, April 1865
LIBRARY OF CONGRESS

me some water, which I drank, and bathed my head and forehead and breast, in order to restore me, if possible, from the fainting condition I was in. As the sun went down and the night came on, it became cooler, and I began to revive and feel renewed vigor. The Confederates gave us nothing to eat. An apple was given me by some one, and that was the only food I had that day. The next day was Sunday. In the morning the Confederates took the officers and the negroes who had been captured in battle and arranged us in an order like this: four officers, four negroes, four officers, four negroes, and so on, until all the officers and negroes were formed into a line of that character. Then they marched us all over the town of Petersburg, through the streets, to show us up to the inhabitants. The idea they had in view, I suppose, was to humiliate the officers. We passed one house, in the doorway of which stood a white woman, with a colored woman on either side of her, and as we passed I heard her say, "That is the way to treat the Yankees; mix them up with the niggers, they are so fond of them, mix them up." I thought to myself that she was very much in the same position that we were. Another woman whom we passed, called out, saying that if she had her way she would put all those Yanks in front of a battery and mow them all down.

A man said to me as we marched along, "They are going to take you down to Andersonville. They are dying down there three or four hundred a day; you will never live to see home again." I thought to myself that his welcome was not, to say the least, hospitable. The guard who was marching along by my side said to me that he did not believe in insulting a prisoner; that he had made up his mind never to insult a prisoner, because he had the feeling that he might some time be in the same position.

We were taken to an island in the river Appomattox, the officers at last being separated from the colored men. About eight o'clock Sunday evening eight hard crackers and a small piece of uncooked bacon were given to each of us. I had had no food except the apple that I spoke of, since the Friday night previous in camp; I went from Friday night to Sunday night without anything to eat. I ate part of the crackers and the bacon, thinking that I would make them go as far as possible, not knowing when I might receive any more. It was dark when they gave us the crackers and the bacon, and in the morning I discovered that the bacon was alive with maggots and that I had been eating it. I scraped off the maggots, and ate the rest of it.

On Monday morning they put us aboard box freight cars. There were no seats in the cars, and we were packed in like so many cattle, and started on our journey to Danville, Virginia. Arriving there, we were imprisoned in a tobacco warehouse, where we remained two or three days. This warehouse the Confederate government had improvised as a place in which to incarcerate prisoners of war, and a very large number of men were confined here. We saw some most revolting sights, men reduced to skeletons and so weak that they could scarcely crawl about. Here we were given boiled bacon and hard crackers for our food.

The enlisted men remained here, but the commissioned officers were taken on board freight cars again, and carried in the same way as before to Columbia, South Carolina. It was a very tedious and trying journey. It was insufferably hot, and very little food was supplied us. We arrived at

Columbia after dark in the evening, and marched directly to the county jail, situated in the city of Columbia.

We were placed in rooms in the jail. The one in which I was had nothing in the way of furniture in it. We simply lay down upon the floor just as we had come from the freight cars. The next day we were distributed around in the rooms on the floor above that on which we were first placed.

The jail stood on one of the principal streets of the city, close to the sidewalk and adjacent to what I took to be the city hall. In the rear of the jail was a yard, surrounded by a high fence and containing out-houses. It was a small yard. In it was a small brick building containing a cook-stove. A pipe from a spring led into the yard, with a faucet from which we drew water, which was of very excellent quality.

The room in which I was placed I should think was in the neighborhood of twenty feet square. There were, as I remember, seventeen of us in that room. There were seven similar rooms, four on one side and three on the other side of a hall running the length of the building. The side of the room towards the outer wall consisted of an iron grating. Between that grating and the outer wall was an alleyway perhaps three feet in width. There were windows in this outer wall, which were also covered with gratings. The room contained nothing whatever in the way of chairs or beds or anything for our comfort. It was absolutely empty of everything, except lice and bedbugs, until we entered it. All along on the angle made by the walls and ceiling were rows of bedbugs, and at night they came down upon us.

Having been divided in these rooms, we organized ourselves into messes, there being a mess in each room. Each mess detailed men from its number to do the cooking. We appointed the highest officer of our number in the prison, Colonel Marshall, as provost marshal. He appointed a lieutenant as adjutant, who kept a roster and detailed two men every day in each of the rooms to do police duty. Their duty was to sweep the floor, and to scrub it when necessity required. No broom was supplied us. We therefore had to purchase one. The men in the room in which I was, clubbed together and bought a broom, of very inferior quality, for which we paid five dollars in Confederate money. There was a tub belonging to the room, very roughly made, in which we brought up water from the yard below whenever we found it necessary to wash the floor. We would dash the water over the floor, and then scrub it with the broom.

We were allowed out in the prison yard each day, at daylight in the morning for an hour, and again in the afternoon for an hour. During the morning hour we all gathered around the one faucet in the yard, to perform our morning ablutions. There were some one hundred and twenty of us, as I remember, and of course we could not all engage in this process at the same time.

The cooks were allowed to go into the brick house of which I have spoken, long before daylight, where they built a fire with wood supplied by the Confederate government, and proceeded to fill a wash-boiler connected with the cook-stove, with water, which they heated and stirred in the corn meal supplied us as the chief article of our diet. This they afterwards baked in two dripping pans, these being the only cooking utensils which the building contained. After they had finished baking this corn-bread, they divided it into pieces about as large as one's hand and perhaps an inch or two thick, and spread it out on boards, which they brought up into the prison about eight or nine o'clock in the morning. A piece of this bread and a tin cup full of cold water constituted our breakfast.

When I entered the prison I had nothing with me but the clothes I had on, and a toothbrush and a small pocket comb. At the time I was taken prisoner I had some twenty or twenty-five dollars in greenbacks, and this I exchanged for Confederate money through one of the guard placed over us, receiving, as I remember, some fifteen or twenty dollars for each dollar of the currency of the United States. With this money I bought me a pint tin cup, paying five dollars for it, Confederate money. A naval officer who had been captured at Fort Sumter a year previous to our imprisonment, and who was also in this prison, gave me a small case knife and a fork made of the handle of a toothbrush. A fellow prisoner who was ingenious with the jackknife, carved a tablespoon out of a piece of wood, of which he made me a present. These articles constituted my kit.

The ration supplied us consisted of cornmeal, rice, and sorghum. The rations were issued to last ten days. They amounted to about a pint of meal a day, a tenth of a pint of rice, and a gill of sorghum. The cornmeal was sometimes good, sometimes it was wormy, sometimes it consisted of the corn and the cob ground up together. The meal was cooked in the way I have described, and twice a day we had a piece of the size I have mentioned. Sometimes we would save our rice and sorghum, and have what we considered a feast. At other times we would sell the sorghum, through the guard, to somebody outside the prison, in exchange for cow-peas, and out of these peas a soup would be made. Of course, it consisted of nothing but the peas boiled in water. We had no meat and no salt. When such an exchange was made, we had the luxury of a pint of this soup.

As I have said, I had no change of clothing, so when I indulged in the luxury of washing day, I had to go without underclothing until my clothes were dry. Of course, each man had to wash his own clothes.

Every now and then it came my turn to wash the floor, and clean up the room as best I could. Retiring at night, consisted in sweeping the floor. We went to bed, of course, upon the floor, wearing the clothes that we had worn during the day. I was fortunate enough to procure a log of wood out in the jail-yard, which I utilized as a pillow, folding up my coat and placing it on top of the wood to make my pillow more comfortable.

Of course, time hung heavy on our hands. We therefore tried to while it away by engaging in games of various kinds. We clubbed together and bought a pack of cards, paying fifteen dollars for them, and they were very poor cards at that. Some one of our number made a checker and chess-board out of a square piece of plank, and whittled out rough checkers and chessmen. We used to tell stories, and indulged largely in telling what we would like to have to eat, and what we would have if we ever got out of that place. I often dreamed at night of having magnificent banquets, and that seemed to be the case with my fellow-prisoners, for we frequently told each other in the morning of the splendid repasts we had had in our dreams. The naval officers of whom I have spoken, some fourteen in number, having been there for a year, and having received their pay in gold regularly, by an arrangement made with the Confederate government on the part of Admiral Dahlgren, had been able to purchase a good many things. They had supplied themselves with a number of books. They had Sir Walter Scott's novels, they had Don Quixote and Gil Blas. The two latter I borrowed of them, and read them in the prison with great interest. Some of the men in the room in which I was having learned that I knew something of Latin, asked me if I would not undertake to teach them Latin, so I obtained from these naval officers a Latin grammar and a Latin Prose Composition, and established a class in Latin. So in one way and another we managed to get through each day.

A portion of each day was occupied by each one of us in a critical examination of our underclothing, in order to make sure that we destroyed the crop of vermin which we found there each day. They were not the kind that are found in the heads of school children, but seemed to infest woolen clothing, and, as we all wore woolen clothing, we were greatly annoyed by them. This process we called "skirmishing," and it was one of our daily duties.

There were guards around the prison in the jail-yard and on the street below at each side of the prison. At the front of the prison there was a large window, which we were ordered not to approach after six o'clock at night. The guard had instructions to fire at any prisoner who might show himself at the window. We not infrequently tantalized the guard by going near enough to be seen by him, and dodging back just as he fired.

We were allowed out in the jail-yard, as I have said, early in the morning. A Confederate corporal would unlock the door, and shout out, "Yanks all out!" Of course, we were counted as we went out, and when we returned we were all drawn up in line and counted again, to make sure that all that went out had returned.

The captain in charge of the jail seemed to be a very excellent man. He was an elderly man, too old for active service in the field, and the men under him were either old men or boys, some of them hardly old enough to carry a musket. This showed to us, as we thought, that nearly all their available men were at the front. The guard was frequently changed; that is to say, the men who served for a few days would disappear and an entirely new set take their places. They wore no uniform, and we therefore concluded that they were rustics and others in the neighborhood, temporarily serving as guards over the prisoners.

One day while I was waiting for the officer to let us return into the prison, we having been allowed out in the yard, I was walking back and forth in the lower hall. While doing so three young girls came up to the sentinel on duty at the front of the building and spoke to him. They were evidently of the class known in the South as "poor white trash," who had come from the country. I heard them say to the guard that they would like to see a Yankee. He immediately pointed to me and said, "There's one." They replied, looking critically at me, "Why, I don't see but what he looks just like other men." What they expected to see I am sure I cannot tell, some monstrous being or other, I presume, for there had been most surprising stories told at the beginning of the war, among the ignorant white and colored people, of the horrible appearance of the Yankees. It was declared that they had horns on their heads, and altogether presented a very devilish aspect.

We used to talk more or less of the possibility of escape. We could easily have gotten away from the prison, because of the inferior quality of the guard. Whenever we were allowed outside, we could have made a rush, and thus gotten away from them. Some of us, of course, would probably have been killed or wounded, but a majority could have escaped from the prison itself. The difficulty was to get to our own lines, the nearest place being the seacoast at Charleston, S. C. This long distance had to be traversed, travelling by night and hiding by day. The Confederates were accustomed to hunt prisoners with bloodhounds, so the chances of ultimate escape were very small.

Two of our number, however, determined to take those chances at the first opportunity. So one night, when a severe storm was raging, the wind blowing, and the rain pouring down, they tied some blankets together as a rope by which they could be let down to the street. Here I may say that some of the prisoners happened to have blankets with them when they were captured, though I myself was not one of the fortunate ones. We had discovered that the sentry on duty when the nights were stormy, was in the habit of retiring within the porch over the front door of the prison; therefore these two men thought if they could reach the ground while the sentry was within the porch, they might possibly make their escape under cover of the darkness.

The plan proved successful. We let them down from the window, and saw and heard no more of them. Whether they were recaptured or not I did not know for years afterwards. They were not brought back to the prison, and I have since learned that they succeeded in getting away. In order to deceive the officer who called us out in the morning, we placed two dummies on the floor in place of the men who had escaped during the previous night. This ruse deceived the prison officials, so the men had a longer opportunity of making their escape; but it was discovered at night when the roll-call was made that there were two men lacking, and, of course, I suppose the two escaped prisoners were at once pursued.

The windows in the prison were sadly lacking in glass, many panes having been broken out. Glass was almost an unknown quantity in the Southern Confederacy at that time, as they manufactured none themselves, and the blockade was so stringent that they could import but little. The consequence was, when winter weather came on, that the prisoners suffered from cold. The captain of the jail fitted up the vacant spaces with boards, and so many panes had to be supplied in this way that it seriously darkened the prison. He also placed a stove in the centre of the hall which I have spoken of as running the whole length of the prison. It was very insufficient in its capacity to heat the prison, nevertheless it was better than nothing. Of course the fuel supplied us was wood.

An old colored woman was allowed to come into the prison whenever she chose, to sell what the southern people call "snacks," to such as were fortunate enough to have money to buy them. The lunches consisted mainly of baked sweet potatoes and flour-bread or biscuit. A New Hampshire officer had quite a little sum of money when he was taken prisoner, and this he had husbanded to the best of his ability, and had some of it left when the cold became quite severe. Through the old colored woman, by paying her liberally for it, he obtained an old carpet that had seen its best days. It was quite ragged and torn. This, those who slept on my side of the room placed over them, and thus had some little protection from the cold weather. We used to sleep spoon-fashion under this carpet, and of course we all had to turn over at the same time to keep the carpet over us. We appointed one of our number to give the word of command whenever he was disposed to have us turn.

Thus we lived week in and week out, until nearly six months had gone by. One day, when I was engaged in teaching my class in Latin, I heard shouts from some of my fellow-prisoners, calling, "Shearman! Shearman! You are wanted!" Making my way toward the direction of the shouts, I found that a Confederate corporal was at the prison door, who informed me that he had good news for me. He took me down stairs, and there I found a Confederate major, who told me the joyful news that I was to be exchanged next morning. I could scarcely believe what he said to be true, for I, in common with the other prisoners, thought we should be compelled to remain there until the end of the war, and when that might be we did not know.

I might say here that we were allowed to write letters home, but they were limited to one side of a half sheet of note paper. The paper and envelopes were of the poorest quality imaginable, and cost an exorbitant price, reckoned in Confederate money. These letters had to be read by the captain in charge of the prison, and forwarded by him to their destination. In my letters I almost always asked my father to do what he could to get me exchanged, but I had no hope that he would be successful. It seems, however, that the two governments had made an arrangement to exchange ten thousand sick men. The exchange was to have taken place at Savannah, and five thousand were exchanged at that point, when General Sherman arrived at Savannah, which compelled a transfer in the place of exchange. The remainder were exchanged at Charleston, South Carolina. Through the influence of General Burnside, a friend of my father's, my name was included in the list of those to be exchanged, although I was not sick. All this I learned after reaching home.

After my interview with the Confederate major, I was taken up stairs again into my portion of the prison, and told my fellow-prisoners of my good luck. There were six others to whom the same glorious news was imparted. Of course, it was the topic of conversation from that time on during the rest of the day and evening. Many of the prisoners took advantage of the opportunity to send letters home by us, and wrote much longer communications than were allowed, we agreeing to secrete them about our persons, and carry them away surreptitiously. They could thus write many things about themselves and their condition that would not pass muster, going through the captain's hands.

I did not sleep a wink that night. The excitement of the news which I had received would not permit me to close my eyes. I might say here, speaking of sitting up nearly all night, that we had no lights in the prison, and when night came on, we had to sit in the darkness until we were ready to lie down upon the floor. Occasionally we would indulge in the luxury of a tallow candle of the poorest quality, for which we paid a dollar in Confederate money. Sometimes a pine knot would be found among the wood which the cooks used. This we would take up into the jail and light in the evening. Of course it afforded light, but it also filled the room with clouds of smoke which escaped through the broken windows. Next morning our faces would be covered with soot.

To come back to the matter of my exchange, on the afternoon of the next day I was duly liberated, with my six companions, and marched to a freight train. I remember that it was a cold day for that region, and that snow was falling. It was the only snow, as I recollect, that we had during the time I was a prisoner. The train of cars soon started on its way to Charleston, S. C. A large number of prisoners were gathered at various points, coming from Andersonville and Florence. We reached Charleston early the next morning, and were marched across the city to the wharves.

Charleston was completely abandoned by its inhabitants because of the siege on the part of our forces, and it was the most desolate looking place I have ever seen in all my life. The damages inflicted by shot and shell were to be seen on every hand. The grass had actually grown in the streets of Charleston, although at the time we were passing through, a light snow was on the ground, adding to the desolation of the scene. General Toombs of Georgia had threatened before the war began that the South would make grass grow in the streets of Boston, and that he would call the roll of his slaves on Bunker Hill. Grass actually did grow in the streets of Charleston as a result of the war.

Arriving at the wharves, we were placed on board of a steam vessel, which proved to be a blockade runner, and were carried out to a fleet of vessels under the walls of Fort Sumter, which our government had provided for the transport of prisoners. I was placed on board a ship called the *United States*, with a number of my fellow-prisoners. Those of us who were officers were assigned by the captain of the ship to staterooms. We found that there were nine hundred prisoners on board from Andersonville and Florence, some of them in the last stages of emaciation. Two or three of them died on the voyage from Charleston to Annapolis, and their bodies were buried in the sea. The Sanitary Commission had an agent on board, with an ample supply of underclothing. I at once got rid of the clothing which I had worn so long in the prison, throwing it overboard, and accepted with alacrity the new and clean clothing given me by the agent of the Sanitary Commission.

We lay at anchor one night in Charleston harbor, and the next day sailed for Annapolis, Md. Arriving at that point, we found each prisoner had been granted a thirty days' leave of absence. I telegraphed my father of my arrival at Annapolis, and found, on reaching home, that he could hardly bring himself to believe it.

We went from Annapolis to Washington to obtain our pay, which had been accumulating during the period of our imprisonment. I purchased new clothing, and then joyfully started for home. I had served nearly three years, and my regiment had been mustered out of service during the period of my imprisonment, its time having expired. Some of its members had re-enlisted, and were consolidated with the Seventh Rhode Island; but I felt that I had done my duty, and that I was entitled to withdraw from the service, so I sent in my resignation direct to the Secretary of War at Washington, accompanying it with a surgeon's certificate of my health, and setting forth the facts of my service and my imprisonment. I obtained the endorsement of the Governor of the State to my application, and it came back in a few days accepted, and I was out of the service. I have often felt that I would have been tempted to return had I known that the war would end as soon as it subsequently did, so as to have had the satisfaction of being in at the close, if possible.

I have never regretted my being in the army during that most trying and critical period of our country. I feel as did the Westerner who said that he would not part with his experiences for a hundred thousand dollars, and he would not go through with it again for a hundred million.

Source: Sumner U. Shearman, *Battle of the Crater and Experiences of Prison Life* (Providence: Rhode Island Soldiers and Sailors Historical Society, 1898; Project Gutenberg, 2014), http://www.gutenberg.org/ebooks/47778.

PRESENTMENT OF THE WING
OF THE ANGEL OF DEATH

CPL. SAM R. WATKINS, CSA

Presentment is always a mystery. The soldier may at one moment be in good spirits, laughing and talking. The wing of the death angel touches him. He knows that his time has come. It is but a question of time with him then. He knows that his days are numbered. I cannot explain it. God has numbered the hairs of our heads, and not a sparrow falls without His knowledge. How much more valuable are we than many sparrows?

We had stopped at Lee & Gordon's mill, and gone into camp for the night.

Three days' rations were being issued. When Bob Stout was given his rations he refused to take them. His face wore a serious, woe-begone expression. He was asked if he was sick, and said "No," but added, "Boys, my days are numbered, my time has come. In three days from today, I will be lying right yonder on that hillside a corpse. Ah, you may laugh; my time has come. I've got a twenty dollar gold piece in my pocket that I've carried through the war, and a silver watch that my father sent me through the lines. Please take them off when I am dead, and give them to Captain Irvine, to give to my father when he gets back home. Here are my clothing and blanket that any one who wishes them may have. My rations I do not wish at all. My gun and cartridge-box I expect to die with."

The next morning the assembly sounded about two o'clock. We commenced our march in the darkness, and marched twenty-five miles to a little town by the name of Lafayette, to the relief of General Pillow, whose command had been attacked at that place. After accomplishing this, we marched back by another road to Chickamauga. We camped on the banks of Chickamauga on Friday night, and Saturday morning we commenced to crossover. About twelve o'clock we had crossed. No sooner had we crossed than an order came to double quick. General Forrest's cavalry had opened the battle. Even then the spent balls were falling amongst us with that peculiar thud so familiar to your old soldier.

Double quick! There seemed to be no rest for us. Forrest is needing reinforcements. Double quick, close up in the rear! siz, siz, double quick, boom, hurry up, bang, bang, a rattle de bang, bang, siz, boom, boom, boom, hurry up, double quick, boom, bang, halt, front, right dress, boom, boom, and three soldiers are killed and twenty wounded. Billy Webster's arm was torn out by the roots and he killed, and a fragment of shell buried itself in Jim McEwin's side, also killing Mr. Fain King, a conscript from Mount Pleasant. Forward, guide center, march, charge bayonets, fire at will, commence firing. (This is where the LL. D. ran.) We debouched through the woods, firing as we marched, the Yankee line about two hundred yards off. Bang, bang, siz, siz. It was a sort of running fire. We kept up a constant fire as we advanced. In ten minutes we were face to face with the foe. It was but a question as to who could load and shoot the fastest. The army was not up. Bragg was not ready for a general battle. The big battle was fought the next day, Sunday. We held our position for two hours and ten minutes in the midst of a deadly and galling fire, being enfiladed and almost surrounded, when General Forrest galloped up and said, "Colonel Field, look out, you are almost surrounded; you had better fall back." The order was given to retreat. I ran through a solid line of blue coats. As I fell back, they were upon the right of us, they were upon the left of us, they were in front of us, they were in the rear of us. It was a perfect hornets' nest. The balls whistled around our ears like the escape valves of ten thousand engines. The woods seemed to be blazing; everywhere, at every jump, would rise a lurking foe. But to get up and dust was all we could do. I was running along by the side of Bob Stout. General Preston Smith stopped me and asked if our brigade was falling back. I told him it was. He asked me the second time if it was Maney's brigade that was falling back. I told him it was. I heard him call out, "Attention, forward!" One solid sheet of leaden hail was falling around me. I heard General Preston Smith's brigade open.

It seemed to be platoons of artillery. The earth jarred and trembled like an earthquake. Deadly missiles were flying in every direction. It was the very incarnation of death itself.

I could almost hear the shriek of the death angel passing over the scene. General Smith was killed in ten minutes after I saw him. Bob Stout and myself stopped. Said I, "Bob, you wern't killed, as you expected." He did not reply, for at that very moment a solid shot from the Federal guns struck him between the waist and the hip, tearing off one leg and scattering his bowels all over the ground. I heard him shriek out, "O, O, God!" His spirit had flown before his body struck the ground. Farewell, friend; we will meet over yonder.

When the cannon ball struck Billy Webster, tearing his arm out of the socket, he did not die immediately, but as we were advancing to the attack, we left him and the others lying where they fell upon the battlefield; but when we fell back to the place where we had left our knapsacks, Billy's arm had been dressed by Dr. Buist, and he seemed to be quite easy. He asked Jim Fogey to please write a letter to his parents at home. He wished to dictate the letter. He asked me to please look in his knapsack and get him a clean shirt, and said that he thought he would feel better if he could get rid of the blood that was upon him. I went to hunt for his knapsack and found it, but when I got back to where he was, poor, good Billy Webster was dead. He had given his life to his country. His spirit is with the good and brave. No better or braver man than Billy Webster ever drew the breath of life. His bones lie yonder today, upon the battlefield of Chickamauga. I loved him; he was my friend. Many and many a dark night have Billy and I stood together upon the silent picket post. Ah, reader, my heart grows sick and I feel sad while I try to write my recollections of that unholy and uncalled for war. But He that ruleth the heavens doeth all things well.

Source: Sam R. Watkins, *"Co. Aytch," Maury Grays, First Tennessee Regiment; or, A Side Show of the Big Show*, 2nd ed. (self-pub., 1882; Chattanooga, TN: Chattanooga Times, 1900), chap. 8, http://www.fullbooks.com/Co-Aytch-1.html.

FORT PILLOW MASSACRE

D. W. GOOCH, USA

"Henry Christian, (colored), private, company B, 6th United States heavy artillery, sworn and examined. By Mr. Gooch:

'Question. Where were you raised? 'Answer. In East Tennessee.

'Question. Have you been a slave? 'Answer. Yes, sir.

'Question. Where did you enlist? 'Answer. At Corinth, Mississippi.

'Question. Were you in the fight at Fort Pillow? 'Answer. Yes, sir.

'Question. When were you wounded? 'Answer. A little before we surrendered.

'Question. What happened to you afterwards? 'Answer. Nothing; I got but one shot, and dug right out over the hill to the river, and never was bothered any more.

'Did you see any men shot after the place was taken? 'Answer. Yes, sir.

'Question. Where? 'Answer. Down to the river.

'Question. How many? 'Answer. A good many; I don't know how many.

'Question. By whom were they shot? 'Answer. By secesh soldiers; secesh officers shot.

'Question. Did you see those on the hill shot by the officers? 'Answer. I saw two of them shot.

'Question. What officers were they? 'Answer. I don't know whether he was a lieutenant or captain.

'Question. Did the men who were shot after they had surrendered have arms in their hands? 'Answer. No, sir; they threw down their arms.

'Question. Did you see any shot the next morning? 'Answer. I saw two shot; one was shot by an officer—he was standing, holding the officer's horse, and when the officer

'Question. Do you say the man was holding the officer's horse, and when the officer came and took his horse he shot the man down? 'Answer. Yes, sir; I saw that with my own eyes; and then I made away into the river, right off.

'Question. Did you see any buried? 'Answer. Yes, sir; a great many, black and white.

'Question. Did you see any buried alive? 'Answer. I did not see any buried alive.

"Jacob Thompson, (colored), sworn and examined. By Mr. Gooch:
'Question. Were you a soldier at Fort Pillow? 'Answer. No, sir, I was not a soldier; but I went up in the fort and fought with the rest. I was shot in the hand and the head.

'Question. When were you shot? 'Answer. After I surrendered.

'Question. How many times were you shot? 'Answer. I was shot but once; but I threw my hand up, and the shot went through my hand and my head.

'Question. Who shot you? 'Answer. A private.

'Question. What did he say? 'Answer. He said, 'G—d d—n you, I will shoot you, old friend.'

'Question. Did you see anybody else shot? 'Answer. Yes, sir; they just called them out like dogs, and shot them down. I reckon they shot about fifty, white and black, right there. They nailed some black sergeants to the logs, and set the logs on fire.

'Question. When did you see that? 'Answer. When I went there in the morning I saw them; they were burning all together.

'Question. Did they kill them before they burned them? 'Answer. No, sir, they nailed them to the logs; drove the nails right through their hands.

'Question. How many did you see in that condition? 'Answer. Some four or five; I saw two white men burned.

'Question. Was there any one else there who saw that? Answer. I reckon there was; I could not tell who.

'Question. When was it that you saw them? 'Answer. I saw them in the morning after the fight; some of them were burned almost in two. I could tell they were white men, because they were whiter than the colored men.

'Question. Did you notice how they were nailed? 'Answer. I saw one nailed to the side of a house; he looked like he was nailed right through his wrist. I was trying then to get to the boat when I saw it.

'Question. Did you see them kill any white men? 'Answer. They killed some eight or nine there. I reckon they killed more than twenty after it was all over; called them out from under the hill, and shot them down. They would call out a white man and shoot him down, and call out a colored man and shoot him down; do it just as fast as they could make their guns go off.

'Question. Did you see any rebel officers about there when this was going on? 'Answer. Yes, sir; old Forrest was one.

'Question. Did you know Forrest? 'Answer. Yes, sir; he was a little bit of a man. I had seen him before at Jackson.

'Question. Are you sure he was there when this was going on? 'Answer. Yes, sir.

'Question. Did you see any other officers that you knew? 'Answer. I did not know any other but him. There were some two or three more officers came up there.

'Question. Did you see any buried there? 'Answer. Yes, sir; they buried right smart of them. They buried a great many secesh, and a great many of our folks. I think they buried more secesh than our folks.

'Question. How did they bury them? 'Answer. They buried the secesh over back of the fort, all except those on Fort hill; them they buried up on top of the hill where the gunboats shelled them.

'Question. Did they bury any alive? 'Answer. I heard the gunboat men say they dug two out who were alive.

'Question. You did not see them? 'Answer. No, sir.

'Question. What company did you fight with? 'Answer. I went right into the fort and ought there.

'Question. Were you a slave or a free man? 'Answer. I was a slave.

'Question. Where were you raised? 'Answer. In old Virginia.

'Question. Who was your master? 'Answer. Colonel Hardgrove.

'Question. Where did you live? 'Answer. I lived three miles the other side of Brown's mills.

'Question. How long since you lived with him? 'Answer. I went home once and staid with him a while, but he got to cutting up and I came away again.

'Question. What did you do before you went into the fight? 'Answer. I was cooking for Co. K, of Illinois cavalry; I cooked for that company nearly two years.

'Question. What white officers did you know in our army? 'Answer. I knew Captain Meltop and Colonel Ransom; and I cooked at the hotel at Fort Pillow, and Mr. Nelson kept it. I and Johnny were cooking together. After they shot me through the hand and head, they beat up all this part of my head (the side of his head) with the breach of their guns.

"Ransome Anderson, (colored), Co. B, 6th United States heavy artillery, sworn and examined. By Mr. Gooch:

'Question. Where were you raised? 'Answer. In Mississippi.

'Question. Were you a slave? 'Answer. Yes, sir.

'Question. Where did you enlist? 'Answer. At Corinth.

'Question. Were you in the fight at Fort Pillow? 'Answer. Yes, sir.

'Question. Describe what you saw done there. 'Answer. Most all the men that were killed on our side were killed after the fight was over. They called them out and shot them down. Then they put some in the houses and shut them up, and then burned the houses.

'Question. Did you see them burn? 'Answer. Yes, sir.

'Question. Were any of them alive? 'Answer. Yes, sir; they were wounded, and could not walk. They put them in the houses, and then burned the houses down.

'Question. Do you know they were in there? 'Answer. Yes, sir; I went and looked in there.

'Question. Do you know they were in there when the house was burned? 'Answer. Yes, sir; I heard them hallooing there when the houses were burning.

'Question. Are you sure they were wounded men, and not dead, when they were put in there? 'Answer. Yes, sir; they told them they were going to have the doctor see them, and then put them in there and shut them up, and burned them.

'Question. Who set the house on fire? 'Answer. I saw a rebel soldier take some grass and lay it by the door, and set it on fire. The door was pine plank, and it caught easy.

'Question. Was the door fastened up? 'Answer. Yes, sir; it was barred with one of those wide bolts.

'James Walls, sworn and examined. By Mr. Gooch:

'Question. To what company did you belong? 'Answer. Company E, 13th Tennessee cavalry.

'Question. Under what officers did you serve? 'Answer. I was under Major Bradford and Captain Potter.

'Question. Were you in the fight at Fort Pillow? 'Answer. Yes, sir.

'Question. State what you saw there of the fight, and what was done after the place was captured. 'Answer. We fought them for some six or eight hours in the fort, and when they charged, our men scattered and ran under the hill; some turned back and surrendered, and were shot. After the flag of truce came in I went down to get some water. As I was coming back I turned sick, and laid down behind a log. The secesh charged, and after they came over I saw one go a good ways ahead of the others. One of our men made to him and threw down his arms. The bullets were surrendered. He did not shoot me then, but as I turned around he or some other one shot me in the back.

'Question. Did they say anything while they were shooting? 'Answer. All I heard was, 'Shoot him, shoot him!' 'Yonder goes one!' 'Kill him, kill him!' That is about all I heard.

'Question. How many do you suppose you saw shot after they surrendered? 'Answer. I did not see but two or three shot around me. One of the boys of our company, named Taylor, ran up there, and I saw him shot and fall. Then another was shot just before me, like—shot down after he threw down his arms.

'Question. Those were white men? 'Answer. Yes, sir. I saw them make lots of niggers stand up, and then they shot them down like hogs. The next morning I was lying around there waiting for the boat to come up. The secesh would be prying around there, and would come to a nigger and say, 'You ain't dead are you?' They would not say anything, and then the secesh would get down off their horses, prick them in their sides, and say, 'D—n you, you aint dead; get up.' Then they would make them get up on their knees, when they would shoot them down like hogs.

'Question. Do you know of their burning any buildings? 'Answer. I could hear them tell them to stick torches all around, and they fired all the buildings.

'Question. Do you know whether any of our men were in the buildings when they were burned? 'Answer. Some of our men said some were burned; I did not see it, or know it to be so myself.

'Question. How did they bury them—white and black together? 'Answer. I don't know about the burying; I did not see any buried.

'Question. How many negroes do you suppose were killed after the surrender? 'Answer. There were hardly any killed before the surrender. I reckon as many as 200 were killed after the surrender, out of about 300 that were there.

Question. Did you see any rebel officers about while this shooting was going on? 'Answer. I do not know as I saw any officers about when they were shooting the negroes. A captain came to me a few minutes after I was shot; he was close by me when I was shot.

'Question. Did he try to stop the shooting? 'Answer. I did not hear a word of their trying to stop it. After they were shot down, he told them not to shoot them any more. I begged him not to let them shoot me again, and he said they would not. One man, after he was shot down, was shot again. After I was shot down, the man I surrendered to went around the tree I was against and shot a man, and then came around to me again and wanted my pocket-book. I handed it up to him, and he saw my watch-chain and made a grasp at it, and got the watch and about half the chain. He took an old Barlow knife I had in my pocket. It was not worth five cents; was of no account at all, only to cut tobacco with.'

"Nathan G. Fulks, sworn and examined. By Mr. Gooch:

'Question. To what company and regiment do you belong? 'Answer. To Company D, 13th Tennessee cavalry.

'Question. Where are you from? 'Answer. About twenty miles from Columbus, Tennessee.

'Question. How long have you been in the service? 'Answer. Five months, the 1st of May.

'Question. Were you at Fort Pillow at the time of the fight there? Answer. Yes, sir.

'Question. Will you state what happened to you there? 'Answer. I was at the corner of the fort when they fetched in a flag for a surrender. Some of them said the major stood a while, and then said he would not surrender. They continued to fight a while; and after a time the major started and told us to take care of ourselves, and I and twenty more men broke for the hollow. They ordered us to halt, and some of them said, 'God d—n 'em, kill 'em!' I said, 'I have surrendered.' I had thrown my gun away then. I took off my cartridge-box and gave it to one of them, and said, 'Don't shoot me;' but they did shoot me, and hit just about where the shoe comes up on my leg. I begged them not to shoot me, and he said, 'God d—n you, you fight with the niggers, and we will kill the last one of you!' Then they shot me in the thick of the thigh, and I fell; and one setout to shoot me again, when another one said, 'Don't shoot the white fellows any more.

'Question. Did you see any person shot besides yourself? 'Answer. I didn't see them shot. I saw one of our fellows dead by me.

'Question. Did you see any buildings burned? 'Answer. Yes, sir. While I was in the major's headquarters they commenced burning the buildings, and I begged one of them to take me out and not let us burn there; and he said, 'I am hunting up a piece of yellow flag for you.' I think we would have whipped them if the flag of truce had not come in. We would have whipped them if we had not let them get the dead-wood on us. I was told that they made their movement while the flag of truce was in. I did not see it myself, because I had sat down, as I had been working so hard.

'Question. How do you know they made their movement while the flag of truce was in? 'Answer. The men that were above said so. The rebs are bound to take every advantage of us. I saw two more white men close to where I was lying. That makes three dead ones, and myself wounded."

Source: B. F. Wade and D. W. Gooch, *Report of the Committee on the Conduct of the War: Fort Pillow Massacre* (Washington, DC: United States Senate, 1864; Project Gutenberg, 2013), http://www.gutenberg.org/ebooks/41787.

BATTLEFIELD TRAGEDY, 1862

CAPT. D. P. CONYNGHAM, USA

If the Civil War was a Brother's War, there could also be additional relationships involved. The following pitiful incident was unlikely to have occurred in any other conflict. It partly accounts for the Civil War's reputation as an American tragedy.

I had a Sergeant Driscoll, a brave man, and one of the best shots in the Brigade. When charging at Malvern Hill, a company was posted in a clump of trees, who kept up a fierce fire on us, and actually charged out on our advance. Their officer seemed to be a daring, reckless boy, and I said to Driscoll, "if that officer is not taken down, many of us will fall before we pass that clump."

"Leave that to me," said Driscoll; so he raised his rifle, and the moment the officer exposed himself again, bang went Driscoll, and over went the officer, his company at once breaking away.

As we passed the place I said, "Driscoll, see if that officer is dead—he was a brave fellow."

I stood looking on. Driscoll turned him over on his back. He opened his eyes for a moment, and faintly murmured "Father," and closed them forever.

I will forever recollect the frantic grief of Driscoll; it was harrowing to witness. He was his son, who had gone South before the war.

And what became of Driscoll afterwards? Well, we were ordered to charge, and I left him there; but, as we were closing in on the enemy, he rushed up, with his coat off, and, clutching his musket, charged right up at the enemy, calling on the men to follow. He soon fell, but jumped up again. We knew he was wounded. On he dashed, but he soon rolled over like a top. When we came up he was dead, riddled with bullets.

Source: "Battlefield Tragedy, 1862," Eyewitness to History, 1999, www.eyewitnessto history.com/malvern.htm; from D. P. Conyngham, *The Irish Brigade and Its Campaigns, With Some Accounts of the Corcoran Legion, and Sketches of the Principal Officers* (1867), reprinted in B. A. Botkin, *A Civil War Treasury of Tales, Legends and Folklore* (1960).

1865

BATTLE OF THE FIVE FORKS

APRIL 1, 1865
GEN. HORACE PORTER, USA

By the spring of 1865, Grant's tenacious persistence meant that Union forces held the Confederacy in a tightening death grip. The area of effective Southern control was limited to far-off spaces in the West and areas in the Carolinas and around Richmond. The latter was where the war would be decided: Lee was stuck in the Petersburg works and the Army of Northern Virginia was running out of room to maneuver. Five Forks, in Virginia's Dinwiddie County, guarded the South Side Railroad, one of the last reliable passages into and out of beleaguered Richmond. On March 31, in an action at the county courthouse, Sheridan's cavalry hit CSA Maj. Gen. George Pickett's force. An alarmed Lee, fearing that the capital might be cut off, ordered Pickett to resist with everything he had so as to hold Five Forks.

It was a hopeless command. Sheridan's cavalry, in tandem with robust V Corps infantry assaults, hit at both left and right Confederate flanks. The woody terrain confused the Southern reserve, who struggled to locate the points of attack. The same confusion delayed the blue jackets, but Sheridan himself rallied his men, who took Five Forks, making Lee's position at Petersburg virtually untenable. If Petersburg fell, everyone knew, Richmond would, too. Here, USA Col. Horace Porter, one of Grant's staff officers who observed the action at close hand and joyously reported the victory to his commander, describes a battle which not only yielded a strategic rail junction but also cost the weakening Confederate army 5,000 prisoners and nearly 3,000 casualties.

A few minutes before noon Colonel Babcock came over from headquarters, and said to Sheridan: "General Grant directs me to say to you that if, in your judgment, the Fifth Corps would do better under one of its division commanders, you are authorized to relieve General Warren and order him to report to him [General Grant] at headquarters." General Sheridan replied in effect that he hoped such a step as that might not become necessary, and then went on to speak of his plan of battle. We all rode on farther to the front, and soon met General Devin of the cavalry, who was considerably elated by his successes of the morning, and loudly demanded to be permitted to make a general attack on the enemy. Sheridan told him he didn't believe he had ammunition enough. Said Devin: "I guess I've got enough to give 'em one surge more." Colonel Babcock now left us to return to headquarters.

About one o'clock it was reported by the cavalry that the enemy was retiring to his intrenched position at Five Forks, which was just north of the White Oak road and parallel to it, his earthworks running from a point about three quarters of a mile east of Five Forks to a point a mile west, with an angle or "crochet," about one hundred yards long, thrown back at right of his line to protect that flank. Orders were at once given to Warren's corps to move up the Gravelly Ron Church road to the open ground near the church, and form in order of battle, with Ayres on the left, Crawford on his right, and Griffin in rear as a reserve. The corps was to wheel to the left and make its attack upon the angle, and then, moving westward, sweep down in rear of the enemy's entrenched line. The cavalry, principally dismounted, was to deploy in front of the enemy's line and engage his attention, and as soon as it heard the firing of our infantry to make a vigorous assault upon his works. The Fifth Corps had borne the brunt of the fighting ever since the army had moved out on March 29; and the gallant men who composed it, and who had performed a conspicuous part in nearly every battle in which the Army of the Potomac had been engaged, seemed eager once more to cross bayonets with their old antagonists.

But the movement was slow, the required formation seemed to drag, and Sheridan, chafing with impatience and consumed with anxiety, became as restive as a racer struggling to make the start. He made every possible appeal for promptness, dismounted from his horse, paced up and down, struck the clenched fist of one hand against the palm of the other, and fretted like a caged tiger. He exclaimed at one time: "This battle must be fought and won before the sun goes down. All the conditions may be changed in the morning. We have but a few hours of daylight left us. My cavalry are rapidly exhausting their ammunition, and if the attack is delayed much longer they may have none left." And then another batch of staff-officers was sent out to gallop through the mud and hurry up the columns. At four o'clock the formation was completed, the order for the assault was given, and the struggle for Pickett's intrenched line began. The Confederate infantry brigades were posted from left to right as follows: Terry, Corse, Stuart, Ransom, and Wallace. General Fitzhugh Lee, commanding the cavalry, had placed W. H. F. Lee's two brigades on the right of the line, Munford's division on the left, and Bosser's in rear of Hatcher's Run, to guard the trains. I rode to the front, in company with Sheridan and Warren, with the head of Ayres's division, which was on the left. Ayres threw out a skirmish-line and advanced across an open field which sloped down gradually toward the dense woods just north of the White Oak road. He soon met with a fire from the edge of these woods, a number of men fell, and the skirmish-line halted and seemed to waver.

Sheridan now began to exhibit those traits which always made him a tower of strength in the presence of an enemy. He put spurs to his horse, and dashed along in front of the line of battle from left to right, shouting words of encouragement, and having something cheery to say to every regiment. "Come on, men," he cried; "Go at 'em with a will! Move on at a clean jump, or you'll not catch one of 'em. They're all getting ready to run now, and if you don't get on to them in five minutes they'll everyone get away from you. I now go for them!" Just then a man on the skirmish-line was struck in the neck; the blood spurted as if the jugular vein had been cut. "I'm killed!" he cried, and dropped to the ground. "You're not hurt a bit!" cried Sheridan. "Pick up your gun, man, and move right on to the front." Such was the electric effect of his words that the poor fellow snatched up his musket, and rushed forward a dozen paces before he fell, never to rise again. The line of battle of weather-beaten veterans was now moving right along down the slope toward the woods with a steady swing that boded no good for Pickett's command, earthworks or no earthworks.

Sheridan was mounted on his favorite black horse, "Rienzi," which had carried him from Winchester to Cedar Creek, and which Buchanan Read made famous for all time by his poem of "Sheridan's Ride." The roads were muddy, the fields swampy, the undergrowth dense, and "Rienzi," as he plunged and curveted, kept dashing the foam from his mouth and the mud from his heels. Had the Winchester pike been in a similar condition, it is altogether likely that he would not have made his famous twenty miles without breaking his own neck as well as Sheridan's. This historic horse derived his name from the fact that he was presented to Sheridan by the Second Michigan Cavalry in the little town of Rienzi, Mississippi, in 1862. After the famous ride he was sometimes called "Winchester." He was of "Blackhawk" blood. He bore Sheridan in nearly all his subsequent battles. When the animal died in 1878, in his twentieth year, his body was stuffed, and now stands in the museum on Governor's Island. The surviving veterans often decorate his body with flowers on Memorial Day.

Mackenzie had been ordered up the road, with directions to turn east on the White Oak road, and whip everything he met on that route. He encountered a small cavalry command and whipped it, according to orders, and then came galloping back to join in the general scrimmage. Soon Ayres's men met with a heavy fire on their left flank and had to change directions by facing more toward the west. As the troops entered the woods and moved forward over the boggy ground and struggled through the dense undergrowth, they were staggered by a heavy fire from the angle and fell back in some confusion. Sheridan now rushed into the midst of the broken lines, and cried out "Where is my battle-flag t**." As the sergeant who carried it rode up, Sheridan seized the crimson-and-white standard, waved it above his head, cheered on the men, and made heroic efforts to close up the ranks. Bullets were now humming like a swarm of bees about our heads, and shells were crashing through the ranks. A musket-ball pierced the battle-flag; another killed the sergeant who had carried it; another wounded an aide, Captain McGonnigle, in the side; others struck two or three of the staff-officers' horses. All this time Sheridan was dashing from one point of the line to another, waving his flag, shaking his fist, encouraging, entreating, threatening, praying, swearing, the true personification of chivalry, the very incarnation of battle. It would be a sorry soldier who could help following such a leader.

Ayres and his officers were equally exposing themselves at all points in rallying the men, and soon the line was steadied, for such troops could suffer but a momentary check. Ayres, with drawn saber, rushed forward once more with his veterans, who now behaved as if they had fallen back only to get a "good ready," and with fixed bayonets and a rousing cheer dashed over the earthworks, sweeping everything before them, and killing or capturing every man in their immediate front whose legs had not saved him. Sheridan spurred "Rienzi" up to the angle, and with a bound the animal carried his rider over the earthworks, and landed among a line of prisoners who had thrown down their arms and were crouching close under the breastworks. Some of them called out: "Wha' do you want us all to go to?" Then Sheridan's rage turned to humor, and he had a running talk with the "Johnnies" as they filed past. "Go right over there," he said to them, pointing to the rear. "Get right along, now. Oh, drop your guns; you'll never need them any more. You'll all be safe over there. Are there any more of you? We want every one of you fellows." Nearly 1500 were captured at the angle.

An orderly here came up to Sheridan, saluted, and said "Colonel Forsyth of your staff is killed, sir." "It's no such thing!" cried Sheridan. "I don't believe a word of it. You'll find Forsyth is all right." Ten minutes later Forsyth rode up. He had been mistaken for the gallant General Winthrop, who had fallen in the assault. Sheridan did not even seem surprised when he saw Forsyth, and merely said "There; I told you so." This incident is mentioned as illustrative of a peculiar trait of Sheridan's character, which never allowed him to be disturbed by camp rumors, however disastrous.

The dismounted cavalry had assaulted as soon as they heard the infantry fire open. The natty cavalrymen, with their tight-fitting jackets, and short carbines, swarmed through the pine thickets and dense undergrowth, looking as if they had been especially equipped for crawling through knot-holes. The cavalry commanded by the gallant Merritt made a final dash, went over the earthworks with a hurrah, captured a battery of artillery, and scattered everything in front of them. Here Custer, Devin, Fitzhugh, and the other cavalry leaders were in their element, and vied with each other in deeds of valor. Crawford's division had moved off in a northerly direction, marching away from Ayres, and leaving a gap between the two divisions. Sheridan became exceedingly annoyed at this circumstance, complained that Warren was not giving sufficient personal supervision to the infantry, and sent nearly all his staff-officers to the Fifth Corps to see that the mistakes made were corrected.

After the capture of the angle I started off toward the right to see how matters were going there. I went in the direction of Crawford's division, on our right. Warren, whose personal gallantry was always conspicuous, had had his horse shot while with these troops. I passed around the left of the enemy's works, then rode due west to a point beyond the Ford road. Here I rejoined Sheridan a little before dark. He was laboring with all the energy of his nature to complete the destruction of the enemy's forces, and to make preparations to protect his own detached command from a possible attack by Lee's army in the morning. He said to me that he had just relieved Warren and placed Griffin in command of the Fifth Corps. I had been sending frequent bulletins to the general-in-chief during the day, and now dispatched a courier announcing the change of corps commanders, and giving the general the result of the round-up. Sheridan had that day fought one of the most interesting tactical battles of the war, admirable in conception, brilliant in execution, strikingly dramatic in its incidents, and productive of immensely important results. I said to him: "It seems to me that you have exposed yourself today in a manner hardly justifiable on the part of a commander of such an important movement." His reply gave what seems to be the true key to his uniform success on the field: "I have never in my life taken a command into battle, and had the slightest desire to come out alive unless I won."

Grant telegraphed to several prominent officers to meet Sherman that evening at headquarters. Late in the afternoon . . . a captured steamer, arrived with Sherman aboard, and General Grant and two or three of us who were with him at the time started down to the wharf to greet the Western commander. Before we reached the foot of the steps, Sherman had jumped ashore and was hurrying forward with long strides to meet his chief. As they approached, Grant cried out, "How'd you do, Sherman!" "How are you, Grant!" exclaimed Sherman; and in a moment they stood upon the steps, with their hands locked in a cordial grasp, uttering earnest words of familiar greeting. Their encounter was more like that of two school-boys coming together after a vacation than the meeting of the chief actors in a great war tragedy. Sherman walked up with the General-in-chief to headquarters, where Mrs. Grant extended to the illustrious visitor a cordial greeting. Sherman then seated himself with the others by the camp-fire, and gave a most graphic description of the stirring events of his march through Georgia.

The story was the more charming from the fact that it was related without the manifestation of the slightest egotism. His field of operations had covered more than half of the entire theater of war; his orders always spoke with the true bluntness of the soldier; he had fought from valley depths to mountain heights, and marched from inland rivers to the sea. Never were listeners more enthusiastic; never was a speaker more eloquent. The story, told as he alone could tell it, was a grand epic related with Homeric power. At times he became humorous, and in a nervous, offhand, rattling manner recounted a number of amusing incidents of the famous march. He said, among other things: "My old veterans got on pretty familiar terms with me on the march, and often used to keep up a running conversation with me as I rode along by their side. One day a man in the ranks had pulled off his shoes and stockings and rolled up his trousers as far as they would go, to wade across a creek we had struck. I couldn't help admiring his magnificently developed limbs, which might have served as models for a sculptor, and I called out to him, 'A good stout pair of legs you've got there, my man.' 'Yes, General; they 're not bad underpinning,' he replied, looking down at them with evident pride. 'I wouldn't mind exchanging mine for them, if you don't object,' I continued. He sized up my legs with his eye, and evidently considered them mere spindle-shanks compared with his, and then looked up at me and said: 'General, if it's all the same to you, I guess I'd rather not swap.'" Sherman then went on to talk about his famous "bummers," saying: "They are not stragglers or mere self-constituted foragers, as many have been led to suppose, but they are organized for a very useful purpose from the adventurous spirits who are always found in the ranks. They serve as 'feelers' who keep in advance and on the flanks of the main columns, spy out the land, and discover where the best supplies are to be found. They are indispensable in feeding troops when compelled, like my army, to live off the country, and in destroying the enemy's communications. The bummers are, in fact, a regular institution.

I was amused at what one of Schofield's officers told me at Goldsboro. He said Schofield's army was maintaining a telegraph-line to keep up communication with the sea-coast, and that one of my men, who was a little more 'previous' than the rest, and was far in advance of my army, was seen up a telegraph-pole hacking away at the wires with a hatchet. The officer yelled out to him: 'What are you doing there! You're destroying one of our own telegraph-lines.' The man cast an indignant look at his questioner, and said, as he continued his work of destruction: 'I'm one o' Billy Sherman's bummers; and the last thing he said to us when we started out on this hunt was 'Be sure and cut all the telegraph-wires you come across, and don't go to foolin' away time askin' who they belong to.'" After the interview had continued nearly an hour, Grant said to Sherman: "I'm sorry to break up this entertaining conversation, but the President is aboard the River Queen, and I know he will be anxious to see you. Suppose we go and pay him a visit before dinner." "All right," cried Sherman; and the generals started down the steps, and were soon after seated in the cabin of the steamer with the President....

Grant said that the President was expecting them aboard his boat, and the two generals and the admiral started for the River Queen. No one accompanied them. There now occurred in the upper saloon of that vessel the celebrated conference between these four magnates, the scene of which has been so faithfully transferred to canvas by the artist Healy. It was in no sense a council of war, but only an informal interchange of views between the four men who, more than any others, held the destiny of the nation in their hands. Upon the return of the generals and the admiral to headquarters, they entered the General-in-chief's hut, where Mrs. Grant and one or two of us were sitting. The chief said to his wife: "Well, Julia, as soon as we reached the boat this morning I was particular to inquire after

Mrs. Lincoln, and to say that we desired to pay our respects to her. The President went to her state-room, and soon returned, saying that she was not well, and asking us to excuse her." General Grant afterward told us the particulars of the interview. It began by his explaining to the President the military situation and prospects, saying that the crisis of the war was now at hand, as he expected to move at once around the enemy's left and cut him off from the Carolinas, and that his only apprehension was that Lee might move out before him and evacuate Petersburg and Richmond, but that if he did there would be a hot pursuit. Sherman assured the President that in such a contingency his army, by acting on the defensive, could resist both Johnston and Lee till Grant could reach him, and that then the enemy would be caught in a vise and have his life promptly crushed out. Mr. Lincoln asked if it would not be possible to end the matter without a pitched battle, with the attendant losses and suffering; but was informed that that was a matter not within the control of our commanders, and must rest necessarily with the enemy. Lincoln spoke about the course which he thought had better be pursued after the war, and expressed an inclination to lean toward a generous policy. In speaking about the Confederate political leaders, he intimated, though he did not say so in express terms, that it would relieve the situation if they should escape to some foreign country. Sherman related many interesting incidents which occurred in his campaign. Grant talked less than any one present. The President twice expressed some apprehension about Sherman being away from his army; but Sherman assured him that he had left matters safe in Schofield's hands, and that he would start back himself that day. That afternoon Sherman took leave of those at headquarters, and returned to his command in the Bat, as that vessel was faster than the one which had brought him up the coast.

Source: Horace Porter, *Campaigning with Grant* (New York: The Century Co., 1906), http://books.google.com/books?id=ZxJCAAAAIAAJ&oe=UTF-8.

STORMING THE PETERSBURG WORKS

APRIL 2-3, 1865
GEN. HORACE PORTER, USA

In the popular imagination, the Civil War was a war of maneuver, with armies in the field struggling for position and tactical advantage at strategic points such as Antietam or Gettysburg. But Petersburg, the longest campaign of the war, was nothing like that. Instead, it presaged the trench warfare of the early twentieth century. The Siege of Petersburg lasted so long—from June 1864 through March 1865—that it included many battles which are remembered individually, such as the Crater, First and Second Deep Bottom, and the Beefsteak Raid. But the essence of Petersburg, after initial Union attempts to blast through Confederate lines came to naught, was Grant patiently extending his lines, forcing Lee to respond in turn. Bit by bit, the Union general forced the weakening and supply-strapped Southerners to expend more men, energy, and matériel to guard ever more ground. Southern supplies, manpower, and morale dwindled, and there was less and less hope that "Marse Robert" could engineer one more battlefield miracle.

News reached Richmond that Sheridan's forces, having pacified the Shenandoah, were on their way to join Grant. Nor was that all: Sherman's troops, having marauded through Georgia and South Carolina, were now heading northward as well. The endgame looked nigh. Desperately grasping at any chance to disrupt Union plans that spelled Confederate doom, Lee ordered a surprise attack by troops led by CSA Maj. Gen. George B. Gordon. The gambit was to strike Fort Stedman, shock federal forces by breaking their continuity in

Interior of the Union Fort Stedman

the field, and force Grant to contract his lines instead of mount-
ing a final assault. On March 25, 1865, Gordon's men went at the
target with every bit of remaining Southern strength. The Confeder-
ates achieved surprise and made initial progress, and captured the
fort and the guns within. But the Union army grasped the situation
and moved with alacrity to contain the breakout. Northern artil-
lery shelled the fort without interruption, while counterattacking
infantry threatened to cut off the salient. Gordon had to order his
soldiers back to their original positions, and the stage was set for
the final Union assault on Petersburg on April 2.

Here, Porter continues his narration, describing the culmina-
tion of the entire 292-day Petersburg campaign. The desperate
attack at Fort Stedman failed to deter Grant's final assault. That
blow fell on April 2. Lee had trimmed from his own flanks in order

to support the Fort Stedman plan; when Grant's Northern troops hit the Confederates on the right, the weakened flank collapsed and the way to the rear was wide open. Ten thousand Confederates were killed, wounded, or captured. Richmond fell the very next day, and Lee found himself without a capital to defend, and with precious few options other than to play for time and hope for succor that could not come.

The hour for the general assault was fixed at four o'clock the next morning. Miles was ordered to march with his division at midnight to reinforce Sheridan and enable him to make a stand against Lee in case he should move westward in the night. A little after midnight the general tucked himself into his camp-bed, and was soon sleeping as peacefully as if the next day was to be devoted to a picnic instead of a decisive battle. Every one at headquarters had caught as many cat-naps as he could, so as to be able to keep both eyes open the next day, in the hope of getting a sight of Petersburg, and possibly Richmond. And now four o'clock came, but no assault. It was found that to remove abatis, climb over *chevaux-de-frise*, jump rifle-pits, and scale parapets, a little daylight would be of material. At 4:45 there was a streak of gray in the heavens, which soon revealed another streak of gray formed by Confederate uniforms in the works opposite, and the charge was ordered. The thunder of hundreds of guns shook the ground like an earthquake, and soon the troops were engaged all along the lines. The general [Grant] awaited for a while the result of the assault at headquarters, where he could be easily communicated with, and from which he could give general directions. At a quarter past five a message came from Wright that he had carried the enemy's line in his front and was pushing in. Next came news from Parke that he had captured the outer works, with 12 pieces of artillery and 800 prisoners. At 6:40 the general wrote a telegram with his own hand to Mr. Lincoln at City Point, as follows: "Both Wright and Parke got through the enemy's line. The battle now rages furiously. Sheridan, with his cavalry, the Fifth Corps, and Miles's division of the Second Corps, which was sent to him since one this morning, is now sweeping down from the west. All now looks highly favorable. Ord is engaged, but I have not yet heard the result in his front." A cheering dispatch was also sent to Sheridan, winding up with the words: "I think nothing is now wanting but the approach of your force from the west to finish up the job on this side." Soon Ord was heard from as having broken through the entrenchments. Humphreys, too, had been doing gallant work. At half-past seven the line in his front was captured, and half an hour later Hays's division of his corps had carried an important earthwork, with three guns and most of the garrison. At 8:30 a.m. a dispatch was brought in from Ord saying that some of his troops had just captured the enemy's works south of Hatcher's Run. The general and staff now rode out to the front, as it was necessary to give immediate direction to the actual movements of the troops, and prevent confusion from the overlapping and intermingling of the several corps as they pushed forward. He urged his horse over the works which Wright's corps had captured, and suddenly came upon a body of 3000 prisoners marching to our rear. His whole attention was for some time riveted upon them, and we knew that he was enjoying his usual satisfaction in seeing so large a capture. Some of the guards told the prisoners who the general was, and they manifested great curiosity to get a good look at him. Next he came up with a division of Wright's corps, flushed with success, and rushing forward with a dash that was inspiriting beyond description. When they caught sight of the leader whom they had patiently followed from the Rapidan to Petersburg, their cheers broke forth with a will, and their enthusiasm knew no limit. The general galloped along toward the right, and soon met Meade, with whom he had been in constant communication, and who had been moving the Army of the Potomac with all vigor. Congratulations were rapidly exchanged, and both went to pushing forward the good work. Grant, after taking in the situation, directed both Meade and Ord to face their commands more toward the east, and close up toward the inner lines which covered Petersburg. Lee had been pushed so vigorously that he seemed for a time to be making but little effort to recover any of his lost ground; but now he made a determined fight against Parke's corps, which was threatening his inner line on his extreme left, and the bridge across the Appomattox. Repeated assaults were made, but Parke resisted them all successfully, and could not be stirred from his position. Lee had ordered Longstreet's command from the north side of the James, and with these troops reinforced his extreme right. General Grant dismounted near a farmhouse which stood on a knoll, from which he could get a good view of the field of operations. He seated himself on the ground at the foot of a tree, and was soon busy receiving dispatches and writing orders to officers conducting the advance. The position was under fire, and as soon as the group of staff-officers was seen, the enemy's guns began paying their respects to the party. This lasted for about a quarter of an hour, and as the fire became hotter and hotter, several of the officers, apprehensive for the general's safety, urged him to move to some less conspicuous position; but he kept on writing and talking, without the least interruption from the shots falling around him, and apparently not noticing what a target the place was becoming, or paying any heed to the gentle reminders to "move on." After he had finished his dispatches he got up, took a view of the situation, and as he started toward the other side of the farm-house said with a quizzical look at the group around him: "Well, they do seem to have the range on us."

The staff was now sent to the various points of the advancing lines, and all was activity in pressing forward the good work. By noon nearly all the outer line of works was in our possession, except two strong redoubts which occupied a commanding position, named respectively Fort Gregg and Fort Whitworth. The general decided that these should be stormed, and about one o'clock three of Ord's brigades swept down upon Port Gregg. The garrison of 300 men, commanded by Lieutenant Colonel J. H. Duncan, with two rifled cannon, made a desperate defense, and a gallant contest took place. For half an hour after our men had gained the parapet a bloody hand-to-hand struggle continued, but nothing could stand against the onslaught of Ord's troops, flushed with their morning's victory. By half-past two 57 of the brave garrison lay dead, and the rest had surrendered. Fort Whitworth was abandoned, but the guns of Fort Gregg were opened upon the garrison as they marched out, and the commander, Colonel Joseph M. Jayne, and 60 men surrendered. About this time Miles struck a force of the enemy at Sutherland's Station, on Lee's extreme right, and captured two pieces of artillery and nearly 1000 prisoners. At 4:40 the general, who had been keeping Mr. Lincoln fully advised of the history that was so rapidly being made that day, sent him a telegram Inviting him to come out the next day and pay him a visit. A prompt reply was received from the President, saying: "Allow me to tender you, and all with you, the nation's grateful thanks for the additional and magnificent success. At your kind suggestion, I think I will meet you tomorrow." Prominent officers now urged the general to make an assault on the inner lines, and capture Petersburg that afternoon; but he was firm in his resolve not to sacrifice the lives necessary to accomplish such a result. He said the city would undoubtedly be evacuated during the night, and he would dispose the troops for a parallel march westward, and try to head off the escaping army. And thus ended this eventful Sunday. . . .

The General was up at daylight the next morning, and the first report brought in was that Parke had gone through the lines at 4 a.m., capturing a few skirmishers, and that the city had surrendered at 4:28 [to] Colonel Ralph Ely. A second communication surrendering the place was sent in to Wright; General Grant's prediction had been fully verified. The evacuation had begun about ten the night before, and was completed on the morning of the 3d. Between 5 and 6 a.m. the general had a conference with Meade, and orders were given to push westward with all haste. About 9 a.m. the general rode into Petersburg. Many of the citizens, panic-stricken, had escaped with the army. Most of the whites who remained stayed indoors; a few groups of negroes gave cheers, but the scene generally was one of complete desertion. Grant rode along quietly until he came to a comfortable-looking brick house with a yard in front, No. 21 Market street, the residence of Mr. Thomas Wallace, and here he and the staff dismounted and took seats on the piazza. A number of the citizens now gathered on the sidewalk, and stood gazing with eager curiosity upon the features of the commander of the Yankee armies. Soon an officer came with a despatch from Sheridan, who had been reinforced and ordered to strike out along the Danville Railroad, saying he was already nine miles beyond Namozine Creek, and pressing the enemy's trains. The general was anxious to move westward at once with the leading infantry columns, but he prolonged his stay until the President came up. Mr Lincoln soon after arrived, accompanied by Robert, who had ridden back to the railroad station to meet him, and by his little son, "Tad," and Admiral Porter. He dismounted in the street, and came in through the front gate with long and rapid strides, his face beaming with delight. He seized General Grant's hand as the General stepped forward to greet him, and stood shaking it for some time, and pouring out his thanks and congratulations with all the fervor of a heart which seemed overflowing with its fullness of joy. I doubt whether Mr. Lincoln ever experienced a happier moment in his life. The scene was singularly affecting, and one never to be forgotten. He said: "Do you know, General, I had a sort of sneaking idea all along that you intended to do something like this; but I thought some time ago that you would so maneuver as to have Sherman come up and be near enough to cooperate with you." "Yes," replied the General; "I thought at one time that Sherman's army might advance far enough to be in supporting distance of the Eastern armies when the spring campaign against Lee opened; but I had a feeling that it would be better to let Lee's old antagonists give his army the final blow, and finish up the job. If the Western troops were even to put in an appearance against Lee's army, it might give some of our politicians a chance to stir up sectional feeling in claiming everything for the troops from their own section of country. The Western armies have been very successful in their campaigns, and it is due to the Eastern armies to let them vanquish their old enemy single-handed." "I see, I see," said Mr. Lincoln; "but I never thought of it in that light. In fact, my anxiety has been so great that I did not care where the help came from, so that the work was perfectly done." "Oh," General Grant continued, "I do not suppose it would have even risen to much of the bickering I mentioned, and perhaps the idea would not have occurred to any one else. I feel sure there would have been no such feeling among the soldiers. Of course I would not have risked the result of the campaign on account of any mere sentiment of this kind. I have always felt confident that our troops here were amply able to handle Lee." Mr. Lincoln then began to talk about the civil complications that would follow the destruction of the Confederate armies in the field, and showed plainly the anxiety he felt regarding the great problems in statecraft which would soon be thrust upon him. He intimated very plainly, in a conversation that lasted nearly half an hour, that thoughts of leniency to the conquered were uppermost in his heart. Meanwhile his son Tad, for whom he always showed a deep affection, was becoming a little uneasy, and gave certain appealing looks, to which General Sharpe, who seemed to understand the mute expressions of small boys, responded by producing some sandwiches, which he offered to him, saying: "Here, young man, I guess you must be hungry." Tad seized them as a drowning man would seize a life-preserver, and cried out "That, I am; that's what's the matter with me!" This greatly amused the President and the General-in-chief, who had a hearty laugh at Tad's expense.

Source: Horace Porter, *Campaigning with Grant* (New York: Century Co., 1906), http://books.google.com/books?id=ZxJCAAAAIAAJ&oe=UTF-8.

NEGOTIATIONS AT APPOMATTOX

APRIL 9, 1865
GEN. ULYSSES S. GRANT, USA

As they fled Petersburg and Richmond, Lee's once-splendid Army of Northern Virginia was ragged and worn out. The tattered remnants had but one remaining hope: to link up with CSA Gen. Joseph E. Johnston's men in North Carolina. Along the way, they might resupply at Lynchburg or Danville. If they could pull this off, the combined Confederate forces might be able to prevent the linkup between Sherman and Grant and at least extend the war. It was a scheme both daring and desperate, but once again, Grant simply refused to yield the initiative. He ordered his own offensive, blocking any westerly retreat and staying relentlessly on Lee's trail. Lee could not shake the pursuit, and instead of racing to resupply and link up with Johnston, the Army of Northern Virginia found itself engaged in a series of running battles all along their hoped-for evacuation route. Slowed and harried, their plan espied and blocked by Union cavalry, they realized that they would never make Danville, much less unite with Johnston's men. Lee's army finally ran out of room. Without food, low on ammunition, and without hope of resupply, they fought a final action at Appomattox Court House on April 9, 1865. Lee's last hope—a fast march to Danville—depended upon Gordon's men holding off the pursuit. But Gordon said, "I have fought my corps to a frazzle." He asked for heavy support from Longstreet's units, but that was a mirage. Taking it all in, Lee made the imperishable admission that marked the end of the attempt to

McLean House, Appomattox, Virginia, scene of Gen. Robert E. Lee's surrender

build an independent Southern republic: "There is nothing for me to do but go and see General Grant and I would rather die a thousand deaths."

The meeting of the two commanders, at the McLean House, marked the end of the war's major actions. Grant and the assembled Union officers treated their vanquished but justly proud foe with magnanimity, stating that officers could keep their sidearms, private horses, and belongings. Furthermore, instead of internment, they could return to their homes. It was this note of proffered grace that signaled the end of the Civil War.

I had known General Lee in the old army, and had served with him in the Mexican War; but did not suppose, owing to the difference in our age and rank, that he would remember me, while I would more naturally remember him distinctly, because he was the chief of staff of General Scott in the Mexican War.

When I had left camp that morning I had not expected so soon the result that was then taking place, and consequently was in rough garb. I was without a sword, as I usually was when on horseback on the field, and wore a soldier's blouse for a coat, with the shoulder straps of my rank to indicate to the army who I was. When I went into the house I found General Lee. We greeted each other, and after shaking hands took our seats. I had my staff with me, a good portion of whom were in the room during the whole of the interview.

What General Lee's feelings were I do not know. As he was a man of much dignity, with an impassible face, it was impossible to say whether he felt inwardly glad that the end had finally come, or felt sad over the result, and was too manly to show it. Whatever his feelings, they were entirely concealed from my observation; but my own feelings, which had been quite jubilant on the receipt of his letter, were sad and depressed. I felt like anything rather than rejoicing at the downfall of a foe who had fought so long and valiantly, and had suffered so much for a cause, though that cause was, I believe, one of the worst for which a people ever fought, and one for which there was the least excuse. I do not question, however, the sincerity of the great mass of those who were opposed to us.

General Lee was dressed in a full uniform which was entirely new, and was wearing a sword of considerable value, very likely the sword which had been presented by the State of Virginia; at all events, it was an entirely different sword from the one that would ordinarily be worn in the field. In my rough traveling suit, the uniform of a private with the straps of a lieutenant-general, I must have contrasted very strangely with a man so handsomely dressed, six feet high and of faultless form. But this was not a matter that I thought of until afterwards.

We soon fell into a conversation about old army times. He remarked that he remembered me very well in the old army; and I told him that as a matter of course I remembered him perfectly, but from the difference in our rank and years (there being about sixteen years' difference in our ages), I had thought it very likely that I had not attracted his attention sufficiently to be remembered by him after such a long interval. Our conversation grew so pleasant that I almost forgot the object of our meeting. After the conversation had run on in this style for some time, General Lee called my attention to the object of our meeting, and said that he had asked for this interview for the purpose of getting from me the terms I proposed to give his army. I said that I meant merely that his army should lay down their arms, not to take them up again during the continuance of the war unless duly and properly exchanged. He said that he had so understood my letter.

Then we gradually fell off again into conversation about matters foreign to the subject which had brought us together. This continued for some little time, when General Lee again interrupted the course of the conversation by suggesting that the terms I proposed to give his army ought to be written out. I called to General Parker, secretary on my staff, for writing materials, and commenced writing out the following terms:

APPOMATTOX C. H., VA.,
Ap 9th, 1865.

GEN. R. E. LEE,
Comd'g C. S. A.

GEN: In accordance with the substance of my letter to you of the 8th inst., I propose to receive the surrender of the Army of N. Va. on the following terms, to wit: Rolls of all the officers and men to be made in duplicate. One copy to be given to an officer designated by me, the other to be retained by such officer or officers as you may designate. The officers to give their individual paroles not to take up arms against the Government of the United States until properly exchanged, and each company or regimental commander sign a like parole for the men of their commands. The arms, artillery and public property to be parked and stacked, and turned over to the officer appointed by me to receive them. This will not embrace the side-arms of the officers, nor their private horses or baggage. This done, each officer and man will

be allowed to return to their homes, not to be disturbed by United States authority so long as they observe their paroles and the laws in force where they may reside.
Very respectfully,

U. S. GRANT,
Lt. Gen.

When I put my pen to the paper I did not know the first word that I should make use of in writing the terms. I only knew what was in my mind, and I wished to express it clearly, so that there could be no mistaking it. As I wrote on, the thought occurred to me that the officers had their own private horses and effects, which were important to them, but of no value to us; also that it would be an unnecessary humiliation to call upon them to deliver their side arms.

No conversation, not one word, passed between General Lee and myself, either about private property, side arms, or kindred subjects. He appeared to have no objections to the terms first proposed; or if he had a point to make against them he wished to wait until they were in writing to make it. When he read over that part of the terms about side arms, horses and private property of the officers, he remarked, with some feeling, I thought, that this would have a happy effect upon his army.

Then, after a little further conversation, General Lee remarked to me again that their army was organized a little differently from the army of the United States (still maintaining by implication that we were two countries); that in their army the cavalrymen and artillerists owned their own horses; and he asked if he was to understand that the men who so owned their horses were to be permitted to retain them. I told him that as the terms were written they would not; that only the officers were permitted to take their private property. He then, after reading over the terms a second time, remarked that that was clear.

I then said to him that I thought this would be about the last battle of the war—I sincerely hoped so; and I said further I took it that most of the men in the ranks were small farmers. The whole country had been so raided by the two armies that it was doubtful whether they would be able to put in a crop to carry themselves and their families through the next winter without the aid of the horses they were then riding. The United States did not want them and I would, therefore, instruct the officers I left behind to receive the paroles of his troops to let every man of the Confederate army who claimed to own a horse or mule take the animal to his home. Lee remarked again that this would have a happy effect.

Source: Ulysses S. Grant, *Personal Memoirs of U. S. Grant* (New York: Charles L. Webster & Company, 1885; Project Gutenberg, 2004), vol. 2, pt. 6, chap. 67, https://www.gutenberg .org/ebooks/5865.

LINCOLN'S LAST HOURS

APRIL 14-15, 1865
CHARLES A. LEALE, MD, USA

The particulars of President Lincoln's assassination at the hands of actor John Wilkes Booth are well known to all. The president and first lady attended the light comedy Our American Cousin *at Ford's Theatre on the night of April 14, 1865. Booth, having free run of the venue, lurked in hiding until he could slip into the presidential box, shoot Lincoln, and flee. The manhunt for the assassin and his partners, and their crackpot plot to kill prominent cabinet members and somehow restart the war, absorbed a shuddering nation. These details are known to history. What can never be fully appreciated is the inestimable loss to both North and South that this murder occasioned. The Second Inaugural Address—frank about the cost of the war as a payment for the bondsman's debt incurred by slavery—determined the absolute necessity to "bind up the nation's wounds, to care for him who shall have borne the battle, and for his widow and his orphan," and above all, redolent with grace about the need for a reconstruction undertaken "with malice toward none; with charity for all," was more than imperishable oratory. It was a promissory note issued by the only man who could redeem it, assuring a grieving and broken country that it could and would rediscover its wholeness and achieve its bright future.*

When Lincoln was killed, the grief was profound across the nation. Southerners uneasily felt that the president's lack of vengefulness was a rare quality indeed; Northerners could not grasp that

429

Ford's Theatre, draped in black following President Lincoln's assassination at the hands of John Wilkes Booth
LIBRARY OF CONGRESS

"Father Abraham," who had steadied their fractious and frequently panicky reactions to the hazards of war, would not shepherd the United States through the peace. Union soldiers, who felt a living bond with their commander in chief, whose suffering so obviously matched their own, keenly missed him. African Americans, newly emancipated or veterans clad in blue, knew in their bones that there was no substitute for the leader who had made his own progress toward understanding the centrality of their plight to the entire national tragedy. At home, Mary Todd Lincoln was crazed by grief. And who could feel more lost than poor Tad, a special needs child whose brother Willie was taken by typhoid fever in 1862, who became his father's main source of emotional support during the war? The loss of Abraham Lincoln was so incalculable, so inconceivable, and so horrendous that it served as a dreadful coda for the worst four years, three weeks, and six days that Americans would

ever experience. Here, one of the doctors attending recounts the pathos of the presidential deathbed.

The people of the United States were rejoicing at the prospect of peace and returning happiness. President Lincoln, after the surrender of General Robert E. Lee, visited Richmond, Virginia, exposing himself to great danger, and on his return delivered an address from the balcony of the White House.

I was then a Commissioned Officer in the Medical Department of the United States Army, having been appointed from my native State, New York, and was on duty as Surgeon in charge of the Wounded Commissioned Officers' Ward at the United States Army General Hospital, Armory Square, Washington, District of Columbia, where my professional duties were of the greatest importance and required constant and arduous attention. For a brief relief and a few moments in the fresh air I started one evening for a short walk on Pennsylvania Avenue. There were crowds walking toward the President's residence. These I followed and arrived just at the commencement of President Lincoln's last public address to his people. From where I stood I could distinctly hear every word he uttered and I was profoundly impressed with his divine appearance as he stood in the rays of light, which penetrated the windows of the White House.

The influence thus produced gave me an intense desire again to behold his face and study the characteristics of the "Savior of his Country." Therefore on the evening of April 14, 1865, after the completion of my daily hospital duties, I told my Ward Master that I would be absent for a short time. As a very large number from the Army stationed near Washington frequently visited the city, a general order was in force that none should be there without a special pass and all wearing uniform and out at night were subject to frequent challenge. To avoid this inconvenience officers stationed in Washington generally removed all signs of their calling when off duty. I changed to civilian's dress and hurried to Ford's Theatre, where I had been told President Lincoln, General Grant, and Members of the Cabinet were to be present to see the play, "Our American Cousin." I arrived late at the theatre, 8.15 p.m., and requested a seat in the orchestra, whence I could view the occupants of the President's box, which on look-ing into the theatre, I saw had been beautifully decorated with American flags in honor of the occasion. As the building was crowded the last place vacant was in the dress circle. I was greatly disappointed, but accepted this seat, which was near the front on the same side and about 40 feet from the President's box, and soon became interested in the pleasing play.

Suddenly there was a cheering welcome, the acting ceased temporar-ily out of respect to the entering Presidential party. Many in the audience rose to their feet in enthusiasm and vociferously cheered, while look-ing around. Turning, I saw in the aisle a few feet behind me, President Lincoln, Mrs. Lincoln, Major Rathbone and Miss Harris. Mrs. Lincoln smiled very happily in acknowledgment of the loyal greeting, gracefully curtsied several times and seemed to be overflowing with good cheer and thankfulness. I had the best opportunity to distinctly see the full face of the President, as the light shone directly upon him. After he had walked a few feet he stopped for a moment, looked upon the people he loved and acknowledged their salutations with a solemn bow. His face was per-fectly stoical, his deep set eyes gave him a pathetically sad appearance. The audience seemed to be enthusiastically cheerful, but he alone looked peculiarly sorrowful, as he slowly walked with bowed head and drooping shoulders toward the box. I was looking at him as he took his last walk. The memory of that scene has never been effaced. The party was preceded by a special usher, who opened the door of the box, stood to one side, and after all had entered closed the door and took a seat outside, where he could guard the entrance to the box. The play was resumed and my atten-tion was concentrated on the stage until I heard a disturbance at the door of the President's box. With many others I looked in that direction, and saw a man endeavoring to persuade the reluctant usher to admit him. At last he succeeded in gaining an entrance, after which the door was closed and the usher resumed his place.

For a few moments all was quiet, and the play again held my attention until, suddenly, the report of a pistol was heard, and a short time after I saw a man in mid-air leaping from the President's box to the stage, bran-dishing in his hand a drawn dagger. His spur caught in the American flag festooned in front of the box, causing him to stumble when he struck the stage, and he fell on his hands and knees. He quickly regained the erect posture and hopped across the stage, flourishing his dagger, clearing the stage before him and dragging the foot of the leg, which was subsequently found to be broken, he disappeared behind the scene on the opposite side of the stage. Then followed cries that the President had been murdered, interspersed with cries of "Kill the murderer!" "Shoot him!" etc., from different parts of the building. The lights had been turned down, a general gloom was over all, and the panic-stricken audience were rushing toward the doors for exit and safety.

I instantly arose and in response to cries for help and for a surgeon, I crossed the aisle and vaulted over the seats in a direct line to the President's box, forcing my way through the excited crowd. The door of the box had been securely fastened on the inside to prevent anyone following the assassin before he had accomplished his cruel object and made his escape. The obstruction was with difficulty removed and I was the first to be admitted to the box.

The usher having been told that I was an army surgeon, had lifted up his arm and had permitted me alone to enter.

I passed in, not in the slightest degree knowing what I had to encounter. At this moment, while in self-communion, the military command: "Halt!" came to me, and in obedience to it I stood still in the box, having a full view of the four other occupants. Then came the advice: "Be calm!" and with the calmest deliberation and force of will I brought all my senses to their greatest activity and walked forward to my duty.

Major Rathbone had bravely fought the assassin; his arm had been severely wounded and was bleeding. He came to me holding his wounded arm in the hand of the other, beseeching me to attend to his wound. I placed my hand under his chin, looking into his eyes an almost instantaneous glance revealed the fact that he was in no immediate danger, and in response to appeals from Mrs. Lincoln and Miss Harris, who were standing by the high-backed armchair in which President Lincoln sat, I went immediately to their assistance, saying I was a United States army surgeon. I grasped Mrs. Lincoln's outstretched hand in mine, while she cried piteously to me, "Oh, Doctor! Is he dead? Can he recover? Will you take charge of him? Do what you can for him. Oh, my dear husband!" etc., etc.

I soothingly answered that we would do all that possibly could be done. While approaching the President, I asked a gentleman, who was at the door of the box, to procure some brandy and another to get some water.

As I looked at the President, he appeared to be dead. His eyes were closed and his head had fallen forward. He was being held upright in his chair by Mrs. Lincoln, who was weeping bitterly. From his crouched down sitting posture it was evident that Mrs. Lincoln had instantly sprung to his aid after he had been wounded and had kept him from tumbling to the floor. By Mrs. Lincoln's courage, strength and energy the President was maintained in this upright position during all the time that elapsed while Major Rathbone had bravely fought the assassin and removed the obstruction from the door of the box.

I placed my finger on the President's right radial pulse but could perceive no movement of the artery. For the purpose of reviving him, if possible, we removed him from his chair to a recumbent position on the floor of the box, and as I held his head and shoulders while doing this, my hand came in contact with a clot of blood near his left shoulder. Remembering the flashing dagger in the hand of the assassin, and the severely bleeding wound of Major Rathbone, I supposed the President had been stabbed, and while kneeling on the floor over his head, with my eyes continuously watching the President's face, I asked a gentleman to cut the coat and shirt open from the neck to the elbow to enable me, if possible, to check the hemorrhage that I thought might take place from the subclavian artery or some other blood vessel. This was done with a dirk knife, but no wound was found there. I lifted his eyelids and saw evidence of a brain injury. I quickly passed the separated fingers of both hands through his blood-matted hair to examine his head, and I discovered his mortal wound. The President had been shot in the back part of the head, behind the left ear. I easily removed the obstructing clot of blood from the wound, and this relieved the pressure on the brain.

The assassin of President Lincoln had evidently carefully planned to shoot to produce instant death, as the wound he made was situated within two inches of the physiological point of selection, when instant death is desired. A Derringer pistol had been used, which had sent a large round ball on its awful mission through one of the thickest, hardest parts of the skull and into the brain. The history of surgery fails to record a recovery from such a fearful wound, and I have never seen or heard of any other person with such a wound, and injury to the sinus of the brain and to the brain itself, who lived even for an hour.

As the President did not then revive, I thought of the other mode of death, apnoea, and assumed my preferred position to revive by artificial respiration. I knelt on the floor over the President, with a knee on each side of his pelvis and facing him. I leaned forward, opened his mouth and introduced two extended fingers of my right hand as far back as possible, and by pressing the base of his paralyzed tongue downward and outward, opened his larynx and made a free passage for air to enter the lungs. I placed an assistant at each of his arms to manipulate them in order to expand his thorax, then slowly to press the arms down by the side of the body, while I pressed the diaphragm upward: methods which caused air to be drawn in and forced out of his lungs.

During the intermissions I also with the strong thumb and fingers of my right hand by intermittent sliding pressure under and beneath the ribs, stimulated the apex of the heart, and resorted to several other physiological methods. We repeated these motions a number of times before signs of recovery from the profound shock were attained; then a feeble action of the heart and irregular breathing followed.

The effects of the shock were still manifest by such great prostration, that I was fearful of any extra agitation of the President's body, and became convinced that something more must be done to retain life. I leaned forcibly forward directly over his body, thorax to thorax, face to face, and several times drew in a long breath, then forcibly breathed directly into his mouth and nostrils, which expanded his lungs and improved his respirations. After waiting a moment I placed my ear over his thorax and found the action of the heart improving. I arose to the erect kneeling posture, then watched for a short time, and saw that the President could continue independent breathing and that instant death would not occur.

I then pronounced my diagnosis and prognosis: "His wound is mortal; it is impossible for him to recover." This message was telegraphed all over the country.

When the brandy and water arrived, I very slowly poured a small quantity into the President's mouth; this was swallowed and retained.

Many looked on during these earnest efforts to revive the President, but not once did any one suggest a word or in any way interfere with my actions. Mrs. Lincoln had thrown the burden on me and sat nearby looking on.

In the dimly lighted box of the theatre, so beautifully decorated with American flags, a scene of historic importance was being enacted. On the carpeted floor lay prostrate the President of the United States. His long, outstretched, athletic body of six feet four inches appeared unusually heroic. His bleeding head rested on my white linen handkerchief. His clothing was arranged as nicely as possible. He was irregularly breathing, his heart was feebly beating, his face was pale and in solemn repose, his eyelids were closed, his countenance made him appear to be in prayerful communion with the Universal God he always loved. I looked down upon him and waited for the next inspiration, which soon came: "Remove to safety." From the time Mrs. Lincoln had placed the President in my charge, I had not permitted my attention to be diverted. Again I was asked the nature of his wound and replied in these exact words: "His wound is mortal; it is impossible for him to recover."

While I was kneeling over the President on the floor Dr. Charles S. Taft and Dr. Albert F. A. King had come and offered to render any assistance. I expressed the desire to have the President taken, as soon as he had gained sufficient strength, to the nearest house on the opposite side of the street. I was asked by several if he could not be taken to the White House, but I responded that if that were attempted the President would die long before we reached there. While we were waiting for Mr. Lincoln to gain strength Laura Keene, who had been taking part in the play, appealed to me to allow her to hold the President's head. I granted this request and she sat on the floor of the box and held his head on her lap.

We decided that the President could now be moved from the possibility of danger in the theatre to a house where we might place him on a bed in safety. To assist in this duty I assigned Dr. Taft to carry his right shoulder, Dr. King to carry his left shoulder and detailed a sufficient number of others, whose names I have never discovered, to assist in carrying the body, while I carried his head, going first. We reached the door of the box and saw the long passage leading to the exit crowded with people. I called out twice: "Guards, clear the passage! Guards, clear the passage!" A free space was quickly cleared by an officer and protected by a line of soldiers in the position of present arms with swords, pistols and bayonets. When we reached the stairs, I turned so that those holding the President's feet would descend first. At the door of the theatre, I was again asked if the President could be taken to the White House. I answered: "No, the President would die on the way."

The crowd in the street completely obstructed the doorway and a captain, whose services proved invaluable all through the night, came to me, saying: "Surgeon, give me your commands and I will see that they are obeyed." I asked him to clear a passage to the nearest house opposite. He had on side arms and drew his sword. With the sword and word of command he cleared the way. We slowly crossed the street. It was necessary to stop several times to give me the opportunity to remove the clot of blood from the opening to the wound. A barrier of men had been formed to keep back the crowds on each side of an open space leading to the house. Those who went ahead reported that the house directly opposite the theatre was closed. I saw a man standing at the door of Mr. Petersen's house, diagonally opposite, holding a lighted candle in his hand and beckoning us to enter. This we did, not having been interrupted in the slightest by the throngs in the street, but a number of the excited populace followed us into the house.

The great difficulty of retaining life during this brief time occupied in moving the President from the theatre to Mr. Petersen's house, conclusively proved that the President would have died in the street if I had granted the request to take him such a long distance as to the White House. I asked for the best room and we soon had the President placed in bed. He was lifted to the longitudinal center of the bed and placed on his back. While holding his face upward and keeping his head from rolling to either side, I looked at his elevated knees caused by his great height. This uncomfortable position grieved me and I ordered the foot of the bed to be removed. Dr. Taft and Dr. King reported that it was a fixture. Then I requested that it be broken off; as I found this could not satisfactorily be done, I had the President placed diagonally on the bed and called for extra pillows, and with them formed a gentle inclined plane on which to rest his head and shoulders. His position was then one of repose.

The room soon filled with anxious people. I called the officer and asked him to open a window and order all except the medical gentlemen and friends to leave the room. After we had given the President a short rest I decided to make a thorough physical examination, as I wished to see if he had been wounded in any other part of the body. I requested all except the surgeons to leave the room. The Captain reported that my order had been carried out with the exception of Mrs. Lincoln, to whom he said he did not like to speak. I addressed Mrs. Lincoln, explaining my desire, and she immediately left the room. I examined the President's entire body from his head to his feet and found no other injury. His lower extremities were very cold and I sent the Hospital Steward, who had been of great assistance to us in removing the President from the theatre, to procure bottles of hot water and hot blankets, which were applied. I also sent for a large sinapism and in a short time one very nicely made was brought. This I applied over the solar-plexus and to the anterior surface of his body. We arranged the bed clothes nicely and I assigned Dr. Taft and Dr. King to keep his head upon the pillows in the most comfortable position, relieving each other in this duty, after which I sent an officer to notify Mrs. Lincoln that she might return to her husband; she came in and sat on a chair placed for her at the head of the bed.

As the symptoms indicated renewed brain compression, I again cleared the opening of clotted blood and pushed forward the button of bone, which acted as a valve, permitted an oozing of blood and relieved pressure on the brain. I again saw good results from this action.

After doing all that was professionally necessary, I stood aside for a general view and to think what to do next. While thus watching several army officers anxiously asked if they could in any way assist. I told them my greatest desire then was to send messengers to the White House for the President's son, Captain Robert T. Lincoln, also for the Surgeon General, Joseph K. Barnes, Surgeon D. Willard Bliss, in charge of Armory Square General Hospital, the President's family physician, Dr. Robert K. Stone, and to each member of the President's Cabinet. All these desires of mine were fulfilled.

Having been taught in early youth to pay great respect to all religious denominations in regard to their rules concerning the sick or dying, it became my duty as surgeon in charge of the dying President to summon a clergyman to his bedside. Therefore after inquiring and being informed that the Rev. Dr. Gurley was Mrs. Lincoln's pastor, I immediately sent for him.

Then I sent the Hospital Steward for a Nelaton probe. No drug or medicine in any form was administered to the President, but the artificial heat and mustard plaster that I had applied warmed his cold body and stimulated his nerves. Only a few were at any time admitted to the room by the officer, whom I had stationed at the door, and at all times I had maintained perfect discipline and order.

While we were watching and letting Nature do her part, Dr. Taft came to me with brandy and water and asked permission to give some to the President. I objected, stating as my reason that it would produce strangulation. Dr. Taft left the room, and again came to me stating that it was the opinion of others also that it might do good. I replied: "I will grant the request, if you will please at first try by pouring only a very small quantity into the President's mouth." This Dr. Taft very carefully did; the liquid ran into the President's larynx producing laryngeal obstruction and unpleasant symptoms, which took me about half a minute to overcome, but no lasting harm was done. My physiological and practical experiences had led to correct conclusions.

On the arrival of Dr. Robert K. Stone, who had been the President's family physician during his residence in Washington, I was presented to him as the one who had been in charge since the President was shot. I described the wound and told him all that had been done. He said he approved of my treatment.

Surgeon General Joseph K. Barnes' long delay in arriving was due to his going first to the White House, where he expected to find the assassinated President, then to the residence of Secretary Seward and his son, both of whom he found requiring immediate attention, as they had been severely wounded by the attempts of another assassin to kill them.

On the arrival of the Surgeon General and Assistant Surgeon General, Charles H. Crane, I reported what we had done and officially detailed to the Surgeon General my diagnosis, stating that whenever the clot was allowed to form over the opening to the wound the President's breathing became greatly embarrassed. The Surgeon General approved the treatment and my original plan of treatment was continued in every respect until the President's death.

The Hospital Steward arrived with the Nelaton probe and an examination was made by the Surgeon General and myself, who introduced the probe to a distance of about two and a half inches, where it came in contact with a foreign substance, which lay across the track of the ball; this was easily passed and the probe was introduced several inches further where it again touched a hard substance at first supposed to be the ball, but as the white porcelain bulb of the probe on its withdrawal did not indicate the mark of lead it was generally thought to be another piece of loose bone. The probe was introduced the second time and the ball was supposed to be distinctly felt. After this second exploration nothing further was done with the wound except to keep the opening free from coagula, which, if allowed to form and remain for a short time, produced signs of increased compression, the breathing becoming profoundly stertorous and intermittent, the pulse more feeble and irregular. After I had resigned my charge all that was professionally done for the President was to repeat occasionally my original expedient of relieving the brain pressure by freeing the opening to the wound and to count the pulse and respirations. The President's position on the bed remained exactly as I had first placed him with the assistance of Dr. Taft and Dr. King.

Captain Robert T. Lincoln came and remained with his father and mother, bravely sustaining himself during the course of the night.

On that awful memorable night the great War Secretary, the Honorable Edwin M. Stanton, one of the most imposing figures of the nineteenth century, promptly arrived and recognized at that critical period of our country's history the necessity of a head to our Government and as the President was passing away established a branch of his War Department in an adjoining room. There he sat, surrounded by his counselors and messengers, pen in hand, writing to General Dix and others. He was soon in communication with many in authority and with the Government and army officials. By Secretary Stanton's wonderful ability and power in action, he undoubtedly controlled millions of excited people. He was then the Master, and in reality Acting President of the United States.

During the night Mrs. Lincoln came frequently from the adjoining room accompanied by a lady friend. At one time Mrs. Lincoln exclaimed, sobbing bitterly: "Oh! that my little Taddy might see his father before he died!" This was decided not advisable. As Mrs. Lincoln sat on a chair by the side of the bed with her face to her husband's his breathing became very stertorous, and the loud, unnatural noise frightened her in her exhausted, agonized condition. She sprang up suddenly with a piercing cry and fell fainting to the floor. Secretary Stanton hearing her cry came in from the adjoining room and with raised arms called out loudly: "Take that woman out and do not let her in again." Mrs. Lincoln was helped up kindly and assisted in a fainting condition from the room. Secretary Stanton's order was obeyed and Mrs. Lincoln did not see her husband again before he died.

As Captain Lincoln was consoling his mother in another room, and as I had promised Mrs. Lincoln to do all I possibly could for her husband, I took the place of kindred and continuously held the President's right hand firmly, with one exception of less than a minute, when my sympathies compelled me to seek the disconsolate wife. I found her reclining in a nearby room, being comforted by her son. Without stopping in my walk, I passed the room where Secretary Stanton sat at his official table and returning took the hand of the dying President in mine. The hand that had signed the Emancipation Proclamation liberating 4,000,000 slaves.

As morning dawned it became quite evident that the President was sinking, and at several times his pulse could not be counted. Two or three feeble pulsations being noticed, followed by an intermission when not the slightest movements of the artery could be felt. The inspirations became very prolonged and labored, accompanied by a guttural sound. The respirations ceased for some time and several anxiously looked at their watches until the profound silence was disturbed by a prolonged inspiration, which was followed by a sonorous expiration.

During these moments the Surgeon General occupied a chair by the head of the President's bed and occasionally held his finger over the carotid artery to note its pulsations. Dr. Stone sat on the edge of the foot of the bed, and I stood holding the President's right hand with my extended forefinger on his pulse, being the only one between the bed and the wall, the bed having been drawn out diagonally for that purpose. While we were anxiously watching in profound solemn silence, the Rev. Dr. Gurley said: "Let us pray," and offered a most impressive prayer. After which we witnessed the last struggle between life and death.

At this time my knowledge of physiology, pathology and psychology told me that the President was totally blind as a result of blood pressure on the brain, as indicated by the paralysis, dilated pupils, protruding and bloodshot eyes, but all the time I acted on the belief that if his sense of hearing or feeling remained, he could possibly hear me when I sent for his son, the voice of his wife when she spoke to him and that the last sound he heard, may have been his pastor's prayer, as he finally committed his soul to God.

Knowledge that frequently just before departure recognition and reason return to those who have been unconscious caused me for several hours to hold his right hand firmly within my grasp to let him in his blindness know, if possible, that he was in touch with humanity and had a friend.

The protracted struggle ceased at twenty minutes past seven o'clock on the morning of April 15, 1865, and I announced that the President was dead.

Source: Charles A. Leale, MD, *Lincoln's Last Hours*, address delivered before the Commandery of the State of New York, Military Order of the Loyal Legion of the United States, February 1909 (Project Gutenberg, 2007), http://www.gutenberg.org/ebooks/24088.

REFLECTING ON THE WAR

Abraham Lincoln *achieved what should have been an impossible rhetorical goal in his Second Inaugural Address, delivered on March 4, 1865. This speech resonated with the most sincere and undying expressions of the great man's humane realism and tender-yet-resolute understanding of why the United States of America was worthy of total love and absolute sacrifice. In just a few paragraphs, "Father Abraham" made sense of four years' worth of savage carnage which tore apart the nation. He named and faced the original American sin, slavery. He admitted the incalculable losses brought by war, and insisted on the imperative for a generous reunion. He reiterated that such a reunion must be free of malice, based upon what he had, in his First Inaugural, termed the "mystic cords of memory" which bound Americans North and South, black and white, together. Because he was taken by the assassin's bullet, every American experienced an irreplaceable loss. His murder meant that no American evaded the Civil War's fearsome toll.*

*While not enough Americans knew it during his lifetime, **Herman Melville** was as significant an American writer as ever put word on paper. His literary output before the war is staggering in its excellence and impact upon American letters:* Typee *(1846),* Omoo *(1847),* Moby Dick *(1851),* Bartleby the Scrivener *(1853),* The Encantadas *(1855),* Benito Cereno *(1855),* The Confidence Man *(1857). In 1866, this magisterial author wrote a meditative poem on the war and the president's martyrdom. "Beware the people weeping," he warns, which turned out to be wise advice.*

While his younger brother, Henry, assisted their father, Charles Francis Adams Sr., the American ambassador in London, **Charles Francis Adams Jr.** *served as a captain in the 1st Massachusetts Volunteer Cavalry. He saw action in several battles, including South Mountain, Antietam, and Gettysburg. Later in the war, he served with forces occupying coastal South Carolina. It was here, watching the many escaped slaves who sought freedom by fleeing to Union lines, that Adams Jr. pondered the racial aspects leading to the war and which inevitably figured into its resolution. Unsurprisingly, since the Adams brothers were part of a deeply literate family, their observations of the war were well written and frequently incisive. Here, Adams Jr. spells out his dawning, and worried, awareness that the black Americans whom he observed embodied the crux of what the war was all about.*

S. A. Cunningham's *recall of the notorious rebel yell is a demonstration of sense memory a generation after the event. In this article in the first issue of* Confederate Veteran *magazine in 1893, the author also recollects the terrible battle conditions that came with it, and why he doesn't wish to re-yell it. Some observers claimed that the difference between the boisterous Confederate yell and the Union soldier's methodical "huzzah" was evidence of America's divided national character. Tocqueville would have been interested in this observation.*

The service career of **Edward Porter Alexander** *stretched from Bull Run to the bitter end. This innovative Georgian was an engineer who reached the rank of brigadier general in the Confederate army. He was a pioneer in the use of observation balloons and signals; it was Alexander who directed the artillery bombardment intended to prepare the way for Pickett's Charge, at Gettysburg. After the war, he was a professor at the University of South Carolina, a railroad executive, a diplomatic surveyor charged with setting the boundary between Nicaragua and Costa Rica, and an author. His memoirs not only recounted his war experiences, but also pondered the war's meaning and the South's future. Like so many Southerners, Alexander needed to figure out how to process the war, given* *that the South devoutly believed in the rightness of its cause, yet failed to achieve the victory secessionists assumed would be theirs. His thoughtful views were delivered in speeches and writings that gained fame and respect, and helped both North and South better grasp the mainstream Southern point of view. In this essay he opines that the nation was better off because it remained united.*

Frederick Douglass *could always be counted upon to point out to his audience what their common sense had ignored or not yet discovered. In his Decoration Day speech in New York City in 1878, he explains, ever so diplomatically, not only what the Civil War amounted to, but also what the black man's war was still about. He was one of the few observers who called Americans to think about more than the memories of Northern and Southern whites. African Americans had their memories, too, and their hopes for a new birth of freedom. The war settled the question of secession, but now it opened the question of emancipation. Reading Douglass, we should ask, where did they get such men?*

USA Pvt. Edward Mott Robbins *makes a fitting final selection for any Civil War collection. His 1918 memoir recounts his experiences fighting in Tennessee, Arkansas, and Georgia from 1862 to 1865. He was no officer, and he was never renowned except by readers of his book, which makes Robbins a suitable spokesman for the hundreds of thousands of common soldiers who bore the war's greatest burdens, carried out the orders of their officers, and fought so long and hard to determine the fate of their country. His notably thoughtful account includes an advisory element aimed at future readers. Using World War I as his reference point at the beginning, he makes this an especially reflective piece.*

Abraham Lincoln in a portrait taken on February 5, 1865

SECOND INAUGURAL ADDRESS

PRESIDENT ABRAHAM LINCOLN, USA

At this second appearing to take the oath of the presidential office, there is less occasion for an extended address than there was at the first. Then a statement, somewhat in detail, of a course to be pursued, seemed fitting and proper. Now, at the expiration of four years, during which declarations have been constantly called forth on every point and phase of the great contest which still absorbs the attention, and engrosses the energies of the nation, little that is new could be presented. The progress of our arms, upon which all else chiefly depends, is as well known to the public as to myself; and it is, I trust, reasonably satisfactory and encouraging to all. With high hope for the future, no prediction in regard to it is ventured. On the occasion corresponding to this four years ago, all thoughts were anxiously directed to an impending civil-war. All dreaded it—all sought to avert it. While the inaugural address was being delivered from this place, devoted altogether to saving the Union without war, insurgent agents were in the city seeking to destroy it without war—seeking to dissolve the Union, and divide effects, by negotiation. Both parties deprecated war; but one of them would make war rather than let the nation survive; and the other would accept war rather than let it perish. And the war came. One eighth of the whole population were colored slaves, not distributed generally over the Union, but localized in the Southern half part of it. These slaves constituted a peculiar and powerful interest. All knew that this interest was, somehow, the cause of the war. To strengthen, perpetuate, and extend this interest was the object for which the insurgents would rend the Union, even by war; while the government claimed no right to do more than to restrict the territorial enlargement of it. Neither party expected for the war, the magnitude, or the duration, which it has already attained. Neither anticipated that the cause of the conflict might cease with, or even before, the conflict itself should cease. Each looked for an easier triumph, and a result less fundamental and astounding. Both read the same Bible, and pray to the same God; and each invokes His aid against the other. It may seem strange that any men should dare to ask a just God's assistance in wringing their bread from the sweat of other men's faces; but let us judge not that we be not judged. The prayers of both could not be answered; that of neither has been answered fully. The Almighty has His own purposes. "Woe unto the world because of offences! for it must needs be that offences come; but woe to that man by whom the offence cometh!" If we shall suppose that American Slavery is one of those offences which, in the providence of God, must needs come, but which, having continued through His appointed time, He now wills to remove, and that He gives to both North and South, this terrible war, as the woe due to those by whom the offence came, shall we discern therein any departure from those divine attributes which the believers in a Living God always ascribe to Him? Fondly do we hope—fervently do we pray—that this mighty scourge of war may speedily pass away. Yet, if God wills that it continue, until all the wealth piled by the bond-man's two hundred and fifty years of unrequited toil shall be sunk, and until every drop of blood drawn with the lash, shall be paid by another drawn with the sword, as was said three thousand years ago, so still it must be said "the judgments of the Lord, are true and righteous altogether"

With malice toward none; with charity for all; with firmness in the right, as God gives us to see the right, let us strive on to finish the work we are in; to bind up the nation's wounds; to care for him who shall have borne the battle, and for his widow, and his orphan—to achieve and cherish a lasting peace among ourselves and with the world.

Source: Abraham Lincoln, Second Inaugural Address, March 4, 1865, Abraham Lincoln Papers, Series 3: General Correspondence, 1837 to 1897, Library of Congress, Washington, DC, http://www.loc.gov/resource/mal.4361300.

THE MARTYR

HERMAN MELVILLE, USA

Good Friday was the day
Of the prodigy and crime,
When they killed him in his pity,
When they killed him in his prime
Of clemency and calm—
When with yearning he was filled
To redeem the evil-willed,
And, though conqueror, be kind;
But they killed him in his kindness,
In their madness and their blindness,
And they killed him from behind.

There is sobbing of the strong,
And a pall upon the land;
But the People in their weeping
Bare the iron hand;
Beware the People weeping
When they bare the iron hand.

He lieth in his blood—
The father in his face;
They have killed him, the Forgiver—
The Avenger takes his place,
The Avenger wisely stern,
Who in righteousness shall do
What the heavens call him to,
And the parricides remand;

For they killed him in his kindness,
In their madness and their blindness,
And his blood is on their hand.

There is sobbing of the strong,
And a pall upon the land;
But the People in their weeping
Bare the iron hand:
Beware the People weeping
When they bare the iron hand.

Source: Herman Melville, *Battle-Pieces and Aspects of the War* (New York: Harper & Brothers, 1866; Project Gutenberg, 2004), https://www.gutenberg.org/ebooks/12384.

"THE FOOT-BALL OF PASSION
AND ACCIDENT"

CHARLES FRANCIS ADAMS PONDERS
THE FUTURE OF FREED SLAVES

Milne Plantation, Port Royal Island
Monday, April 6, 1862

Here I am on the Milne Plantation in the heart of Port Royal Island. Cotton fields, pine barrens, contrabands, missionaries and soldiers are before me and all around me. A sick missionary is in the next room, a dozen soldiers are eating their suppers in the yard under my window and some twenty negroes of every age, lazy, submissive and as the white man has made them, are hanging about the plantation building just as though they were not the *teterrima causa* of this consuming *bella* [Adams' Latin words refer to a quote by the Roman poet Horace meaning "the most shameful cause of war".] The island is now just passing into its last stage of spring. The nights are cool, but the days are hot enough to make the saddle no seat of comfort. The island, naturally one of the most delightful places in the world, is just now at its most delightful season.

The brown unhappy wastes of cotton fields unplanted this year and with the ragged remnants of last year's crop, still fluttering in the wind, do not add to its beauty, but nothing can destroy the charm of the long plantation avenues with the heavy grey moss drooping from branches fresh with young leaves, while the natural hedges for miles along are fragrant with wild flowers. As I canter along these never ending avenues I hear sounds and see sights enough to set the ornithologist and the sportsman crazy. Nor are less inviting forms of animal life wanting, for snakes cross your path more frequently than hares and, even now, the soldiers under my window are amusing themselves with a large turtle, a small alligator and a serpent of curious beauty and most indubitable venom, a portion of the results of their afternoon's investigation.

One can ride indefinitely over the island and never exhaust its infinite cross-roads and out-of-the-way plantations, but you cannot ride fifteen minutes in any direction, however new, without stumbling over the two great facts of the day, pickets and contrabands. The pickets are recruits in active service without models—excellent material for soldiers and learning the trade, but scarcely soldiers yet. The contrabands were slaves yesterday and may be again tomorrow, and what slaves are any man may know without himself seeing who will take the trouble to read [Frederick Law] Olmsted's books. No man seems to realize that here, in this little island, all around us, has begun the solution of this tremendous "nigger" question.

The war here seems to rest and, for the present, Port Royal is thrown into the shade, and yet I am much mistaken if at this minute Port Royal is not a point of greater interest than either Virginia or Kentucky. Here the contraband question has arisen in such proportions that it has got to be met and the Government is meeting it as best it may. Some ten thousand quondam [former] slaves are thrown upon the hands of an unfortunate Government; they are the forerunners of hundreds of thousands more, if the plans of the Government succeed, and so the Government may as well now decide what it will do in the case of the success of its war plans. While the Government has sent agents down here, private philanthropy has sent missionaries, and while the first see that the contrabands earn their bread, the last teach them the alphabet. Between the two I predict divers results, among which are numerous jobs for agents and missionaries, small comfort to the negroes and heavy loss to the Government. Doubtless the world must have cotton and must pay for it, but it does not yet know what it is to pay for it if the future hath it in store that the poor world shall buy the next crop of Port Royal at prices remunerative to Government.

The scheme, so far as I can see any, seems to be for the Government, recognizing and encouraging private philanthropy and leaving to it the task of educating the slaves to the standard of self-support, to hold itself a sort of guardian to the slave in his indefinite state of transition, exacting from him that amount of labor which he owes to the community and the cotton market. The plan may work well; if it does, it will be the first of the kind that ever has. Certainly I do not envy the slaves its operation. The position of the Government is certainly a most difficult one. Something must be done for these poor people and done at once. They are indolent, shiftless, unable to take care of themselves and plundered by every comer—in short, they are slaves. For the present they must be provided for. It is easy to find fault with the present plan. Can any one suggest a better? For me I must confess that I cannot. I think it bad, very bad, and that it must end in failure, but I can see no other more likely to succeed.

This is the solution of the negro question I take it no one but the missionaries and agents will contend. That is yet to come, and here as elsewhere we are looking for it, and trying to influence it. My own impression is that the solution is coming—may already in some degree be shadowed out, but that it is a solution hurried on by this war, based on simple and immutable principles of economy and one finally over which the efforts of Government and individuals can exercise no control.

This war is killing slavery. Not by any legal quibble of contrabands or doubtful theory of confiscation, but by stimulating free trade. Let any man ride as I do over this island. Let him look at the cotton fields and the laborers. Let him handle their tools and examine their implements, and if he comes from any wheat-growing country, he will think himself amid the institutions and implements of the middle ages—and so he would be. The whole system of cotton growing—all its machinery from the slave to the hoe in his hand—is awkward, cumbrous, expensive and behind the age. That the cultivation of cotton is so behind that of all the other great staples is the natural result of monopoly, but it is nonetheless disgraceful to the world, and to give it an impulse seems to have been the mission of this war. The thorough and effectual breaking up of its so much prized monopoly will be the greatest blessing which could happen to the South, and it seems to be the one probable result of this war. Competition involves improvement in ruin, and herein lies the solution of this slavery question. Northern men with Northern ideas of economy, agriculture and improvement, are swarming down onto the South. They see how much behind the times the country is and they see that here is money to be made. If fair competition in the growth of cotton be once established a new system of economy and agriculture must inevitably be introduced here in which the slave and his hoe will make room for the free laborers and the plough, and the change will not be one of election but a sole resource against utter ruin. The men to introduce this change or any other are here and are daily swarming down in the armies of the Government, soon to become armies of occupation. A new tide of emigration has set in before which slavery has small chance.

But how is it for the African? Slavery may perish and no one regret it, but what is to become of the unfortunate African? When we have got thus far we have just arrived at the real point of interest in the "nigger" question. The slaves of whom I see so much here may be taken as fair specimens of their race as at present existing in this country. They have many good qualities. They are good-tempered, patient, docile, willing to learn and easily directed; but they are slavish and all that the word slavish implies. They will lie and cheat and steal; they are hypocritical and cunning; they are not brave, and they are not fierce—these qualities the white man took out of them generations ago, and in taking them deprived the African of the capacity for freedom.

My views of the future of those I see about me here are not therefore encouraging. That they will be free and free soon by the operation of economic laws over which Government has no control, I thoroughly believe; but their freedom will be the freedom of antiquated and unprofitable machines, the freedom of the hoes they use which will be swept aside to make way for better implements. The slave, however, cannot be swept aside and herein lies the difficulty and the problem. My impression from what I see is that Emancipation as a Government measure would be a terrible calamity to the blacks as a race; that rapid emancipation as the result of an economic revolution destroying their value as agricultural machines would be a calamity, though less severe; and finally, that the only transition to freedom absolutely beneficial to them as a race would be one proportioned in length to the length of their captivity, such a one in fact as destroyed villeinage in the wreck of the feudal system.

Were men and governments what they should be instead of what they are, the case would be different and all would combine in the Christian and tedious effort to patiently undo the wrongs they had done, and to restore to the African his attributes. Then the work could be done well and quickly; but at present, seeing what men are, and how remorselessly they throw aside what has ceased to be useful, I cannot but regard as a doubtful benefit to the African anything which by diminishing his value increases his chances of freedom. A revolution in cotton production springing from competition may work differently by gradually changing the status of the African from one of forced to one of free labor but I do not regard this as probable. The census already shows not only that cotton can everywhere be cultivated by free labor, but also that the best cotton now is so cultivated, and the most probable result of a permanent reduction in the price of cotton would seem to me to be a sudden influx of free white emigration into the cotton fields of the South. Such a result would produce untold advantages to the South, to America and to the white race; but how about the blacks? Will they be educated and encouraged and cared for; or will they be challenged to competition in the race, or go to the wall, and finally be swept away as a useless rubbish? Who can answer those queries? I for one cannot; but one thing I daily see and that is that no spirit exists among the contrabands here which would enable them to care for themselves in a race of vigorous competition. The blacks must be cared for or they will perish, and who is to care for them when they cease to be of value?

I do not pretend to solve these questions or do more than raise them, and their solution will come, I suppose, all in good time with the emergency which raises them. But no man who dreams—at all of the future can wander over Port Royal Island at present and mark the character and condition of its inhabitants, without having all these questions and many more force themselves upon his mind. I am a thorough believer in this war. I believe it to have been necessary and just. I believe that from it will flow great blessings to America and the Caucasian race. I believe the area of freedom will by it be immensely expanded in this country, and that from it true principle of trade and economy will receive a prodigious impetus throughout the world; but for the African I do not see the same bright future. He is the foot-ball of passion and accident, and the gift of freedom may prove his destruction. Still the experiment should and must be tried and the sooner it is tried the better. . . .

Source: "Charles Adams Forecasts the Future," HistoryNet.com, March 17, 2017, adapted from Worthington Chauncey Ford, ed., *A Cycle of Adams Letters* (New York: Houghton Mifflin Co., 1920), https://www.historynet.com/charles-adams-forecasts -future.htm.

THE REBEL YELL REMEMBERED

S. A. CUNNINGHAM, CSA

Many people think of the three measured huzzas given now and then as "the rebel yell." It is shocking to an old Confederate to consider such deception. The venerable widow of Rear Admiral Raphael Semmes, in attending a Confederate reunion at Memphis a couple of years ago, modestly expressed her wish to hear "the rebel yell." Something of an old time cheer came from the throats of men who gladly tried to compliment the wife of the eminent naval commander. Kellar Anderson, who was of the Kentucky Orphan Brigade and had heard the yell, wrote a reminiscence for the *Memphis Appeal*. It is this saint Anderson, called Captain and again Gen. Anderson, who honored his native Kentucky, his adopted Tennessee and American heroism some months ago at Shoal [?] Creek, in defying the miners who had captured him and demanded ransom for his head, when it seemed but madness to refuse their demands. One thing is sure, he had heard "the rebel yell."

There is a Southern mother on this stand who says she wants to hear the rebel yell once more. The announcement transforms, and in an instant I find myself acting the humble part of file-closer to Company I, Fifth Kentucky Infantry, with pieces at the right shoulder, the brigade in route column. With the active, strong, swinging stride of the enthusiastic trained soldier, they hold the double quick over rocks, logs, gullies, undergrowth, hill and vale, until amid the foliage of the trees above them, the hurling shell and hissing shot from the enemy's field guns gives notice that if retreating they have missed the way. Yet, there is no command to halt. Direct, on unchanged course, this battle-scarred and glory-mantled battalion of Kentucky youths continues, and as they reach the open woods, in clarion tones comes the order, "Change front, forward on first company," etc. The order executed found them formed on ground but recently occupied by a battalion of their foes, and few of these had left their positions. The battalion of Kentuckians was in battle array where once were they, but now the ground was almost literally covered with the Federal dead, the entire length of our regiment of 700 men. Men, did I say? Soldiers is the word; there were few men among them, they being youths, but soldiers indeed. The increasing spat, whirl and hiss of the minnie balls hurrying by, left no doubt of the fact among these soldiers. They are about to enter the action again and forward is the order. "Steady, men, steady; hold your fire; not a shot without orders. It is hard to stand, but you must not return it. We have friends in our front yet. They are being hard pressed, and their ammunition is almost expended, but they are of our proudest and best, and Humphries' Mississippians will hold that ridge while they have a cartridge."

It is nearing sunset, and after two days of fearful carnage—aye, one of the best-contested battles of the times, the enemy has been driven pell-mell from many parts of the field. Our losses are numbered by thousands, and we are now advancing in battle array, the little red flag with blue cross dancing gaily in the air over heads of those who were there to defend it. The last rays of the setting sun had kissed the autumn foliage when we stepped into open ground and found that we were amid the wreck of what a few short minutes ago had been a superb six-gun battery! The uniform of the dead artillerymen and the gaily caparisoned [cloth-covered] bodies of the many dead horses proclaimed this destruction the work of our friends. We look upon the dead, pull our cartridge boxes a little more to the front and resolve once more to face the destruction we are now entering.

The boom of artillery increases. The rattle of musketry is steady—aye, incessant and deadly. The sulphurous smoke has increased until almost stifling. Only fifty yards of space separates us from the gallant Mississippians we are there to support. They have clung to the ridge with a death-like grip, but their last cartridge has been fired at the enemy, and their support being at hand these sturdy soldiers of Longstreet's corps are ordered to retire. Simultaneously the support was ordered forward.

As the Mississippians retired, the deep-volumed shouts of the enemy told us plainer than could words that the enemy thought they had routed them. Oh, how differently we regarded the situation! If they might have seen them as we—halting, kneeling, lying down, arranging themselves in columns of files behind the large trees to enable us to get at the enemy with an unbroken front, each man as we passed throwing cap high into the overhanging foliage in honor of our presence—then I imagine their shouts would have been suppressed. "Steady in the center! Hold your fire! Hold the colors back!" The center advanced too rapidly. We are clear of our friends now, only the enemy in front, and we meet face to face on a spur of Mission Ridge, which extends through the Snodgrass farm, and we are separated by eighty yards.

Thud! and down goes Private Robertson. He turned, smiled and died. Thud! Corporal Gray shot through the neck. "Get to the rear!" said I. Thud! Thud! Thud! Wolf, Michael, the gallant Thompson. Thud! Thud! Thud! Courageous Oxley, the knightly Desha, and duty-loving Cummings. And thus it goes. The fallen increase, and are to be counted by the hundreds. The pressure is fearful, but the 'sand-digger' is there to stay.

"Forward! Forward!" rang out along the line. We move slowly to the front. There is now sixty yards between us. The enemy scorn to fly; he gives back a few paces; he retires a little more but still faces us, and loads as he backs away. We are now in the midst of his dead and dying, but he stands as do the sturdy oaks about him. We have all that is possible for humans to bear; our losses are fearful, and each moment some comrade passes to the unknown. At last Humphries' Mississippians have replenished boxes and are working around our right. Trigg's Virginians are uncovering to our left. I feel a shock about my left breast, spin like a top in the air, and come down in a heap.

I know not how long before came the sounds "Forward! Forward! Forward!" I rise on my elbow. Look! Look! There they go, all at breakneck speed, the bayonet at charge. The firing appears to suddenly cease for about five seconds. Then arose that do-or-die expression, that maniacal maelstrom of sound; that penetrating, rasping, shrieking, blood-curdling noise that could be heard for miles on earth and whose volumes reached the heavens; such an expression as never yet came from the throats of live men but from men whom the seething blast of an imaginary hell would not check while the sound lasted. "The battle of Chickamauga is won."

Dear Southern mother, that was the Rebel yell, and only such scenes ever did or ever will produce it. Even when engaged, that expression from the Confederate soldier always made my hair stand on end. The young ones and youths who composed this unearthly music were lusty, jolly, clear-voiced, hardened soldiers, full of courage, and proud to march in rags, barefoot, dirty and hungry, with head erect to meet the plethoric ranks of the best equipped and best fed army of modern times. Alas, now many of them are decrepit from ailment and age, and although we will never grow old enough to cease being proud of the record of the Confederate soldier, and the dear old mothers who bore them, we can never again, even at your bidding, dear, dear mother, produce the Rebel yell. Never again; never, never, never.

Source: S. A. Cunningham, "The Rebel Yell Remembered," *Confederate Veteran* 1, no. 1 (January 1893).

THE POINT OF VIEW

BRIG. GEN. EDWARD PORTER ALEXANDER, CSA

The raison d'être of the following pages is not at all to set forth the valor of Confederate arms nor the skill of Confederate generals. These are as they may be, and must here take their chances in an unpartisan narrative, written with an entirely different object. That object is the criticism of each campaign as one would criticize a game of chess, only to point out the good and bad plays on each side, and the moves which have influenced the result. It is far from being a grateful task, and the writer is, moreover, painfully conscious of his limitations in his effort to perform it adequately. But it is of great importance that it should be attempted even approximately not only for the benefit of general history, but more particularly for that of military students and staff officers. These will find much of value and interest in the details, pointing out how and why the scale of battle was turned upon each occasion. It is only of recent years since the publication by the War Department of the full Official Reports of both armies, in 135 large volumes that it has become possible to write this story, even approximately. History, meanwhile, has been following the incomplete reports of the earlier days which, sometimes, as at Seven Pines (or Fair Oaks), have deliberately concealed the facts, and has always felt the need of the personal accounts covering the incidents of every march, skirmish, and battle. Only among these can be traced the beginnings, often obscure and accidental, of the most important events; and these must ever form an inexhaustible mine for the study by the staff-officer of the practical working and details in every department of an army.

As to the causes of the war, it will, of course, be understood that every former Confederate repudiates all accusations of treason or rebellion in the war, and even of fighting to preserve the institution of slavery. The effort of the enemy to destroy it without compensation was practical robbery, which, of course, we resisted. The unanimity and the desperation of our resistance even to the refusal of Lincoln's suggested compensation at Fortress Monroe, after the destruction had already occurred, clearly show our struggle to have been for that right of self-government which the Englishman has claimed, and fought for, as for nothing else, since the days of King John. It has taken many years for these truths to gain acceptance against the prejudices left by the war, even though it has been notorious from the first that no legal accusation could be brought against any one, even Mr. Davis. With the adoption of this view by leading English authorities, not to mention distinguished Northern and Republican authors, the South may be content to leave all such questions to the final verdict of history, admitting itself too close to the event to claim impartiality.

One thing remains to be said. The world has not stood still in the years since we took up arms for what we deemed our most invaluable right, that of self-government. We now enjoy the rare privilege of seeing what we fought for in the retrospect. It no longer seems so desirable. It would now prove only a curse. We have good cause to thank God for our escape from it, not alone for our sake, but for that of the whole country and even of the world. Had our cause succeeded, divergent interests must soon have further separated the States into groups, and this continent would have been given over to divided nationalities, each weak and unable to command foreign credit. Since the days of Greece, Confederacies have only held together against foreign enemies, and in times of peace have soon disintegrated. It is surely not necessary to contrast what would have been our prospects as citizens of such States with our condition now as citizens of the strongest, richest, and strange for us to say who once called ourselves "conquered" and our cause "lost," the freest nation on earth. The statistics of our commerce, our manufactures, and our internal improvements are an object-lesson of the truth of old Aesop's fable, pointing out the increased strength of the separate sticks when bound together into a fagot. That the whole civilized world shares with us in the far-reaching blessings and benefits of our civilization, wealth, and political power is manifest in our building the Panama Canal, and again, in the Treaty of Peace between Russia and Japan, negotiated through the influence of our President. These are but the first-fruits of what the future will develop, for our Union is not built to perish. Its bonds were not formed by peaceable agreements in conventions, but were forged in the white heat of battles, in a war fought out to the bitter end, and are for eternity.

Source: Edward Porter Alexander, "The Point of View," in *Military Memoirs of a Confederate: A Critical Narrative* (New York: Charles Scribner's Sons, 1907), https://archive .org/details/militarymemoirso00alex.

Frederick Douglass in 1870
LIBRARY OF CONGRESS

SPEECH DELIVERED IN MADISON SQUARE, NEW YORK, DECORATION DAY, 1878

FREDERICK DOUGLASS, USA

Friends and Fellow Citizens: In this place, hallowed and made glorious by a statue of the best man, truest patriot, and wisest statesman of his time and country; I have been invited—I might say ordered—by the Lincoln Post of the Grand Army of the Republic, to say a few words to you in appropriate celebration of this annual national memorial day . . . We tender you on this memorial day the homage of the loyal nation, and the heartfelt gratitude of emancipated millions. If the great work you undertook to accomplish is still incomplete; if a lawless and revolutionary spirit is still abroad in the country; if the principles for which you bravely fought are in any way compromised or threatened; if the Constitution and the laws are in any measure dishonored and disregarded; if duly elected State Governments are in any way overthrown by violence; if the elective franchise has been overborne by intimidation and fraud; if the Southern States, under the idea of local self-government, are endeavoring to paralyze the arm and shrivel the body of the National Government so that it cannot protect the humblest citizen in his rights, the fault is not yours. You, at least, were faithful and did your whole duty. Fellow-citizens, I am not here to fan the flame of sectional animosity, to revive old issues, or to stir up strife between the races; but no candid man, looking at the political situation of the hour, can fail to see that we are still afflicted by the painful sequences both of slavery and of the late rebellion. In the spirit of the noble man whose image now looks down upon us we should have "charity toward all, and malice toward none." In the language of our greatest soldier, twice honored with the Presidency of the nation. "Let us have peace." Yes, let us have peace, but let us have liberty, law, and justice first. Let us have the Constitution, with it thirteenth, fourteenth, and fifteenth amendments, fairly interpreted, faithfully executed, and cheerfully obeyed in the fullness of their spirit and the completeness of their letter. . . .

My own feeling toward the old master class of the South is well known. Though I have worn the yoke of bondage, and have no love for what are called the good old times of slavery, there is in my heart no taint of malice toward the ex-slaveholders. Many of them were not sinners above all others, but were in some sense the slaves of the slave system, for slavery was a power in the State greater than the State itself. With the aid of a few brilliant orators and plotting conspirators, it sundered the bonds of the Union and inaugurated war. . . .

Nevertheless, we must not be asked to say that the South was right in the rebellion, or to say the North was wrong. We must not be asked to put no difference between those who fought for the Union and those who fought against it, or between loyalty and treason. . . .

But the sectional character of this war was merely accidental and its least significant feature. It was a war of ideas, a battle of principles and ideas which united one section and divided the other; a war between the old and new, slavery and freedom, barbarism and civilization; between a government based upon the broadest and grandest declaration of human rights the world ever heard or read, and another pretended government, based upon an open, bold and shocking denial of all rights, except the right of the strongest.

Good, wise, and generous men of the North, in power and out of power, for whose good intentions and patriotism we must all have the highest respect, doubt the wisdom of observing this memorial day, and would have us forget and forgive, strew flowers alike and lovingly, on rebel and on loyal graves. This sentiment is noble and generous, worthy of all honor as such; but it is only a sentiment after all, and must submit to its own rational limitations. There was a right side and a wrong side in the late war, which no sentiment ought to cause us to forget, and while today we should have malice toward none, and charity toward all, it is no part of our duty to confound right with wrong, or loyalty with treason. If the observance of this memorial days has any apology, office, or significance, it is derived from the moral character of this war, from the far-reaching, unchangeable and eternal principles in dispute, and for which our sons and brothers encountered hardship, danger, and death. . . .

. . . though freedom of speech and of the ballot have for the present fallen before the shot-guns of the South, and, the party of slavery is now in the ascendant, we need bate no jot of heart or hope. The American people will, in any great emergency, be true to themselves. The heart of the nation is still sound and strong, and as in the past, so in the future, patriotic millions, with able captains to lead them, will stand as a wall of fire around the Republic, and in the end see Liberty, Equality, and Justice triumphant.

Source: Frederick Douglass, "Speech Delivered in Madison Square, New York, Decoration Day," 1878, Library of Congress, Manuscript Division.

DON'T BELITTLE THE CIVIL WAR

PVT. EDWARD MOTT ROBBINS, USA

We think of the present war [World War I] as the most terrible experience of humanity, and are apt to think of our present sacrifices as something unheard of before. But any of our old veterans who went through the civil war know that measured by any standpoint—cost, men engaged, casualties, property loss, or general awfulness the civil war was enormously more costly and terrible to America than this war was or could have become if it had lasted for several years.

In fact we have only had a mere taste, a faint suggestion of what the men and women of the '60s went through.

The world war has cost us eighteen billion dollars. The civil war cost us $5,160,000,000. The amount of wealth now in the country is fifteen times what it was in 1860. Had the cost mounted up to 77 billion we might begin to feel it pinch as they did. We should have to spend sixty billion more before we should make the money sacrifice they did.

The lives lost in the civil war was in round numbers 600,000. The population was then 27,400,000—about one-fourth of what it is now. Four times 600,000 is 2,400,000. If every soldier sent over seas were killed we should have a smaller proportion of gold stars by a quarter of a million than they did.

Out of a population of 27,400,000 there were mustered in during the '60s 3,730,000. Multiplying again by four we get 14,920,000. If we had kept on sending two million a year to France for six more years to come we would begin to feel the drain on our male population here at home as they did in 1865. And this takes no account of the billions of dollars' worth of property destroyed and the disruption of business in nearly half our territory. In this war we have faced nothing of this kind.

Nor has the fighting been anything like so savage and terrible as when both sides were Americans, the best soldiers in the world. Phil Sheridan sat on his horse beside Prince Charles when Metz was taken from the French in 1870. Looking at the serried lines of Germany's best soldiers he said to the Prince, "Give me two divisions of the Sedgwick sixth corps of the Union army and I could cut my way through your army of Prussians."

In the last hundred years the world has seen no other such fighting as was done by the Blue and Gray. The three most destructive battles in the last century outside the civil war were the battle of Waterloo in 1815, where the victors lost 20 per cent of their men; Vioville, between the Germans and the French in 1870, where the casualties were 20 per cent, and the battle of Plevno in 1870 where the Prussians lost 8 per cent in their battle with the Turks. But in the battle of Antietam the casualties of the victors were 23 per cent, at Gettysburg 20 and at Chickamauga 27 per cent.

Germany boasts of her "shock troops." In the civil war our boys were all "shock troops." And they were only boys. We see the few gray haired veterans with us to-day and forget that of those wonderful boys of 1860, 1,151,438 of them were mere striplings under 18 years old. But what terrible fighters they became! They were shock troops, for they knew but one way to fight. That was at close quarters after the roar of musketry, with bayonets and clubbed rifles.

The present method of long range shooting and trench fighting shows no such savage intensity of fighting or terrible slaughter as these men faced, and it knows no such losses.

At Gettysburg the First Minnesota lost 82 per cent of its men in fifteen minutes of the second day. At Petersburg the First Maine lost 70 per cent of its men in seven minutes. At Gettysburg the 141st Pennsylvania lost 76 per cent. And remember, these were killed or wounded and not a man "missing," as they didn't surrender.

And how about the Gray? First Texas at Antietam 82 per cent, 21st Georgia at Manassas 78 per cent, 26th North Carolina at Gettysburg 72 per cent, 6th Mississippi at Shiloh 71 per cent. They printed no casualty lists then. The day after one of these battles the whole Chicago Tribune would not have been big enough to hold the names.

An eminent British officer recently said, "The Americans still hold the record for hard fighting." And now the sons and grandsons of the men who shook hands at Appomattox, lineal descendants of the best infantry that ever marched on the globe, have had a chance to send the shivers of fear down the spine of the hun and America has repeated itself under the Stars and Stripes. But let us not forget the deeds of their heroic fathers who set a world record for terrific fighting that is not likely to ever be broken.

Source: Dr. Edward M. Robinson, *Civil War Experiences, 1862–1865* (1919; Project Gutenberg, 2012), http://www.gutenberg.org/ebooks/38859.